# Praises for Identity Theft Handbook: Detection, Prevention and Security

"No one in the world is more knowledgeable about Identity Theft than Mr. Biegelman. This book has it all—well-written and researched, chock full of illustrative examples, and insightful tips on how to reduce and prevent this burgeoning crime."

> —Joseph T. Wells, CFE, CPA, Founder and Chairman, Association of Certified Fraud Examiners

"In the same way he has unselfishly shared his vast knowledge on the establishment of financial investigations units and world-class compliance programs, Mr. Biegelman has once again delivered what will undoubtedly become the authoritative work on Identity Theft. What makes his latest book so powerful is that it can both be utilized as a primer to college students pursuing careers in economic crime investigations while at the same time serve as an invaluable desk reference to veteran financial crime investigators. With his latest work, Marty has further solidified his iconic status in the investigative and fraud prevention field."

> —Scott Moritz, Executive Director, Daylight Forensic & Advisory

"Biegelman's Identity Theft Handbook provides a thorough discussion of the history and typology of identity theft and fraud that is enriched by significant and poignant cases from investigative files. One cannot help but be impressed by the permutations and resiliency of this crime, the dogged determination of those who investigate and prosecute offenders and those who research the motivations and methods of offenders in an effort to devise technologies and countermeasures to detect and prevent identity theft. Although I have studied identity theft from the legal perspective for several years, the Handbook has provided me with different perspectives on identity theft. This is an ideal read for those whose daily tasks involve fighting identity theft, but also those wish to learn about this crime for the first time. It should also be mandatory reading for legislators, regulators, and other policymakers seeking to define and resolve issues of data privacy."

> —George E. Curtis, J.D., Executive Director, Economic Crime Institute & Professor of Criminal Justice, Utica College

"Martin has done it again! This book is a must-read for anyone who cares about protecting their financial health and reputation as well as those of us who protect and counsel others. As a former federal prosecutor and now private practitioner, I have seen the devastating financial and emotional impact that identity theft can cause. Each year I advise numerous corporate and individual clients, from major league athletes, celebrities, and corporate executives to physicians, attorneys and banking and investment professionals, on how they should protect themselves and their clients against the fastest-spreading financial disease— identity theft. Martin's latest book provides insightful guidance, extremely helpful suggestions, and practical examples that will be your best defense against identity theft. Every fiscally responsible adult needs to read this book."

> —George A. Stamboulidis, Esq., Managing Partner of the New York office and head of the White Collar Defense & Corporate Investigations Team at Baker Hostetler LLP

"Identity theft, the fastest growing white collar crime, preys upon the assets and reputations of businesses and consumers, even the deceased. Sadly it is one of the few crimes in which the victim must often first prove their innocence before anyone will pay attention. Law enforcement cannot give identity theft the attention it needs due to the sheer volume and the fact that it crosses so many jurisdictions, often world-wide thanks to the Internet. No consumer or business is immune from its reach and all would be well advised to read this book by a renowned, innovative investigator with a unique blend of knowledge, story-telling ability, and experience as a federal investigator and now as an industry fraud expert in one of the largest companies in the world. Martin Biegelman has devoted his life to fighting crime, protecting consumers and businesses, and teaching thousands of investigators and auditors."

> —Kenneth Hunter, Former Chief Postal Inspector, Former President & CEO, Council of Better Business Bureaus

"The issue of identity theft is one of the most important and controversial of our time. Martin does a masterful job of bringing value to both the naive consumer and the educated professional with his new book on the subject. He set the bar very high with his previous works and his latest on Identity Theft continues the trend."

> —Dan Wachtler, President & CEO, IPSA International, Inc.

"Some executives will read this book after they discover that private information they were entrusted to hold on to, was not held tight enough. Others will read Martin Biegelman's Identity Theft Handbook before a leak occurs. I recommend the latter."

> —Roy Snell, CEO, Society of Corporate Compliance and Ethics

Over the past several years, identity crimes have captured the interest and imagination of the media, the public, and, yes, fraudsters. Nonetheless, professional publications on this subject have been scarce. With *Identity Theft Handbook: Detection, Prevention and Security*, Martin Biegelman fills the need for one comprehensive volume addressing all of the various aspects of identity frauds. Drawing on his many years of experience and his well-recognized expertise in the field of fraud fighting, Mr. Biegelman has produced the definitive book on this subject. Richly researched, yet written in an accessible and interesting style, Mr. Biegelman's *Identity Theft Handbook: Detection, Prevention and Security* will undoubtedly become the primary resource for fraud examiners, researchers, academics, member of law enforcement, and anyone else interested in identity theft.

> —William J. Kresse, MS, JD, CPA, CFE, Associate Professor and Director of Graduate Programs in Fraud Examination, Graham School of Management, Saint Xavier University, Chicago, 2007 ACFE Educator of the Year

# Identity Theft Handbook

# Identity Theft Handbook

*Detection, Prevention, and Security*

**Martin T. Biegelman**

**WILEY**

JOHN WILEY & SONS, INC.

**Library of Congress Cataloging-in-Publication Data**
Biegelman, Martin T.
  Identity theft handbook : detection, prevention and security / Martin T. Biegelman.
    p. cm.
  Includes index.
  ISBN 978-0-470-17999-4 (cloth)
    1. Identity theft—United States.   2. Identity theft—United States—Prevention.   I. Title.
  HV6679.B54 2009
  332.024—dc22                                                                2008037343

Printed in the United States of America

10 9 8 7 6 5 4 3 2 1

*This book is dedicated to the men and women of the United States Postal Inspection Service. These outstanding law enforcement professionals were fighting the scourge of identity theft and protecting consumers and businesses long before the crime was named.*

# Contents

# Contents

# About the Author

**Martin T. Biegelman, CFE, CCEP,** is Director of Financial Integrity for Microsoft Corporation in Redmond, Washington. In 2002, he joined Microsoft to create and lead a worldwide fraud detection, investigation, and prevention program based within Internal Audit. In addition to focusing on preventing financial fraud and abuse, his group promotes financial integrity, fiscal responsibility, and compliance in a COSO framework of improved business ethics, effective internal controls, and greater corporate governance. He works closely with Microsoft's executive leadership, the Office of Legal Compliance, Internal Audit, and others in protecting Microsoft from financial and reputational risk.

He has more than 30 years of experience in fraud detection and prevention. Prior to joining Microsoft, he was a Director of Litigation and Investigative Services in the Fraud Investigation Practice at BDO Seidman, LLP, an international accounting and consulting firm. He is also a former federal law enforcement professional, having served as a United States Postal Inspector in a variety of investigative and management assignments. As a federal agent, he was a subject matter expert in fraud detection and prevention. He retired as the Inspector in Charge of the Phoenix, Arizona, Field Office of the Postal Inspection Service. He also served as a technical advisor in the filming of the Showtime movie *The Inspectors II* on the subject of identity theft.

Mr. Biegelman is a Certified Fraud Examiner as well as an adjunct faculty member, Regent Emeritus, and Fellow of the Association of Certified Fraud Examiners (ACFE). He is a Certified Compliance and Ethics Professional, a member of the Society of Corporate Compliance and Ethics, and an adjunct faculty member. He serves on the Board of Directors of the ACFE Foundation, the Board of Advisors for the Economic Crime Institute at Utica College, and the Accounting Advisory Board for the Department of Accounting and Law in the School of Business at the University at Albany, State University of New York. He is also a member of ASIS International and the High Technology Crime Investigation Association.

He is a sought-after speaker and instructor on identity theft, white-collar crime, corruption, security, fraud prevention, and corporate compliance. He has written numerous articles on fraud-related subjects including identity theft, corporate crime, Internet fraud, check fraud, fraud prevention, corporate investigations, and the Sarbanes-Oxley Act. Mr. Biegelman is the author of *Building a World-Class Compliance*

*Program: Best Practices and Strategies for Success* and coauthor of *Executive Roadmap to Fraud Prevention and Internal Control: Creating a Culture of Compliance.* He is also a contributing author to *Fraud Casebook: Lessons from the Bad Side of Business.*

He is the 2008 recipient of the Cressey Award bestowed annually by the Association of Certified Fraud Examiners for lifetime achievements in the detection and deterrence of fraud.

Mr. Biegelman has a Bachelor of Science degree from Cornell University and a Master of Public Administration from Golden Gate University.

# Foreword

The magnitude of the identity theft and fraud problem is enormous. Identity fraud was identified as one of the top priorities of the Department of Justice, just prior to the terrorist attacks of 9/11. Naturally, everyone's priorities changed after 9/11. The impact of identity theft and identity fraud is reaching a proportion and a level of sophistication by the criminal element that prompt coordination by governments, multinational corporations, and citizens is required if we are going to have any significant impact.

*Identity Theft Handbook: Detection, Prevention, and Security* is also very timely, considering the woes of our financial services/banking industry. Current poor economic trends, oil prices, and mortgage lending problems threaten the confidence in our financial services industry. It must be protected from further damage from identity theft and identity fraud.

*Identity Theft Handbook: Detection, Prevention, and Security* is a great beginning to understanding the history and complexity of the identity theft and identity fraud problem. Biegelman gives an excellent view of the history of the identity theft problem in the United States. The past method of operation for criminals committing these crimes provides a framework for understanding the origins of their new methods and indicates how much the criminal element has grown.

In the Postal Inspection Service, we separate identity crimes into two areas: identity theft and identity fraud. Identity theft is the act of stealing your identity. This often includes your Social Security Number, driver's information, date of birth, and so on. Biegelman gives a very clear picture of the old days of Dumpster diving to obtain personal identifying information to the newest threats dealing with today's very technologically savvy, borderless, international organized criminals.

In today's world, two of the common ways of stealing identities are computer intrusion and infiltration. We have seen far too many examples of computer intrusion.

As Biegelman outlines, infiltration is when the criminals intentionally gain employment in a company to access large quantities of personal information or bribe existing employees to steal the information. The use of technology to maintain massive quantities of data has opened up greater opportunities for infiltration as a prime method for stealing your identity.

Identity fraud is the use of your personal information to obtain money, products, or services, using your identity and your credit. Biegelman takes us from the old days of submitting a fraudulent, handwritten application for a credit card, to the use of online banking systems to defraud on a grander scale.

*Identity Theft Handbook: Detection, Prevention, and Security* provides insight that may be helpful in preventing victimization. Governments, corporations, and individual citizens all can learn how to better protect personal identifying information and to reduce fraud.

The Postal Inspection Service is at the forefront of the Department of Justice's new efforts to combat international organized crime. Governments must coordinate investigations, prevention, and awareness in order to reduce the crimes and protect commerce. We also play a key role with the Departments of Justice and Homeland Security in ensuring that identity theft and identity fraud are not used for funding terrorist activities. Virtually every major terrorist event involved identity theft; many involved identity fraud for funding terrorist activities.

Corporations play a key role in future mitigation of identity crimes. Self-audits and due diligence are needed to protect that valuable information you have entrusted to them: your identity. Also, their corporate brand reputation, fraud losses, and customer loyalty all depend on the protection of that information.

Finally, individual citizens must be as savvy as the criminals seeking to steal their identity. The new methods of stealing your identity require you to understand and use technology to protect yourself. Understanding the dos and don'ts of protecting your identity are key, but that will stop only some of the criminals' methods.

In all, Biegelman has more than accurately captured the challenges of both today and tomorrow in the world of identity theft and identity fraud. Here we get a clear picture of the challenges to come and the opportunities to meet those challenges. Now we need action. I hope some of the leaders in both business and government who read this book (as well as the average citizen) are prompted to get involved and take action. The consequences of inaction are grave.

**Kenneth R. Jones**
Deputy Chief Inspector
U.S. Postal Inspection Service
Washington, DC
August 2008

# Preface

This is the book that I have always wanted to write. In fact, I have been preparing for it for 30 years, since my early days investigating mail theft and credit card fraud. "Identity theft" was not even a term then. That would come in the 1990s. The crime had many names, but it was always the same. Identity theft was and is an evil with a life of its own. It has grown from just an American problem into a worldwide epidemic that shows no signs of ending.

My first experience with identity theft was in 1978, when I was a newly hired United States Postal Inspector in the New York metropolitan area. I heard other inspectors tell stories of fraudulent credit card applications and the resulting credit card frauds, the ease of obtaining personal information and phony identification to perpetrate this crime, how foreign nationals were behind many of the schemes, and how much money the banks and growing credit card industry were losing. It seemed like such a simple crime to commit.

By 1981, I was assigned to a team of federal agents investigating mail theft involving credit cards, checks, and other valuables sent through the mail. I saw firsthand how identity theft occurred and how easy it was to perpetrate. It still would be years before the crime would get the name "identity theft." At the time we called it credit card fraud, fraud apps (for credit card application fraud), true name fraud, and the Crime of the '80s. As I investigated case after case, I came to the realization that this was not just any typical fraud.

Back then there were not many in law enforcement involved in fighting this crime. As the epidemic grew, more and more federal, state, and local law enforcement agents would learn about and start investigations into identity theft. Even though we were making arrest after arrest of defendants involved in this crime, other fraudsters just took their places. It felt like we were fighting a losing battle. We realized that prevention needed to be embraced and evangelized to the public as well as the financial services industry. Perhaps education and awareness could stem the tide.

By the mid-1980s, other agents and I were speaking about the growing problem to anyone who would listen but especially to law enforcement, credit card and bank investigators, and the media. I said things like "It's a major problem throughout the country; the problem is growing so much that it is overwhelming law enforcement agencies; cooperation between banks, credit bureaus and law enforcement is essential to address the problem; and it's a growing problem and can destroy the credit industry as we know it if we don't stop it." I made these comments on a 1985 video for the TransUnion credit bureau to show to its employees, financial services employees, and law enforcement. The video was titled *Crime of the 80s.*

In September 1986, I had the honor of testifying before the United States Senate about emerging criminal groups, credit card fraud, and the phony identification used to perpetrate this crime. Nowhere in the hearings transcript is the phrase "identity theft" but every person there was describing it as they spoke. In writing this book, I looked at my testimony and was struck by something I said. Asked about the impact on victims, I responded:

> *Basically, it is a horror story for the individual. The banks assume the losses so the individual does not have to pay the losses out of his pocket, but the real problem is the effect on the individual's credit rating. . . . I know of cases where the people, a year or two after the fraud, and after they have contacted the credit bureaus to clear up their name, they still have problems getting credit, including credit cards, mortgages, and other loans.*

Ultimately, the greatest impact that identity theft has is on the victim, and that is something we must do a better job of addressing. I have met thousands of victims of fraud in my career as a criminal investigator: not just victims of identity theft but of all varieties of fraud. I have seen people from all walks of life who have lost not only their money but also hope. They were good people who falsely believed in the fraudsters to whom they gave their life savings. There is nothing good about being a victim, and that is especially true for identity theft. Even when victims of identity theft did not lose any money, they still lost their most important asset: their good name.

In a memorable cartoon strip on the first Earth Day in 1971, the title character of the Walt Kelly comic strip *Pogo* uttered the famous quote "We have met the enemy and he is us." Pogo was reflecting on the sad state of the environment and the growing problem of pollution when he made this comment. Yet, Pogo's timeless quote is just as relevant to our loss of privacy over the years and how we as a society provide fraudsters with all the tools they need for identity theft. We hold some responsibility for identity theft, and we are the ones to stop it. Famed poet and philosopher George Santayana once said: "Those who cannot learn from history are doomed to repeat it." We need to remember Santayana's words as they relate to identity theft.

I like to believe that we can turn the tide of identity theft. I still believe it is all about prevention. That is also why I wrote this book. I intend it to be a handbook both in name and premise. A handbook is a detailed and comprehensive guide, manual, and reference. I want to provide as much information and cover as many aspects of identity theft as possible. To do that and provide context, I have included numerous stories and case studies about the criminals who commit this crime and the law enforcement professionals who hunt them down. Often they tell their stories in their own words. Through these accounts, you will learn much about the many ways identity theft occurs and its effect on all of us.

This handbook details the history and evolution of identity theft, the impact on individuals and businesses, key legislation, the global reach of this crime, privacy rights and the loss of privacy, case studies that illustrate the various methods employed by fraudsters, the role of technology, research and trends, the future growth and challenges of this crime, and prevention recommendations. I have included anecdotes, news stories, government reports, and other information related to identity theft that I have personally collected since the late 1970s.

The United States Postal Inspection Service is the leading federal law enforcement agency fighting identity theft since the 1960s. It devoted investigative resources to credit card fraud, mail theft, and identity theft long before anyone else did, and it continues to be a thought leader in detecting and preventing these interrelated crimes. The Inspection Service provided me access to closed case files as well as to the inspectors who are subject matter experts in identity theft. These inspectors shared many experiences that I have included in this book.

In a few instances, I changed the names of victims, witnesses, and defendants as well as locales and dates for specific privacy and/or safety concerns. The essential facts of these cases remain the same.

Throughout the book are unique profiles of criminals whom I have ignominiously admitted to the "Identity Theft Hall of Infamy" for their criminality. I also profile the honorable and dedicated professionals working to put these fraudsters behind bars and prevent the growth of identity theft in sections entitled "Thought Leaders in Identity Theft Investigation, Research, and Prevention."

As you read this book, you may come away with a feeling of dread. Be afraid, be very afraid for what identity thieves have done. These criminals have taken our good names and reputations as their very own. Once they start, they cannot stop. They are addicted to identity theft; it becomes their heroin. But we have the power to stop them and it will take a great deal of work. Education, awareness, technology, and prevention are important tools in stopping the spread of this fraud. It is my pleasure to provide all that and more in this book. Read and learn.

# Acknowledgments

With each book I write, the more I realize that my success is the direct result of the efforts and contributions of others. This book is no exception. I have had exceptional support from many people who provided their experiences, stories, materials, and thought leadership.

First and foremost, I thank my son, Daniel Biegelman, who, as with my previous books, provided extraordinary assistance. Daniel was involved in research, writing, editing, and proofing. His countless hours and tireless dedication helped make this book a reality.

A special note of thanks to my executive editor at John Wiley & Sons, Tim Burgard, who strongly encouraged me to write this book and, as before, guided me through the writing and publishing process. Tim has continuously supported my literary adventures and has given me the unique opportunity to express my thoughts and experiences in writing. I also want to acknowledge Helen Cho and Dexter Gasque at Wiley, who have been invaluable in helping me get through issues large and small in the production process. They are true professionals.

Chief Postal Inspector Alexander Lazaroff and Deputy Chief Inspector Kenneth Jones of the United States Postal Inspection Service gave me unique access to their highly skilled law enforcement professionals who are subject matter experts in identity theft. This amazing opportunity allowed me to tap some of the best minds in the business for this book.

Postal Inspector Phil Garn provided me the excellent content for Chapter 14 as well as other material. He devoted untold hours sharing his firsthand knowledge and experience of how identity theft severely impacted San Diego. I am extremely grateful for his assistance.

A special thank you to Brad Kleinknecht, Henry Herrera, Patricia Sweeney, Phil Bartlett, Larry Katz, Mike McCarthy, Bob Hoffman, Don Landisi, Patrick Bernardo, Robert Diaz, Brian Huenefeld, Ken Male, Richard Petry, Mark Shaw, Walley Wang, Scott Mathews, Dave McGinnis, Jack Galvin, Mike Colaiacovo, Jim Antonino, Debbi Baer, Joseph Wolf, Jane DeFillippo, Joseph Jakubiec, Carl Clapper, John Murphy, Steven Maciag, Mark Carr, Raymond Marvez, Tony Galetti, Dave Collins, Thomas Kerns, Bob Vincent, Tony Haskett, Ralph Perez, Randy DeGasperin, Dave Colen, Eddy Boucher, Dominick Pinto, Bernard Ferguson, Melisa Llosa, Jody Kowahl, Mike

Casadei, Bob Northrop, Bob Joy, Tom Buggie, Ron Pry, Rick Ruhland, George Eller, John Wisniewski, Sally Wolfe, Joe Clark, Rick Johnson, Joe Byers, Tom Kelly, Dennis Kelleher, Don Gattie, Rudy Green, Mike Egner, Al Dockus, Paul Hinman, and Brendan O'Brien. These Inspection Service personnel, past and present, provided me insight and shared many experiences and considerable expertise that I have included in this book.

I would also like to acknowledge the late Robert "Buzz" Jones, Jr. He was an extremely dedicated Postal Inspector with an innate ability to solve even the most difficult of cases. That special skill was on display when he was the case agent in a series of identity theft-related homicides profiled in this book. Buzz especially enjoyed working with and teaching new inspectors. He is missed.

My sincere thanks to those who those who provided ideas, content, interviews, and assistance: Shannon Grayer, Brock Phillips, Kevin Barrows, Don Rebovich, George Curtis, Todd Hutton, Georgia Hanif, Julie Werner-Simon, Jackie Fishman, Byron Hollis, Scott Moritz, George Stamboulidis, Joe Wells, Dick Carozza, John Gill, Joel Bartow, Catherine Grant, Bill Kresse, Kathleen Hanold Watland, John Lucki, Steve Reed, Harry Megerian, William Zabotka, and Thomas Cooney.

When I wanted someone to read my draft manuscript and give me honest feedback, I again turned to my old and wise friend, DeWayn Marzagalli. DeWayn, a former federal agent extraordinaire, provided the constructive and thoughtful comments I needed. As always, he offered ongoing advice and encouragement that was much needed and appreciated.

Although this work is solely mine and does not reflect the views and opinions of Microsoft Corporation, I would like to thank my company for allowing me to write this book.

And, last but not least, my gratitude to my wife Lynn, who was indispensable as she again spent many hours reviewing the manuscript and providing insightful feedback. Lynn's constant encouragement, wisdom, and attention to detail were essential to my writing. Her patience as I again spent all my free time engrossed in the book, is exceptional.

# Identity Theft Handbook

# CHAPTER 1

# The Identity Theft Explosion

Imagine seeing a disaster unfold before your very eyes, one constantly growing larger and more destructive. It continually evolves to the changing environment and resists all attempts to blunt its impact. You and thousands of others try to stop this disaster, but all actions are futile. Despite all the warnings, you are powerless to do anything but observe the massive impact on individuals, organizations, and businesses. While I could easily be describing a major earthquake, hurricane, or tsunami, the actual culprit is a crime. But this is not just any crime. It is an extraordinary wrong that is more like an unstoppable force in its devastation. The crime is identity theft, and it has grown and evolved over the last 35 years to take on a relentless life of its own.

Identity theft is the fastest-growing financial crime in the United States and the world. Several years ago CBS News reported that someone's identity is stolen every 79 seconds. A Federal Trade Commission (FTC) survey in 2006 found that 8.3 million American adults were victims of identity theft. That same study estimated the total identity theft losses to be $15.6 billion, a figure significantly down from a similar FTC study in 2003 that found total losses to be $47.6 billion. Of note, the 2006 study indicated that changes in survey methodology may be the reason for the difference, rather than an actual drop in incidence levels.

Whatever the exact losses, the growth of identity theft has been striking. *Kiplinger's Personal Finance* magazine in its July 1995 edition reported that the credit reporting bureau Experian received 600 to 700 identity theft complaints each day. MasterCard International reported that identity theft represented 96% of member banks' fraud losses in 1997. Identity theft losses grew from $450 million in 1996 to over $2 billion in 1999.

According to the FTC, fraudulent use of credit cards accounted for 50% of all identity theft complaints in 2000. Identity theft complaints involving the misuse of Social Security numbers (SSNs) jumped from 27,000 in 1998 to 73,000 in 2002, according to the Social Security Administration.

As a result of stronger data-loss notification laws, more than 500 incidents of data breaches were reported between 2005 and the first half of 2007, involving more than 155 million records. The lost data came from the theft of laptops, intrusions by hackers, and general carelessness and disregard for data security. Breaches have affected government agencies, hospitals, financial services firms, and a host of other companies.[1]

## WHAT IS IDENTITY THEFT?

During identity theft, criminals acquire key pieces of personal identifying information—such as name, address, date of birth, SSN, mother's maiden name, employment information, credit information, and other vital facts—in order to impersonate and defraud the victim. This information enables the thief to commit numerous forms of fraud, including taking over the victim's financial accounts; applying for loans, credit cards, and Social Security benefits; purchasing homes and cars; and establishing services with utility and phone companies.

Simply put, identity theft is the stealing of your good name and reputation for financial gain. Yet not everyone can agree on a suitable meaning of the term. The definition of this crime differs among law enforcement, regulatory agencies, and the many studies on this subject. The United States Postal Inspection Service states that "[i]dentity theft occurs when a crook steals key pieces of personal identifying information to gain access to a person's financial accounts."[2] The United States Secret Service calls it identity crimes and defines it as "the misuse of personal or financial identifiers in order to gain something of value and/or facilitate other criminal activity."[3]

The President's Identity Theft Task Force Report issued in April 2007 stated that "[a]lthough identity theft is defined in many different ways, it is, fundamentally, the misuse of another individual's personal information to commit fraud."[4] The report goes on: "Criminals must first gather personal information, either through low-tech methods—such as stealing mail or workplace records, or 'dumpster diving'—or through complex and high-tech frauds, such as hacking and the use of malicious computer codes."[5] More detailed information on the Task Force Report can be found in Chapter 18.

The October 2007 study entitled *Identity Fraud Trends and Patterns: Building a Data-Based Foundation for Proactive Enforcement* issued by the Center for Identity Management and Information Protection at Utica College in Utica, New York provided detailed new research on identity theft. For a more detailed discussion of this study, please see Chapter 19. The study agreed with the President's Task Force that the fraudulent use of personal identifying information—name, address, SSN, date of birth—are elements of identity theft but fraud involving credit cards, debit cards, and ATM cards are not. The report stated: "While the theft of a credit card may result in fraudulent charges, it does not result in the theft of an identity."[6] The study went on to quote a line from the President's Task Force: "For example, a stolen credit card may lead to thousands of dollars in fraudulent charges, but the card generally would not provide the thief with enough information to establish a false identity."[7]

I generally agree with these definitions but respectfully disagree with the idea that a theft of a person's credit card, including name and related credit card number, is not identity theft. I take a much larger and more victim-oriented view of identity theft. Therefore, I prefer the definition used by the Federal Trade Commission's Consumer Sentinel. Consumer Sentinel is an information sharing network that provides law enforcement with access to consumer complaints received by the FTC. Identity theft is "when someone appropriates your personal identifying information (like your Social Security number or credit card account number) to commit fraud or theft."[8] When a fraudster steals a victim's credit card, the criminal poses as that person, fraudulently using the name and linked credit card number to steal money and property that will be charged to the victim's account. Although the ultimate financial loss will be borne by the financial institution or credit card issuer, the true card holder is still a victim. There are various degrees of identity theft, but I do not think there is a single person who would not be outraged knowing that someone had stolen and used his or her credit card or other financial access device.

## IT IS NOT ROCKET SCIENCE

It is very easy for criminals to obtain our personal information and our identities. Everything from low-tech to high-tech thievery is readily available. It seems that not a day goes by without hearing about another news story on identity theft. Due to this publicity, almost everyone knows about this crime. It has been called everything from credit card fraud to true name fraud to identity fraud to the Crime of the '80s, and since the mid-1990s, identity theft. It was called credit card fraud first because in the early days, it primarily involved the theft of personal identifying information for submitting fraudulent credit card applications. The stolen information came from a variety of sources: Dumpster diving; insiders at banks, credit bureaus, and the post office; mail theft from collection boxes and residences were but some of the ways the fraudsters obtained personally identifiable information.

The growth of credit card fraud paralleled the rise of credit card use in this country starting in the early 1970s. Once people began to accept credit card use and heavy marketing by the banking industry spurred their growth, fraudsters had a new avenue for their criminal enterprise. These criminals would steal personal information and apply for credit cards in the victims' names. I would like to say they were ingenious, but in reality it was pretty easy to do. They used simple means to obtain identity information because then as now, personal information, the keys to our personal vault, was so readily available.

The old standby of getting down and dirty in Dumpster diving has been effective whenever individuals or businesses do not safeguard information. Unfortunately that is all too often. Dumpster divers look in the trash for discarded credit card statements, canceled checks, preapproved credit card offers, medical records, mortgage applications, and any other documents that contain your name, address, date of birth, SSN, or other information. In the days before shredders were commonplace, fraudsters found mother lode after mother lode of personal information. And they still find gold today.

Mail theft is another valuable source of personal data for identity thieves. The beauty of the mail system is that Americans receive mail delivery to their homes and businesses six days a week, 52 weeks a year. There is a never-ending supply of bank and brokerage statements, credit card bills, convenience checks, credit card offers, and a wealth of other personal and financial information for identity thieves. We lock our homes, our cars, and our businesses to protect what is inside, but how many of us have a locking mailbox?

As Internet access gets faster and cheaper, more and more people worldwide use it for business and pleasure. Do you know anyone who does not have Internet access either at home or work? Very few, I would say. Fraudsters have found how easy it is to do business—fraudulent business—using the Internet. They use spam, phishing, pharming, vishing, hacking, planting malicious codes, and whatever new technology breakthrough they can exploit to steal passwords, financial information, and other identifying data. If you are not familiar with some of these terms, you will learn all about them in Chapter 3. The increasing reporting of large-scale data breaches are the result of these technology attacks as well as plain old human failure. Story after story involves laptops left unsecured in cars or hotel rooms without encryption. No wonder we have the problem we do; we make it so easy for identity thieves.

In the early 1980s, professionals such as lawyers, stockbrokers, physicians, and others with good credit ratings were likely victims. Fraudsters often applied for jobs as night watchmen, security guards, and cleaning people at major businesses, where at night they would have free access to search through personnel files, employees' desks, and other belongings to obtain names, home addresses, job titles, and SSNs for credit card fraud. They often passed this data to confederates throughout the country for further fraud. In 1985, identity thieves did just that when they infiltrated CBS News in New York City and stole personal information on hundreds of CBS employees, including famed news anchor Walter Cronkite and *60 Minutes'* Ed Bradley.

The crime began to evolve. Fraudsters subverted postal employees so that they would turn over mail containing credit cards. Identity thieves would infiltrate Social Security offices, banks, brokerages, and credit bureaus to fraudulently access victims' credit reports and then do credit card and bank frauds with the stolen identities. They used post office boxes to obtain fraudulently ordered credit cards. Postal Inspectors would arrest these identity thieves when they came to pick up the cards at post offices. They then began to use a new business industry called commercial mail receiving agencies (CMRAs) or mail drops to open mail boxes in the names of their victims and receive the fraudulently requested credit cards.

By the mid-1980s, this crime began to hit the media's radar screen. More and more victims complained to financial institutions and law enforcement. In 1982 and 1984, Congress enacted legislation that made access device fraud, including credit and debit card fraud, specific crimes. The United States Secret Service was given primary authority for the investigation of access device fraud. Postal Inspectors who had been working credit card frauds since the 1960s were now joined by Secret Service agents. Still the crime grew.

Identity theft has grown tremendously since those early years because criminals have found out how easy it is and how available personal information is. The associated crimes currently include identity takeovers of company names, committing insurance fraud under stolen names of physicians, and stealing information from family home-pages and resumes found online. The Internet and online databases make obtaining personal information just a mouse click away.

## THOUGHT LEADER IN IDENTITY THEFT INVESTIGATION

### Edward Stroz

Following a 16-year career as a Special Agent for the Federal Bureau of Investigation, Edward Stroz founded Stroz Friedberg, LLC in 2000 and now serves as its copresident. Stroz Friedberg is a technical and consulting services firm specializing in digital forensics, e-discovery, and corporate investigations. Stroz has assisted clients in responding to Internet extortions, denial-of-service attacks, hacks and unauthorized access, and theft of trade secrets and has pioneered the concept of incorporating behavioral science into the methodology for addressing computer crime and abuse.

Stroz is an expert in addressing the threat of computer crime and abuse posed by insiders and has coauthored a book on the subject. He has supervised numerous forensic assignments for federal prosecutors, defense attorneys, and civil litigants and has conducted network security audits for major public and private entities. In 1996, while still a Special Agent, he formed the FBI's Computer Crime Squad in New York City, where he supervised investigations involving computer intrusions, denial-of-service attacks, illegal Internet wiretapping, fraud, money laundering, and violations of intellectual property rights, including trade secrets. Here Stroz provides his perspective on the evils of identity theft and fighting back:

*Imagine you are at home having dinner with your family and you hear an unexpected knock on the door. You answer the door and meet two FBI agents who want to question you about threatening email messages that have been traced as having originated from your home. You find it hard to believe this could be true. However, in the interview with the FBI, it becomes clear that the wireless network in your home was hacked remotely by the true perpetrator to commit a crime by making threats and extortionate demands to people completely unknown to you. In essence, your identity and that of your household were compromised, and used to provide cover to an intruder. While not an everyday occurrence, I've seen this kind of identity theft scenario played out over my career in law enforcement and as a consultant.*

*Identity theft is essentially the theft of information. It's information "about you" as an individual person, and there is some reason that it would be valuable to a thief. That value could be purely monetary—as simple as the thief using your credit in order to buy things. But the value of your information may have nothing to do with money, as the scenario recounted above shows.*

*(Continued)*

*And there are other forms of identity theft. Using a stolen identity can allow a wanted person to evade capture, or a suspected terrorist to pass through a security checkpoint unrecognized in order to get on an airplane. I have been involved with computer hacking cases in which stolen identities were used to make it look as though someone else was behind the crime, and to get them in serious trouble.*

*Each of these examples represents different types of problems, and it's important to make distinctions among them. As with any type of fight, it is important to know something about your adversary. The different types of identity thieves can be categorized into "threat agent" profiles in order to fight this problem. The term "threat agent" is often used to describe the individual behind the attack and the method used to execute the attack.*

*The simplest type of identity theft is targeted against consumer credit/debit cards. These are often stolen in bulk (large computer files that contain numerous card numbers) and used a few times before being discarded. This activity is more of a "property crime," which, while serious, is sometimes more manageable. This is because stealing money or credit will show up right away in business records as there is a vendor alongside you in the fight. Within days or weeks, the unauthorized activity will show up on a credit card or bank statement, bringing the problem to light. While this represents a real problem, it is probably not the biggest threat to our society.*

*Identity theft for the purpose of actually assuming your identity in order to move through society unimpeded is different from that of stealing a credit card number, and is harder to fight. Here you are up against a smarter and more dedicated adversary, with much greater value to a threat agent in the form of a terrorist, than a property crime thief. Fighting that type of adversary is primarily done by law enforcement.*

*Nobody really knows where these problems will lead. Greater security almost always comes at the price of decreased convenience and privacy. The technologies with the least inconvenience will likely be in high demand. For example, retinal scans, already in use at some airports to speed people through security, will probably gain increasing acceptance as a form of biometric (something you "are") recognition. Fingerprint scanners are increasingly featured on laptop computers. It seems that opting in for biometrics as a form of protection is going to be the most useful technology for countering identity theft without inconveniencing people to an unacceptable level.*

## EARLY DAYS OF CREDIT CARDS

In the early years of credit card issuance, the cards generally had very low purchasing limits. Purchasing caps of $300 to $500 were not uncommon, and it usually took a formal application with a good payment history to raise a card's limit. Although American Express offered cards that appeared to have no spending limit, the balance could not be carried over and had to be paid off by the end of the billing cycle. American Express was much more selective with regard to potential customers than other card issuers, such as Visa, MasterCard, department stores, and gasoline companies.

Initially, credit card transactions were processed manually from the merchant making an imprint on the sale or charge slip at the store to reconciling slips at the bank and posting charges to customers' accounts. Although a card might have a limit of $500, criminals would make multiple purchases under recognized floor limits, which they learned from trial and error. When financial institutions reconciled the charges at the end of the cycle, the total charges would far exceed the card's limit. It was not uncommon for small businesses to send in charges a month or more past the normal cycle. The store might wait until it had several charges to send in its charge slips, and this would delay the posting of the particular charges. So it might take several months to determine the true losses on the card. This manual process carried through the early days of automation as many smaller merchants were not "online." The online electronic process was gradually phased in and equipment became more affordable for smaller merchants.

As local banks began to issue their own cards and more banking functions became automated, far more cards were issued, including ones mistakenly linked to other accounts. San Diego–based Postal Inspector Phil Garn related a case where a doctor applied for a $50,000 loan for a piece of diagnostic medical equipment. The bank accidentally issued a card linked to the loan account with a $50,000 limit. This card was then stolen from the mail. The crook had no idea what the limit was and, luckily for the victim, only charged a few thousand dollars. Despite the low limits on credit cards, criminals were able to run up charges so quickly that they frequently far exceeded the card's limit. It was common to find cards with $500 limits but which had over $1,800 of fraudulent charges.

At this time, both newly issued cards and reissued cards were "live cards." They could be used immediately upon arrival. There was no activation procedure, either in person or on the phone, and there was no online banking. Most merchants manually ran the card through a device that embossed an imprint of the card onto a carbon sales slip that the customer had to sign. This turned out to be a great paper trail for investigators, not only for suspects' handwriting but for fingerprints. However, these copies rapidly disappeared as banks began to microfilm the slips and destroy the originals due to the sheer quantity of slips and physical storage limits. The microfilmed copies would preclude fingerprint analysis and make it hard to get a positive forensic identification on the handwriting.

Later, merchants would be able to make queries via telephone, and larger merchants would be able to run the card through their own magnetic card readers to get an authorization code. These codes became commonplace; however, at the time, the codes could also be manually overridden at the point of sale at the merchant's discretion and liability. If access to credit was denied, criminals would often engage in social engineering, telling the merchant a story about how their vindictive ex-spouse canceled their card or had intentionally reported it stolen.

The criminal would also demand to speak to the credit card company on the telephone at the store. The criminal would then put on a dramatic one-sided conversation, finally coming up with an authorization code, usually a sequence of letters and numbers, which he or she would provide to the merchant, who would write the number down on the charge slip and finish the transaction. Although this authorization code was not valid, it would appear to have a correct sequence of numbers and letters for the particular card being used. Magnetic credit card readers would eventually come down in price and become commonly used, as they are now. Today nearly every merchant has an electronic credit card terminal for approving purchases. There is no doubt that today's technology has helped to significantly decrease fraud at the point of sale.

## LIMITING LOSSES

Detection and prevention of credit card fraud were also very much on the minds of the credit card issuers. During these years, each card issuer, such as American Express, Visa, and MasterCard, would also issue lists of lost/stolen credit card numbers, typically printed in books similar to the size of telephone books. These warning lists allowed subscribing merchants to check the account number when the customer presented a card to make a purchase. It was a time-consuming process, as the type was very small and it was hard to find a suspect card's number in the endless pages of listed numbers.

Merchants did not always check the warning lists even though they would be liable for fraudulent charges. European merchants would hang on to this countermeasure for much longer than the United States. Criminals who stole bulk shipments of new or reissued credit cards in the United States would use the cards immediately after the theft and then send the cards in bulk to criminal associates in Europe, where the printed lost/stolen lists were at least a month behind. After charging purchases up to the cards' limits in Europe, the cards were sent to Asia, where they would be reencoded. It was not unusual for a stolen Visa card to be magnetically reencoded with a MasterCard account number and fraudulently used.

In the 1970s and 1980s, billing processes were far more manual and much slower than today. Electronic point-of-sale terminals had yet to come into existence. Charges would typically post during the following month and be mailed to a customer in a statement for a 30-day period, although it was not uncommon for some charges to show up 60 or 90 days later. This was due to merchants physically mailing in their sales slips and the increased time needed for processing and posting.

When unauthorized charges appeared, a lengthy process to dispute these charges could take months. Problems even could continue for years, as sometimes these unpaid balances were not removed from people's credit histories. Inspector Garn relates how he would often get panicked calls from victims six to 18 months after he first talked to them about their stolen credit cards. The victims had filed affidavits of forgery and had cleared their accounts with the financial institutions but were now trying to buy a car or close on a house. Unfortunately, the fraudulent charges still appeared on their credit records.

Even though victims may have cleared one fraudulently used card, criminals often applied for additional cards or utility services in the names of the victims. These new cards would be sent to another address controlled by the fraudsters; then after use and nonpayment, the account would appear as unpaid and delinquent. After hearing from the first few panic-stricken callers, Inspector Garn would tell victims to check their credit histories on an ongoing basis to see if any additional charges appeared. He often felt helpless in not being able to do more for these victims; even arresting the scammers did not stop the credit problems.

Customers were also responsible for the fraud charges or some portion of them, until lawsuits and public opinion caused banks to change their policies. It became highly embarrassing when victims who had an average monthly balance of a few hundred dollars and a history of on-time payments could show the news media thousands of dollars charged in a few days, all obvious fraud. Financial institutions also found they could pass the losses off to their customers in the form of higher interest rates. It was not until the losses from fraud cut into the banking institutions' profits that changes occurred and proactive fraud prevention became routine.

In the early 1980s, a bank investigator for a major financial institution in New York decided that he would create his own fraud detection process for the increasing number of fraudulent credit card applications his bank was receiving. These applications were being submitted using stolen identities and contained the names, birth dates, Social Security numbers, and employment histories of the victims. This bank investigator correctly assumed that the bulk of these thousands of fraudulent applications were being submitted by members of Nigerian Criminal Enterprises who were a plague on the credit card industry at the time.

At this point, credit card applications were completed by hand and mailed in for processing. After finding that the fraudsters had a very distinctive style of handwriting, this investigator began to manually review each submitted application looking for these handwriting characteristics. They included the signature being underlined, periods on both sides of middle initials in names, period after signatures, reversal of first and last names, European-style date, a colon used in place of decimals, dashes or slashes, letters A and E connected to the next letter, dashes between names or nouns, as well as other misspelled words and strange abbreviations. Although this process by itself was not totally conclusive as to the existence of fraud, this investigator was very successful in identifying suspect applications that needed additional scrutiny.

Both federal and state authorities would investigate and prosecute identity theft—although it was yet to have that name—but many considered the fraud a "victimless" crime. Banks and credit card issuers ultimately made the individuals whole for fraud losses. When I was working these cases in Brooklyn, New York, a federal prosecutor told me that he would not accept any credit card fraud cases for prosecution unless I could specifically detail the prevention efforts in place by the victim financial institution. This prosecutor felt that the banks were not doing enough to stop identity theft and that they were using law enforcement to fix the problem. I went back and told this to the bank investigators I was working with. Some banks had excellent prevention efforts; others sadly did not.

I remember making a prevention recommendation that was quickly rejected as cost prohibitive. The fraudulent credit card applications submitted by criminals contained stolen identity information, but one piece of information could be used to quickly determine the validity of the application. To ensure that an application would be approved, the thieves would include the victim's actual employer but would substitute a telephone number controlled by the suspect for the actual work number. This was done so that when a credit card issuer called to verify employment, the fraudster or his accomplice would verify employment. I recommended that when verifying the credit card application, a call be made to the named employer asking to speak directly to the named employee but not using the telephone number on the application. Instead, the employer's number would need to be obtained through the telephone directory or calling Directory Assistance. The financial institutions advised me that while my suggestion was sound in theory and would quickly determine if a person had submitted the application in question, the extra steps and time would be financially burdensome.

There were many prosecutions in the early years, but the jail sentences were not significant enough to have a deterrent effect. The crimes continued to grow. As a consequence, although criminals were apprehended and successfully prosecuted, offenders did not receive long prison sentences, and the lure of the money brought on recidivism. A felony or even a misdemeanor conviction would have a major impact on an average person, but the short sentences the fraudsters received sent a clear message to recidivists that identity theft was extremely profitable.

## JAIL ORDER FRAUD

There are always opportunities for creative and resourceful criminals to fleece an unsuspecting public. For those hardened fraudsters focused on committing identity theft, even confinement in a prison was not a barrier to committing this crime. During the summer and fall of 1981, Ricky Lee Bishop and Howard A. Jones were inmates at the Pulaski County Prison Farm in Virginia. Bishop was in prison on unrelated credit card fraud charges, serving a three-year sentence. Jones was a frequent prison guest with a history of criminal offenses including Grand Larceny and Obtaining Money by False Pretenses. Due to good behavior in prison, both Bishop and Jones were participating in a weekend furlough program where they were permitted to return home on Saturdays and Sundays.

Prison did not stop the pair from returning to a life of crime. While serving their sentences, Bishop and Jones were able to obtain the credit card numbers of people who had stayed at the Red Carpet Inn in Pulaski. Prisoners assigned to work on garbage collection details with the Pulaski County Sanitation Department obtained the stolen credit card numbers from the inn, one of the stops for the garbage pickup. The inmates would go through the trash at the hotel and recover discarded credit card receipts. It was believed that this was how Bishop and Jones found the credit card numbers used for the fraud.

Back in 1981, multiple part credit card slips with carbon paper inserts were used for sales transactions. The slips contained the purchaser's name, credit card number, expiration information, and signature. Often merchants discarded the slips after the transactions were completed. Fraudsters quickly found that Dumpster diving was a simple and easy way to obtain personal information for fraudulent purposes. It worked for these two inmates; it is no different today for those who fail to properly shred documents containing pertinent information.

After obtaining the credit card numbers, Bishop and Jones ordered merchandise by telephone from various companies located in Richmond, Chicago, Atlanta, Dallas, and Decatur. One of the companies was Best Products, a now-defunct chain of catalog sales and retail stores that was located in Richmond, Virginia. The inmates used the addresses of girlfriends and relatives as the delivery addresses for the merchandise. They would then arrange to pick up the packages on weekends when on furlough. On several occasions, Bishop would personally return the merchandise to Best Product stores located in Roanoke and Lynchburg for cash refunds.

The case was investigated by the Postal Inspection Service. The scheme lasted from July to November 1981 and Bishop and Jones received only about $4,400. The defendants used telephones to order the merchandise and the mails were used to ship the merchandise. As a result, they were charged with federal violation of Wire Fraud, Mail Fraud, and Use of Fictitious Names. Both defendants pleaded guilty in October 1982, and each received three additional years to their existing prison sentences.

There are lessons to learn from this case. Although the amount of the fraud was relatively small, and the individual credit card holders did not suffer any losses, there still was an impact. The credit card holders needed to close out their accounts and obtain new ones. The true card holders did nothing wrong yet were subject to this crime because the motel owners discarded the credit card slips. The simple act of shredding the slips would have prevented the possibility of this crime occurring. But in those years few people thought of destroying personal and financial information. There will always be hidden opportunities for criminals to defraud society. It is up to us to remove those opportunities through increased vigilance and prevention.

## IDENTITY THEFT WAS NOT A HIGH PRIORITY

The owner of an alternative press wrote in 1981 that "[t]he supposed problem of 'ID fraud' generates low-level interest among law enforcement people, both state and federal. The prevailing attitude among prosecutors, born out of practice, is that laws are already in existence to combat the types of crimes associated with false ID."[9] To most people, this opinion was the correct one. It was also perceived this way because relatively small numbers of consumers had been victimized by this crime. Yet the crime was still in its infancy.

The time period between the late 1960s and early 1980s saw the birth and growth of a new crime. It was just beginning to spread and evolve to a more damaging offense. The years to come, from the mid-1980s through the new millennium, would see an explosion of identity theft that would burn the existence of this crime into everyone's mind.

## NOTES

1. Byron Acohido and Jon Swartz, "Credit Bureaus Fight on State, Federal Levels against Freezes," *USA Today*, June 26, 2007, 1B.
2. United States Postal Inspection Service, Publication 280 (August 2003), www.usps.com/postalinspectors/pub280txt.htm.
3. United States Secret Service, *Financial Crimes*, www.ustreas.gov/usss/criminal.shtml.
4. President's Identity Theft Task Force, *Combating Identity Theft: A Strategic Plan* (April 2007), 2, www.idtheft.gov/reports/StrategicPlan.pdf.
5. Ibid.
6. Gary R. Gordon, Donald J. Rebovich, Kyung-Seok Choo, and Judith B. Gordon, *Identity Fraud Trends and Patterns: Building a Data-Based Foundation for Proactive Enforcement*, Center for Identity Management and Information

Protection, Utica College, Utica, NY(October 2007), 10, www.utica.edu/academic/institutes/cimip/research.cfm.

7. President's Identity Theft Task Force, *Combating Identity Theft*, 3.
8. Federal Trade Commission, Consumer Fraud and Identity Theft Complaint Data, January–December 2007, February 13, 2008, 74, www.ftc.gov/opa/2008/02/fraud.pdf.
9. Barry Reid, *The Paper Trip II* (Fountain Valley, CA: Eden Press, 1985), 5.

# CHAPTER 2

# Game of the Name: How It All Began

It can be argued that the future of identity theft was set with the advent of the Social Security number. When the government first issued Social Security numbers (SSNs) in late 1936, their stated purpose was to track each American's earnings and to provide a retirement safety net. The government assured everyone that the SSN was not intended to be used as a national identification card. For many years, right on the face of the card were the words "For Social Security Purposes—Not For Identification." Unfortunately, that was not to be the case.

In 1961, the Federal Civil Service Commission began using the SSN as an identification number for all federal employees. The following year, the Internal Revenue Service began to use the SSN as its taxpayer identification number (TIN) for individuals.[1] The Tax Reform Act of 1976 authorized the states to use SSNs in their programs for public assistance, driver's licenses, motor vehicle registration, and taxation. Over time, the SSN became the universal identification tool. It quickly became the identifier for driver's licenses, tax returns, medical records, college registration, banking and credit, and so much more.

Social Security numbers have become universally recognized as the gateway to our personal and financial information. We are asked for that number constantly. When we go to the doctor, we need to complete a medical form with not only our SSN but pages of other personal information. When we open a bank account or credit card, we are asked for our SSN and all the other personal information. We are asked for our SSN when we open a cellular telephone account, or utilities for water, electrical, or gas service. The same goes when we purchase a car. We generally provide a credit application that contains all our personal information, starting with our SSN. This also includes our name, home address, date of birth, employer, and bank and credit card information. A credit check is run to determine if we are creditworthy. Think about what would happen if an identity thief was working at that car dealership.

## FIRST IDENTITY THEFT VICTIM

When President Franklin Delano Roosevelt signed the Social Security Act into law in 1935, he had no way of knowing what the future would hold for that seemingly innocent Social Security number and its eventual connection to fraud. Within a year, the first Social Security cards were sent to working Americans. Not long after, the misuse of SSNs began. Hilda Schrader Whitcher may have been the first identity theft victim, well before credit and credit cards were the norm. If nothing else, her SSN was the most used and abused number ever issued.

In 1938, wallet manufacturer E.H. Ferree Company of Lockport, New York, came up with a novel approach to market its products. As a marketing ploy, the company decided to include a sample Social Security card in each wallet to show that the cards could easily fit inside. The cards were new to Americans, and by the end of 1937, over 37 million had been distributed. A company executive decided to use a copy of the actual card of his secretary, Hilda Schrader Whitcher, for the insert. The sample card was about half the size of the actual one, printed all in red, with the word "specimen" written diagonally across the face. Thousands upon thousands of these wallets were eventually sold at Woolworth's stores and other department stores throughout the country. Each contained Whitcher's facsimile Social Security card.

It did not take long for enterprising people to make use of Whitcher's number. Untold thousands of people began using it and by 1943, more than 5,700 people were known to be using Whitcher's number as their own. Although the Social Security Administration (SSA) publicized that it was improper to use another person's number, that did not stop the abuse. The SSA eventually voided the number and gave Whitcher a new one. I would imagine that she was very careful to safeguard her number after that. Still, her original number continued to be used for many years. It was being used in 1977 by as many as 12 people. In all, the SSA determined that over 40,000 people had used Hilda Schrader Whitcher's SSN over the years.[2]

What is not known is how many times the number was used for fraudulent purposes. SSNs were not used for credit in those early years, and there would have been few opportunities to benefit financially other than for SSA benefits. It can be readily assumed that most of the abusers were uninformed about how to properly obtain their own individual numbers. With so many people using her number as their own, it must have been a nightmare for Whitcher and the SSA to determine her correct benefits.

## IDENTITY FRAUD CONNECTION

The Department of Justice in *The Criminal Use of False Identification: The Report of the Federal Advisory Committee on False Identification* issued in November 1976 used the term "ID fraud" in describing identity crimes. The committee studied the growing use of phony identification and how the identification documents that people carry "have become the currency of fraud."[3] The report opined on the availability of "how-to" books that were being offered from the underground press at the time about creating and using new identities to commit fraud and concluded that the use of false identification to obtain goods and services was commonplace: "We have found clear evidence of widespread abuses in identification documents commonly used in our society . . . through the fraud committed; they also undermine the trust among individuals upon which our commercial and governmental institutions depend."[4]

The report also debated the use of publicity to increase fraud awareness among the general public. There was a concern that "publicity of fraud increases fraud" and by implication that the education process would "convince more people to try it."[5] Wisely, the report concluded that this was not the case. Even in 1976, abundant information was available on how to obtain and use phony identification. Criminals will always find the means to commit fraud. Publicizing the scope of the problem and prevention was paramount to protect businesses and individuals. "Educating the potential innocent victims of ID fraud—a significant portion of our U.S. populace—and prosecuting offenders may provide a far greater benefit than any hypothetical danger from exposure of victims to the facts of false ID use."[6]

When I first started speaking publicly in the mid-1980s about the threat of identity theft and its various forms, some people told me that it was not a good idea to talk so openly. They would say, "Why provide so much information; aren't you just teaching potential fraudsters, and adding to the problem?" Their concern was that by discussing the various details of how identity theft is perpetrated, it would give criminally minded people the information needed to commit it. I remember saying that fraudsters did not need me to educate them; a wide variety of readily available publications could teach them all they needed to know. They were already too busy committing identity theft. That was well before the Internet and the World Wide Web that today provides a plethora of information. It was not the identity thieves we needed to educate, it was and is the victims and potential victims of identity theft.

## HISTORY OF CREDIT CARDS

The acceptance of credit cards by the general public gave rise to many related crimes that developed over the years. Criminals would deal in lost, stolen, and counterfeit cards as well as those obtained through submission of fraudulent credit card applications. Each of these crimes touched on identity theft although that term was not commonly used until many years later. If it were not for credit cards, I am convinced we would not have the extensive identity theft problem we have today. The simplicity of the crime in the early days and the abundance of readily available personal information set the stage for its staggering growth and impact. For that reason, it is fitting and necessary to know the history of credit cards and how they have become an indispensable part of our everyday existence.

Although the use of credit cards became commonplace in the 1970s, credit cards in various forms had been around for most of the twentieth century. In 1914, Western

Union Telegraph Company offered its best customers a metal charge card that required a settlement of outstanding charges each month. It was the first consumer credit card and included deferred payments. These dogtag-style metal plates became commonplace and were later used by other retailers for their credit cards. They were embossed with the customer's name and address.

In 1924, a chain of California gas stations issued the first cardboard credit cards, setting the stage for the widespread use of oil and gas credit cards. This was an important development. The popularity of the automobile whetted the American public's appetite for travel and stoked the desire to be able to pay for gas anywhere. In the 1930s, department stores began to offer credit cards to their customers, and most used the metal plate–style cards. Major department stores, including Bloomingdales, the now-defunct Gimbel's chain, and others, found that these cards were a customer draw as more and more people wanted them. By the 1940s, trendy restaurants and nightclubs offered their own credit cards that could be used only at the particular business establishment.

In 1948, the first bank credit card was introduced through a bank in Brooklyn, New York. It was called "Charg-it" and had similar payment terms to today's credit cards. Only local purchases could be made, and the cardholder had to have a bank account at that bank through which payments were made.[7] The first bankcard, the Charg-it would not be the last and would open the door for other such cards and changes that would make them far more customer friendly.

In 1950, a visionary named Frank MacNamara conceived of a universal credit card that could be used at restaurants throughout New York City. The beauty of his idea was that instead of receiving monthly statements from each restaurant, as had been the norm, the cardholder would receive one statement each month for all restaurant activity. Thus was born the Diners Club credit card. The Diners Club card grew in popularity over the years and became the standard that others would emulate.

Long Island, New York banker Arthur Roth saw the future of credit and wanted to be in on it. His Franklin National Bank established a bank credit card for its customers in 1951. The card was a revolving credit card and could be used at stores and restaurants in the Long Island area. The card had no fees or interest but the balance had to be paid monthly. The bank made its money from the transaction fees paid by merchants accepting the cards. Franklin National Bank would eventually become European-American Bank (EAB), a powerhouse in banking. Citigroup would eventually purchase EAB. Many other banks also started issuing their own credit cards around this time.

In 1958, American Express got into the credit card business and its card quickly grew in popularity. The Hilton Hotel chain then came out with its own Carte Blanche credit card to compete with Diners Club and American Express. Although the big three credit card companies competed with each other, fraud had not yet emerged as a major problem. There were isolated stories of people without adequate income receiving cards and then going on huge spending sprees, unable to pay the subsequent statements. Yet the business model foretold future problems. The original model had been to extend credit to only the most worthy of customers, but the need to continually add new customers was critical to success. The result was that not all recipients of cards were as creditworthy as others.

In his excellent book on the history and evolution of credit cards entitled *The Credit Card Catastrophe*, author Matty Simmons asked, "In the rush to get more members, would cards be given to people only with dreams and no real way of paying for those dreams?"[8] We would see many more examples of this in the years to come as the marketing arm of credit card issuers sometimes won out over the security department concerns.

Bank of America, a venerable financial institution, also wanted to be part of the credit card action. In 1958, it launched its BankAmericard and offered a revolving credit account. It started a campaign of sending unsolicited credit cards to people in California to grow its customer base. At the time, banks could do business only in the state where they had their charter. In order to reach the huge numbers of potential cardholders nationwide, BankAmericard worked out an ingenious interchange agreement with banks throughout the country. This agreement came to fruition in 1966, and the use of credit cards grew as millions more signed up. BankAmericard would eventually become the Visa card in 1976.

Also in 1966, another group of banks created a bank cooperative and named it the Interbank Card Association, to compete with BankAmericard. In 1969, this group purchased the rights to use the name Master Charge from the California Bank Association. The Interbank Card Association (ICA) was an umbrella organization for Master Charge and "governed by consensus among its member banks."[9] It managed the various functions related to credit card administration including payments, authorizations, and settlement of charges for the association members. In 1979, Master Charge would be renamed MasterCard. The competition in the late 1960s resulted in large mailings of unsolicited credit cards. People received cards even though they may have not have been creditworthy or able to pay the charges. Children, the deceased, and family pets also got credit cards.

Large numbers of cards were stolen from the mail by Postal Service employees and others, resulting in an increasing amount of fraud losses to the industry. Criticism of the practice of mailing unsolicited cards was extensive, even reaching the mainstream in a widely read 1970 *Life* magazine article. As *Life* observed: "American banks have mailed 100 million cards to unsuspecting citizens and have offered each recipient not only a handful of 'instant cash' but a dreamy method of buying by signature after the lettuce runs out."[10] By this time, more than 1,400 banks offered its customers either Bank-Americard or Master Charge cards.

Congress reacted as expected and in 1970 passed a law forbidding the mailing of unsolicited cards. It enacted the Fair Credit Reporting Act and later the Fair Credit Billing Act in 1974 that amended 1968's Truth in Lending Act. But the stage was already set. Americans were becoming addicted to credit and their credit cards. And the threat of fraud and identity theft was only beginning.

## GROWTH OF CREDIT CARD FRAUD

Early credit card schemes commonly involved the use of stolen or lost cards and false statements made in the applications for cards. Credit card frauds began as relatively simple crimes. Law enforcement investigated and prosecuted criminally minded individuals only, rather than people who just became financially overextended. A white-collar crime manual from 1977 cautioned investigators

> *to avoid becoming collection agencies in such cases by carefully analyzing referrals to be sure that the requisite criminal intent is present, e.g., to avoid cases in which a credit card holder badly overextended himself and fell hopelessly into debt—opposed to cases where he never intended to pay.*[11]

In the early years of investigating credit card fraud, federal agents, and in particular Postal Inspectors, would use the Mail Fraud Statute for federal prosecution. Many of the cases involved the theft of credit cards from wallets and purses, often by pickpockets and prostitutes. The thieves would then use the stolen cards. The billing statements for the various charges would be mailed by the merchants to the credit card companies for processing and then to the true holders of the cards. The theory was that since the mails were used for the processing of the transaction, the act of mailing the billing statement was in furtherance of the crime. As a result, the Mail Fraud Statute would apply.

There were also numerous thefts of credit cards from the U.S. Mails. The mail has always been an attractive target for criminals. Mail theft had been common since the creation of the American Postal Service in 1775. By the 1800s, laws had been enacted to criminalize mail theft, then called mail depredations. Credit cards provided another valuable item to steal from the mail. In one example, the theft of credit cards from the mail by gangs and individual criminals in Chicago in the 1966–1967 period resulted in fraud losses of $6 million.[12]

From the late 1960s until 1974, large numbers of credit card fraudsters all over the country were prosecuted and convicted using the Mail Fraud Statute. Although the prosecutions were not stopping the problem, at least it was not growing. An estimate of losses in credit card fraud in 1969 was $100 million, primarily due to the widespread mailings of unsolicited credit cards by the credit card industry. After Congress prohibited such mailings, fraud losses declined.

Traditional organized crime found that credit cards were another source of income for their criminal activities. In 1970, Salvatore "Bill" Bonanno, the son of former mob boss Joseph "Joe Bananas" Bonanno, went to jail for four years after Postal Inspectors and the Federal Bureau of Investigation caught him fraudulently using someone else's credit card. Organized crime would continue this criminal activity and in the early 1980s would counterfeit credit cards in the names of unsuspecting victims. By 1973, data suggested that credit card fraud losses were down to between $40 and $60 million. In that year, it was estimated that 200 million credit cards were in circulation in the United States with annual theft losses of 1.5 million cards.[13]

As a result of the Truth in Lending Act legislation (also called the Consumer Credit Protection Act), American consumers were better protected in the use of credit cards and credit-related transactions. The act required clear disclosures in the granting of credit and credit card practices. In addition, a new statute to fight credit card fraud was created: Title 15, United State Code, Section 1644, Fraudulent Use of Credit Cards, was enacted in 1970. This statute was used to prosecute defendants for the "use of any counterfeit, fictitious, altered, forged, lost, stolen, or fraudulently obtained credit card to obtain money, goods, services, or anything of value which within any one-year period has a value aggregating $5,000 or more."[14] In 1974, the amount was lowered to $1,000 as many of the credit cards frauds were less than $5,000.

By 1974, credit card fraud losses began to climb significantly; losses were estimated to be at $460 million for the year.[15] The criminals who had been so active stealing credit cards from the mail back in 1966 and 1967 when millions of unsolicited cards were sent out were again active. Plus, there were new mail thieves added to the mix. Mail theft of credit cards was becoming more and more of a problem with the growing consumer base of credit card users. People now had multiple credit cards, and new customers were being signed up at a record rate. Credit card applications were readily available, and everyone wanted credit cards.

The commentary from 1974 that follows is illustrative of how the credit card fraud application process by fraudsters has changed over the years but also remained the same:

> *One false application procedure is either to observe a user's card number during the course of a credit card transaction or to obtain this information by retrieving the carbons of credit card charge slips from merchant's trash containers. Public records are then studied to gather background information about the cardholder: address, homeowner, or renter, occupation, etc. This is used to apply for a card from another issuer. A change of address is indicated. Or the defrauder might notify the issuer of the card held by a legitimate user that the latter is changing his address—and "please send me an additional card for my wife."*

> *Sometimes a fictitious name is used on the application. Frequently, the applicant is listed as a doctor or lawyer in the belief that issuers are reluctant to embarrass those in the professions by conducting a thorough check. Credit references may be stores which are known to be unresponsive to inquiries about their customers' credit status. On occasion, employees of card issuers have been bribed to approve false applications. Cards obtained through false applications might be used safely for up to two months in conjunction with counterfeit identification documents.*[16]

Technology advances and other changes have done away with some of these elements and steps. Those old charge slips with carbon paper inserts are no more. Public records are now readily available on the Internet. Credit checks are made through the various credit bureaus.

In February 1975, four family members and another person involved in fraudulently obtaining credit cards were sentenced to prison after being convicted of mail fraud. According to the *Economic Crime Digest* that provided commentary on the prosecution of these fraudsters: "The five defendants used college catalogs to collect the necessary personal and professional information on professors to complete the false applications" and as a result, "forty-nine credit cards were obtained and used with forged identification to purchase goods valued at approximately $217,000."[17]

*The Cost of Crimes Against Business*, a January 1976 United States Department of Commerce publication, warned of the rapid rise in the cost of crime impacting America. Among the concerns were credit card–related crimes and the need to do more to prevent this growing problem. The study advised that "close scrutiny of credit card applicants, aggressive attention to delinquent accounts. . . . and expulsion from the plan of merchants who engage in improper practices, can help banks keep their credit card losses to a minimum."[18] Unfortunately, this advice was not enough to stem the tide of future events and the rise of identity theft.

In 1977, the Hennepin, Minnesota County Attorney charged a gang of Nigerian nationals with defrauding insurance and credit card companies throughout the United States. A St. Paul, Minnesota Postal Inspector assisted in the investigation and provided additional details of the fraud scheme in a memorandum included in the criminal complaint. The inspector stated, "Operating in concert with other Nigerian aliens residing across the United States, they have conducted a scheme to defraud, with the primary victims being the credit card industry."[19] The criminal complaint further stated that "recently arrived Nigerians would collaborate with more settled individuals in preparing applications for credit cards and escaping detection in utilizing the fraudulently obtained cards. The suspects allegedly use a variety of names including Anglicized versions of their own names and will assume each other's identity in order to make identification more difficult."[20]

In 1979, the problem of identity theft came to the attention of law enforcement in Atlanta, Georgia. Shortly after, complaints on credit card fraud started to increase with information coming in from victims. Soon the focus was on Nigerian nationals involved in these crimes. In 1981, the Georgia Bureau of Investigation (GBI) organized a task force to investigate the increasing incidents of credit card fraud. At first the criminals used their own names and addresses but added other phony information. This made arrests easy, but fraudsters soon learned from their mistakes.[21]

The identity thieves in Georgia became much more sophisticated in their crimes in the years between 1981 and 1985. Individual fraudsters were joined by gangs involved in identity theft. They began to steal entire identities of others and use them for credit card applications. A Special Agent of the GBI found that stolen "background information included names, Social Security numbers, dates of birth, addresses, and the number of dependents. . . . The investigation revealed that they got this information by infiltrating legitimate businesses or corrupting people who were already employed in those legitimate businesses."[22]

## EVEN POSTAL EMPLOYEES WILL STEAL

Rick Johnson is a retired Postal Inspector. During his career with the Inspection Service, he had an internal crimes assignment in Jacksonville, Florida, in the late 1980s. Internal crimes are internal mail theft investigations generally involving postal employees and contractors. Mail theft can involve anything that is delivered via the U.S. Mails and that can include items of value such as checks, birthday cards with cash, registered mail containing rare coins, securities, and of course credit cards.

One case that Inspector Johnson investigated involved a strange coincidence that would prove the downfall of a credit card thief. Johnson was investigating 32 AT&T Universal credit cards that had been stolen from the mails over a period of time. The cards had been used for numerous fraudulent charges, but none was made in Jacksonville. The charges were spread out all over the country.

Inspector Johnson began poring over the receipts to find at least one clue that might break the case. He came across a charge made at Knott's Berry Farm in the Los Angeles area. The charge was made to a credit card issued to a Billy T. Smith and the receipt contained a Florida driver's license number issued to a Billy T. Smith. It turned out there was a Billy T. Smith working as a mail handler at the Jacksonville General Mail Center.

Inspector Johnson eventually confronted him, and Smith admitted to stealing all the 32 subject credit cards and using them in other states. He stole the Billy T. Smith credit card because it had his exact name on it. He took his daughter to Knott's Berry Farm; she wanted a big teddy bear so he used the stolen card to purchase it. The postal employee was shocked when the clerk asked for identification. He said he normally would have made some excuse as to why he did not have identification and left. However, his daughter wanted the teddy bear, and he had the perfect identification so he showed his driver's license to the clerk.

The employee said it was the only mistake he made in all the fraudulent transactions, and it turned out to be his undoing. By showing his true identification to the clerk, he was eventually identified as the mail thief. He was very impressed that the Postal Inspector had been able to catch him and told him so. Smith was prosecuted in late 1988. He pleaded guilty to mail theft and resigned from the Postal Service. He received a 13-month prison sentence and was ordered to pay $35,000 in restitution.

## RECIDIVISM IS COMMON

Between December 1996 and May 1998, a Nigerian national conducted a scheme wherein he assumed the identities of at least five victims utilizing their valid Social Security numbers. Using these identities, he obtained North Carolina identification cards, contracted for mail delivery at commercial mail receiving agencies, and opened bank accounts. He deposited stolen, counterfeit, and otherwise fraudulent checks and convenience checks into these accounts. He wrote checks for merchandise and withdrew funds. One of the identities he stole was that of a former U.S. Ambassador. The investigation was jointly conducted by Postal Inspectors and Secret Service agents.

Investigating officers did not know the suspect's true identity at the time but they had incriminating evidence. Based on bank surveillance photos, a John Doe arrest warrant was obtained and the photo was circulated to police in North Carolina. On May 9, 1998, an alert Greensboro Triad Airport police officer recognized the suspect as he was awaiting a flight at the airport and he was arrested. He provided a false name when arrested, and it took two months to determine his true identity.

At that point, it was learned that the defendant had been the subject of three prior Postal Inspection Service investigations in New York and New Jersey dating back to 1985, all for credit card fraud. In one of the cases, the defendant had in his possession a number of credit cards that were part of 100 credit cards stolen from the mails in Houston, Texas. Besides using stolen credit cards, he obtained other cards through fraudulent credit card applications using victims' personal information. The most recent fraud was in excess of $200,000. He pleaded guilty to using stolen Social Security numbers and opening bank accounts using fraudulent names.

Imagine my surprise as I was researching material for this book and came across a very familiar case study. The case was one I investigated when I was a Postal Inspector in New York. I immediately recognized the fraudster's name; I had arrested him for the first time on December 17, 1985, in Staten Island, New York, for credit card fraud. He pleaded guilty in February 1986 and in April of that year was sentenced in Brooklyn Federal Court to two years in prison to be followed by deportation. Not only did prison time not work, deportation obviously did not either. Recidivism is unfortunately quite common for identity thieves; the punishments are not sufficient to be effective deterrents when the crime is so easy and lucrative.

## MAIL THEFT AND PHONY ID

On March 30, 1998, a resident in an apartment complex in Pickerington, Ohio, reported to the local police department and Postal Inspectors that he was receiving credit cards that he had not applied for. The postal customer reported he had been contacted by various banks and that over $10,000 in convenience checks associated with credit cards mailed to his apartment were being negotiated in the Houston, Texas, area. The postal customer also informed the authorities that on the two prior mail delivery days, he witnessed an unknown male driving a white vehicle removing mail from his mailbox.

That same day, Postal Inspectors and police detectives conducted surveillance in the area of the victim's mailbox. Within a short time, a male driving a white vehicle was observed entering the apartment complex and removing mail from the victim's mailbox. The subject was arrested as he was leaving the scene in his car. In the car were several pieces of mail addressed to the victim, credit cards and mail addressed to other victims, as well as a list of numerous names, SSNs, and birth dates of other victims. He was charged with theft of mail.

When the defendant was booked, he gave a phony name, provided a home address that turned out to be a mail receiving agency, and had a Washington State driver's license in the alias. He also falsely provided an SSN that was found to belong to a female. It was later determined that the defendant previously had been arrested in Las Vegas and Atlanta for credit card fraud and deported in 1990. He illegally reentered the country under an alias as a temporary U.S. visitor in 1996.

## THE CIRCULATION: A SOUTHERN CALIFORNIA CRIME SYNDICATE

The Circulation was an organized group of individuals involved in mail theft, identity theft, and other crimes for the purpose of supporting their methamphetamine habits. The Circulation membership was primarily Filipino, but group members came from other backgrounds as well. The U.S. Postal Inspection Service identified over 100 individuals as members of the Circulation operating as separate groups in the San Fernando Valley, Los Angeles, and Long Beach, California. Postal Inspectors believe that the gang has stolen the identities of more than 1,000 people since 1996.

The Circulation found it easy to use financial crimes to feed their drug habits. Methamphetamine is a particularly nasty and addictive drug that quickly consumes the lives of its users. The drug puts users on a nonstop path of crimes to raise money for more of the drug. The crimes usually began with mail theft. Mail was stolen by various methods, including internal theft through employment with the Postal Service as mail clerks and carriers, and external theft by breaking into mailboxes in apartments and residential housing. Often gang members used stolen or counterfeit Postal Service "Arrow" keys: keys that are used by postal employees to access collection boxes, apartment boxes, and storage boxes. The thieves would pose as joggers running by mailboxes and removing mail. In fact, the Circulation referred to "jogging" and "boxing" to describe stealing incoming and outgoing mail from Postal Service boxes.

Mail stolen by the gang would be sorted at area hotels or safe houses and grouped into checks, credit card information, bank statements, and something they called "profiles." Profiles were the personal identifying information stolen from victims that was maintained for later use in identity theft. The checks were generally found in outgoing mail as payment for credit cards, utilities, mortgages, loans, and other payment purposes. The Circulation would chemically wash the stolen checks in chemicals such as acetone and brake fluid to remove the original inked writing and enable the fraudsters to rewrite the checks with new payment information including payee and check amount. (See Chapter 6 for more information on mail theft, check washing, and identity theft.)

The Circulation would use these altered checks to obtain cash through fraudulently opened bank accounts and make payments on credit cards obtained through identity theft. Although this may not make sense at first, payments like these can temporarily inflate the account balance and allow suspects to withdraw the additional funds before the bank realizes the account holders deposited a "bad" check. This is a common approach that is used by many identity thieves, not just the Circulation.

Stolen credit card information was used to purchase merchandise from mail order companies. The fraudsters would provide a different address than the true credit card holder at which to receive the ordered merchandise. At times, they would request that the credit card company change the account address to reflect the new one provided by the fraudster. When they were successful in changing account addresses, the Circulation members would order additional credit cards to be mailed to the new address. These cards allowed the gang to make additional purchases and cash advances until the credit card issuer was alerted to the fraudulent use and canceled the card. The purchased items included computers, big-ticket electronics, hotel rooms, and rental cars.

The "profiles" maintained by the Circulation included victim names, SSNs, dates of birth, driver's license numbers, mother's maiden names, and other personally identifiable information (PII). Besides obtaining this information from mail theft, the Circulation would use collusive employees at car dealerships, hotels, retail establishments, medical facilities to obtain PII. This PII would originate on employment applications, applications for credit and loans, goods and services documents, medical files, and other sources. Members of the Circulation would use these profiles personally to fraudulently obtain credit cards, for payments of personal services such as utilities, and to sell to other criminals.

In April 2001, two members of the gang were arrested in Burbank, California, on charges of credit card fraud, forgery, identity theft, and methamphetamine possession. In their possession at the time of the arrest were scores of credit cards and a list of names and account numbers from potential identity theft victims, including people from South America and Germany. The credit card and bank account information in their possession had a potential fraud loss value of $23 million. As was common practice for this group that financed their drug use with their criminal activities, these two defendants also had methamphetamine in their possession. Criminals, methamphetamine use, and identity theft are a potent and dangerous mixture, and one that will be a recurring theme throughout this book.

## NOTES

1. The President's Identity Theft Task Force, "Combating Identity Theft: A Strategic Plan" (April 2007), 23, www.idtheft.gov/reports/StrategicPlan.pdf.
2. Social Security Administration, "The Story of the Most Misused Number of All Time," www.ssa.gov/history/ssn/misused.html.
3. United States Department of Justice, *The Criminal Use of False Identification: The Report of the Federal Advisory Committee on False Identification* (November 1976), 2.
4. Ibid., 5.
5. Ibid., 16.
6. Ibid.
7. Emily Starbuck Gerson and Ben Woolsey, "A Not-So-Brief History of Credit Cards," www.creditcards.com/history-of-credit-cards.php.
8. Matty Simmons, *The Credit Card Catastrophe: The 20th Century Phenomenon That Changed the World* (New York: Barricade Books, 1995), 81.
9. Company history of MasterCard International, Inc, www.answers.com/topic/mastercard-1?cat=biz-fin.
10. Quoted in Simmons, *Credit Card Catastrophe*, 119.
11. Herbert Edelhertz, Ezra Stotland, Marilyn Walsh, and Milton Weinberg, *The Investigation of White-Collar Crime: A Manual for Law Enforcement Agencies* (Washington, DC: Law Enforcement Assistance Administration, United States Department of Justice, April 1977), 287.
12. U.S. Department of Commerce, *The Cost of Crimes Against Business* (January 1976), 23.
13. Charles E. O'Hara, *Fundamentals of Criminal Investigation*, 3rd ed. (Springfield, IL: Charles C Thomas, 1973), 358.
14. Title 15, United States Code, Section 1644.
15. U.S. Department of Commerce, *Cost of Crimes Against Business.*
16. Chamber of Commerce of the United States, *A Handbook on White Collar Crime: Everyone's Problem, Everyone's Loss,* 1974, 34.
17. National District Attorneys Association, *Economic Crime Digest* 2, no. 3 (August–October 1975), 168.
18. U.S. Department of Commerce, *Cost of Crimes Against Business.*
19. National District Attorneys Association, *Economic Crime Digest* 4, no. 3 (January–February 1978), 6.

20. Ibid.
21. Testimony of Steve Simmons, Special Agent, Georgia Bureau of Investigation, Hearings on Emerging Criminal Groups: Nigerian Criminal Activities, before the Permanent Subcommittee on Investigations of the Committee on Governmental Affairs, United States Senate, 99th Congress, 2nd Ses., September 17, 1986, 38.
22. Ibid.

# CHAPTER 3

---

# How Identity Theft Occurs

Everyone is vulnerable to identity theft because we possess something very valuable that criminals crave: our name and reputation. William Shakespeare recognized the value of a person's good name and the impact of misuse, as evidenced by these lines in his classic play *Othello*:

*Good name in man and woman, dear my lord, is the immediate jewel of their souls.*

*Who steals my purse steals trash; 'tis something, nothing;*

*'Twas mine, 'tis his, and has been slave to thousands;*

*But he that filches from me my good name,*

*Robs me of that which not enriches him.*

*And makes me poor indeed.*[1]

These lines were uttered by Iago, a villainous and vengeful character in the play, to Othello. Iago was referring to the damage from libel and slander and his reluctance to discuss a fabricated affair between Othello's wife, Desdemona, and one of Othello's officers. While Iago's words speak volumes about one's good name and reputation, he was also talking about the damage caused by identity theft. Stealing one's very life through personal and financial information can have a lasting impact.

## CRIMINAL ROLES OF IDENTITY THIEVES

In an October 2007 study, the research described the various roles that defendants play in the commission of identity theft crimes.[2] (For a more detailed discussion of this study, see Chapter 19.) A list of the criminal actions of identity thieves follows.

- Steal or obtain personal identifying information (e.g., personal identifying information that can be captured from credit card databases, client and employee records, credit card receipts, bank statements, stolen mail, checks)
- Steal or obtain personal identifier documents (e.g., driver's licenses, birth certificates, Social Security cards, employee badges)
- Steal or obtain bank cards (credit, debit, automated teller machine [ATM])
- Alter identification documents (e.g., driver's licenses, Social Security cards, birth certificates, employee badges)
- Produce counterfeit identification documents (e.g., driver's licenses, Social Security cards, birth certificates, employee identification cards)
- Distribute personal identifier information to others (so that they can use it for personal gain)
- Sell identification documents (genuine and counterfeit)
- Use identification documents for own use (offenders use genuine or counterfeit documents for personal gain)
- Use identification documents to obtain more identification documents (e.g., using a utility bill and birth certificate to procure a driver's license)
- Direct others' activities (within an organized crime group, giving instructions or orders to the others in the group)
- Other (includes credit card skimming, encoding or re-encoding bank cards)[3]

## HOW IDENTITY THIEVES STEAL YOUR GOOD NAME

Cunning criminals have long known how easy it is to commit identity theft. Since this crime began its growth in the 1970s, we have seen a progression from simple to complex schemes. Interestingly enough, although fraudsters embraced technology to carry out identity theft, they never completely forgot their roots. Dumpster diving, mail theft, fraudulent credit card applications, lost or stolen wallets and purses, and insider access continue to provide vast sources of information for identity thieves. The only limitation to the many types of identity theft, as well as the new ones yet to come, is the very imagination of these crooks and advances in technology.

The President's Identity Theft Task Force in its April 2007 report defined identity theft as "the misuse of another individual's information to commit fraud." The definition also describes the three stages in the life cycle: (1) the identity thief acquires a victim's personal information; (2) the identity thief attempts to use the stolen information; and (3) the identity thief is successful in the crime using the proceeds while the victim is harmed.[4] Many of the ways that identity theft occurs are discussed next.

## Account Takeover Fraud

Account takeover fraud is the fraudulent access and/or manipulation of existing financial account information, such as a checking account, by an unauthorized individual or individuals. Postal Service change-of-address forms are often used to divert mail from the actual address to another controlled by the identity thief. The President's Identity Theft Task Force Report defines existing account fraud as occurring "when thieves obtain account information involving credit, brokerage, banking, or utility accounts that are already open" and defines new account fraud as the use of "personal information, such as Social Security numbers, birth dates, and home addresses, to open new accounts in the victim's name, make changes indiscriminately, and then disappear."[5] Account takeover is also called identity takeover. Stolen personal information such as names, Social Security numbers (SSNs), dates of birth, and account information is used to "(1) make unauthorized use of existing credit or other financial accounts or (2) establish new accounts, apply for loans, etc."[6]

## Bank and Loan Fraud

Criminals may open bank accounts in your name. The fraudsters will falsify the information on account applications using stolen personal information and provide phony identification claiming to be you. They obtain checks for the account and then write numerous bad checks on that account until it is drained dry. They may attempt to cash stolen and altered checks through the account. Identity thieves have been known to chemically "wash" checks to remove the inked writing so they can forge the checks with different payees, check amounts, and their signatures. This illegal process is called check washing and is covered in detail in Chapter 6. Scammers also obtain a variety of loans in your name—business, personal, student, auto, mortgage, and home equity— that are not repaid.

## Counterfeit or Altered Cards

Counterfeiting and altering credit cards has long been an illegal practice by fraudsters. Criminals counterfeit credit cards with varying degrees of quality. In the early days, some were simple white or blue pieces of plastic cut to the size of credit cards and embossed with stolen information including cardholder name, account number, and expiration date. Thus, the term "white (or blue) plastic fraud" was born. The phony cards often were used at collusive merchant establishments and required a conspiracy between the fraudster and the merchant or a merchant's employee for the transaction to be successful. Generally, the merchant would imprint a credit card sales draft with the white plastic and deposit it into the business account. This merchant then would split the credit card charge proceeds with the fraudster. White plastic schemes effectively ended with the advent of electronic point-of-sale terminals that read the magnetic stripes on the cards.

In 1984, I worked undercover to investigate a group of collusive merchants in Queens, New York, dealing in white plastic. The store owners thought I was a fraudster with a never-ending supply of embossed white plastics with stolen credit card numbers. They were all too happy to run my white plastics through their accounts for fraudulent transactions and share the "cash splits" with me. Even I was surprised that merchant after merchant had no problem in doing these fraudulent transactions with me. Their only surprise was when we arrested them.

Today, criminals with technology skills can easily counterfeit credit cards using skimming techniques to "skim" existing information from one card to another for fraudulent use. Skimming bypasses the need to actually counterfeit a credit card and the need to re-create holograms and other credit card security features. (See the "Skimming" section later in this chapter.)

Altered credit cards are actual credit cards that have been lost or stolen and changed by fraudsters to reflect new account holder information. Various methods are employed to alter cards for use. Some are high-quality alterations but most can be easily detected as altered. With advances in technology, altered cards are not the problem they were in the 1980s.

## Downloading Deceptive Software

Identity thieves may offer you free music, antivirus protection, or other applications. If you fall for this too-good-to-be-true offer and download or open unknown attachments, you may expose yourself to surreptitious installation of spyware on your computer. Once this spyware is installed, identity thieves can use it to record your keystrokes and obtain passwords, bank account information, and other sensitive information.

## Dumpster Diving

Nothing is more low tech than Dumpster diving as a source of personal information. For far too long, individuals and businesses simply disposed of their financial records and other personal documents by just throwing them into the garbage. Enterprising criminals were more than willing to "get down and dirty" in the trash looking for, and often finding, valuable information. The increased focus on identity theft prevention has resulted in more and more shredding of documents. Yet we still regularly read of businesses that simply dump boxes of mortgage applications, medical files, consumer credit reporting information, and other financial documents into the garbage, information that then is found by identity thieves.

Dumpster diving is still an easy and vast source of information for identity thieves, and not only in the United States. In 2003, methamphetamine users in Edmonton, Alberta, Canada, found that Dumpster diving in the trash of call centers was especially valuable. They discovered "copies of credit card transactions, loan applications, customer-service reports, employment manuals, internal phone directories" as well as "credit check information from Equifax, credit card numbers to make payments, Social Security numbers, dates of birth, and addresses."[7] The wealth of information was then used for identity theft. Equally important, none of these documents had been shredded before being discarded.

## Employment Fraud

Fraudsters use your name, SSN, and other personal information to pose as you for employment. This may be done by people who are in this country illegally and do not have SSNs of their own. They may hijack your resume if it is available online. Job seekers who post resumes online that contain too much personal information are at risk from identity thieves who are on the prowl for such data. People using your SSN for employment may or may not contribute to Federal Insurance Contributions Act (FICA) payroll taxes (Social Security and Medicare), a fact that will impact your Social Security benefits in the future.

## Fraudulent Credit Card Applications

Identity thieves use stolen personal information to complete fraudulent credit card applications. The fraudsters will use a victim's true name, SSN, date of birth, employment, and other available information but not the victim's actual home address. Instead, they provide an address where they can receive the card. Identity thieves have used post office boxes, commercial mail receiving agencies, and residences rented for the purpose of receiving credit cards. Often numerous fraudulent applications are completed and submitted in the belief that the greater number provides a better chance of some getting approved and cards issued. Ingenious criminals will change home and work telephone numbers to ones where they can receive inquiries from the credit card issuers. The widespread use of cell phones has made this easier for the thieves. In the past, they had to have a physical location to set up telephone service and await possible calls from banks and credit card issuers verifying employment, income, and other information. Now they can go about their criminal ways while awaiting those calls.

## Government Benefits and Documents Fraud

Government benefits or documents fraud can include a wide range of fraudulent activity. Using your name and personal information, scam artists apply for various government benefits, obtain driver's licenses, receive SSNs and benefits, file fraudulent tax returns to obtain refunds, and receive other government documents and benefits.

## Hacking and Electronic Intrusions

The computer and Internet age have ushered in a new breed of criminals who use technology for fraud and abuse. These computer hackers steal information from both individuals and businesses by penetrating firewalls, intercepting data during transmission, attacking unprotected home wireless networks, and other means. Hackers have traditionally created computer viruses more for status and bragging rights than for financial gain. "But now hackers are mixing with fraudsters and organized crime rings" and "viruses are being used illegally for financial gain, and they are becoming part of the modern criminal's toolbox."[8]

Criminals will use variations of viruses to take over multiple computers, often all over the world, and turn them into "zombies." This results in a botnet, a large-scale network that criminals can control remotely and use for malicious purposes. Botnets can control tens of thousands of unprotected computers and are used most often to "distribute spam email, spread viruses, attack other computers and servers, and commit other kinds of crime and fraud."[9] With more and more people leaving their computers on and continuously connected to the Internet, highly skilled cybercriminals "can cover their tracks since they act through other people's computers."[10] Botnets are some of the fastest-growing Internet dangers today. Unless your computers and networks are adequately protected, they can be easily infected and controlled. (More information about botnets and wireless networks can be found in Chapter 17.)

### Insider Threat

It is not just career criminals and organized crime gangs that are responsible for the growing problem of identity theft. Insiders play a key role in this crime. There are several definitions of insiders. The most common insiders are criminally minded employees working at banks, credit bureaus, and other businesses where personally identifiable information (PII) is found. The failure to secure and limit access to computers, networks, and databases can allow unauthorized entry and data breaches by fraudster employees and others. "Criminals also may bribe insiders, or become employees themselves to access sensitive data at companies."[11]

But the identity thieves may also be your friends and relatives, the people you least suspect. Several years ago in Morena Valley, California, a woman was "devastated to learn that her sister stole her identity and that of their Alzheimer's-afflicted mother and used them to open fake credit cards and utility accounts and forge checks."[12] In a similar case, a woman in Downey, California, had her identity stolen. The purloined information was used to empty her bank accounts and open credit card accounts in her name that were used for thousands of dollars in fraudulent purchases. Who was the identity thief who did this to her? "It was her husband who fled to his native Pakistan with nearly $60,000 of her money."[13]

### Lost and Stolen Credit Cards

Just because some criminals have turned to technology to commit fraud does not mean they all have. Do not forget that the old standards still work. Fraudsters have continued to use the time-tested methods of pickpocketing and thefts to steal wallets, purses, computer bags, and other opportunistic pilfering. Credit cards and checking account information are the usual targets of these thefts. Lost and stolen credit cards traditionally have been an easy means of financial gain for fraudsters. Lost wallets and purses containing credit cards, Social Security cards, driver's licenses, and other personal information give identity thieves the information they need for fraud. The same goes for stolen wallets, purses, and personal belongings.

Long before the other forms of identity theft occurred, thefts of credit cards and other PII from vehicles, residences, the workplace, unsecured lockers, and by professional pickpockets were a common means for financial abuse. The 2006 Identity Theft Survey Report of the Federal Trade Commission (FTC) released in November 2007 reported that 16% of victims had their PII stolen by people they personally knew. The same study found that 5% of victims had their PII compromised through the theft of their wallet or purse.[14]

## Mail/Telephone Order Fraud

Mail/telephone order fraud is also called no card present fraud, as the actual credit card is not physically present for the transaction. Such transactions are usually conducted by telephone or mail. The scammer, after fraudulently obtaining a victim's credit card, attempts to use it to purchase merchandise or services over the phone or by mail. With advances in card security, such as the Card Security Value (CSV), it is harder to commit mail or telephone order fraud using another's credit card. On a system using CSV, customers are prompted for the three- or four-digit number on the back of the credit card. Only a person with the card in hand can provide this number, as it is not stored in any system.[15]

## Mail Theft

Each and every day, the United States Postal Service delivers millions of pieces of mail containing checks, credit cards, financial statements, and a host of other important and valuable documents and items. For this reason, mail is a highly prized target for identity thieves and other criminals. Mail theft has been a concern since the creation of the Postal Service in the United States. Mail thieves have always used imaginative ways to steal mail and commit identity theft. In 2002, mail thieves employed a "sticky device" to steal mail from Postal Service collection boxes. A sticky device is a heavy object covered with a strong glue substance, either pine tar or melted mousetrap glue, with an attached string. While one suspect acts as a lookout, the other suspect drops the sticky device into a collection box through the mail slot. The deposited mail adheres to the glue, the heavy object is pulled up, and the outgoing mail is then stolen.

This was not the first time that a sticky device was used. In 1996, Postal Inspectors found it being used to steal mail from snorkel boxes in the Los Angeles area. Snorkel collections boxes are named for the snorkel-like opening on the street side so customers in their cars can drive up to the box and deposit outgoing mail from the driver-side window. A "teeth device" was installed inside the collection box that prevented the removal of mail adhered to the sticky device. This modification completely eliminated the problem at the time. It was not until 2002 that the problem resurfaced. It seemed that due to routine maintenance and collection box replacement, most of these modified boxes had been removed from service. The sticky device modification was again installed in collection boxes, and the threat ended.

Fishing for mail, which is obviously a low-tech version of the much newer phishing, has been a common technique for identity thieves for many years. I investigated a case of a mail thief in the early 1980s who was not as imaginative in his technique. I was working as a Postal Inspector in Brooklyn, New York, when I received a telephone call from the New York Police Department that they had apprehended a mail thief. The not-too-bright criminal had tried to reach down the mail slot of a collection box to steal mail and got his arm stuck. He had attempted this in the early-morning hours when he thought no one would see him.

With his arm stuck in the box, he was spotted by police officers on patrol. The police extricated the thief from the collection box and held him for me. While I was processing him on attempted mail theft charges, I learned that he had been arrested for mail theft twice before and had served time in prison for these crimes. I remember telling the embarrassed criminal that he needed to find another line of work because he definitely was not good at his current one.

Mailbox fishing has been a particularly vexing problem over the years. Collection boxes placed in front of post offices are often a target due to the volume of mail deposited. The design of the box allows a person to reach in and, if the box is completely full, simply remove the mail. The answers are modifications and ongoing collection of the mail by postal employees, and these have been implemented. In addition, numerous collection and storage box thefts occurred as a result of lost or stolen Postal Service Arrow keys. In one of the easier methods, criminals would simply break into the box with a crowbar or screw driver. The Postal Service has responded by hardening collection and mailboxes with stronger security, improved locking devices, and other modifications that reduce the possibility of mail theft using these techniques.

Although modifications greatly help, they will not completely reduce the possibility of break-ins and theft. One simple prevention method is for the public to deposit outgoing mail only inside a post office. If mail is deposited in outside boxes, it should always be deposited during the day and around collection time to ensure that it will not sit overnight when it could be stolen. (More prevention recommendations can be found in Chapter 20.)

In 1996, Postal Inspectors in Puerto Rico uncovered a mail theft scheme where an adult recruited juveniles to steal mail. The juveniles were instructed to collect information flyers from local supermarkets and "deliver" them to residential mailboxes on the first of the month. While inserting the circulars, the juveniles were told to remove any government checks that might be inside the box. This mail theft technique was designed to lessen the chance of discovery as it appeared the juveniles were simply putting the flyers inside area mailboxes.

In July 2007, Postal Inspectors and other law enforcement agents arrested 10 identity thieves; most of them were from Kenya. The defendants stole the mail and identities of hundreds of victims, primarily elderly people in nursing homes. The criminals used the information to file fraudulent federal and state tax returns. More than 365 fraudulent tax returns were involved. The potential losses exceeded $13 million and impacted victims in more than 27 states. This was one of the largest tax fraud cases ever uncovered.

Not Received Items (NRI) is the credit card industry terminology for nonreceipt of new or replacement credit cards mailed to the authorized cardholder. Often these NRI cards have been stolen at some point in transit. Postal employees have been found to be involved in mail thefts, but cards are also stolen by external parties during or after the mail delivery process. The Card Activation Program (CAP) detailed in Chapter 11 has helped to significantly reduce NRI losses over the years.

## Medical Identity Theft

Medical identity theft is a relatively new variation where criminals use a victim's personal information to obtain medical care and file fraudulent medical claims. This ominous mutation of the crime leaves victims with a double whammy. Not only are they vulnerable to the financial losses associated with identity theft; they also are subject to a more serious health threat through commingled diagnoses and treatments in their medical files. (Much more can be found on medical identity theft in Chapter 8.)

## Phishing

The term "phishing" is a take-off on the word "fishing" where scam artists use tempting emails as bait to lure unsuspecting victims to part with account numbers, passwords, and other financial information. The spoofed Web sites look so real that people can be easily fooled into thinking they are at the actual site of their financial institution. According to the Anti-Phishing Working Group, the term "was coined in the 1996 timeframe by hackers who were stealing AOL accounts by scamming passwords from unsuspecting users."[16]

In phishing schemes, victims get hooked if they fall for the bait. Identity thieves send unsuspecting people e-mails that by all appearances seem to be legitimate correspondence from banks, brokerages, or online service companies, such as eBay or PayPal. A common theme used by fraudsters is to inform the recipient that there has been an unauthorized access of their online account. The recipients are urged to click on a link for additional important information that needs to be acted on. Usually the e-mails ask that you provide your personal information to verify your account. Once done, the crooks have all the information they need for fraud. This is social engineering at its worst.

## Pharming

Hackers use pharming or domain spoofing to redirect a legitimate Web site's traffic to a phony site they control. The phony site looks real with logos and other information similar to the true site. In phishing, fraudsters primarily employ social engineering, tricking the recipient into clicking on the spoofed site. Pharming is more insidious, as it directly attacks and alters domain name servers (DNS). DNS are the large directories of common and specific Internet Protocol (IP) addresses, such as www.microsoft.com. Pharming will corrupt your local DNS server by redirecting your Web request to the fake site. You think you are at the correct site, but you are not. Once you are at the imposter site, you will be asked to provide personal information that will be used by the thieves. The name "pharming" refers to the large amount of PII that criminals can potentially harvest using this method.

## Pretexting

"Pretexting" is a term coined by the private investigation industry to describe the practice of obtaining personal information about others under false pretenses. It is defined the same way by the FTC. Individuals involved in pretexting will sell the personal information they covertly and, often illegally, obtain to others who may use it to commit identity theft and other crimes.

The FTC has been active in targeting information brokers who deal in the personal and financial information of others without their knowledge and consent. In April 1999, the

FTC filed the first federal case against information brokers for pretexting.[17] The legal action was against a private investigation firm in Denver that was illegally obtaining and selling consumers' private financial information. More recently, in December 2007, the United States Attorney for the Western District of Washington indicted 10 private investigators around the country on charges they used identity theft and other illegal methods to obtain and sell PII from unsuspecting victims. The PII was sold to law firms and others for use in litigation without the victims' knowledge.[18]

## Reshipping or Forwarder Scams

Beginning in 2003, many Internet vendors saw a steady increase in the number of fraud attempts. Much of the increase in credit card fraud on the Internet can be directly attributed to a credit card scam from Nigeria known as the reshipping or forwarder scam.

Professional fraudsters in Africa surf Internet chat rooms looking for young marks. They give the young victim a story of how unfair the trade tariffs are in Africa on computer items. They ask the victim to accept orders from several merchants at the victim's home, and they ask the victim to forward the items to an address in Lagos, Nigeria, or elsewhere. They offer to pay the forwarder $100 per package (which would be more than any tariff). The naive victim agrees and begins to receive packages. Each order is on a different stolen credit card for an amount that is usually less than $500, an amount often frequently used as a limit for fraud screening on orders in the industry. Of course, the victim never gets paid for forwarding the goods.

Some victims have decided just to keep all the merchandise, occasionally resulting in telephonic death threats. The typical victim of the Nigerian scam is a male between the ages of 15 and 24, and the fraudsters often pose as young women. Some have even sent a photo of a pretty young blonde, who is supposed to be the person with whom the mark is chatting. Police all over the United States have been finding mail drop forwarders who have been duped into forwarding stolen merchandise. The more advanced scammers use accomplices in the United States who rent warehouse space to use as a staging area for sending stolen goods overseas. Many such warehouses have been raided in Atlanta, Houston, Miami, and other cities, and authorities have found computer equipment and office supplies stacked to the ceiling, all bound for Nigeria.[19]

## Skimming

Skimming has been used by identity thieves for a number of years. A skimming device is a portable credit card reader used to surreptitiously capture the account data contained on the magnetic stripe of credit cards. Once this information is obtained, it can be placed on a counterfeit card and fraudulently used. Law enforcement has known of this problem for many years. It has been especially prevalent at restaurants, gasoline service stations, and other establishments where employees swipe cards out of sight of the cardholders. Dishonest restaurant employees have used portable, palm-size skimming devices to secretly copy the credit card account information of people dining at the establishment and paying with their card. When unsuspecting guests provide the credit card for payment, the server surreptitiously skims it through the device to record the data. Some of these skimmers are small enough to fit inside a jacket pocket.

Ingenious criminals have been known to install skimming machines over the fronts of ATM machines to capture account information when victims try to use the ATM. Miniature cameras are placed at the side of the ATM to record the PIN number entered by the cardholder. No transaction occurs so the cardholder assumes the ATM is broken. Unfortunately, the damage is done, with the account information and PIN captured for later fraudulent use. A disturbing case in Rhode Island in 2007 at several Stop & Shop supermarkets further reinforces the brazenness of identity thieves. The fraudsters replaced checkout lane credit and debit card readers with look-alike skimming devices. The resulting fraud and arrests reinforced this as a growing way to steal personal information.

Restaurants have been an especially fertile ground for identity thieves over the years. I remember cases where criminally minded restaurant employees would sell bags of credit card carbons to identity thieves. The carbons contained the cardholder's name, card number, and expiration date. This was in the days before electronic verification, and the information was used to create counterfeit credit cards. Today, restaurants are facing intrusions from poorly protected wireless networks as well as old-fashioned employee collusion and theft of information. Restaurants continue to be a significant source of stolen credit card information "Since January 2005, restaurants represented about 40% of incidents in which intruders gained unauthorized access to credit card information."[20] Now MasterCard, Visa, and other financial institutions are cracking down on restaurants for not protecting customers' credit card information. The credit card companies are requiring increased security procedures designed to lessen fraud.

## Smishing

As if we do not have enough to worry about, smishing is emerging as a new threat to cell phone users. Smishing is phishing using a cell phone's text messaging capability to obtain confidential information. The potential victim receives a text message with instructions to visit an imposter Web site for any number of legitimate-sounding reasons. People who follow the instructions are subjected to a pattern of deception similar to that in phishing schemes. Smishing gets its name from a mash-up of phishing and SMS (short message service) text messaging.

## Social Engineering

Social engineering is a crucial tool used by identity thieves, like all con men, to manipulate unsuspecting people into divulging confidential information. They also trick others into believing they are someone other than who they truly are. According to Wikipedia, social engineering is "a collection of techniques used to manipulate people into performing actions or divulging confidential information."[21] To be even more effective, social engineering is usually performed via telephone or email, and the perpetrator does not come into contact with the subject of the deception. Social engineering is used by identity thieves to convince victims to provide personal and financial information about themselves. This trickery can take many forms, including simple ruses over the telephone or more involved uses of pretexting, phishing, vishing (to be described), or the installation of malware, spyware, and keystroke-logging software.

## Spearfishing

Spearfishing is a form of phishing where specific organizations and individuals are targeted by fraudsters to collect sensitive information. Unlike phishing where millions of generic emails are blasted out, spearfishing is directed at a particular person whom the crooks have identified. In April 2008, thousands of corporate executives received emails that looked like an official government notice that they were being served with a subpoena. Each of the emails was personally addressed to the potential victim with his or her name, organization, and telephone number. The recipient was ordered to appear before a Grand Jury and a link was embedded in the email for viewing the actual subpoena. Anyone who opened the link downloaded keystroke-logging software to capture account numbers and passwords. The term "whaling" is also used when the targets are the rich and powerful, such as corporate executives.

## Telephone and Utilities Fraud

Identity thieves use stolen personal information to open telephone, cell phone, and utility accounts in your name and then do not make the payments, thereby impacting your credit score. In an FTC study released in February 2008 of consumer complaints related to identity theft, 18% of complaints related to telephone or utilities related identity theft. According to this study, only credit card fraud was a more common form of identity theft.[22]

## Vishing

Vishing is a new fraud development similar to phishing where the recipient receives a voice message purportedly from a bank or credit card issuer. The message states that there is an important matter that needs to be addressed, and a telephone number is left to return the call. The message sounds legitimate, but the phone number given is that of the fraudster. When the number is called, callers are asked to punch in their account number, PIN, SSN, and/or other personal information. The victim's information is collected at the other end of the line and later used for fraud. In January 2008, the FBI issued a warning to the public on the increase of vishing attacks and the various versions of the schemes. The caution was posted on FBI's Cyber Investigations Homepage under "New E-Scams and Warnings" and stated:

> These attacks against US financial institutions and consumers continue to rise at an alarming rate. Vishing operates like phishing by persuading consumers to divulge their Personally Identifiable Information (PII), claiming their account was suspended, deactivated, or terminated. Recipients are directed to contact their bank via a telephone number provided in the e-mail or by an automated recording. Upon calling the telephone number, the recipient is greeted with "Welcome to the bank of . . ." and then requested to enter their card number in order to resolve a pending security issue.
>
> For authenticity, some fraudulent e-mails claim the bank would never contact customers to obtain their PII by any means, including e-mail, mail, or instant messenger. These e-mails further warn recipients not to provide sensitive information when requested in an e-mail and not to click on embedded links, claiming they could contain "malicious software aimed at

*capturing login credentials." Please beware—spam e-mails may actually contain malicious code (malware) which can harm your computer. Do not open any unsolicited e-mail and do not click on any links provided.*

*A new version recently reported involves the sending of text messages to cell phones claiming the recipient's on-line bank account has expired. The message instructs the recipient to renew their on-line bank account by using the link provided.*

*Due to rapidly evolving criminal methodologies, it is impossible to include every scenario. Therefore, be cognizant and protect your PII. Beware of e-mails, telephone calls, or text messages requesting your PII.*[23]

---

## IDENTITY THEFT HALL OF INFAMY

### Jeffrey Webster Lawson

Jeffrey Webster Lawson was one of the most professional identity thieves operating in the United States. He was smart, persistent, and extremely careful not to get caught. It took years to track him down and put him behind bars. Lawson was in many ways the invisible man because law enforcement was unable to get their hands on him. They knew his name but did not know the phony identities he was always using until the day they finally caught him. He confounded and outsmarted his pursuers for years in his identity theft crime spree throughout the United States.

Lawson was a crafty mail thief who targeted the mailboxes in wealthy neighborhoods. There he would find valuable mailings containing financial and personal information. Once he had his victims' mail, he would take over their identities, weaving convincing tales to entice unsuspecting people to assist him in stealing the proceeds of bank and brokerage accounts. He had been a financial advisor in Chicago and used his knowledge to manipulate the system for his benefit.

Lawson traveled the country for years committing his crimes. He would find a promising city and set up shop posing as either an attorney or businessperson. He would open a small office with a telephone answering service and an official-sounding phone message. He used business addresses located in large office buildings. He distributed business cards that helped reinforce the impression of a successful businessman. Lawson would rent a home or apartment in an affluent area in a further attempt to establish roots and respectability. But this was all a ruse, for his intention was to spend only a few months in each city and, while there, rip off as many wealthy people as possible in his identity theft schemes.

THE PHOENIX CAPER
Postal Inspector Michael Casadei was one of most accomplished federal criminal investigators in the United States. In his 33-year law enforcement career, he investigated thousands of mail theft, identity theft, robbery, burglary, mail bomb,

*(Continued)*

and other criminal cases in Illinois, California, Arizona, and other states. In 1996, Inspector Casadei began investigating a series of mail thefts in the affluent Paradise Valley, Arizona, community adjacent to Phoenix. Although he did not know it at the time, Lawson was the culprit. It would take three years of good detective work and a little luck to finally capture Lawson. Inspector Casadei would later comment that Lawson was the most professional mail thief he had ever dealt with.

In Arizona, Lawson claimed he was a divorce attorney representing rich clients. He rented a home in upscale Scottsdale. He had been in the area before and had lived in Tempe and Mesa, where he committed prior identity theft scams. He always dressed well, wearing Rolex watches to portray wealth and success. He favored luxury cars, usually Mercedes, and he used several of them in his schemes. Lawson targeted Paradise Valley for his mail thefts because it is home to the rich and famous of Phoenix. The homes there are big and expensive with large pieces of property. Their rural mailboxes are often secluded from view and easy to steal from.

Lawson was imaginative and no ordinary mail thief. He would steal mail from mailboxes every day and recycle the mail from each day's theft. Recycling is a unique form of mail theft, and Lawson specialized in it. In recycling, mail is stolen each day over an extended period. The mail is carefully opened using a variety of methods. Documents with signatures are especially prized for forgery purposes. The victim's signature is traced using a glass plate with an illuminating light below. The contents are photocopied, replaced in the envelope, and resealed. The envelope is then returned to the homeowner's mailbox the next day. This is done day after day, each time stealing the new mail while replacing it with the prior day's mail that has been examined and copied.

Hardly anyone realized that their mail was delivered a day late as long as they received some mail each day. To ensure the success of the scheme, Lawson made sure to steal and recycle the mail shortly after the carrier made his or her daily delivery. Lawson continued this recycling process for 30 straight days, building quite a profile on his victims. Just think of how much important mail the average person receives in a month's time. Bank and brokerage statements, copies of canceled checks, mortgage bills, credit card statements, credit card offers, utility bills, and correspondence are just some of the many mailings that people can receive. Now think of how much information can be obtained about a person from the contents of those mailings.

Lawson developed profiles on his victims that he would keep from year to year. These profiles contained the personal data he gleaned from the mail thefts including names, SSNs, birth dates, banking information, brokerage accounts, and other key information. When he was later arrested, he had victim profiles going back many years. There were files on people who never knew they were victims of mail theft due to Lawson's use of covert recycling.

Once Lawson obtained personal and financial information from victims, he would assume their identities to clean out their accounts, but not completely. Often these accounts were very large accounts. In some cases, the account holders did not know they were victims until Inspector Casadei contacted them. One victim had $100,000 withdrawn without knowing it. Lawson would call the brokerage firms posing as the account holder and request that additional checks be mailed to the account of record. Knowing approximately how long it would take to receive checks in the mail, Lawson would go to the target's mailbox each day until the checks arrived. The homeowner had no idea that additional checks had been ordered under his or her name and would not miss them when Lawson stole them from the box. Using these checks, he would write large checks on the accounts, then repeat this process over and over again.

Many identity thieves employ change-of-address tactics for account takeovers. They file fraudulent change-of-address orders with the Postal Service, redirecting a victim's mail to an address they control. The mail and the information therein are then used for identity theft. These schemes are usually quickly discovered when a victim stops receiving mail at home or the office. Lawson did not need to use this approach; he was obtaining the checks from the actual address and controlling the distribution of new checks that the victim had no idea were even requested.

TARGETING STRIPPERS

Lawson also targeted young women to unwittingly assist him in emptying the accounts of his victims. His targets of choice were strippers. He frequented high-end strip clubs and with his expensive suits, ostentatious display of money, jewelry, and suave manner, he had an air of authority and trust. Using aliases, he befriended the strippers at these clubs and won their confidence. He always tried to limit his contact with them and had "someone from his firm" deal with them. This person was usually his criminal associate. Lawson told the women he was a successful divorce attorney with rich female clients. His clients were going through painful divorces from abusive spouses and needed to hide money that was rightfully theirs. The stories of allegedly battered spouses looking to protect themselves and keep their money hit a chord with the strippers. They were sympathetic, and that was exactly what Lawson was hoping for.

Lawson asked the strippers to help shelter this money by depositing it into their bank accounts. The money would be maintained in the bank accounts until the divorce was finalized. By safeguarding the client's money, they would earn fees of 10%. He knew that the nature of the strippers' business was generally cash and that they made large amounts of money. Banks would not necessarily notice large deposits into their bank accounts as they already had a history of such deposits from their work. The strippers fell for the pitch and deposited checks received from Lawson: the blank brokerage and personal checks he had stolen from the mail and that he had filled out. In one case, three checks totaling $90,000 were deposited.

Once the checks were deposited, Lawson had the women withdraw amounts typically around several thousand dollars. He would tell them the money was

*(Continued)*

41

needed for legal fees or other client expenses. This would be done several times and usually each time the money was given to Lawson's associate. Lawson himself was always concerned about being caught on surveillance cameras.

The withdrawals were always kept under the limits that would trigger banks to suspect possible money laundering or other criminal violations and the issuance of a Suspicious Activity Report (SAR). Lawson knew how long it would take before the mail theft victims, the brokerage firms, and the strippers' banks would learn of the theft of funds, and he made sure to stop withdrawals then and disappear. The strippers would be left holding the bag and trying to explain the deposits and withdrawals to authorities.

Although not as clever as the stripper scam for negotiating checks, Lawson used another tactic too. He posed as a car trader and drew up a business agreement with a Phoenix dealer to buy and sell used cars. He had the unsuspecting person deposit stolen checks that allegedly came from car sales and withdraw cash for Lawson or his associate to purchase additional cars. Again, others would be left holding the bag when Lawson absconded.

Inspector Casadei first learned of this case from bank investigators who reported the negotiation of bad checks. This led to mail theft reports in Paradise Valley and interviews of the many strippers who fell for Lawson's silver tongue. Inspector Casadei went to every strip club in Phoenix and interviewed the employees. Each woman Inspector Casadei interviewed told him the same story. Even though every stripper had been given a phony name by Lawson, the inspector was able to obtain a large amount of evidence. Yet he was unable to identify or locate Lawson.

Although Lawson had an associate assisting him, neither ever wanted to go anywhere near a bank to negotiate a check. They had a fear of being caught on bank cameras or identified by tellers or security officers. They had others do their dirty work, and anytime they felt possible heat, they dropped everything and took off. Their extreme level of caution protected them from discovery and arrest for a very long time. They would walk away from well-furnished homes when they felt they might be at risk of discovery. They would not take anything they could not fit into a car.

WHAT HAPPENS IN VEGAS DOES NOT ALWAYS STAY IN VEGAS

Inspector Casadei found that Postal Inspectors in other states were investigating similar identity theft schemes and after comparing notes, it was clear that Lawson was responsible. The FBI also was hunting Lawson, who had stolen mail and did identity theft and bank fraud in Texas, Illinois, Colorado, Florida, California, Georgia, Nevada, and Arizona. He would work his fraud in one state and then move to another and another, always one step ahead of the law.

Try as he might to track down Lawson, Inspector Casadei hit a dead end. Banks in Phoenix were no longer reporting bad checks, and it looked like the suspects had left town. Inspector Casadei then found that checks stolen in Tempe, Arizona, were deposited into an account in Las Vegas, Nevada. He assumed that Lawson was or had been there. Inspector Casadei asked everyone he spoke with to contact him if they were ever approached by a smooth-talking attorney who wanted them to cash some checks. His hard work paid off as he soon learned that Lawson was back.

Law enforcement then went one step further to find him. They tapped his cell phone calls to his mother. Lawson was always changing cell phones so the feds tapped incoming calls to his mother and traced them back to him in "Sin City." The FBI finally grabbed him in the Fashion Show Mall on the Las Vegas strip in 1999 on an old warrant out of Chicago originally issued in the mid-1990s. Once in custody, all the cases in other jurisdictions came down on Lawson. He was now facing multiple prosecutions and many years in jail.

The fraud perpetrated in Las Vegas was similar in many ways to his modus operandi. He again posed as a well-dressed attorney and used aliases including Steve Wilson, Michael Andres, William Watkiss, and Ron Porter. He targeted young women in strip clubs and casinos. He said he needed to hide money and requested their assistance for a fee. Once the women deposited the stolen checks, they would withdraw amounts of money and return it to Lawson or his associate, who then gave them their cut. As before, he would quickly disappear, never using the same alias again. This time he was not so lucky.

CONFESSION

After the arrest, Lawson agreed to cooperate and was interviewed by Inspector Casadei. Lawson provided an astonishing story of his life of crime. He admitted to stealing mail and identities of untold numbers of victims across the country and cashing over $5 million in checks in more than 10 years of criminal activity. In that period, he had repeated the theft and check-cashing activity in Phoenix and Tucson three or four times. Based on just Inspector Casadei's cases, Lawson was responsible for approximately $450,000 in fraud in 1999 in Phoenix and Las Vegas.

There were a number of ongoing investigations into Lawson's activities. He finally agreed to an all-inclusive plea that would resolve his outstanding criminal cases throughout the United States. He pleaded guilty in federal district court in Chicago. He was sentenced on February 8, 2001, to six years and three months in prison and $2,230,018 restitution. Theodore Shaw, his longtime partner in crime, received two years and three months in prison and court ordered restitution of $433,307.

**NOTES**

1. William Shakespeare, *Othello*, Act 3, Scene 3, 155–161.
2. Gary R. Gordon, Donald J. Rebovich, Kyung-Seok Choo, and Judith B. Gordon, *Identity Fraud Trends and Patterns: Building a Data-Based Foundation for Proactive Enforcement*, Center for Identity Management and Information Protection, Utica College, Utica, NY (October 2007), 43, www.utica.edu/academic/institutes/cimip/research.cfm.
3. Ibid.

4. The President's Identity Theft Task Force, "Combating Identity Theft: A Strategic Plan" (April 2007), 2–3, www.idtheft.gov/reports/StrategicPlan.pdf.

5. Ibid., 3.

6. United States General Accounting Office, "Identity Theft: Prevalence and Cost Appear to be Growing, Report to Congressional Requestors," March 2002, 35.

7. Byron Acohido and Jon Swartz, "Meth Addicts' Other Habit: Online Theft," *USA Today,* December 15, 2005, 10A.

8. Cassell Bryan-Low, "Growing Number of Hackers Attack Web Sites for Cash," *Wall Street Journal,* November 30, 2004, A1.

9. Microsoft Corporation, "Zombies and Botnets: Help Keep Your Computer under Your Control," January 3, 2007, www.microsoft.com/protect/computer/viruses/zombies.mspx.

10. Bryan-Low, "Growing Number of Hackers."

11. President's Identity Theft Task Force, "Combating Identity Theft," 15.

12. Yochi J. Dreazen, "Identity Theft as an Inside Job Is Increasing," *Wall Street Journal,* July 31, 2002, B1.

13. Ibid.

14. Federal Trade Commission, "2006 Identity Theft Survey Report" (November 2007), 31–32, www.ftc.gov/os/2007/11/SynovateFinalReportIDTheft2006.pdf.

15. Martin T. Biegelman and Joel T. Bartow, *Executive Roadmap to Fraud Prevention and Internal Control: Creating a Culture of Compliance*, (Hoboken, NJ: John Wiley & Sons, 2006), 219.

16. Anti-Phishing Working Group, www.antiphishing.org/word_phish.html.

17. Federal Trade Commission News Release, "Consumers' Private Financial Information Obtained and Sold Illegally; FTC Alleges," April 22, 1999, www.ftc.gov/opa/1999/04/touchtone.shtm.

18. U.S. Department of Justice, Office of the United States Attorney, Western District of Washington News Release, "Ten Indicted for Pretexting in 'Operation Dialing for Dollars,'" December 6, 2007, www.usdoj.gov/usao/waw/press/2007/dec/torrella.html.

19. Biegelman and Bartow, *Executive Roadmap,* 215–216.

20. Robin Sidel, "Card Companies Crack Down on Restaurants," *Wall Street Journal,* March 25, 2007, B1.

21. Social Engineering (Security) Wikipedia, //en.wikipedia.org/wiki/Social_engineering_(computer_security).

22. Federal Trade Commission, Consumer Fraud and Identity Theft Complaint Data, January–December 2007, February 13, 2008, 3, www.ftc.gov/opa/2008/02/fraud.pdf.

23. Federal Bureau of Investigation, "New E-Scams & Warnings," January 17, 2008, www.fbi.gov/cyberinvest/escams.htm.

# CHAPTER 4

# Student Loan Fraud and the Theft of Identity

As credit card fraud was leaving its wicked mark on individuals and financial institutions in the 1980s, another form of identity theft was continuing its assault on these same victims. Some fraud schemes are just so good and effective that they never go out of style. That is the case with student loan fraud, one of the earliest forms of identity theft. Common in the early 1970s and into the 1980s, it still occurs today. With the spiraling cost of college education, the great majority of students need some form of financial aid. The United States Department of Education gives out more than $80 billion in grants and loans each year. With so much money in financial assistance and federal education funds available, it is inevitable that identity thieves will want a big piece of that pie.

As in most identity theft schemes, the fraudster applies for financial assistance posing as another person, purportedly a student. The victim's identity and personal information is fraudulently obtained in any number of ways. Once the identity thief receives the funds, the money is spent and, of course, the loan is never repaid. As a result, the victim is eventually listed as defaulting on the loan. This can be especially problematic for actual students when they apply for financial aid and are denied because of their apparent history of default. The problem is just as bad for nonstudents whose identities are stolen and used in this fashion. When they apply for mortgages and other personal loans, they learn their credit history is damaged and they have to begin to restore their credit and reputation.

There are a number of variations of student loan fraud. Although identity theft is a common type of student loan fraud, there are other ways to defraud the system. In 2003, about $365 million of the $12 billion awarded each year to low-income undergraduate students went to those who misrepresented their family's actual annual income. This underreporting of family income on the financial aid applications resulted in increased, and fraudulent, payments to the students. Other examples of student loan fraud involve fraudsters who never attend the school or who drop out after receiving the loan funds.

## GROWTH AND IMPACT OF STUDENT LOAN FRAUD

Modern-day identity theft had its roots first in student loans and then credit cards. In terms of financial damage, fraudulent credit card use has had a greater impact on individuals and businesses over the years. That is not meant to minimize the toll of student loan fraud. However, the acceptance of credit cards in America allowed for a much greater financial impact through identity theft and related financial crimes. It is no coincidence that the leap from student loan fraud to credit card fraud occurred. The explosion of identity theft parallels the adoption and widespread use of credit cards. It did not happen overnight, as the use of credit cards grew slowly at first.

Prior to the enormous spike in credit card fraud in the 1980s, the outbreak of student loan fraud that started in the early 1970s laid the groundwork for the proliferation of identity theft. New York was particularly hard hit by student loan fraud. The New York State Higher Education Services Corporation (HESC) was one of the first organizations to recognize the seriousness and impact of student loan fraud. The HESC is a leading guarantor of student loans, grants, and scholarship programs. In 1979, it established a fraud unit to address the problem of student loan fraud. By 1980, it had identified hundreds of suspect loan applications due to phony Social Security numbers (SSNs), similar addresses used multiple times, and other fraudulent information found on the applications.[1]

The HESC found that a large number of the student loan applications had foreign names; along with the fraudulent identifying information, the investigators suspected that the applicants might not be eligible for benefits. Loan program benefits are earmarked for U.S. citizens and permanent resident aliens. The HESC reported this growing fraud to the Federal Bureau of Investigation and the U.S. Department of Education. Soon the Immigration and Naturalization Service (INS) in New York got involved in the fraud against federally guaranteed student loans. In 1982, these three federal agencies started an informal task force to tackle the problem.[2]

The task force identified and arrested numerous illegal aliens for student loan fraud. Due to the nature of student loans at the time, most of the individual fraud losses were under $10,000. The vast majority of the defendants were found to be Nigerian nationals in the United States illegally. Many of the fraudsters had phony identification and fraudulently obtained credit cards in their possession. While investigating these loan frauds, the task force realized it had encountered the proverbial tip of the iceberg. It would learn that credit card fraud was the much larger fraud but that both student loan fraud and credit card fraud were connected to identity theft.[3]

Subsequently, in 1983, the INS formed the Entitlement Frauds Unit to investigate, prosecute, and deter fraudsters from defrauding the government-financed student loan programs. The continuing investigations found an abundance of credit card fraud schemes intermingled with the loan frauds. Fraudsters had obtained employment in banks and other financial institutions with access to account holder information. Additional investigations by the INS uncovered other ingenious ways fraudsters used to infiltrate companies to obtain personal information.[4]

The INS conducted sweeps in New York City for illegal aliens working as security guards at private security companies. A number of those arrested had been assigned security guard work at New York Telephone Company. While working there, the security guards would steal the names, SSNs, and other personal information of contract employees. This stolen information would then be used for fraudulent credit card applications in the names of the victim contract workers, but the home address would be that of a mail drop controlled by the fraudsters.[5]

In January 1983, a government crackdown on student loan fraud netted 19 foreign students who falsely claimed they were either citizens or resident aliens. The grand jury investigation in San Francisco resulted in charges of mail fraud, making false statements to the United States Government, and falsely claiming eligibility for student loan benefits. The amount of student loan fraud totaled $77,509. These arrests brought the total number of those prosecuted for student loan fraud to over 100 in that one-year period ending in January 1983.[6]

A sad but prophetic comment was made by an INS Special Agent and one of the key members of the student loan fraud task force when he testified on Nigerian criminal activities before the Senate Permanent Subcommittee on Investigations on September 17, 1986. Although he was speaking about Nigerian criminal activity, the comments apply to the overall identity theft problem no matter who the perpetrator is. The Special Agent said, "The ready availability of fraudulent identification documents will enable Nigerians to continue their schemes unchecked." He added, "Their overall activities in the United States can be likened to economic terrorism."[7]

## FINANCIAL FLEECING 101: THE CASE OF JOHN EDWARD CHRISTENSEN

In 1999, at the very mature age of 58, John Edward Christensen decided to return to school. But a college education and degree were the last things on his mind. His only goal was a financial fleecing of the federal student aid program. Christensen devised an identity theft scheme to defraud lenders, schools, and the United States Department of Education that would ultimately net him $313,000 and a trip to prison. He perpetrated the fraud in and around Phoenix, Arizona, between 1999 and 2003.

Identity fraudsters continually use imagination in their crimes, and Christensen was no different. He obtained a list of prison inmates' names and then contacted them via the mails posing as an attorney. In his letters, he offered the prisoners his assistance in their criminal cases and possible appeals of their sentences. The inmates were all too happy to have someone help and readily provided personal information that Christensen then used in his identity theft scheme. Christensen applied for financial aid in 57 stolen names and received financial aid under 43 of those names.

Christensen generally focused on community colleges, as many identity thieves do. Community colleges usually have cheaper tuitions, resulting in more money for the fraudsters after paying the enrollment fees. "They're applying online for financial aid, enrolling online, they stay enrolled for 30 days and then move on," an official from the Department of Education's Office of Inspector General said at the time.[8] "The object I had was to not be dropped out of the courses for the first 30 days. If I didn't drop out, and the instructor didn't drop me out, I was going to get the money," said Christensen.[9]

Christensen's comeuppance came on September 2, 2003. He was at Mesa Community College in Mesa, Arizona, where he was picking up a student aid check under one of the stolen names. An alert financial aid officer recognized him as the person who had previously received a student aid check in another name. Although Christensen tried to flee the scene, he was quickly caught and arrested. He identified himself using one of the stolen identities but that did not work. On his person were phony identifications in several different names.[10] A search of his residence found further evidence of his identity theft activity. The house and car he was driving were purchased using a stolen identity. He was also receiving Social Security benefits under a stolen identity.

He pleaded guilty on January 20, 2004, in federal district court in Phoenix to charges of Student Aid Fraud and Identity Theft. He also forfeited money seized from 10 bank accounts and his home. On March 22, 2004, Christensen was sentenced to 41 months in prison, followed by three years probation and court-ordered restitution.

## A FAMILY AFFAIR OF FRAUD

Between January 2000 and March 2004, Ann Armstrong, a 64-year-old grandmother in Las Vegas, Nevada, orchestrated a $1 million identity theft scheme using student financial assistance. She brought four of her children and three of her grandchildren into the conspiracy. Together, they used the identities of 65 people to obtain federal student aid at colleges in Arizona, Colorado, Maryland, Nevada, and Texas. The focus was on schools that offered distance learning and online classes.

An observant financial aid officer at Truckee Meadows Community College in Reno, Nevada, noticed that a number of students applying for financial assistance had the same address and telephone number on their applications. This was reported to the Office of Inspector General of the U.S. Department of Education, which began an investigation. Armstrong and her family cashed or deposited the student aid checks at banks using phony identification. Just in their home state of Nevada, they received 76 federal grants and loans totaling over $400,000. The balance of the fraud was conducted in the other four states.[11]

Armstrong and her family were indicted in June 2004. She pleaded guilty on October 19, 2005, to conspiracy to commit student loan fraud and student loan fraud. In her guilty plea, Armstrong admitted "the object of the conspiracy was to fraudulently obtain federal student financial aid through the use of false applications which were submitted by fax and email. Financial aid checks were received through the mail and the funds obtained through the use of false identification documents."[12] "When individuals fraudulently and illegally receive federal student aid grants and loans, less money is available for deserving students," said the United States Attorney for Nevada at the time.[13]

On February 24, 2006, Armstrong was sentenced to 57 months in prison, three years of supervised release, and ordered to pay $662,000 in restitution. Under the federal sentencing guidelines, she received an enhanced sentence because she was the leader of the conspiracy, directed the activities of the other family members, and received the bulk of the fraudulent proceeds. All of her family members also pleaded guilty, and most were sentenced to prison terms.

## TRYING TO MAKE AMENDS

In order to combat the ongoing problem of student loan fraud, the Department of Education's Office of Federal Student Aid and Office of Inspector General (OIG) began a public awareness campaign to alert the general public, and specifically students, their families, schools, and financial institutions, about identity theft. They created a Web site at www.ed.gov/misused that offers a wealth of information about identity theft related to student loans and grants, how the fraud is committed, recommendations for prevention, and how to report identity theft involving federal education dollars.

The awareness campaign also created videos using convicted fraudsters discussing how they committed identity theft. These videos help to educate potential victims about the extent of the problem and steps to follow to stop from becoming a victim. Christensen and Armstrong agreed to appear in the prevention videos to alert the public about the evils of this crime.

The DVD entitled *FSA* [Federal Student Aid] *Identity Theft: We Need Your Help* was released in 2003 and features Christensen discussing his techniques for committing identity theft. The second DVD is entitled *Identity Theft: It's Not Worth It* was released in January 2007 and features Armstrong telling how she regretted her criminal acts and how her life and that of her family were destroyed. Both DVDs are available through the Department of Education.

Other identity thieves who have been arrested have also been featured in identity theft deterrence videos. For example, fraudster Abraham Abdallah appears in the 1985 TransUnion-produced *Crime of the '80s* video after his first arrest for identity theft. He claimed to have learned his lesson and promised to go straight. That turned out to be an empty promise; he returned to a life of crime and identity theft and was arrested numerous times over the next 16 years before his front-page-making arrest in 2001 resulting in a lengthy prison sentence. Abdallah is profiled in Chapter 12.

## COMPROMISE OF STUDENT LOAN DATA

Data breaches have been in the news over the last few years. The highly lucrative $85 billion student loan business is particularly susceptible. Media stories have detailed how lenders may have misused students' personal information for the purpose of "trolling for marketing data they can use to bombard students with mass mailings or other solicitations."[14]

The National Student Loan Data System was created in 1993 to assist in determining whether students are eligible for financial aid and assistance in collecting loan payments. The database contains confidential information that includes names, addresses, telephone numbers, birth dates, SSNs, and financial information, such as loan balances. Approximately 29,000 university financial aid officers and 7,500 loan company employees have access to this extremely sensitive information, which is protected by federal privacy laws.[15]

The U.S. Department of Education is concerned about inappropriate use of the system and has increased monitoring to ensure compliance. Particularly disconcerting is data mining by companies looking for potential customers for loan consolidation. Lenders also have given unauthorized access to marketing firms and collection agencies. This not only violates privacy laws but opens the more than 60 million student loan borrowers to potential misuse of their personally identifiable information (PII) and identity theft. Although there have not been any significant identity theft cases surfacing from these breaches, it may only be a matter of time.

## ADMISSION TO THE IVY LEAGUE THROUGH ID THEFT

A constant theme throughout this book is how fraudsters involved in identity theft employ various means to steal identities and profit from their financial crimes. I have been speaking and writing about my Potato Chip Theory of Fraud for many years. Simply put, just as a person is often unable to eat only one potato chip and will eat one after another, once criminals start committing fraud, they cannot stop. Committing fraud becomes addictive. Assuming a scammer does not get caught, the swindler will commit fraud after fraud, even branching out to new frauds to steal money and other things of value.[16] Although this chapter is on student loan fraud, as you will learn, identity thieves can steal in many different ways.

In 1999, then 21-year-old Esther Reed vanished without a trace, leaving friends and family in Washington State deeply concerned. The young woman already had a troubled life. Her parents' divorce had had a deep impact on her. Her mother's death from cancer may have been the final straw. Although considered very smart, Reed dropped out of high school. She turned to stealing and was facing criminal charges of possession of stolen property. So it was not a complete surprise that she would leave town. No one heard from her or knew where she was; some even assumed she was dead.

In reality, Reed was busy, very busy honing a new skill: identity theft. Over the next several years, she stole the identities of a number of women and obtained admission to the prestigious Ivy League schools of Harvard and Columbia, as well as California State University, Fullerton. Not much is known about Reed's secret life between the time she dropped out of sight in 1999 and when she was finally arrested on February 2, 2008, in suburban Chicago, thanks to a tip made to the *America's Most Wanted* television show. What we do know is that she was very active in stealing the lives of others. She used the names Liz Reed, Natalie Bowman, Natalie Fisher, Brooke Henson, and others.[17]

Someone using the name Natalie Bowman started attending Cal State Fullerton in the fall of 2002. It is believed that someone was Reed. She was later accepted at Harvard, but it is unknown if she actually attended the university. In October 2003, she began using the name of Brooke Henson. The real Henson lived in Travelers Rest, South Carolina, and went missing on July 4, 1999. She was never seen again and is feared dead. There is no evidence that Reed had anything to do with Henson's disappearance. Yet, as of the writing of this book, it is unknown how Reed learned of Henson and why she decided to steal Henson's identity.

In October 2003, Reed obtained a State of Ohio identification card using Henson's name, date of birth, and SSN. In December 2003, she received a high school equivalency diploma in Ohio using Henson's name and then took the SAT college admission examination using Henson's identification. In May 2004, Reed applied to Columbia University using Henson's name and was accepted in June 2004 to the School of General Studies. She started classes at Columbia in August 2004. Reed also fraudulently applied for and received more than $100,000 in student loans in Henson's name.[18]

In February 2005, Reed applied to the South Carolina Department of Vital Statistics for a duplicate birth certificate of Henson using the Ohio identification card, the Columbia University student identification card, and Henson's SSN. In April 2006, Reed received a United States Passport in Henson's name.[19] Her downfall began in 2006 when she applied for a job. The prospective employer did a background check on her assumed name of Henson and "found a Web site dedicated to the missing woman."[20] Suspicious, she contacted the New York City Police Department, who began an investigation.

Further evidence emerged. A "skeptical boyfriend had rummaged through her purse and discovered identification for seven different people, including Brooke Henson and Esther Reed."[21] He also contacted the police, and although they concluded that the woman claiming to be Henson was in reality Reed, she disappeared before an arrest could be made. The connection to the missing Henson was finally made, and the feds got involved in the investigation.

The United States Secret Service in South Carolina conducted a detailed investigation and uncovered significant evidence against Reed. They also learned that Reed had used credit cards in the names of other people. The identity theft was more than just an attempt to gain an education; it was also to steal and commit fraud. Reed was indicted in United States District Court for the District of South Carolina in the summer of 2007 on charges of aggravated identity theft, mail fraud, wire fraud, and fraudulent use of someone else's Social Security number. She eventually made the United States Secret Service's Most Wanted List.

After being profiled on *America's Most Wanted*, an anonymous tipster provided information that helped locate Reed. The tipster provided an email address that Reed was using and from that law enforcement found another alias, Jennifer Myers. The federal agents on her trail discovered an Iowa driver's license in Myers's name and a car registered to Myers with Iowa plates. Using this information, the feds then tracked her to a hotel in Tinley Park, Illinois, where she was arrested.[22]

After her arraignment in federal court in Chicago on February 4, 2008, Reed agreed to speak to the press interested in her case. She made some bizarre comments. "Obviously I did things wrong" but she added, "I wouldn't have changed what happened." She refused to say why she used Henson's name or what she did all those years using other people's identities.[23] The sad thing is that in this identity theft case, there is more than just a stolen identity and a financial impact. As Brooke Henson's family told *America's Most Wanted*, "they have been victimized twice—first when Brooke disappeared and now again—knowing that someone is living as Brooke."[24]

No matter the eventual criminal sentence imposed on Reed, there are a number of unanswered questions. How was she able to take the SAT, Graduate Record Examination, and apply to colleges including two Ivy League schools and get accepted, all the while using stolen identities? Was any kind of due diligence used to scrutinize the personal identifying information provided? Obviously not. This sad case should be a wake-up call to institutions of higher learning everywhere.

On August 19, 2008, Reed pleaded guilty to fraud and identity theft charges in federal court in Greenville, SC. She is facing the prospect of many years in prison and the many questions about her life on the run are still unanswered.

## MORE CASES

In May 2007, an escaped murderer pleaded guilty to bank fraud and identity theft charges related to his stealing the identity of another person and applying for student loans using that person's name and SSN. Beginning in 1999 and continuing to 2002, the defendant, Ivan Orta Cuprill, submitted applications for financial aid to attend the State University of New York at Old Westbury using a stolen identity. The loan funds were subsequently disbursed but Cuprill never repaid the loans. Special Agents of the Department of Education OIG arrested Cuprill for the student loan fraud in July 2006, but investigators did not know his true identity. The continuing investigation discovered that Cuprill was a fugitive on the run from a 27-year prison term for murder and other crimes in Puerto Rico. Cuprill escaped from jail in 1994 and successfully hid in plain sight until his arrest for the student loan fraud. He will now spend the next 30 years behind bars.[25]

In but another example of the ease of conducting student loan fraud, a Tucson, Arizona man was arrested on November 9, 2007, and charged in a fraudulent scheme to obtain numerous student loan frauds. Between 2003 and 2007, the defendant submitted more than 200 student loan applications via the Internet through various email accounts he maintained. He used both his own name and that of people whose identities he had stolen. Thanks to technology, all necessary documentation for the loans including falsified proof of employment and residence verification were faxed to the financial institutions. The defendant received 42 student loans totaling $624,287 for attendance at Stanford University, George Washington University, University of Arizona, and Scottsdale Culinary Institute. He never attended any of these educational institutions, although he received the loan funds. In all, he applied for more than $10 million in student loans but only received a fraction of that amount.[26]

## IT IS NOT JUST AN AMERICAN PROBLEM

Student loan fraud and identity theft is not isolated to the United States. It is a worldwide problem, and the United Kingdom has been especially hard hit in recent years. The government-owned Student Loans Company (SLC) is a U.K. organization established to provide financial services, including loans and grants, to students attending colleges and universities in England, Northern Ireland, Scotland, and Wales. For many years the SLC accepted just a birth certificate for loans up to £6,000 per student per year.

Once fraudsters learned this, they quickly exploited it. A major student loan fraud against the SLC started with the theft of hundreds of blank birth certificates. Eventually, more than 200 of the stolen birth certificates were used to create phony identities to obtain student loans.

In one of the largest student loan frauds in the U.K., an identity thief used 17 stolen identities to enroll himself in five different degree programs in one university. Adeleke Adebayo was clearly not a student, but that did not stop him. He collected more than £65,595 (approximately $130,000) in fraudulent loans with the many identities. He also claimed to be attending classes at other U.K. universities for which he was receiving loans. In March 2007, he was sentenced to four years in prison. His girlfriend received 18 months in jail for assisting him in creating the phony identities.[27]

Although this is an especially egregious case, it is by far not the only one. In another investigation, an identity thief enrolled in a university and received student loans although he never took the required preparatory examinations or attended class lectures. The bigger problem is that the university system and the SLC have limited knowledge as to the true identities of their students or whether they are actually attending classes. As one investigator stated, "We are talking about a criminal industry, a large-scale criminal industry." As such, the Universities and Colleges Admissions Service, a clearinghouse for student applications to U.K. universities, has doubled the size of its fraud investigations team.[28]

## DEPARTMENT OF EDUCATION'S OUTREACH PREVENTION PROGRAM

The United States Department of Education (ED) and its OIG have developed a proactive student loan fraud prevention program. The OIG conducts audits, investigations, and inspections of educational programs and operations and is the law enforcement agency within the ED responsible for fighting fraud, waste, and abuse. Exhibit 4.1 includes key messages from its excellent resource Web site.

**Exhibit 4.1    U.S. Department of Education Guidance to Students to Prevent Identity Theft Fraud**

---

### Identity Theft Alert to Students

Protect your Social Security number and other personal information. Don't let identity thieves rob you of your educational future!

Being a student does not safeguard you against identity theft, one of the fastest growing consumer crimes in the nation. Identity thieves don't steal your money; they steal your name and reputation and use them for their own financial gain. They attempt to steal your future! Identity theft literally steals who you are, and it can seriously jeopardize your financial future.

Imagine having thousands of dollars of unauthorized debt and a wrecked credit rating because of identity theft. Also, the unfortunate reality of identity theft is that it is you, the victim, who is responsible for cleaning up the mess and re-establishing your good name and credit. The experience of thousands of identity theft victims is that this frustrating experience often requires months and even years.

*(Continued)*

**Exhibit 4.1   (Continued)**

In fact as a student, you may even be more vulnerable to identity theft because of the availability of your personal data and the way many students handle this data. A recent national survey of college students found that:

- Almost half of all college students receive credit card applications on a daily or weekly basis. Many of these students throw out card applications without destroying them.
- Nearly a third of students rarely, if ever, reconcile their credit card and checking account balances.
- Almost 50 percent of students have had grades posted by Social Security number.

All of these factors make students potential identity theft victims. In addition, as a student, you may be surprised to learn how many of your daily activities expose you to this crime. For example:

- Do you use your personal computer for online banking transactions?
- Do you use your personal computer to buy merchandise or purchase tickets for travel, concerts, or other services?
- Do you receive credit card offers in the mail? Do you discard these documents before you shred all of them?
- Do you store personal information in your computer?
- Do you use a cell phone?
- Do you use your Social Security number for identification?
- Do you have a student loan?

You probably answered yes to at least one of these questions about daily transactions that you routinely perform. Each of these routine actions places you at risk of being a victim of identity theft because each of these transaction requires you to share personal information such as your bank and credit card account numbers, your Social Security number, or your name, address, and phone number. This is the same personal information that identity thieves use to commit fraud.

The first step to prevent identity theft is awareness of how and when you use your personal information. By keeping close tabs on your personal information, you can reduce your chances of becoming an identity theft victim. Let's start with credit cards.

- Memorize your Social Security number and passwords. Don't record your password on papers you carry with you.
- Don't use your date of birth as your password.
- Shred pre-approved credit applications and other financial documents before discarding them.
- Order credit reports every year from each of the major credit reporting agencies and thoroughly review them for accuracy.
- Never give personal or financial information over the phone or Internet unless you initiated the contact.

- Don't carry your Social Security card or birth certificate with you.
- Report lost or stolen credit cards immediately.
- Check your monthly credit card and bank statements for unusual activity.
- Use a firewall program on your computer, especially if you leave your computer connected to the Internet 24 hours a day.
- Do not download files sent to you by strangers or click on hyperlinks from people you don't know.

Students applying for or using student loans should also:

- Use caution when using commercial financial aid services over the Internet or telephone. U.S. Department of Education services are free and password-protected. Before deciding to use a for-fee financial aid advice service, visit the Looking for Student Aid site.
- Apply for federal student aid at www.fafsa.ed.gov. After completing the Free Application for Federal Student Aid (FAFSA) electronically, remember to exit the application and close the browser.
- Don't reveal your PIN to anyone, even if that person is helping you fill out the FAFSA. The only time you should use your PIN is on secure ED systems.
- Shred receipts and copies of documents with personal information if they are no longer needed.
- Review your financial aid award documents and keep track of the amount of student aid you applied for and have been awarded.
- Report all lost or stolen student identification immediately.

Source: www.ed.gov/about/offices/list/oig/misused/index.html

## NOTES

1. Testimony of Richard G. Palak, Special Agent, Immigration and Naturalization Service, Hearings on Emerging Criminal Groups: Nigerian Criminal Activities, before the Permanent Subcommittee on Investigations of the Committee on Governmental Affairs, United States Senate, 99th Congress, 2nd Session, September 17, 1986, 26.
2. Ibid.
3. Ibid., 27.
4. Ibid., 28.
5. Ibid.
6. "Nineteen Aliens Are Indicted in Student Loan Fraud," *New York Times*, January 21, 1983, http://query.nytimes.com/gst/fullpage.html?res=9505EFD61138F932A15752C0A965948260.
7. Testimony of Richard G. Palak, 30.
8. Andrea Coombes, "Identity Thieves Head Off to College," *Wall Street Journal*, October 25, 2005, D3.

9. Ibid.

10. U.S. Department of Justice, Office of the United States Attorney, District of Arizona, Press Release, "Thief Admits Identity Scam Used to Get $300,000 in Student Loans," January 20, 2004, www.ed.gov/about/offices/list/oig/invtreports/az012004.html.

11. U.S. Department of Education, News Release, "U.S. Department of Education Office of Inspector General Launches New DVD: *Identity Theft: It's Not worth It*," January 18, 2007, www.ed.gov/news/pressreleases/2007/01/01182007.html.

12. U.S. Department of Justice, Office of the United States Attorney, District of Arizona, News Release, "Woman Sentenced to Almost Five Years in Federal Prison For Student Loan Fraud," February 24, 2006, www.usdoj.gov/usao/nv/home/pressrelease/february2006/armstrong022406.htm.

13. Ibid.

14. Amit R. Paley, "Student Loan Data Misused, Officials Say," *Seattle Times*, April 16, 2007, A5.

15. Ibid.

16. For more information on the Potato Chip Theory of Fraud, please see Martin Biegelman and Joel Bartow, *Executive Roadmap to Fraud Prevention and Internal Control: Creating a Culture of Compliance*, (Hoboken, NJ: John Wiley & Sons, 2006), 37–38.

17. *America's Most Wanted* television show, Esther Elizabeth Reed, Capture #974, February 2, 2008, www.amw.com/fugitives/capture.cfm?id=42967.

18. *United States of America v. Esther Elizabeth Reed*, Indictment, United States District Court, District of South Carolina, www.amw.com/pdf/indictment.pdf.

19. Ibid.

20. Jennifer Sullivan, "Feds Searching for Local Woman in ID Theft Cases," *Seattle Times*, November 1, 2007, B1.

21. Jennifer Sullivan, "A Disappearance, Stolen Identities and a Trail of Clues," *Seattle Times*, January 11, 2007, A1.

22. *America's Most Wanted* television show, Esther Elizabeth Reed, Capture #974.

23. Ibid.

24. Ibid.

25. U.S. Department of Justice, Office of the United States Attorney, Southern District of New York, News Release, "Escaped Murderer Pleads Guilty to Bank Fraud and Identity Theft," May 14, 2007, www.ed.gov/about/offices/list/oig/invtreports/ny052007.html.

26. "Tucson Man Faces Criminal Charges in Fraudulent Student Loan Scheme," LawFuel.com, November 18, 2007, lawfuel.com/show-release.asp?ID=16133.

27. Matthew Chapman, "Fake Students Net Loan Millions," BBC News, May 5, 2007, news.bbc.co.uk/1/hi/education/6624019.stm.

28. Ibid.

# CHAPTER 5

# Nigerian Criminal Enterprises

Organized criminal gangs have long been a plague on society. The traditional organized crime of the Mafia or La Cosa Nostra that developed in the United States in the early twentieth century set the stage for a myriad of other nontraditional gangs and groups that have sprung up over the years. They include Russian mobsters who came to this country after the fall of the former Soviet Union, Chinese tongs, Japanese Yakuza, Colombian drug cartels, and others who have gained a foothold in the United States. For most of these groups, drug trafficking, extortion, protection rackets, and other crimes of violence are the norm. One organized crime group, more than any other, has made financial crimes their focus and turned identity theft into their specialty. They are members of Nigerian organized crime often called Nigerian Criminal Enterprises (NCE) by law enforcement in this country.

For more than 30 years, a very small percentage of Nigerian nationals living in America have been involved in a criminal conspiracy to commit various white-collar crimes, defrauding banks and other financial institutions, businesses, insurance companies, government agencies, and private citizens. Like other immigrants, Nigerians come to this country in search of higher education and a better way of life, but some gravitate to a life of crime. Over the years Nigerian scam artists have committed credit card and bank frauds, identity theft, insurance fraud, healthcare fraud, student loan fraud, check kiting, confidence schemes, entitlement frauds, money laundering, counterfeiting, tax frauds, and numerous other scams.

In the early 1990s, federal agents and prosecutors began to use the term "West African criminal activity" when referring to Nigerian fraudsters because of a concern that our government was portraying all citizens of a particular country as engaging in criminal activity. This occurred after protests from the Nigerian government that law enforcement branded all Nigerians as criminals based on the actions of only a few. In reality, while countries such as Sierra Leone, Ghana, Togo, Senegal, Guinea, and the Ivory Coast are in West Africa, almost all of the "West African criminal activity" was committed by Nigerians. As a result, the United States Department of Justice then instituted a new terminology because of the explosive growth of Nigerian fraud schemes. It designated this type of organized and widespread activity as Nigerian Criminal Enterprise schemes.

I want to again emphasize that not all Nigerians or West Africans are involved in criminal activity. The great majority of these people are honest, hardworking, and law-abiding and contributing members of society. Law enforcement limits its investigations to crimes committed by individuals, not by national origin. Former Deputy Attorney General Eric H. Holder Jr. made the same point in a speech he gave on Nigerian Organized Crime in Washington, DC, on November 9, 1999:

> As we discuss the topic of Nigerian Organized Crime, I want to emphasize from the outset that our focus is not on the millions of law abiding Nigerians, at home and abroad, whose rich tradition and culture we admire and whose contributions to our society we value; rather our focus is on Nigerian criminal elements that now dominate crime emanating from West Africa.[1]

## FBI RECOGNIZES THE GROWING IDENTITY THEFT THREAT

The Federal Bureau of Investigation's New York Field Office recognized the growing identity theft threat by Nigerian nationals in early 1984 with the publication of an informational memorandum that made its way through the law enforcement community. At that time, the FBI was conducting investigations into credit card fraud, student loan scams, and other crimes perpetrated by these early identity thieves. The FBI recognized that this problem was not going away and would have a much bigger impact in the years to come. Thus, the organization wanted to warn and educate others in law enforcement. The memo was entitled "Nigerian Fraud Group" and was intended to provide an overview of the fraudulent activities of foreign nationals in the United States.

The memo detailed the work of the FBI, the Immigration and Naturalization Service (INS), and the United States Department of Education in investigating systematic, multimillion-dollar fraud schemes conducted by Nigerian nationals. The scams involved everything from defrauding U.S. government agencies, to banks, credit card issuers, insurance companies, and social welfare services. The FBI reported that this criminal activity was especially prevalent in New York, California, Massachusetts, Illinois, Texas, Arizona, Washington, DC, Georgia, Wisconsin, Minnesota, North Carolina, and Rhode Island. The fraudsters were found to be well educated and quite adept at defrauding financial institutions. The memo stated that various investigations found scam artists working in financial institutions in the New York metropolitan area and assisting other Nigerian nationals in defrauding these institutions.

The FBI memo also covered the origin of the problem. Apparently, student loan fraud was the impetus. In the early 1970s, banks in New York State started receiving fraudulent loan applications in the names of college professors. The professors had not submitted the applications, and their personal information was used without their knowledge. The information in the applications was correct except for the home address, which was one used by the fraudster. The banks learned through investigation that the applications were being submitted by Nigerian nationals who were college students in the United States on student visas. The professors' names came from college yearbooks.

The FBI also learned that these fraudsters were submitting student loans through the Guaranteed Student Loan Program in variations of their names claiming they were U.S. citizens. They also used the names and identifying information of fellow students from their schools for loans. This information was readily available on campus as schools commonly used Social Security numbers for student identification. The criminals exploited a weakness in the student loan program; because the loans were guaranteed by the government, the banks knew that they would recover any losses from default. Thus, there was little if any scrutiny of the loan applications for false information.

The report went on to describe the many other frauds committed by this criminal group, including staged vehicle accidents, welfare fraud, passport fraud and creating phony identification, check fraud, submission of fraudulent tax returns, scam marriages to obtain citizenship, narcotics trafficking, counterfeiting, and, of course, credit card fraud through the submission of fraudulent card applications. Many in federal law enforcement knew about the existence and activities of these fraud artists, but the report was an awakening to others in state and local law enforcement who were just beginning investigations into these criminals.

## GENESIS OF THE PROBLEM

Fraud is nothing new in the United States. It has been a problem facing law enforcement and the public for well over 100 years. Yet the Nigerian crime problem was something not seen before. Nigeria's oil prosperity of the 1970s and early 1980s helped compound the problem. A mass migration to the country's capital, Lagos, grew out of control. Many people wanted a piece of the newfound wealth, and they wanted it right away. This also led to rampant corruption throughout the government and a complete lack of institutional accountability. There was a desire to have what others in the world had. Individuals who gained an education and worked hard found they could make only a meager living. Yet they saw criminals living the good life with luxury cars and all the trappings of wealth. The result was cynicism and distrust. The United States was viewed as the land of opportunity. The criminal element found out how easy it was to exploit America's financial institutions.

Nigerian criminal gangs not only understood the U.S. financial system but became skilled at learning new ways to attack it. They saw how easy it was to commit fraud. The fraudsters were well educated and able to counter fraud prevention techniques instituted by the banks, credit card issuers, businesses, and government. Those who came to the United States with criminal intent quickly learned about these frauds from others already in the country, causing the problem to grow. In an arrest made by Postal Inspectors in November 1997 of a Nigerian national for credit card fraud, the suspect admitted that he opened private mailboxes at a mail drop several months earlier with a friend. The suspect stated that he had recently arrived in the United States from Nigeria and that his friend was tutoring him in credit card fraud schemes.

Law enforcement has found that most Nigerians involved in criminal activity do not operate as part of large gangs. They are able to carry out these scams either individually or in small groups. Some operate in organized cells, which may consist of a leader and numerous soldiers. Some of these cells are bound by tribal loyalties. The drug smuggling gangs have a more traditional organized crime structure, but this is not usually seen in fraud activity. The gang members often travel all over the United States when conducting their various fraud schemes. They also maintain contact and correspondence with others involved in this fraud throughout the country.

## CREDIT CARD AND IDENTITY FRAUD

Nigerian fraud activity plays an important part of credit card fraud in the United States. In the early 1970s, Nigerian fraudsters began committing student loan fraud and then progressed to credit card fraud. They became masters of credit card application fraud by obtaining and using a victim's personal information. They then used this information fraudulently to obtain credit cards, bank accounts, and loans.

Nigerian credit card fraud schemes continually evolved to avoid law enforcement detection and prosecution. They subverted postal employees to turn over to them mail containing credit cards. Scam artists rented apartments in inner city areas to receive these credit cards, knowing that it is much harder for law enforcement to closely watch these locations. They infiltrated Social Security offices, banks, brokerages, and credit bureaus as employees to steal personal information on potential victims. These fraudsters spread their criminal activities throughout the United States.

Scammers obtained unsuspecting individuals' credit and biographical information and submitted false applications in these names to banks, department stores, oil and gas companies and other credit card issuers. They targeted prominent professionals, such as lawyers, stockbrokers, doctors, and others who were likely to have good credit ratings. Using the stolen information, the fraudsters completed numerous credit card applications and submitted them to various issuers. They would seek out credit card issuers that did not do a thorough investigation on applicants or were attempting to expand their cardholder base.

## HIGHLY CONFIDENTIAL IDENTITY THEFT "TRAINING MANUAL"

In the spring of 1985, I was attending a credit card investigators' meeting in New York City. One member had an exciting discovery he wanted to share with the group. Law enforcement in another state had executed a search warrant of the residence of a suspected identity thief who happened to be a Nigerian national. While searching the apartment for evidence of credit card fraud and identity theft, the law enforcement officers had found the mother lode of damning proof that a training school on fraud existed. It was allegedly a training manual of how to conduct credit card fraud. Someone from the law enforcement agency prepared a cover page for the manual entitled "Training Manual" and wrote "Used by Nigerian fraud artists to obtain new identities in order to perpetrate credit card frauds." Each of the 70 pages was stamped "Confidential: For Law Enforcement Use Only"—obviously this was done after it was seized by the police.

For years, bank and credit card investigators as well as law enforcement believed that Nigerian nationals had training centers in Nigeria that trained future fraudsters in identity theft–related crimes. Following their training and indoctrination, these students came to the United States, either legally or illegally, to commit fraud on the American public and business community. Many believed this to be the case because of the explosion of identity theft in the mid-1980s and the expertise of the fraudsters committing it. Although there was no doubt that criminals were teaching each other, I always discounted the idea of a "Fraud University" somewhere in Lagos where hundreds of eager students listened to pearls of fraud wisdom from their criminally minded professors. There was no need for formal training programs; there already was a wealth of information available to anyone with an interest. As soon as I heard of this training manual, I had my doubts.

It turned out that the manual seized by police was a copy of a readily available book published in the United States. The book covered in detail how to obtain new identities and commit various forms of fraud, including credit card fraud. This book, and others like it, was at the time and continues to be easily available to anyone with an interest. Many of them state that the information therein is intended for educational purposes only and not for any illegal activity. Considering that this "educational" guide was found in the residence of identity thieves, I would have to assume that they found the information useful.

In writing this book, I reread my copy of this "Training Manual," now more than 23 years after I first received it. I was struck with the enduring relevance of the information. Among page after page of instructions on how to obtain identity information and related comments were these pointers:

- Criminals were told to peruse the obituary columns for the recently deceased and take over that person's identity. A suggestion was to write to the funeral home posing as an "old friend" who had just seen the obituary in the paper and asking for the deceased's date and place of birth to confirm that this was indeed the old friend. With that information, a duplicate birth certificate can be ordered. A similar case where the identities of deceased people were used in a long-running identity theft case is profiled in Chapter 15.

- Once a birth certificate is obtained, getting a Social Security card is next. If assuming the identity of a deceased person, the guide reminded the reader to remember to ask for a duplicate card, not a new one, to dispel possible suspicions.

- Credit card and other personal information can be easily obtained from the garbage. This was true in 1985 and it is just as true today. Shredding any and all personal and financial information is a must. (See Chapter 20 for a detailed discussion on the importance of document shredding.)

- The average American is not focused on security and will too easily divulge personal information to almost anyone.
- Good con artists can call unsuspecting victims and use a variety of stories to obtain their dates of birth, SSNs, and other information. One scheme discussed was how to pose as a bank representative or law enforcement officer and ask for the person's assistance in an investigation of identity theft. Part of the cooperation would be to provide their personal information.
- Another scheme was to call and tell people they had won a prize contest. All they had to do was provide personal identification to claim the award.
- People do not thoroughly examine their monthly credit card statements so they often will miss discovering fraud on their cards.

I did find an interesting comment about the role of law enforcement when discussing the number of arrests and convictions for credit card fraud in 1983. "Credit card criminals face a higher probability of being struck by lightning than being convicted of credit card fraud" was the sad but true statement.

## CHECK FRAUD

Nigerian criminals are also involved in various check schemes including check forgery and kiting. Check fraud goes well with the other financial crimes that are carried out. Using the identities they have stolen, criminals open numerous checking accounts. They use the fraudulently obtained credit cards for identification when opening the accounts and later when passing the checks. The scammers are also using advances in technology to commit fraud. They are stealing business and corporate checks and using computers and scanners to change payees and payment amounts. They then negotiate these fraudulent checks through various accounts they have set up. In 1998, 75 percent of the counterfeit checks that were negotiated in Houston, Texas, resulted from Nigerian Criminal Enterprises.[2] Fast forward to today, and much is still the same. In October 2007, Postal Inspectors and other law enforcement officers arrested 77 scammers as part of a global fraud crackdown on counterfeit checks bound for the United States. Investigators intercepted more than $2.1 billion in phony checks from schemes in Nigeria and other countries.

## ADVANCE FEE OR "419" FRAUD

Nigerian fraudsters based in their home country and throughout the world are committing "419 frauds," or advance fee frauds, on American and international businesses. These imaginative frauds appeal to a person's greed and are very successful. Victims are blinded by the possible riches they are offered and forget to use common sense. Although law enforcement agencies such as the United States Secret Service warn people about these frauds, people continue to fall victim. "A large number of victims are enticed into believing they have been singled out from the masses to share in multi-million dollar windfall profits for no apparent reason."[3]

The "419" refers to the Nigerian criminal code statute for this kind of crime. Nigerian scammers target businesses in an old-fashioned confidence swindle offering huge sums of money from the Nigerian government. Although this scheme seems implausible at first glance, it has achieved remarkable success among unwitting victims. It started in England and spread to the United States, then to businesses in Asia, Europe, Canada, and elsewhere.

When the scam first started in the early 1990s, fraudsters used the mails to convey the phony pitch. Companies were contacted by a mysterious Nigerian businessman or government official with a fictitious title. There are many variations, but all generally advise that one can receive a substantial portion of millions of dollars for moving this money out of Nigeria and into a foreign bank account. In one letter, the writer states that he is operating with the knowledge of the Nigerian government. He explains that a large sum of money—usually from $10 to $20 million—is available if the American business will act as the accepting agent. The American firm is told it can receive a fee of 30% or more. The balance is to be paid to the Nigerian accomplices. Of course, victims are told that they need to pay up-front or advance fees to be used as bribes to expedite the deal. At times, these advance fees supposedly are used to pay taxes or legal expenses.

The most common 419 frauds involve business proposals for the transfer of funds from overinvoiced contracts, sales of crude oil below market prices, purchase of real estate, contract fraud, goods and services on consignment, disbursement of money from wills, and conversion of hard currency. A variation of this scam involves Nigerians sending these letters to churches offering large sums of money to be donated if "taxes" are paid. Once the taxes are paid, the church hears nothing further. It is believed that victims lose hundreds of millions of dollars annually in this 419 fraud. Many victims do not report their victimization to law enforcement due to fear or embarrassment.

These scam letters were initially produced in factories in and around Lagos. A typical operation may have had dozens or even hundreds of people typing or writing these letters in an office or warehouse. They were signed with phony names and titles and mailed to unsuspecting victims all over the world. The United States Secret Service in conjunction with Nigerian police authorities raided many suspected 419 factories in Lagos. In one action, approximately 6 million letters ready for mailing were seized. The problem was so pervasive that at one point in 1998, the Central Bank of Nigeria took out full-page fraud advisories in major U.S. newspapers to warn Americans.

An interesting discovery was made by the Postal Inspection Service when it examined the mailing envelopes used to transmit the 419 letters. The Nigerian postage stamps were counterfeit. That should not have been much of a surprise when you think about the nature of fraudsters. Postage for the millions of letters that flooded the mail throughout the world would have cost the scammers hundreds of thousands if not millions of dollars. So, of course, they did not pay for postage; they simply used readily available Nigerian counterfeit stamps. This was also the break that law enforcement needed to put a damper on the scheme. Since the envelopes bore counterfeit stamps, they were deemed not to be official mail and could be the subject to seizure. The Postal Inspection Service, in conjunction with Nigerian authorities, seized and destroyed millions of these scam letters as they entered the United States through New York's JFK Airport Mail Facility. Nevertheless, these enforcement actions were unable to stem the constant flow of these letters.

With the exponential growth of the Internet, the 419 scam quickly migrated to electronic mail delivery. With a simple keystroke, millions and millions of 419 emails could be sent to millions and millions of potential victims throughout the world—all without the risk of seizure by law enforcement. A simple measure of whether this scam works is this: The fraudsters would not continue to send these 419 emails unless people continue to fall victim. Plus, with millions of emails being sent with minimal up-front costs, con artists need only a few victims to actually take the bait.

The United States Secret Service has this to say about reporting 419 scams and possible criminal investigations:

*If you have received an e-mail or fax from someone you do not know requesting your assistance in a financial transaction, such as the transfer of a large sum of money into an account, or claiming you are the next of kin to a wealthy person who has died, or the winner of some obscure lottery, DO NOT respond. These requests are typically sent through public servers via a generic "spammed" e-mail message. Usually, the sender does not yet know your personal e-mail address and is depending on you to respond. Once you reply, whether you intend to string them along or tell them you are not interested, they will often continue to e-mail you in an attempt to harass or intimidate you. If you receive an unsolicited e-mail of this nature, the best course is to simply delete the message.*

*Due to a number of aggravating circumstances—the use of false names, addresses, stolen/ cloned/prepaid cell phones and remote e-mail addresses—verifying the location of and subsequent prosecution of these persons or groups is difficult. The act of sending an e-mail soliciting your assistance in a financial transaction is not a crime in itself. The installation of a credible spam filter and contacting your Internet Service Provider may help deter these unsolicited e-mails. However, there is currently no available program to completely block these types of messages.*

*If you have suffered a significant financial loss related to advance fee fraud, please contact your local Secret Service field office. Telephone numbers are available at www.secret service.gov or on the inside cover of your local telephone directory. Any investigation regarding this type of fraud will be conducted on a case by case basis at the discretion of the local Secret Service office and U.S. Attorney's Office.*[4]

## SENATE HEARINGS

On September 17, 1986, the Permanent Subcommittee on Investigations of the United States Senate Governmental Affairs Committee held hearings on the Nigerian crime network and the growth of credit card fraud, as identity theft was then called. I testified before this subcommittee as a result of my work investigating nontraditional organized crime, credit card fraud, and identity theft. Although these hearings took place more than 20 years ago, the findings are still relevant today. Among the Senate findings at that time were these:

- During its lengthy investigation, the subcommittee staff determined that members of the Nigerian crime network have become especially adept at credit card fraud, bank fraud, insurance fraud, and entitlement fraud, and have recently moved into the areas of narcotics trafficking and distribution. The staff also found numerous examples of marriage fraud, visa and passport fraud, and customs and currency violations.

- In virtually all the known criminal cases involving Nigerians, the individuals have been found to be in possession of or using false documents.

- An analysis of the Nigerian crime network reflects three identifiable elements. The first and most common is the individual who learns how to commit fraud from another Nigerian, perhaps for a fee. The second identifiable element has been labeled by some law enforcement officers as the "cell" group. Consisting of between 3 and 15 members, the cell usually has an identifiable leader who controls the group's criminal activities. The third element is more of a structured hierarchy where the leader has clearly insulated himself from direct criminal activity. Below the leader are various cell leaders who control smaller groups involved in criminal activities

- The subcommittee staff has been unable to conclusively determine whether Nigerians are being formally trained in fraudulent schemes in classes of some sort (in the United States and/or Nigeria) or through written manuals. Allegations of such training have been made by a number of law enforcement officials, generally through informant information.

- Although increasing numbers of Nigerians are being arrested for criminal violations, the criminal justice system often breaks down after arrest. Many Nigerians have avoided serious criminal sentences, either because their individual nonviolent fraud schemes resulted only in fines and probation, because the individual absconded, or because federal authorities chose to deport the individual rather than prosecute. In many jurisdictions, especially the federal system, prosecutors do not pursue financial fraud cases because of the relatively small dollar amounts that are involved.

- Investigators from the law enforcement and banking communities are unanimous in their belief that credit card frauds perpetrated by Nigerians in this country are the most prevalent and the most sophisticated here, perhaps by a wide margin.

- One basic credit card scheme used by Nigerians involves the fraudulent use of an individual's legitimate identifying information, such as name, SSN, employer, and so on. By using correct information on a credit card application, an applicant can virtually ensure the receipt of a card because in most instances the individual whose information is being used has a stable job and a good credit history. The major distinction would be the address on the application.

- Investigators have also uncovered numerous cases of check-kiting schemes perpetrated by Nigerians operating independently from credit card frauds. These schemes generally involve opening checking accounts without having the money to do so. They include setting up accounts with out-of-town checks and then writing checks or demanding cash prior to the clearance of the original deposited check, which eventually bounces.

- In one case described to the Permanent Subcommittee on Investigations staff by U.S. Customs investigators, a Nigerian used fraudulent documentation to obtain a $1 million letter of credit from a Nigerian bank for a dummy import/export company.

The individual was able to withdraw over $1 million from a Seattle bank before the fraud was discovered.

- An internal Immigration and Naturalization Service memorandum obtained by the subcommittee (dated October 1985) states: "Over the past few years it has become evident on a nationwide basis, aliens from West Africa, primarily Nigeria, Ghana, and Liberia, are abusing our entitlement systems in a most organized and methodical way."
- With the exception of the student aid programs, it appears that little effort is being made by federal agencies to determine the extent of fraud being perpetrated by ineligible aliens.
- Recent statistics suggest that 40,000 to 50,000 Nigerian nationals are residing in the United States, with perhaps half attending school. Law enforcement officers uniformly state that virtually all Nigerians they arrest entered the country with a student visa (whether they are currently students or not).[5]

I had the honor of testifying before the Senate Permanent Subcommittee on Investigations on September 17, 1986. I was one of a relatively small number of law enforcement officers active in the investigation and prosecution of Nigerian nationals for fraud. My many cases in the New York metropolitan area involving Nigerians and others in credit card and bank fraud brought me to the attention of the subcommittee staff in 1986. I had significant experience and expertise in this area and had been on television news programs discussing this growing problem. Although a little dated, my testimony is striking in that little has changed since 1986, except that identity theft has exploded worldwide.

*Mr. Chairman, I am a Postal Inspector assigned to the New York Division. My area of responsibility includes mail fraud investigations in the New York metropolitan area. Additionally, I am the credit card coordinator, and investigate cases involving credit card fraud.*

*I would like to address some of the specific criminal activities in the New York City area, which are not limited exclusively to Nigerian perpetrators, but typify the schemes in which Nigerian nationals are heavily involved. I would like to stress that we are not investigating all Nigerian nationals, but rather crimes against the Postal Service committed by individuals, an inordinate number of whom turn out to be Nigerian nationals.*

*In my research related to my investigations, I have found that individuals from Nigeria are involved in increasing numbers in schemes to defraud banks and other government and financial institutions. While some of the individuals are committing student loan frauds, check kiting, insurance fraud, drug and gun smuggling, and other crimes, by far the most prevalent crime being committed in the New York area involves credit cards.*

*The criminals fraudulently obtain law abiding individuals' credit and biographical information, and submit false applications under these names to banks, department stores, oil companies, and other credit card issuing companies. They are quite skillful in obtaining information on other people.*

*Many major companies and businesses employ security guards to patrol their offices at night. The criminals obtain guard positions which are generally low paying and hard to fill. I have found that many of the ones I investigated and arrested are employed as security guards in private security in New York.*

*When assigned to a building at night, these individuals have free rein to patrol the office. They will go through personnel files, employees' desks, and other belongings to obtain names, job titles, Social Security numbers, home addresses, and other personal information. The information which they obtain, besides being found in personnel files is also found on resumes, pay stubs, bills, and other personal materials in the offices.*

*Once armed with this personal information, the criminals with their knowledge of the American credit system apply for credit cards. They will complete credit card applications and submit them to numerous banks and other issuers, using the names they have found, sometimes to 30 or 40 issuers in this one name.*

*They will list the name, employment, and Social Security number on the application. They will list the current home address of the person as a previous address, and then use a mail receiving agency as the current address. In addition, they also use a post office box or possibly an apartment controlled by the false applicant. The current address associated with the name is used as a previous address to throw off credit bureau inquiries, which may list this home address. Generally, the credit bureau believes the person has recently moved, since the addresses match.*

*While all issuers verify credit card applications, generally this is limited to a credit bureau check of the credit history of the person, and a check with the applicant's employer. Since the applicant's name and other personal information is correct, the credit check will show this individual's credit profile.*

*Thus, the credit check will help approve the application. Additionally, since the person whose name is being used has no idea his identity is being used for this fraud, even a check with the individual's personnel office will only verify that, indeed, the person does work there, then, of course, the application will be approved.*

*Once a criminal receives a credit card, it is quickly used to the limit of the card for cash advances and high ticket items such as stereos, televisions, and VCRs, which are easily fenced. Then the card is used for additional purchases under the floor limit of the card. Floor limits are amounts that are used to determine when a merchant must call in for a verification of a charge. If a purchase is kept under the floor limit, a fraudulently obtained credit card can be used for months without detection.*

*I have personally seen false application credit cards issued with a $2,000 limit on the card, but ultimately $8,000 was charged to the card because of charges under the floor limit. When the bills are sent to the suspect address, they are, of course, ignored. After several months of non-payment, the credit card issuers call the collection agencies to attempt collection. When no one is found at the mail drop or apartments listed on the applications, collection agencies go to credit bureau files, and check the name and Social Security number of the applicant named. At this point, the unsuspecting citizen's address is found, and that person is contacted. Then it is learned that a fraud has taken place. Unfortunately, this can be many months or even a year after the initial fraud has occurred, and chances of locating the suspect at this time are almost non-existent.*

*One major bank in New York City has reported to me that it lost $1.4 million through this type of fraud in 1985, and that it expects to lose $2 million in 1986. An official of MasterCard* *advised me that he believes many banks and other credit card issuers mistakenly write off these frauds as bad debts and failure to pay, and never report them for investigation.*

*I have had cooperating Nigerians tell me that they do not want to belong to a group or a gang because then they would have to split the proceeds of the fraud. By working individually, they can keep all the proceeds themselves. Besides, this crime is so simple and lucrative, a gang isn't necessary for this crime to be successful.*

*All of these agencies that I have been discussing, particularly the Secret Service and the Postal Inspection Service, participated in a task force in 1985. The task force also consisted of Immigration and Naturalization Service agents, New York City Police Department detectives, and bank investigators from the major banks in New York.*

*The purpose of this task force was to identify those involved in false application fraud, to determine the extent of the involvement of these individuals, and successfully investigate and prosecute.*

*One example of the effectiveness of this task force was an operation conducted on November 7, 1985, when simultaneous search warrants were executed at eight safe houses in Brooklyn, New York. We arrested five Nigerian nationals for credit card fraud. We executed the search warrants and found the following items:*

*Approximately 100 fraudulent application credit cards, dozens of completed and partially completed false applications for credit cards, numerous phony identification cards, including driver's licenses, Social Security cards, college I.D.s, birth certificates, W-2 forms, and passports, a list of over 1,000 names and respective credit card numbers, a list of CBS employees, including name, Social Security number and other personal information, security guard uniforms, and numerous televisions, stereos, VCRs, radios, and answering machines. Additionally, two other Nigerian individuals involved with this gang were subsequently arrested.*

*Although investigations do enjoy limited successes, I believe the most effective method to fight these abuses is through prevention. Other inspectors and I, in conjunction with the Inspection Services' prevention program, regularly provide fraud prevention training to the industry and the public to further help in combating this problem.*[6]

## NIGERIAN CRIMINAL ENTERPRISES

The United States Department of Justice (DOJ) recognized the enormity of the problem created by Nigerian criminal activities. In 1996, then U.S. Attorney General Janet Reno announced the Nigerian Criminal Enterprise Initiative to focus investigation and prosecution resources on the problem of Nigerian criminal activity with a particular emphasis on fraud and forgery crimes. Although there had been an investigative focus on Nigerian criminal activity in years past by many federal law enforcement agencies, this was the beginning of a concerted effort to attack the problem. In the years prior to 1996,

*the Nigerian criminal enterprises have exploited financial institutions, insurance companies, government entitlement programs, and individual citizens of the United States. Law enforcement officials in the United Kingdom, Canada, Germany, Australia, South Africa, Russia and other countries have also experienced high crime rates attributable to the Nigerian criminal enterprises.*[7]

These remarks by then Deputy Attorney General Eric H. Holder Jr. on the subject of Nigerian Organized Crime at the Eighth International Nigerian Crime Conference in Washington, D.C. on November 9, 1999 provide context on the state of the problem at the time:

> *Nigerian organized criminal activity has escalated dramatically over the last decade, posing an ever-increasing threat, not only within the United States, but also on a global scale. Nigerian criminal enterprises have proven to be particularly adept at taking advantage of opportunities created by the rapid globalization of transportation and communications, and are now engaged in a broad range of criminal activity that reaches across borders and victimizes citizens, businesses and financial institutions in Africa, Europe, Canada, the United States and around the world.*

> *In the past, defining the scope and extent of Nigerian criminal activity has been difficult because Nigerian criminal groups are highly fluid in personnel and in methods of operation. Although there is a degree of structure to these organizations, their hierarchical makeup and relationships are not comparable to those of more traditional criminal organizations. In terms of structure, NCEs seem to range from independent entrepreneurs to highly organized syndicates. These groups are able to change and adapt as needed, both in the nature of the criminal activities they pursue and in the members they use. This flexibility allows them to remain in operation and to insulate themselves from law enforcement.*

> *The pervasiveness of Nigerian crime has required us to devise a coordinated and comprehensive plan with participation by all U.S. agencies. In September of 1996, under the leadership of Attorney General Reno, the Departments of Justice, State, and Treasury and other law enforcement agencies began to develop the Nigerian Crime Strategy to identify and combat Nigerian criminal groups. The Strategy targets both domestic and international Nigerian criminal activity, and emphasizes increased coordination of U.S. law enforcement, the sharing of investigative leads and information, enhanced cooperation with our foreign law enforcement counterparts to coordinate multinational cases and investigations, and improving coordination and dialogue with the Government of Nigeria, especially Nigerian law enforcement officials, so we can strengthen their ability to combat crime occurring within Nigeria, and assist in combating crimes committed elsewhere in the world by individuals and organizations located in Nigeria.*[8]

In July 1999, an initial investigation by law enforcement in Brooklyn and Queens, New York, into heroin trafficking by a "highly organized group" of Nigerian nationals ultimately discovered much more than just drug dealing. The gang had also stolen the identities of more than 1,300 people throughout the country. The criminals forged financial documents to commit this large-scale identity takeover scheme affecting individuals and financial institutions in more than 21 states. In just one of their many schemes, banks and credit card companies lost more than $1.4 million with most of the defrauded funds sent to Nigeria.[9]

Here is what the FBI has to say today about African criminal enterprises including Nigerian groups involved in fraud:

> *African criminal enterprises have developed quickly since the 1980s due to the globalization of the world's economies and the great advances in communications technology. Easier*

*international travel, expanded world trade, and financial transactions that cross national borders have enabled them to branch out of local and regional crime to target international victims and develop criminal networks within more prosperous countries and regions. The political, social, and economic conditions in African countries like Nigeria, Ghana, and Liberia also have helped some enterprises expand globally.*

*African criminal enterprises have been identified in several major metropolitan areas in the U.S., but are most prevalent in Atlanta, Baltimore, Chicago, Dallas, Houston, Milwaukee, Newark, New York, and Washington, D.C. Nigerian criminal enterprises are the most significant of these groups and operate in more than 80 other countries of the world. They are among the most aggressive and expansionist international criminal groups and are primarily engaged in drug trafficking and financial frauds.*

*Nigerian groups are famous globally for their financial frauds, which cost the U.S. alone an estimated $1 billion to $2 billion each year. Schemes are diverse, targeting individuals, businesses, and government offices. The advent of the Internet and e-mail have made their crimes more profitable and prevalent.*

*The FBI participates in two initiatives to bolster efforts to combat African criminal enterprises:*

- *The Department of Justice Nigerian Crime Initiative coordinates the federal investigations of Nigerian criminal enterprises by using joint task forces in six major U.S. cities.*
- *The Interpol West African Fraud annual conference brings together law enforcement agents from around the world to discuss and share information about the financial frauds perpetuated by criminal enterprises whose members are predominantly West African, and specifically Nigerian Criminal Enterprises.*[10]

## ONGOING THREAT OF FRAUD

The problem of Nigerian Criminal Enterprises will not be solved in the near future. This is something that was many years in the making. It transcends individuals and encompasses the political, economic, and societal conditions in Nigeria. Although these conditions may have contributed to the crime problem, we as citizens and fraud investigators must deal with it. Now that Nigerian Criminal Enterprises are recognized as a serious threat to the public, businesses, and government of the United States and other countries, fraud examiners must use all their skills to detect and prevent these schemes. Once again, education and improved prevention techniques will be a major factor in how well we succeed.

## NOTES

1. Remarks of Eric H. Holder, Jr., Deputy Attorney General, United States Department of Justice, on Nigerian Organized Crime at Eighth International Nigerian Crime Conference, Washington, DC, November 9, 1999, www.justice.gov/archive/dag/speeches/1999/nigerianspch.htm.
2. Testimony of Mr. Tom Kneir, Deputy Assistant Director, Criminal Investigative Division, Federal Bureau of Investigation, Combating International Crime in Africa

Hearing before the Subcommittee on Africa of the Committee on International Relations, House of Representatives, 105th Congress, 2nd Session, July 15, 1998, commdocs.house.gov/committees/intlrel/hfa50884.000/hfa50884_0.HTM.

3. United State Secret Service, "Criminal Investigations: Advance Fee Fraud," www.secretservice.gov/criminal.shtml.

4. Ibid.

5. Emerging Criminal Groups Hearing before the Permanent Subcommittee on Investigations of the Committee on Governmental Affairs, United States Senate, 99th Congress, 2nd Session, September 17, 1986, www.lib.ncsu.edu/congbibs/ senate/099dgst2.html.

6. Ibid.

7. Testimony of Mr. Tom Kneir, Deputy Assistant Director, Criminal Investigative Division.

8. Ibid.

9. Remarks of Eric H. Holder, Jr., Deputy Attorney General.

10. Federal Bureau of Investigation, "African Criminal Enterprises," www.fbi.gov/hq/ cid/orgcrime/africancrim.htm.

# CHAPTER 6

# Methamphetamine, the Mails, and Check Washing

Identity theft has many variations, and all of them are damaging. Yet some have more than just an economic impact when a destructive drug is involved. For much of the 1990s, and even now in the new century, mail theft has been the crime du jour in certain parts of the country. It is not just any kind of mail theft but an insidious, narcotic-driven crime that precipitates identity theft. It is a crime that creates an unholy marriage between the drug methamphetamine (also called meth, speed, and many other names) and the mails. This M&M is not a sweet candy but a bitter poison that destroys lives, threatens confidence in the mails, and results in thousands and thousands of new identity theft victims.

The widespread availability and use of methamphetamine in the American Southwest and on the West Coast contributed to the interrelated growth of mail theft and identity theft. It is a unique story. In the late 1980s, as meth use increased, addicts needed money either to purchase or to make the drug, as it can be easily made at home or in makeshift labs. They turned to Dumpster diving and mail theft to obtain financial instruments and personal information they could use for crime. The considerable amount of information and documents found in the garbage of homes and businesses helped fuel a raft of financial crimes.

The meth users then discovered something that would eventually contribute to an even greater mail theft problem and a huge spike in identity theft. The chemicals used to manufacture meth, or speed, as it is also commonly known, could also be used to remove the inked writing from checks stolen from the mail. The fraudsters then would rewrite the checks with new payees and check amounts and negotiate the checks. "Check washing" spread throughout the western states. Armed with stolen financial information and identities of victims, and the new check-washing capability, meth addicts found it was easy to commit fraud. As the vicious cycle continued, mail theft increased as a source of stolen checks and other personal information.

To be fair, the 2006 Identity Theft Survey Report of the Federal Trade Commission (FTC) found that only 2% of identity theft victims reported that their personal information was stolen from the mails. Yet 56% of these survey respondents did not know how their personal information was obtained. Based on my experience, I will venture to guess that a good percentage of the number came from mail theft. Mail theft, both external and internal, is a continuing problem, even when it is not identity theft related.

## MAIL THEFT PROBLEM

Mail theft is nothing new. It has been a problem in the United States for over 200 years. In the Old West, mail theft from stagecoaches and trains was common. Mail theft is still commonplace in the first decade of the twenty-first century. The only difference today is where and how the mail is stolen. Robberies of mail carriers; burglaries of post offices; break-ins of mail vehicles, collection boxes, and residential mailboxes; and internal theft by postal employees are all ways to attack and steal mail. The mails may contain valuables, such as cash, precious metals, jewelry, credit cards, and checks. Besides items of obvious value, the mails contain personal and financial information, stolen to commit identity theft. Stealing large amounts of mail allows scam artists to easily obtain all the information needed to assume a victim's identity.

Mail theft occurs in a variety of ways, but serious criminals are on the lookout for large volumes of mail that accumulate before collection or delivery. Volume mail thefts or volume attacks target postal vehicles, collection boxes, apartment mail panels, and neighborhood delivery and collection box units (NDCBUs) where large quantities of mail can be found. The most popular targets for volume mail thefts are NDCBUs and apartment panels. By attacking these units, thieves can steal more mail at one location. The Postal Service experienced 3,435 volume attacks in fiscal year (FY) 1999, 3,929 volume attacks in FY 2000, and 6,752 volume attacks in FY 2001, at the height of the problem. The vast majority of volume attacks occurred in the western states and was attributable to users of the drug methamphetamine, commonly called "meth heads" or "tweakers."

Much of the problem centered on the American Southwest. The mail theft problem in Arizona and other western states can be likened to the mythical creature the hydra. Cut off one of the seven heads of this serpent and it is quickly replaced with two new heads. No matter how many heads are cut off, there are always more than before. This analogy also applied to the mail theft problem because of the vast methamphetamine epidemic and the legions of addicted users who gravitated to mail theft. Meth addicts are heavily involved in the theft of mail to fund their drug habits. As each one was arrested, two more meth heads were ready to steal more mail.

Arizona, Nevada, and California are the top three states for number of mail theft victims, according to a 2006 FTC report on victim complaint data. They are followed by Texas, Florida, Colorado, Georgia, New York, Washington, and New Mexico. It is not surprising; seven of these states have big problems with meth. With Arizona and Nevada leading the victim survey, it is understandable why Phoenix, Tucson, and Las Vegas have led the nation in the total number of volume mail thefts. These thefts centered on NDCBUs as well as apartment mailbox panels. The suspects target incoming and outgoing mail containing checks and other financial information. They break into these mailboxes through a variety of means including the use of counterfeit keys, prying open the locked panels, and even removing entire mailbox units from their metal anchors.

A Postal Inspector who worked in Texas in the late 1970s and early 1980s told me he saw the early impact of meth-related mail theft. He advised that the theft and negotiation of checks stolen from the mail as well as the submission of fraudulent credit card applications financed drug labs in northern Texas and Oklahoma. The meth heads would steal cars for their crime sprees, and almost every car recovered contained trash bags full of stolen mail. He reported that the crime was so new that the local police and bank investigators thought that the victims whose mail was stolen were involved in the fraud until law enforcement were educated on the modus operandi of tweakers.

## CHECK WASHING: A NEW SPIN ON MAIL THEFT

The primary reason for mail theft is to obtain checks that can be "washed." Check washing is a mail theft–related crime that is easy to accomplish. Mail thieves know that outgoing mail contains checks being mailed to pay mortgages, utilities, credit cards, and other bills. Once the checks are stolen, the thieves "wash" the checks in a chemical solution to erase the inked writing. The checks are actually soaked in commonly available chemicals that remove only the handwritten portions.

The chemicals that check washers often use include acetone, benzene, bleach, carbon tetrachloride, chloromice T, clear correction fluids, brake fluid, and other bleaching agents. Some of these chemicals are also used in the manufacture of methamphetamine. After the washed check is dried, a new amount and payee are filled in. The criminal uses counterfeit identification in the name of the true account holder, but with his or her own photo, to negotiate the check.

Often the washed checks are rewritten and made payable to the thieves using their own names or other names. The checks are then negotiated at various banks, check cashers, department stores, and convenience stores. A commonly used technique to wash checks goes like this: First one obtains a 16-ounce plastic soft drink bottle; the top portion of the bottle is cut off, then brake fluid and acetone are poured into the bottom half of the bottle. Next the check is dipped in the solution. and it is swirled around until the writing disappears. After the check is allowed to dry, it is ready to rewrite and fraudulently cash.

To further illustrate the problem, Postal Inspectors arrested a woman who was stealing mail from unlocked mailboxes in the more rural areas of Las Vegas. She would wash the stolen checks right inside her car. She had a laptop computer, laminator, and all the necessities to make up bogus identification right there. In some cases, tweakers presented washed checks that were still wet and smelling of acetone. Once a bank teller stalled a suspect attempting to cash a washed check by telling him she would try to dry off the check using the hand dryer in the restroom.

## ALL "METHED" UP: THE DRUG CONNECTION

Methamphetamine is a powerfully addictive stimulant drug that produces feelings of mental alertness and well-being. It also causes increased activity, decreased appetite, and a host of undesired effects. Like cocaine, meth is a central nervous system stimulant. Users report that these stimulants produce a sense of euphoria, strength, and control as well as postpone fatigue, suppress the appetite, increase metabolism, and act as an aphrodisiac that heightens and prolongs sexual pleasure. Methamphetamine's effects last significantly longer than those of cocaine (two to four hours for meth that is "snorted" versus one hour for cocaine) and it is a cheaper product, particularly when there is easy access to the precursor, ephedrine, and other synthesis materials.

Due to lower prices as compared to cocaine, meth appeals to a wide range of users. That includes workers who are in monotonous and repetitious occupations, those who hold down more than one job, or those who work exceptionally long hours. It is used to fight fatigue. Occasional usage, whether to fight fatigue or not, can quickly turn into an addiction with disastrous occupational, family, and health consequences. Work behavior can quickly turn from superhuman to substandard, and poor or erratic performance becomes the norm. The user may also become not only more aggressive but combative and paranoid, which causes problems both at work and home.

Like many addictions, the desire for the drug can replace commitment to family and common sense. Users will do outrageous things, including neglecting or even selling their children, for the drug. Methamphetamine makes the body work harder and has other health consequences, such as heart and organ damage, dental decay, and malnutrition. Users have a heightened risk of sexually transmitted diseases, such as AIDS and hepatitis B and C, as they turn to prostitution to pay for the drug and/or engage in sex with multiple partners for entertainment. Nervous energy causes users to pick at sores and scabs, which worsen with poor diets and create scarred skin.

There are few accepted medical reasons for the use of meth other than the treatment of narcolepsy and attention deficit disorder (ADD). The drug can be smoked, snorted, orally ingested, or injected. It is often called meth, speed, crank, crystal meth, glass, or ice. Former White House Drug Czar Barry McCaffrey said methamphetamine has a "serious potential nationally to become the next crack cocaine epidemic."[1] He added that meth "remains one of the most dangerous substances America has ever confronted."[2] Unfortunately, that epidemic has already arrived. It is estimated that 4.7 million people have tried meth, and its use has spread across the country.

Methamphetamine was first synthesized from ephedrine in 1887. In 1932, it was sold in the United States as a nasal spray for the treatment of inflamed nasal passages. Meth abuse first became a problem in the 1930s and 1940s when it was used by Allied and Axis troops supposedly to improve soldiers' performances. Meth was widely available in the 1940s and 1950s via prescription, and this availability resulted in abuse.

The second epidemic of methamphetamine abuse occurred in the 1960s. In 1970, meth was classified as a controlled substance. Generally out of favor by drug users for much of the 1970s, it emerged in the 1980s in Hawaii and other western states. New and simple methods to manufacture meth helped fuel its growth. Outlaw biker gangs on the West Coast soon got involved in the manufacture, use, and distribution of the drug. The drug's availability made it the "poor man's cocaine," and San Diego became a focal point of meth use in California.[3] (For more information on the impact of meth, mail theft, and identity theft on an American city, see Chapter 14.)

In the late 1980s, a smokable form of meth was introduced and eventually spread throughout the western United States. By the 1990s, there was heavy methamphetamine use and production in the western states with a continuing spread eastward. In 1995, meth overtook cocaine as the primary illegal drug used in the Phoenix, Arizona, area. Meth is also commonplace in rural Arizona and many rural communities throughout the country. The drug is easily manufactured in clandestine drug labs.

A clandestine drug laboratory is a small chemical lab designed to make deadly, illegal drugs quickly and cheaply. These labs are often called mom-and-pop labs because of the ease with which they can be set up. The drug of choice for most of these labs is methamphetamine. The equipment necessary to manufacture meth can range from highly specialized chemical apparatus to ordinary pots and pans, coffee filters, glass cookware, hot plates, and other common household items. Due to the ease of production, it is the most commonly manufactured illegal drug today. The labs can be located in rental apartments or houses, motel rooms, mini-storage units, motor homes, or other vehicles. In fact, mobile meth labs are quite common.

Thirty-two chemicals can be cooked together in various combinations to make meth, including everything from brake fluid to drain cleaner to red phosphorous, a highly flammable chemical that can easily combust when mixed with water or air and a nearby flame. Lithium batteries, grain alcohol, distilled water, and anhydrous ammonia are also used to make meth. When mixed together, these chemicals create toxic fumes that can cause liver and kidney failure, severe lung damage, and cancer.

Ingredients found in cold medicine, such as pseudoephedrine, can also be mixed with household products and chemicals to make meth. Individuals who manufacture meth often purchase large quantities of cold medicines. For this reason, it was important to stop the bulk sales of these over-the-counter drugs. In 1999, Arizona enacted a law forbidding retailers from selling cold medicine in large quantities. Similar laws are now commonplace throughout the United States. Restricting the over-the-counter sale of these cold medicines has helped but not eliminated the problem.

People living in or near the potentially toxic environment of a meth lab can suffer life-threatening illnesses. These chemicals can seep into food stored in the house, into the walls and floors, and into clothes and other items. Short-term exposure can cause breathing problems, disorientation, and seizures. Long-term effects include fatal kidney and lung disorders, brain damage, strokes, and death. Chemicals used to produce methamphetamine, such as red phosphorus and acetone, are highly toxic and the residual "soup" from the manufacture contaminates properties, creating serious health risks to unsuspecting tenants and neighbors as well as costing significant amounts to clean up or abate. In addition, the risk of explosions and fires from these toxic mixes poses life-threatening issues.

Meth users suffer from a destructive addiction cycle. When using meth, addicts can stay up for 10 days straight with no need for food. Then they are driven into a severely depressed state followed by worsening paranoia, belligerence, hallucinations, and aggression. This period is known as tweaking; from this comes the term "tweaker." A tweaker always craves more meth and will often do anything to obtain it. Eventually meth users collapse from exhaustion, finally awakening to begin the cycle again. Eighty-five percent of those who try meth will become addicts.

Methamphetamine has had a dramatic impact on criminals and crime and has propelled traditional problems of fraud and forgery into the current epidemic of identity theft. Meth users turned to traditional street crimes—burglary, auto theft, prostitution, and forgery—to support their habits. Unlike heroin addicts or crack cocaine users who can devote only a small portion of their day to committing crimes to support their habits, meth users can stay up for days at a stretch committing crimes before crashing for a few hours or days, then going right back to committing crime.

## ORIGIN OF THE PROBLEM

The Arizona problem began in the mid-1980s when gangs of thieves and individuals did Dumpster diving, obtaining checks thrown away by banks and check manufacturers. These thieves started the check-washing process. This method of altering checks evolved from the gangs trying to wash off words like "spoiled" or "void" stamped on the discarded checks. Once they were successful, they began stealing checks from the mail and washing the "pay to" and "dollar amount," then reissuing the check in any name and amount they chose.

Volume mail thefts began in the late 1980s with most of the activity restricted to apartment complexes. In the early 1990s, thefts from NDCBUs began to increase. Thieves would pry open the rear doors of these units and remove all the mail. During this time, there was an influx of meth users into Arizona from California. The thieves counterfeited identification documents and cashed the checks. By 1994, counterfeiting of Arrow keys became a major problem as thefts from collection boxes greatly increased. Attacks on NDCBUs and apartment panels also increased. More than 90% of the volume break-ins were committed by meth addicts who financed their drug habit by stealing mail.

Thieves often use stolen bicycles that they pedal through the neighborhoods while breaking into mailboxes. Frequently they carry stolen mail in backpacks or in plastic garbage bags attached to their bicycles. They open the mail receptacles with small needle-nose pliers, screwdrivers, or other pry tools. Then they open the mail, remove the checks, and dump the envelopes and contents. Large quantities of stolen mail have been recovered from hotel rooms, rental vehicles, and abandoned apartments once used by these thieves as well as in Dumpsters and empty lots.

One particular type of mail theft is called "red flagging." Mail thieves, on foot, on bicycles, or in cars, will look for residential mailboxes with the red flag up. The red flag on residential mailboxes is there to notify the mail carrier that residents have placed outgoing mail in the box for pickup. The red flag in the up position has a different meaning for these thieves. It means "steal me." These criminals then take the outgoing mail looking for checks to wash and negotiate. They usually are most active in the evening and early-morning hours before the mail carrier has had a chance to pick up the mail and there is less chance of being seen stealing the mail.

Another way that these criminals steal mail is by walking from residential mailbox to residential mailbox delivering business flyers. They make photocopies of a legitimate flyer and place them in the mailboxes while removing mail already in the boxes. Depositing unstamped mail matter in a mailbox is against the law but it commonly occurs and can be done to mask mail theft. Again, the thieves are mostly looking for outgoing mail containing checks they can wash.

The monies these fraudsters obtain from forging and fraudulently negotiating the checks are used primarily for the purchase of methamphetamine and other illegal substances as well as to manufacture meth. In 2002, it was estimated that check washing cost consumers and financial institutions $815 million a year. Identity theft is the crime of choice for meth heads. It is financially lucrative and can be accomplished in many different ways. It is generally a nonviolent, white-collar crime that usually results in lesser criminal penalties than crimes such as robberies and burglaries. Computers, the Internet, and the availability to connect almost anywhere provides "anonymity and speed with which to work."[4]

Examples of cases involving mail theft, check washing, identity theft, and meth investigated by Postal Inspectors follow.

Subsequent to a routine traffic stop, police in Arizona arrested two occupants of a vehicle on drug violations. Police discovered among the personal property of the occupants five personal checks stolen from the mail in Chandler, Mesa, Scottsdale, and Tempe, Arizona. Postal Inspectors were contacted and interviewed the suspects. The suspects were husband and wife. Both admitted that the stolen checks had been washed and were to be cashed at a later date. A search warrant was obtained for the motel where the couple had been staying. Six additional stolen checks were recovered, including one that was still soaking in the washing solution. An eight-month-old boy and a six-year-old girl were found alone at the hotel room when officers arrived. The Division of Family Services took the two young children into protective custody. The husband and wife both admitted to being methamphetamine users.

Another case involved the arrest of a mail theft suspect. He had in his possession two small plastic bags containing a substance believed to be methamphetamine. He also possessed two checks, one of which had been chemically altered. The checks recovered from the suspect were determined to be stolen from the U.S. Mail. The suspect's fingerprints were identified on stolen mail and other items containing "practice" signatures seized during the search. It was learned that the suspect would provide washed checks to individuals who would negotiate the checks. The suspect kept 50% of the proceeds from the negotiated checks. He is believed to have stolen, chemically altered, and forged hundreds of checks stolen from rural-type mailboxes in the Phoenix area for the last several years.

In yet another case, Postal Inspectors arrested a woman suspected of a series of mail thefts in New Mexico, Colorado, Nebraska, Utah, and Idaho. A search of her car found significant evidence of her crimes, including checks, credit cards, counterfeit IDs, forged birth certificates, financial documents, drugs, and guns. The defendant was believed to have stolen more than $1 million worth of checks from the mail.

## CHANGING FACE OF CHECK FORGERY

Technology has offered criminals greater opportunities to commit financial crimes without having to resort to check washing and the dangerous chemicals needed for the process. With advances in technology, counterfeiting checks has become commonplace. Counterfeiters use computers, scanners, readily available software, laser printers, and color printers to create high-quality checks that are hard to detect as phony. They also use computers and scanners to create bogus identification documents for use in negotiating these checks.

In one case involving a gang operation, stolen canceled checks that came from curbside mailbox thefts were scanned into check-writing software. The graphic images were edited and printed onto blank check stock using laser jet printers and computers available at the local retail photocopy store. Another method used by the gang involved lifting or washing the payee information, dollar amount, and other unwanted data from the check by swabbing portions of the check with chemical solvents or by erasure or obfuscation with correction tape or correction fluid. In some cases, company logos and account numbers were cut from other documents and pasted onto the master. A copy of the master was made, which helped to further hide any obvious alterations. The master copy was used to transfer the now-altered check image onto blank check stock using ordinary photocopy machines. The blank counterfeit checks were completed on a typewriter and negotiated.

Postal Inspectors in San Francisco arrested an individual for mail theft, possession of counterfeit postal keys, and access device fraud. The suspect's occupation was a locksmith and computer technician. During the period prior to the suspect's arrest, the Postal Service received numerous reports of volume attacks on street mailboxes and apartment mailboxes throughout the San Francisco area. Upon arrest, the suspect had in his possession over 500 pieces of U.S. Mail, including checks and credit cards associated with many of the reported volume attacks. He also had in his possession counterfeit postal keys and phony California driver's licenses. The suspect additionally had a computer containing templates for making California driver's licenses and a Versa-Check software program to create personal and business checks. VersaCheck software is readily available at office supply stores. It is used to create and print custom checks in minutes using a home personal computer and an inkjet or laser printer. Criminals can use this software to create counterfeit checks using the information they have stolen.

In another case, Postal Inspectors executed a search warrant at the residence of an individual suspected of being involved in mail theft and forgery. The search resulted in the discovery of the VersaCheck computer program, blank VersaChecks, blank cashier's checks, a computer printer and scanner, document-producing computer programs, and a paper cutter.

In December 2000, two defendants who were meth addicts were arrested at a motel in Washington State. The search of their room *found "numerous" pieces of stolen mail; a counterfeit Postal Service key; seven Washington state drivers' licenses, each bearing the photo of [the defendants] but containing a different name; counterfeit checks; and supplies to create false identification documents, including a computer, digital camera, printer, and scanner.*[5]

The two defendants had been convicted previously for mail theft and bank fraud and were serving jail terms when they escaped and started this new mail and identity theft spree.[6]

In yet another case investigated by Postal Inspectors, two defendants participated in a scheme to defraud Phoenix area major retailers, such as K-Mart and Target, to purchase merchandise with checks stolen from the mail that were chemically washed. The thieves later returned the merchandise to the stores for cash. They used false Arizona driver's licenses, which they produced on their laptop computer, to facilitate purchasing the merchandise. The defendants used software programs Corel Draw, PhotoShop, and Corel PrintShop to make the phony licenses. A digital camera was used to take the photographs for the false identification.

## PREVENTION EFFORTS

The Postal Service realized that while it could not stop the spread of meth, it could make it much harder for criminals to obtain source information from mail theft. The result was an increased focus on security enhancements. At one time, postal vehicles were a major object of attack. Security modifications have been installed that make it harder to break into these vehicles, resulting in a lessening of this problem. Similar efforts have been implemented to upgrade security for collection boxes. The Postal Service is deploying collection boxes that are less vulnerable to attack, hardening existing boxes with reinforcements and different locks, anchoring the boxes in a manner that renders them more difficult to remove, and implementing high-security collection box locks with keys that are virtually impossible to counterfeit.

The Postal Service strengthened the security of NDCBUs by reinforcing areas where attacks usually occur and reinforcing rear doors and other points of entry, all in an effort to improve security. A significant effort was undertaken in target areas to educate law enforcement officials and the public about security and prevention practices. There have been numerous television, newspaper, and radio spots focusing on public awareness of the volume mail theft problem. The focus has been to advise members of the public on how to best protect themselves from losses. The public was provided with several alternatives to using NDCBU outgoing mail slots. The media spots were a constant reminder to the public to make thinking about prevention part of their daily lives.

Improved security features hardened other mailboxes against attack. The Postal Service researched and tested high-security boxes that could withstand attack by almost any tool. They succeeded in developing a secure cluster box unit (CBU) that was deployed throughout Phoenix. CBUs are free-standing mailboxes located at central points in a community for the delivery of mail. In many parts of the country, they are used in place of individual mailboxes in front of homes and businesses. In FY 2004, 5,716 high-security CBUs were deployed in Phoenix area. Although mail thieves have attempted to break into these reinforced boxes, to date not a single one has been compromised. As a result, volume mail theft attacks have significantly declined since 2005.

Financial institutions are also doing more to protect the public. More banks are requiring non-account holders, those opening new accounts, and those purchasing bank checks and money orders to provide a fingerprint to the face of each check they are cashing. A thumb or index fingerprint is placed on the lower center of the face of the check between the memo and signature lines. If the check bounces or is forged, evidence is available for a law enforcement investigation.

To prevent or lessen the possibility that someone can "wash" a stolen check, these procedures are recommended to the general public:

- Write out in full the payee, memo, and amount portions of the checks. Fill up the entire line with letters or a squiggly line.
- Use thick, dark ink to write checks. Roller-ball, thick felt tip, and fountain pens are best; ballpoint and permanent ink pens are the most easily altered.
- Purchase checks through institutions that use tamper-resistant paper and ink.

Here is how to detect a washed check:

- The finish on the check paper may look or feel softer than the original.
- The finish may feel bumpy.
- The ink color may be slightly changed.
- The paper color may have a grayish tint.
- The watermark may have been washed off or lightened.

Much more information on preventing mail theft and other aspects of identity theft can be found in Chapter 20.

## THE PROBLEM CONTINUES TODAY

Although the increased focus on prevention in the last few years has reduced mail theft and check washing, the crime continues to be a problem. In my discussions with Postal Inspectors while writing this book, I was told that check washing is not as prevalent as it once was, but it is still present. Investigators are still encountering washed checks, especially by those meth heads who are not computer savvy. Banks and merchants are still accepting washed checks, especially high-quality ones that are hard to detect as washed. Unfortunately, most tweakers involved in identity theft are very computer literate and have easy access to computers. The tools of the trade today for these criminals include computers, printers, high-quality graphics software, Internet access, online services for Internet telephone accounts, and an abundance of personal and financial information.

Arizona continues to provide the "perfect storm" for the highest incidence of identity theft in the country. Along with the fastest-growing population in the country comes the need for mortgages and other loans, the mailing of financial information, and the opportunity for mail thieves to commit identity theft. The ongoing meth problem is still a factor. Some of the highest meth abuse is reported in the Phoenix area. Arizona has become an importation and distribution point for meth in the United States from so-called super labs operating in Mexico and elsewhere. This results in one of the highest incidences of identity theft in the country.

Other states also continue to see the problem. Meth-fueled crimes including identity theft persist in other states as well. In the Seattle, Washington, area in 2007, a law enforcement task force focusing on meth-related crimes arrested 11 people for identity theft and forgery.[7] But we may be starting to see the light at the end of the tunnel. Some researchers believe the worst of the meth epidemic may be past. Research indicates that the meth epidemic peaked in 2004 and 2005.[8] One drug-testing firm hired by companies to test job applicants and employees found far fewer people tested positive for meth in 2006 than in 2004 or 2005.[9] An aggressive law enforcement approach is also helping.

As mentioned, pseudoephedrine is used in popular cold and allergy medications as well as being a key ingredient in the creation of meth. For many years, meth heads purchased large quantities of these over-the-counter decongestants to manufacture the highly addictive drug. In order to reduce the manufacture and availability of meth, drug makers, the federal government, and many states have taken strong actions. Under a recent federal law, people who buy medications containing pseudoephedrine must show photo identification. In addition, there is a limit of how much can be purchased.

The great majority of states have enacted legislation to restrict products that contain pseudoephedrine, and the major drug makers have introduced new lines of decongestants that do not contain this ingredient. Pfizer is working to create a pseudoephedrine medication that cannot be used to make meth.[10] Limiting the availability of pseudoephedrine is critical in reducing the manufacture of meth and the related crimes that come with its use. As a result of these restrictions and government enforcement actions, there has been a decrease in the small mom-and-pop meth labs.

## NOTES

1. Peter Grier and James N. Thurman, "Illegal Drug Use Tapers Off, But Supplies are Plentiful," *Christian Science Monitor*, March 24, 2000, www.nationalfamilies.org/publications/about_nfia/use_tapers.html.
2. "Clinton's Anti-Drugs Adviser Reports Substantial Progress," Media Awareness Project, March 22, 2000, www.mapinc.org/drugnews/v00/n397/a08.html.
3. Diana Hunt, Sarah Kuck, and Linda Truitt, "Methamphetamine Use: Lessons Learned," National Institute of Justice, July 31, 2006, 4–5, www.ncjrs.gov/pdffiles1/nij/grants/209730.pdf.
4. Ibid.
5. Sam Skolnik, "Meth Use Linked to Jump in ID, Mail Thefts," MSNBC, July 23, 2001, www.msnbc.com/local/pisea/m71111.asp.
6. Ibid.

7. Jennifer Sullivan, "30 More Arrests in Meth-Crime Probe," *Seattle Times*, August 18, 2007, B5.
8. Martha Irvine, "Meth Use Declining, Says Feds and States," *Seattle Times*, April 2, 2007, A4.
9. Ibid.
10. Donna Leinwand, "Drugmakers Take Action to Foil Meth Crooks," *USA Today*, June 29, 2005, 3A.

# CHAPTER 7

# The Violent Side of Identity Theft

The criminals who commit identity theft have innumerable motives. While most relate to greed and financial gain, there have been cases of violent acts done in concert with and in furtherance of identity theft. There is a mistaken perception that white-collar crimes do not involve violence. Violent behavior can easily surface whenever criminal activity occurs. Violence often invades the realm of fraud and white-collar crime, and we have seen it again and again in identity theft cases.

I learned this unfortunate lesson in 1983 when I was leading an investigation of a gang involved in credit card fraud, mail theft, welfare fraud, and bank fraud in Brooklyn, New York. Identity theft was the focus and most lucrative of their crimes. The gang leader was a young man with a minor criminal record and no prior history of violence. At most, these crimes would have landed him in jail for five years, and probably much less. We infiltrated his gang with two undercover informants to gain evidence against him. Sadly, when he thought that law enforcement was getting too close and he suspected the true allegiance of the informants, he murdered them with bullets to the back of their heads. Now he is serving a life sentence behind bars. I have never forgotten the violent side of identity theft.

# IDENTITY THEFT HALL OF INFAMY

## George Kalomeris

In the 1990s, an investigation with connections to Maryland, Delaware, and North Carolina uncovered the unthinkable: that identity theft would be the stimulus for murder. The criminal murdered two people to steal their identities and their estates. One murder was not enough for this homicidal identity thief; he wanted more of what belonged to others, so he killed again.

The investigation focused on George Kalomeris, a resident of both Maryland and North Carolina. Ultimately, Kalomeris admitted to killing two people, one a Delaware resident and the other a North Carolina resident, to obtain their financial assets. He pleaded guilty to the homicides, but the story leading up to his plea and life sentence is chilling. State, local, and federal authorities were involved in the investigation, including the Postal Inspection Service; Federal Bureau of Investigation (FBI); Montgomery County, Maryland, Police Department; United States Attorney for the District of Maryland; Attorney General for Delaware; a North Carolina District Attorney; Greenville, North Carolina, Police Department; and Delaware State Police.

The details of the events leading up to the homicides and the subsequent consequences come from the statement of facts signed by Kalomeris on November 17, 1998, included in his federal plea agreement and incorporated into his plea agreements in Delaware and North Carolina. The details also come from the November 18, 1998, press release issued by the United States Attorney for the District of Maryland.

George Kalomeris resided in Maryland when he got married in 1994. Shortly after, the couple moved to Greenville, North Carolina. They lived in an apartment complex, and Kalomeris became friends with Gary Wayne Thomas, who lived in the same complex. In the course of their friendship, Kalomeris learned that Thomas was an alcoholic and was the beneficiary of a $1 million trust controlled by a bank in Greenville. Thomas's grandfather had established the trust fund for him years earlier. A checking and savings account had also been established in Thomas's name. He received monthly deposits varying between $1,500 and $3,000.

Kalomeris was envious of Thomas's good fortune and wanted it for himself. He planned to take control of Thomas's trust fund by assuming his identity. In July 1996, Kalomeris and Thomas were smoking marijuana when Kalomeris shot and killed Thomas. Kalomeris then hid the body and started his identity takeover. He opened Thomas's mail to learn about his victim's financial history. He canceled Thomas's health insurance, requested bank information on Thomas's account, took over Thomas's apartment, and sold Thomas's car.

To conceal Thomas's disappearance and give the appearance that he was alive, Kalomeris, acting as Thomas, contacted the bank and the trust fund and advised that he (Thomas) relocated to Maryland for the purpose of rehabilitation of his alcohol addiction. Once back in Maryland, Kalomeris advised the bank of the change of address. In December 1996, Kalomeris began using Thomas's money by writing checks from the account. Between December 1996 and July 1997, he wrote 20 checks on Thomas's account, payable to various payees, including a company that Kalomeris had set up, creditors of Kalomeris, and others including a relative. The total amount of the checks written was $18,055. No one had any clue that Thomas was dead; everyone believed he had moved to Maryland.

By August 1997, Kalomeris had run through much of the funds in the bank account and needed money. Desperate, he decided to again turn to murder for financial gain. He had another victim in mind. Thomas Wayne Jones was a 57-year-old paraplegic living on a farm in rural Delaware. Kalomeris had met Jones because Kalomeris's father and stepmother owned property near Jones's home. Kalomeris knew that Jones was wealthy and collected rare and valuable coins.

On August 13, 1997, Kalomeris drove from Maryland to Delaware for the purpose of robbing and killing Jones. At Jones's home, Kalomeris shot Jones in the back of the neck. Thinking that Jones would soon die, Kalomeris dumped the body in the wooded area behind the home. Back in the house, Kalomeris cleaned up the evidence of the shooting and then stole financial information about Jones, valuable gold coins, and Jones's checkbook. Kalomeris then returned to Maryland taking Jones's wheelchair. He even abandoned Jones's dog by the roadside.

On August 14, 1997, Kalomeris negotiated a check drawn on Jones's checking account and also paid a debt he owed. Kalomeris then sold some of the gold coins he stole from Jones. He disposed of the wheelchair as well as the gun used to shoot Jones. Unbeknownst to Kalomeris, Jones was found alive a little more than a day after the shooting. Although in very bad shape, Jones was able to identify Kalomeris as the shooter.

On August 20, 1997, police arrested Kalomeris for the attempted homicide of Jones. While he was incarcerated, Kalomeris told his wife about the Thomas account and asked his wife to access funds from it. Around the time Kalomeris was arrested, a financial institution in New York was contacted by a person who may or may not have been Kalomeris regarding an account in the name of Jones and a request was made to change Jones's mailing address to a different rural address in Delaware. Kalomeris later claimed that he had no recollection of making the address change.

Kalomeris was concerned about Jones testifying against him. In September 1997, Kalomeris approached an inmate at the Montgomery County Detention Center with a murder-for-hire scheme to kill Jones for $10,000. Kalomeris gave detailed information to the inmate about where to find Jones. He also asked the inmate to kill a couple in Frederick, Maryland: Kalomeris's father and stepmother.

*(Continued)*

Kalomeris explained to the inmate that the way to make money was to "assume the identity" of wealthy persons whose disappearance would not be noticed.

The money for the hit on Jones came from Thomas's account with the assistance of Kalomeris's wife. While in jail, Kalomeris continued to defraud the Thomas account by sending letters to the bank in the name of Thomas to give the appearance that he was still alive. Kalomeris's wife continued to withdraw money each month from Thomas's account using an automated teller machine (ATM) card.

The inmate whom Kalomeris approached cooperated with law enforcement authorities, resulting in the additional arrest of Kalomeris for federal solicitation to commit murder. Unfortunately, Jones died in September 1998 from injuries related to the shooting. On November 16, 1998, Kalomeris was indicted in Delaware for the murder of Jones. When documents in Thomas's name surfaced during the investigation of the solicitation to commit the murder of Jones, the Montgomery County Police Department, Homicide Division, began investigating Thomas's disappearance.

Kalomeris pleaded guilty to federal charges of solicitation to commit murder, money laundering, and bank fraud as well as state homicide charges. As part of his plea agreement, Kalomeris agreed to assist North Carolina law enforcement authorities in locating Thomas's body. On November 18, 1998, Kalomeris directed North Carolina authorities to the skeletal remains of Thomas.

On March 9, 1999, Kalomeris was sentenced in federal court to 395 years in prison without the hope of parole. If by some miracle he lives that long, he would then face life without parole in Delaware and a minimum of 45 years imprisonment in North Carolina for the state murder charges. Kalomeris's wife was not implicated in the homicides, but she pleaded guilty to bank fraud charges and was sentenced to a short prison term.

## CHICAGO PARCEL BOMB MURDER CASE

Another case from the files of the Postal Inspectors illustrates how murder and violence can be involved in identity theft. On February 15, 2000 at 10:45 p.m., a parcel bomb exploded in the living room of a residence in Chicago, Illinois. The package was a videocassette recorder box with two pipe bombs inside, of which only one exploded. But that was more than enough. When Marcus Toney, the intended victim, opened the package, he was killed instantly. Toney was a 37-year-old college custodian. A friend of Toney's also in the room suffered non–life-threatening injuries as he was shielded from the full blast of the bomb by Toney's body.

Investigation by the Postal Inspection Service, Alcohol Tobacco and Firearms, and Chicago Police Department determined that the bomb was placed at the residence and made to look as if it had been mailed. Toney was in the process of divorcing his wife, Lisa, and they had been living apart for several months. The survivor of the blast told authorities that the wife's boyfriend, Sienky Lallemand, had been threatening Toney. Toney was also the recent victim of identity theft, and he had learned that the boyfriend was the culprit.

The investigating officers interviewed the wife, who denied any involvement in the murder or the identity theft. Lisa Toney agreed to take a polygraph and failed the test when asked if she had any knowledge of her husband's murder. She then admitted knowledge of her boyfriend's involvement in her husband's identity theft. Her lawyer refused to allow her to answer any further questions about the homicide.

There was much more to learn about Lisa Toney and Sienky Lallemand. Lisa Toney began her affair with Lallemand in 1998. Not long after, she started talking about murdering her husband. She told Lallemand that her husband had a $50,000 life insurance policy and owned property. At first, Lallemand wanted no part of homicide and instead suggested stealing Marcus Toney's identity for financial gain. Sienky Lallemand had a predisposition for identity theft as he had prior convictions for credit card fraud in Indiana and Michigan.

The two then went about their identity theft scheme, obtaining and using credit cards in the husband's name. They also leased a Lexus SUV and a Mercedes-Benz in Marcus Toney's name. The person who leased the Lexus presented an Indiana driver's license as identification. While it had the name and identifying information of Marcus Toney, the licenses's photograph was that of Sienky Lallemand. Overall, the identity theft losses in Marcus Toney's name exceeded $220,000.[1]

At some point, Marcus Toney learned that his wife and her boyfriend were involved in the identity theft of his good name. On February 1, 2000, he told a bank investigator that his wife and Lallemand were fraudulently using credit cards in his name. After learning that her husband was going to alert the police about the fraud, Lisa Toney and Lallemand decided to end his life by sending him the parcel bomb.[2] They placed a FedEx label on the package to make it appear more authentic. After receiving the parcel, Marcus Toney removed the label and placed it in another room of his house. It was recovered by the investigators, and the handwriting on it was found to belong to Lallemand.

For some reason, Marcus Toney did not open the bomb parcel right away. It sat in his home for three days before he opened it and it exploded. When it was clear that Toney had not opened the box and was still alive, Lallemand called him and left a voicemail intended to convince him to open the package. "Why don't you just open your little gift, and, uh, you know, take a look at what I sent you?" was the message Lallemand left.[3] When the bomb exploded and Lallemand learned that Toney was dead, he went on the run.

When federal agents captured Lallemand in Los Angeles on May 31, 2000, he was living with an executive of the *COPS* television show. The woman was aware that he was a fugitive and helped him flee by purchasing an airline ticket for him to travel to Los Angeles. Lallemand had convinced the executive to pay for plastic surgery to alter his appearance and prevent him from being caught.[4] She was convicted and sent to prison for aiding and abetting Lallemand in his escape.

Lallemand avoided the death penalty by pleading guilty to the homicide and identity theft charges. During his sentencing hearing, he was given the opportunity to address the court. Rather than ask forgiveness, Lallemand stated, "It's really a day for the family to seek justice."[5] He never offered an apology for his crimes and was sentenced to life in prison without the possibility of parole. He also agreed to testify against Lisa Toney in her trial on similar charges. She was convicted and also sentenced to life in prison. What started as an identity theft ended as a homicide, leaving numerous lives forever devastated.

## MAIL THEFT TURNED VIOLENT

The circumstances and outcomes in some identity theft cases can be far from typical. At times, they open a Pandora's box of violence and evil. That was the result of an investigation that started in a very straightforward manner. On April 11, 2004, Postal Inspector Mark Shaw in Gary, Indiana, received a telephone call from a local police department reporting that patrol officers had found several bags of mail in a trash Dumpster. Inspector Shaw responded to the location and found almost 200 pieces of rifled first-class mail. He determined that the mail was outgoing mail placed in Postal Service collection boxes for pickup. Also found in the mail bags were numerous personal checks, blank check stock, and what appeared to be counterfeit checks.

As he searched through the bags, Inspector Shaw discovered eight counterfeit Indiana driver's licenses. Two of the licenses had the same photograph of a male but in two different names. Four of the licenses had the same photograph of a female but in four different names. The remaining two licenses contained the same photograph of another female but in two different names. Inspector Shaw observed that five names on the licenses were the same names and return addresses on the mail found in the Dumpster.

Inspector Shaw had been a Postal Inspector for 11 years at the time and had investigated numerous mail theft, identity theft, and counterfeiting cases. It was clear to him that the mail had been stolen for the purpose of obtaining identity and checking account information for use in manufacturing counterfeit identification and checks. The phony identification would be used so the thieves could pass the counterfeit checks at financial institutions and retail merchants.

Criminals are not always smart. Also found in the Dumpster was a receipt for lodging at a nearby motel in the name of Jane Parker. Inspector Shaw went to the motel and after being told by the front desk manager that Parker was still in the room, Inspector Shaw called for police backup. After the police arrived, they went to Parker's room, knocked on the door, and a male opened it. Inspector Shaw quickly recognized him as the same person on the counterfeit driver's licenses that were found in the Dumpster. The male was asked for his name and stated that he was Richard Zane, but that was an alias. In his possession were a backpack and a briefcase, each containing a laptop computer.

At the same time, Inspector Shaw observed a female in the motel room whom he recognized as the same person in the photographs on four of the counterfeit driver's licenses. A second female was observed in the room; she also identified herself with an alias. In the room, the investigators also found what appeared to be a white powdery substance and drug paraphernalia. The three suspects were taken in for booking.

A subsequent search of the motel room found more stolen mail, counterfeit driver's licenses, personal checks, blank check stock, a computer printer, digital camera, and controlled substances and drug paraphernalia. Evidence found in the motel room tied the suspects to the stolen mail and phony identification found in the Dumpster. Attention now turned to the three suspects in custody at the police station. Their fingerprints were sent to the FBI to determine their true identities. Each was then interviewed.

Jane Parker was determined to be the real name of the first woman. The other woman was identified as Annie Steen. The male who claimed he was Richard Zane was identified as Ryan Williams, a fugitive with outstanding arrest warrants from Florida,

Georgia, and Ohio. Steen confessed and admitted she was involved in mail theft, identity theft, and check fraud. She told quite a story. Originally from Missouri, she had moved to Georgia six months earlier and met Williams. In January 2004, Steen and Williams traveled to Atlanta for the purpose of cashing checks with fake identities that they acquired through mail theft. Steen explained that they obtained the mail by placing "mail stops" in collection boxes to get banking and personal information from bills and payments victims had sent through the U.S. mail. Steen and Williams would then use the phony identifications to negotiate checks.

Steen described a mail stop or mail slide as a piece of metal that was placed in a Postal Service collection box to intercept mail deposited by postal customers. The device trapped incoming mail so it could not drop to the bottom of the box. The thieves would later retrieve the mail and the mail stop. Steen stated that two weeks earlier, she joined Williams and Parker on a road trip to Indiana to make money by stealing mail from collection boxes. When they arrived in Indiana, they again used mail stops to steal outgoing mail. They used the motel room as a base of operations. The counterfeit checks and phony IDs were created and printed using a laptop belonging to Williams. Williams, Steen, and Parker were charged with theft of mail on April 11, 2004, in United States District Court, Northern District of Indiana.

This was far from the end of the case. Inspector Shaw had also been investigating checks stolen from the mail in La Porte, Indiana, during January 2004 that were subsequently altered and negotiated. The inspector had not been able to identify any suspects in those mail thefts. A break came after the arrests of Williams, Steen, and Parker. With information provided by the FBI, a suspect was identified and interviewed on April 17, 2004. Mandi Ann Gordon admitted to forging signatures on these checks and then negotiating them. Gordon identified Ryan Williams as her partner in crime and stated that he had been the one who stole the mail containing these checks in La Porte, Indiana, and gave them to her to cash. Gordon stated that Williams had "washed" the checks to remove the inked writing so that she could rewrite it with different information. She would then forge the account holders' signatures on the fronts of the checks and the endorsements on the backs. Inspector Shaw obtained an arrest warrant for Gordon and she was prosecuted.

We now need to step back in time a few years to see how we got to this point. Postal Inspectors in Ohio had arrested Williams for identity and mail theft in 2000. Williams's partner in crime at the time was Carl Langdon. Both men were convicted for their offenses. Williams received two years in prison and Langdon received four years, as he had an extensive record of arrests and convictions. After serving their time, Williams headed for Georgia and Langdon for Indiana. After the arrests of Parker, Steen, Williams, and Gordon, Inspector Shaw informed Inspector Richard Petry (who was assigned to the Indianapolis office of the Postal Inspection Service) of the arrests and advised him that Langdon was in Indianapolis, probably up to no good. Inspector Petry then started on Langdon's trail.

Postal Inspectors knew that Langdon was a career criminal and worked with Williams but could not connect him with the crimes of Williams, Steen, Parker, and Gordon. Actually, Langdon had learned something from his prior crimes and jail time. He kept a low profile and now let others in his crew do his dirty work. He no longer handled stolen mail and checks so his fingerprints would not be left as evidence to be used against him. He had others forge the checks. He was a planner and directed others but always got his fair share of the proceeds. Postal Inspectors knew that even the smartest criminals make mistakes; it was only a matter of time before Langdon would slip up. Yet even the street-smart inspectors were shocked by what Langdon would eventually do.

Inspector Petry developed a confidential informant (CI) who told him that Langdon was committing mail theft and bank fraud. The CI told of how he cashed counterfeit checks for Langdon in Indiana and Ohio. The CI also said that Langdon was planning a home invasion robbery of a drug dealer where he would kill the home's occupants and steal their cash and drugs. This turned out to be a ruse. Langdon was really planning to kill the CI as he was upset with him for leaving his fingerprints on one of the counterfeit checks cashed in Ohio. Langdon was concerned that the CI would be identified and eventually lead the police to him.

Unfortunately, neither the CI nor the investigators knew this was Langdon's plan at the time. Of course, Langdon had no idea that this person was acting as a confidential informant. Langdon wanted to lure the CI to his home, then murder him, and bury the body where it would never be found. Langdon asked the CI to assist in the home invasion robbery by driving the getaway car and he agreed. The Postal Inspectors and the police thought this was a great opportunity to catch career criminal Langdon in the act of a violent crime. At the time, it was thought to be just another case of a bad guy robbing another bad guy.

The robbery was to take place on November 4, 2004. Inspector Petry placed a body transmitter on the CI for both personal safety and evidentiary purposes. This was standard operating procedure, and the CI was very fortunate that Inspector Petry followed it. The CI met Langdon at a prearranged location and got into his car. Langdon told the CI that they needed to return to his house as he had left something he needed for the robbery. Once inside the house, the investigators heard sounds of a struggle coming over the CI's body transmitter. Fearing for the CI's safety, the police broke into the house and subdued Langdon after a brutal fight. Several officers suffered injuries when Langdon resisted arrest.

The CI was found unconscious and barely breathing. A piece of rope had been used in the attempt to strangle him. A search of Langdon's car found a body bag, bags of concrete, a shovel, a pickax, a change of clothes, and a pair of work gloves. In the garage, a trash can held construction-strength trash bags and bottles of acid. Nearby was a new, hard plastic children's wading pool. Langdon did not have children; it was believed that the pool was to be used to dispose of the body. A subsequent search of Langdon's home by Inspector Petry found a laptop computer used for fraud as well as other evidence of counterfeiting and identity theft.

Langdon was charged with attempted murder and resisting arrest. During the trial in March 2005, Langdon's courtroom antics disrupted the proceedings and angered the trial judge. At one point, Langdon grabbed the physical evidence used against him and threw it into the air, causing the trial to be stopped temporarily. During closing arguments, as he was being led out of the courtroom, Langdon lunged toward the prosecutor. Quick-acting bailiffs stopped Langdon before he reached the prosecutor. The jury convicted Langdon of all counts in deliberations lasting just two days.

In May 2005, Langdon was sentenced to 50 years in prison. His sentence was enhanced due to his extensive criminal record. Defiant until the end, he denied he ever tried to kill the CI and claimed law enforcement had blown everything out of proportion. He also claimed that he had been a model citizen. He obviously forgot the eight prior felony convictions he had received for a variety of crimes including identity theft, mail theft, and forgery. Langdon was oblivious to the fact that he had committed crimes of a most serious nature and would now be paying for it for much of the rest of his life. Inspector Petry reflected on the strange paths that criminal investigations take by stating "Justice is often served when criminals least expect it."[6]

Inspector Shaw later contemplated the events leading up to the attempted murder and remembered something Langdon had told the CI when they were cashing stolen checks. Langdon said, "If the Postal Inspectors get involved, that's who we gotta watch out for—those are the guys that know everything."[7] Langdon was right and probably never realized how true his statement was when he made it. He will have the rest of his life to ponder his crimes. Williams, Steen, Parker, and Gordon all entered guilty pleas and were convicted. Williams and Gordon were sentenced to jail terms while the other two received probation. This case clearly illustrates the lesson that identity thieves can destroy lives, both figuratively and literally.

## AN IDENTITY THIEF TURNS HIS BRUTALITY ON LAW ENFORCEMENT

Kurt Sohrbeck had a criminal history with stints in prison going back to the 1970s. After a number of years of various criminal activities, he turned to identity theft. "He was a prolific identity thief dating back to early 1990s. He hasn't used his real name since about 1992," said Washington State Patrol Detective Erik Noren. "He assumes other people's IDs and he's very, very difficult to track."[8] At least three people had the unfortunate experience of knowing firsthand what it was like to be an identity theft victim of Sohrbeck's. He stole their identities, received Washington State driver's licenses in their names, made numerous credit charges in their names, and created huge legal and financial problems for them.

In one case, a victim learned that a new Volvo was purchased in his name in 2001. Although stealing one's identity to buy a car is bad enough, there was much more to come. The identity thief got into a serious accident with the car. The fraudster, again using the name and identity of the victim, ran up almost $250,000 in medical bills at a hospital in Bellevue, Washington. Of course, the thief did not pay the bills, leaving the victim to face the wrath of collection agencies that then came after him. "It was a nightmare," the victim said. "There was a period there where every week someone would call trying to collect something I knew nothing about."[9]

A second victim believes that Sohrbeck stole his identity when he lost his wallet in Reno in 2003. The wallet contained his driver's license and other personal information. Sohrbeck began using this victim's name and identifiers to obtain construction jobs in Washington State. The fraudster also sullied the victim's good name by being cited for road rage and driving under the influence in January 2005. An arrest for reckless driving and attempting to elude police followed in February 2007. Then in December 2007, the identity thief was again charged with theft. In all three of these arrests, the scammer identified himself with the victim's name. The police had no idea that he was using a stolen identity. The suspect failed to show up for any of his court appearances, and arrest warrants were issued in the name of the unsuspecting victim.[10]

This incident provides another example of how the system does not always work to protect our identities. Sohrbeck was able to obtain a valid driver's license in this victim's name using the victim's 1978 date of birth. Sohrbeck had to appear in person at the licensing office to apply for and get his photograph taken. At the time, the victim was 30 years old; Sohrbeck was clearly much older, probably in his 50s. That is at least a 20-year age discrepancy. Why did no one from the Washington State Department of Licensing notice this inconsistency and check further? I would expect that Motor Vehicles Department employees are trained to look for things like this.

A third victim fared no better than the other two. In January 2007, he offered employment to the fraudster, not knowing his true motives. The victim described himself as a very trusting person and even opened his home to the thief. Although the construction job lasted only a few days, the damage was done. Shortly after, Sohrbeck obtained a Washington State driver's license in the victim's name. He purchased a truck and opened several credit card accounts in the victim's name. "I'm mad at myself, but I don't know that I'd change anything," said the victim. "I believe there's more honest people out there than bad."[11]

In addition to identity theft, Sohrbeck had a violent streak. His history of violence included an assault on a Washington State police officer during a routine traffic stop. Detective Noren was investigating and tracking Sohrbeck in February and March 2008 on pending criminal charges of assault and identity theft when the trail went cold. Given Sohrbeck's criminal record in 11 states and his travel around the country, it was easy to see that he would skip town. Washington State issued an all-points bulletin for Sohrbeck's arrest. Police believe that Sohrbeck has used at least nine aliases and probably many more. "He's someone who has just figured out how to get a free ride in life," Noren said. "This guy just ruins people."[12]

While on the run, Sohrbeck headed to New Mexico. On March 13, 2008, a Lincoln County, New Mexico, sheriff's sergeant spotted the fugitive's truck in southern New Mexico. The deputy attempted to pull over Sohrbeck, but the fugitive came out of his vehicle shooting and severely wounded the deputy.[13] Sohrbeck fled the scene, leaving the deputy by the roadside fighting for his life. Luckily, the deputy survived and is recovering.

An extensive manhunt ensued to locate Sohrbeck. It did not take long to find him. Shortly after the shooting, he abandoned his truck and set out on foot and bicycle. On March 26, 2008, Sohrbeck was located in Otero County, New Mexico, and was fatally shot by a deputy sheriff when he failed to respond to the officer, exhibited aggressive and threatening behavior, and was attempting to reach into his pants pocket for something. According to police reports, Sohrbeck told the deputy that he "was not going to be taken."[14] Police later found a folding box cutter in his back pocket.

News of Sohrbeck's demise quickly reached one of his many identity theft victims in Washington State. "[Sohrbeck] didn't deserve to die for [stealing my identity]—that's only money," he said. "But when I heard he hurt a cop . . . there has to be a trade-off there. That's way over the line."[15]

## NOTES

1. Steve Warmbir, "Man Admits He Sent Bomb, Killed Girlfriend's Husband," *Chicago Sun-Times*, March 13, 2002, www.highbeam.com/doc/1P2-1428580.html.
2. Daniel Silver, "Trial Starts for Woman Accused of Helping Murder Her Husband," Medill News Service, February 19, 2003, mesh.medhill.northwestern.edu/mnschicago/archives/2003/02/trial_starts_fo_1.html.
3. Warmbir, "Man Admits He Sent Bomb."
4. Ibid.
5. Steve Warmbir, "Man Who Blew Up Lover's Husband Gets Life in Prison," *Chicago Sun-Times*, September 18, 2003, www.highbeam.com/doc/1P2-1501200.html.
6. Postal Inspector Richard Petry's written comments to the author on January 31, 2008.
7. Postal Inspector Mark Shaw's written comments to the author on November 21, 2007.
8. KOMO 1000 News, "Identity Theft Suspect Sought in Deputy's Shooting," May 13, 2008, www.komoradio.com/news/16658971.html.
9. Caleb Heeringa, "Police Seek Identity Thief: Man Rack Up Debt, Arrests in Names of at Least 3 People, *Bellingham Herald*, March 9, 2008, www.bellinghamherald.com/477/story/346318.html.
10. Ibid.
11. Ibid.
12. Ibid.
13. "Reward Increased for Information Leading to Man Who Shot Deputy," *Bellingham Herald*, March 15, 2008, www.bellinghamherald.com/northwest/story/352715.html.
14. Associated Press, "Deputy Involved in Fatal Shooting in Cloudcroft on Paid Leave," *Las Cruces Sun-News*, March 27, 2008, www.lcsun-news.com/ci_8716775.
15. Caleb Heeringa, "Details Unfold in Shooting Death of County Man," March 28, 2008, www.bellinghamherald.com/102/story/363866.html.

# CHAPTER 8

# Medical Identity Theft

In the last decade, there has been an ominous twist to identity theft. It is one that should have been as plain as the nose on one's face. This growing threat is medical identity theft. The Federal Trade Commission (FTC) defines medical identity theft as occurring

> *when someone uses your personal information without your knowledge or consent to obtain, or receive payment for, medical treatment, services, or goods. Victims of medical identity theft may find that their medical records are inaccurate, which can have a serious impact on their ability to obtain proper medical care and insurance benefits.*[1]

The FTC's 2006 Identity Theft Survey Report provided key findings on medical identity theft. Three percent of all identity theft victims indicated that a fraudster had obtained medical treatment, services, or supplies using their stolen personal information. That translates to approximately 250,000 victims for calendar year 2005.[2] Anyone who receives medical care is potentially a victim. Yet some people may be at an even higher risk. "People 50 and older are at the greatest risk because they often have some kind of government-issued insurance, such as Medicare or Medicaid," states Pam Dixon, executive director of the World Privacy Forum, a nonprofit research and consumer education organization that closely monitors medical identity theft.[3]

## IT IS OFTEN AN INSIDER

The Social Security number (SSN), the key to our financial vaults, is also commonly our medical identifier. This creates another avenue for identity theft. As valuable as stolen personal information is, some types are even more prized. While resumes go for about 7 cents on the black market, pilfered medical records bring $50 to $60 each. There is a gold mine of valuable data inside medical files in doctors' offices, hospitals, and clinics everywhere.

Far too often, the crook who steals your medical identity is not some Dumpster diver or ingenious hacker but a trusted healthcare worker. Although cases of medical identity theft are not as common as other types of identity theft, they are a growing problem. "We have the anecdotal information that it is increasing," says Dixon. "We do see some of that where someone steals a wallet or they steal someone's name. That does happen. But the preponderance of cases are happening from insider jobs."[4]

These criminally minded insiders have easy access to the information. Patients' medical files contain a wealth of information for an enterprising criminal. The standards of security for medical files vary considerably. There are no requirements for hospitals or doctors to lock medical files. Many files are maintained in lockable storage cabinets, but I wonder how many are actually secured when the office closes for the day.

A patient coordinator at a clinic in Weston, Florida, stole medical data on approximately 1,130 patients and sold the information to her cousin. Both were eventually arrested and convicted for their crimes.[5] While locking files may discourage some from identity theft, when a corrupt insider is involved, the problem is even more complex and challenging. Criminal rings also see the value in medical information. Organized gangs have even gone so far as setting up fake clinics to obtain patient information for use in healthcare fraud and identity theft. In one case, they lured elderly Medicare patients to a clinic near San Jose, California "by offering free transportation, a nutritional supplement and skin oil."[6] Phony doctors performed superficial examinations on the victims and then submitted fraudulent medical claims in their names to the tune of over $1.1 million.

Yet medical files are not the only source of personal information. Patient wristbands used during hospital stays may contain SSNs in addition to other identifying information. A few years ago, I had day surgery and was given a wristband. Although the hospital did not place my SSN on the band, it did include my full name and date of birth. During hospital stays, wallets and purses containing personally identifiable information (PII) are often left unlocked in hospital rooms and provide another source of access for scammers.

## UNPROTECTED MEDICAL FILES

In 1994, in Pasadena, California, the 24-year-old son of a psychiatrist stole personal information from the unprotected medical records in his father's medical office. The son occasionally worked in the father's office and had access to all patient records. When his father was away, the fraudster went through about 60 patient files and took names, SSNs, dates of birth, addresses, and other identifying information. He used this information to obtain the patients' credit reports and opened a mailbox at a commercial mail receiving agency (CMRA) in nearby Arcadia, California.

With help of the credit reports, the fraudster was able to take over the patients' identities and change their addresses to his mailbox. He opened a bank account and obtained checks in the name of one patient. The scammer then applied for and received credit cards in the names of dozens of patients. These cards were mailed to his CMRA mailbox. The CMRA owner became suspicious when he noticed the large quantity of credit reports and credit cards coming to the box in so many different names shortly after the box had been opened. The mail included correspondence from banks in Europe. Fortunately, the CMRA owner had previously worked with Postal Inspectors on fraud cases and quickly alerted them.

Due to the mail drop owner's swift action, the young man was caught before he was able to use any of the credit cards and receive any proceeds of the criminal activity. When questioned by Postal Inspectors, he said that his plan was to run up the credit cards and transfer the proceeds to banks in Western Europe. In fact, he was in the process of opening bank accounts in Switzerland and Luxembourg.

Had it not been for a sharp CMRA operator, the young man would have succeeded in ruining the credit of dozens of his father's patients. The victims were all people who were suffering with various forms of mental health issues and were further distressed to learn that their personal information had been stolen from their medical files. Although none of their money was stolen, the peace of mind of a rather vulnerable group of people certainly was impacted. Unfortunately, justice was not served; prosecutors declined to charge the suspect because there were no financial losses.

That did not sit well with many of the victims who, although they had not lost any money, still had their identities stolen. Some of the victims wanted to dole out their own brand of justice to the young man, but cooler heads prevailed.

## BEING YOUR OWN DETECTIVE

Being a victim of identity theft can become so frustrating that you may feel the need to take matters into your own hands. That was the case of Eric Drew, who turned detective to track down the medical identity thief who victimized him. Drew was a leukemia patient. Besides having to deal with his illness, Drew learned that someone was impersonating him and using his credit for purchases at an area department store. After learning that the store had a surveillance tape of the suspect, he convinced the employees to give him the video. Drew got a local television station to run the tape, and the culprit was identified as a lab technician at Seattle Cancer Care Alliance—the same facility where Drew was receiving care for his leukemia. Seattle Cancer Care Alliance claimed that it did not know how the employee was able to steal Drew's personal information.[7]

## SNOOPING EYES

As much as we would like to think that our medical records are confidential and viewed only by those who need to know, recent experience shows just the opposite. Hospital employees and other healthcare providers have abused their insider privileges to pry into patients' files, especially those of hospitalized celebrities, to sell medical details to the tabloids. In 2008, several UCLA Medical Center employees were disciplined or fired for snooping into the medical records of Britney Spears, George Clooney, Farrah Fawcett, and other stars. The subsequent inquiry found that one employee viewed as many as 32 electronic medical files of celebrities, politicians, and high-profile patients. Noncelebrities fared no better. This same unauthorized employee also accessed the medical files of 61 other patients.

Although there was no evidence that these unauthorized employees did anything other than leak medical ailments to the media, those with fraudulent intentions have the same uncontrolled access. These breaches of patient confidentiality are particularly troublesome. Medical records, without exception, should be safe from prying eyes. Consequences for violators need to be more severe than just being fired. Civil and criminal ramifications should be considered in all such cases. Patients and their medical records' privacy are protected by both state and federal laws, which carry penalties of prison and/ or fines for illegal breaches.

## THEFT AND FRAUDULENT USE OF PHYSICIAN NAMES AND LICENSES

Identity thieves have resorted to the theft of physicians' names, medical license information, tax identification numbers, and other related information to defraud various state and local medical services programs. One scheme was reported by the California Attorney General and the California Department of Health Services in December 1999, when the California Medi-Cal Program was defrauded. The Medi-Cal Program provides basic healthcare services for California residents who are poor, disabled, elderly, or otherwise qualified. According to the California Attorney General, this scheme resulted in fraud losses in excess of several million dollars in 1999. The identity theft worked in this way:

- Criminals fraudulently obtained doctors' names and copies of their medical licenses. This was often accomplished through improper access to various personnel files at hospitals where the doctors were employed. Other PII was also stolen from the files.
- Once fraudsters had this information in their possession, they would apply to the Medi-Cal Program and obtain a new provider number in the victim doctor's name. Fraudsters would also claim that the doctor had moved and provide the new address where future payments should be sent.
- The identity thieves then would forge the doctor's name on claim forms for medical services never performed and submit phony bills to the Medi-Cal Program. As another unknowing victim of this scheme, Medi-Cal would pay the doctor, believing he or she was the legitimate service provider.
- Once the criminals received the payments, they forged the true doctor's signature on the checks and negotiated them. The Medi-Cal Program generally had no idea this fraud was occurring. Even a reporting tool that should have caught this failed: The 1099 tax forms subsequently mailed out to document payments to participating

providers were sent to the addresses provided by the fraudsters. One of the many consequences of this crime was the tax liability faced by victims whose identities were stolen and who had payments made in their names.

- Another aspect of this insidious crime was that patients' identities were also stolen and used to falsely receive Medi-Cal benefits. The victims had no knowledge that their accounts were being used to defraud the Medi-Cal Program.[8]

In announcing the prevention awareness and heightened enforcement campaign to fight physician identity theft and related false medical claims in December 1999, then California Attorney General Bill Lockyer stated:

*We want to see Medi-Cal scams shrivel up by exposing the practices of these swindlers early and encouraging preventive measures. Our first alert covers a major scheme we discovered to bilk Medi-Cal of millions of dollars using confidential physician and patient information stolen from hospital files.[9]*

As a result, California put new procedures into place to prevent this fraud, including increased scrutiny and review of all new requests for provider numbers and changes of address. As a further internal control, original providers were contacted to verify that they had actually submitted a request for a new payment location. Doctors were told to protect their license information by placing a statement on any copy of their license provided to hospitals or others. The recommended statement is *Copy Provided for Use by (name of hospital/clinic) Only.* Another recommendation was for hospitals and other medical providers to place their business stamp on all file copies of physician licenses.

The enhanced focus on prevention and prosecution paid off in just a few months. In July 2000, six suspects were arrested in Los Angeles in a large Medi-Cal fraud and identity theft scheme. According to the California Attorney General's July 6, 2000 press release, the defendants illegally purchased "physicians' medical licenses and identification from Los Angeles-area hospital employees in a sophisticated fraud, identity theft, and money laundering conspiracy." The criminals then "submitted phony applications to the Department of Health Services under these doctors' names requesting Medi-Cal provider numbers that are required in order to bill the State's $20 billion Medi-Cal program."[10]

The defendants recruited codefendants who obtained the names and personal information of thousands of hospital patients who were Medi-Cal beneficiaries. "As with the victimized doctors, the names and identification of these beneficiaries were taken from various hospitals without the knowledge or consent of either the hospitals or the patients." Subsequently, fraudulent medical claims were submitted claiming medical treatment by the victimized doctors.[11]

The defendants created phony businesses and opened mail drop boxes to receive the payment checks from the state. The defendants also opened bank accounts using fraudulent identification documents in the names of the victimized doctors in order to cash the state payment checks. In addition, the defendants laundered the stolen proceeds through the business of a codefendant. The attorney general said at the time that "[s]chemes such as this one victimize not just the taxpayers, but also patients and medical doctors. Seven physicians and more than a thousand patients had their identities stolen, and it has resulted in well over a million dollars in fraudulent claims being paid by Medi-Cal."[12]

## LIFE-AND-DEATH CONSEQUENCES

Imagine the shock and concern that Linda Weaver experienced in 2007 when she received a hospital bill for the amputation of her right foot. She did not need to look down at her two very intact feet to know this was bunk. As she came to learn, an identity thief had stolen her identity, including her SSN and insurance identification number. Posing as Linda Weaver, the fraudster had the costly amputation performed. To make matters far worse, Weaver later found that the thief's medical information was merged into her medical file. Her medical chart now listed her as having diabetes—the criminal's condition, not hers. Just think of all the life-threatening complications she or anyone else in this situation could potentially face. The wrong blood type listed in the file, not documenting a heart condition, and allergies or intolerance to certain medication can result in trauma or death. "I now live in fear that if something ever happened to me, I could get the wrong kind of medical treatment," said a clearly troubled Weaver.[13] As more and more health records are computerized and available on the Web to medical providers, there is the fear that more data breaches and medical record compromises will occur.

## IT STARTED WITH AN INNOCENT ADVERTISEMENT

Medical identity theft victim Joe Ryan fared even worse. He knew something was wrong when he received a $44,000 bill for colon surgery from Littleton Adventist Hospital in Colorado. But that was only the start of his misery. Ryan made the mistake of providing his SSN and date of birth to a salesman to purchase a magazine ad. Ryan was placing an ad in the magazine and was told that this personal information was needed. What Ryan would later learn was that the salesman was a career criminal on parole who needed the surgery and used Ryan's good name and credit. Ryan went through reams of red tape and bureaucracy before he finally convinced the hospital that he had not been the one who had the surgery. Unfortunately, it came too late: His credit was damaged, his credit cards were canceled, and he faced foreclosure on his residence and had to take out a loan just to get by.[14]

## ARIZONA'S IDENTITY THEFT PROBLEM

Arizona has long been a hotbed for identity theft as discussed in Chapter 6. Year after year, it ranks near the top among states for number of victims. Again in 2007, the state had the greatest number of reported identity theft victims. In 2002, the theft of personal information including the SSNs of 562,000 military patients of TriWest Healthcare Alliance in Phoenix set the stage for the numerous data breaches that continue to the present. In response to the huge problem of identity theft, the Arizona state legislature enacted a law, which took effect in January 2005, that prevented health insurers from using SSNs on medical benefits identification cards. The law also restricts how Social Security–related information can be mailed to members of medical benefit plans. SSNs should never have been used as medical identifiers. Yet the numbers were readily available; everyone had one; and no one anticipated the problem. Prior to enactment of the law, a number of health insurers had already changed over to randomly selected numbers out of a concern for privacy protection and fraud prevention.

## HEALTH INSURANCE PORTABILITY AND ACCOUNTABILITY ACT

The Health Insurance Portability and Accountability Act (HIPAA) is sweeping legislation that has had an enormous impact on healthcare providers and patients. HIPAA was enacted by Congress in 1996 and covers everything from healthcare access, portability, and renewal, to preventing healthcare fraud, to effects on research and clinical care. It is also known as the Kennedy-Kassebaum Act after the two Senate sponsors of the bill. A key component of HIPAA is to encourage electronic transactions of medical information and heightened safeguards to protect the security and confidentiality of medical information.

The provisions of HIPAA apply to healthcare providers and plans, public health agencies, self-ensured employers, colleges and universities involved in medical studies, life insurance companies, vendors, and others. There are both civil and criminal penalties for noncompliance, including fines and imprisonment. The most severe penalties involve up to 10 years in prison and a $250,000 fine for offenses related to the criminal sale, transfer, or use of personally identifiable health information.

HIPAA called on the Department of Health and Human Services (HHS) to ensure that providers secure electronic files in the same way they secure physical paper records, improving overall informational security. The stated goal was to assure individuals that their health information is properly protected while at the same time allowing important uses of the information to protect the health and well-being of the individual and the public at large. The act covers both health plans and healthcare providers who transmit health information in electronic form.[15]

The HHS federal privacy standards generally went into effect beginning April 14, 2003, with an extension to 2004 for small health plans to comply. The privacy rules enacted to carry out HIPAA's requirements protect consumers from having their personal health information exploited, disclosed, or otherwise misused, whether by insurance companies, employers, or anyone else. In many cases, consent from the patient must be obtained before information can be disclosed, and when it is disclosed, it often must be limited to the minimum amount of protected health information needed.[16]

Healthcare providers and plans must provide notice to their patients of how their medical information will be used. These notices are generally signed and dated by the patient and maintained in the medical file with a copy provided to the patient. A key component of the privacy regulations allows patients to access their medical records and make corrections to any identified errors or mistakes. This is especially important if a person is victimized by medical identity theft and the fraudster's medical information is incorporated into the victim's medical records. For more information on federal privacy standards to protect patients' medical records, visit the HHS Protecting the Privacy of Patient's Health Information site at www.hhs.gov/news/facts/privacy.html.

## HEALTHCARE RECORDS ON THE WEB

As more and more services and information move online, it is only natural that healthcare records will too. There are many benefits to this innovative concept. In theory, patients will be able to access and better manage their medical records. They can keep detailed and up-to-date records on family medical history, immunizations, prescriptions, allergies, lab results, and doctor visits. In an emergency, either the patient or someone with authorization can quickly access the online health record and provide it to the treating health practitioner at whatever medical facility the patient is brought. It is also believed that online tools will dramatically drive down the spiraling cost of healthcare.

President George W. Bush lobbied for electronic medical records in an attempt to reduce healthcare costs and prevent medical errors. Former HHS Secretary Tommy Thompson has been a strong proponent of online health records. "To achieve these goals, Americans deserve a seamless and secure national health information infrastructure," he said.

*This system must provide accurate, complete patient data to providers wherever they are, in time to be useful—even in an emergency. It must allow doctors to prescribe medications electronically, so the medications can be checked for safety before they are administered. And it must do all this without revealing personally identifiable information without the patient's consent.*[17]

Several hundred vendors, including insurance, technology, and Internet companies, are competing to provide digital medical records as nationwide providers. Everyone from Aetna and United HealthCare to Microsoft and Google are getting involved in the business. Microsoft's personal health record tool is called HealthVault. It is a "search engine supported service to help patients coordinate disparate pieces of health-care information, from lab results to X-rays and daily blood pressure and allergy readings."[18] Only patients will be allowed access to their medical information, and Microsoft promises safety and security for these highly sensitive digital records.

HIPAA requires minimum privacy and security standards for access, disclosure, and other purposes. As a general rule, HIPAA prevents the disclosure of medical information for marketing purposes. HIPAA's strong rules apply only to "covered entities," which are defined as healthcare providers, health insurers, health plan administrators, and billing services. The rules apply to the covered entities and not to the actual medical record. Companies vying for the online medical record business, such as technology and Internet companies are not considered covered entities under HIPAA, and they may or may not follow its privacy and security standards.

According to HHS, only 14% of medical practices in the United States maintain electronic medical records. HHS would like to see that number rise to 50% by 2014. However, a Forrester research study found that only 20% of consumers want to access their medical information online. There may be some good news on the horizon for those interested in using online medical records. In a 2007 Harris Interactive poll, 76% of adults over 55 regularly use the Web to research their medical conditions. People may very well embrace online medical records in the not-too-distant future.

## NATIONAL HEALTH INFORMATION NETWORK

The National Health Information Network (NHIN) is an ambitious government and private sector initiative that would create a nationwide system of readily accessible electronic medical records. In theory, it would provide government healthcare agencies and providers the ability to quickly and easily share patient information. It would connect every medical record of patients with all of their healthcare providers, insurers, pharmacists, labs, and claims processors.[19] As stated on their HHS Web site, the NHIN

> is the critical portion of the health IT [information technology] agenda intended to provide a secure, nationwide, interoperable health information infrastructure that will connect providers, consumers, and others involved in supporting health and healthcare. The NHIN will enable health information to follow the consumer, be available for clinical decision making, and support appropriate use of healthcare information beyond direct patient care so as to improve health.[20]

Although the NHIN is still in the early implementation stages, there are many concerns as to its safety and security. No matter how secure the NHIN database will claim to be, history tells a different story in light of the many large-scale data breaches of the last few years. In a major breach of medical records, for example, "two computers and a disc containing the confidential records of close to 200,000 patients of a medical group in San Jose, California were posted for sale on Craigslist.org."[21] Everything including names, dates of birth, SSNs, medical histories, billing records, and insurance information was contained on the disc. An employee of the medical group was the culprit, and he was subsequently charged with the crime. Again, a trusted insider was responsible. The threat of an insider breach puts greater concerns on whether patient information can be truly protected from breaches in any form.

## THOUGHT LEADER IN IDENTITY THEFT PREVENTION

### Byron Hollis

Byron Hollis is the managing director of the Blue Cross and Blue Shield Association's (BCBSA) National Anti-Fraud Department. BCBSA is a federation of independent Blue Cross and Blue Shield companies. Hollis is responsible for providing national strategic leadership and support to the antifraud programs at the

*(Continued)*

39 independent Blue Cross and Blue Shield companies, which collectively insure more than 100 million customers. He is also responsible for direction and leadership of the BCBSA Federal Employee Program Special Investigations Unit.

Hollis's background includes a law degree from the Thomas Goode Jones Law School at Faulkner University and an undergraduate degree in criminal justice from Auburn University. His public service career includes working as a deputy sheriff, a district attorney's investigator/child support enforcement officer, and finally as a deputy district attorney.

Hollis believes that medical identity theft is a dangerous, albeit not well understood, crime that threatens the health and welfare of individuals while adding to the burden of healthcare costs in this industry. He states, "The danger and impact of ID theft, especially medical ID theft, is not generally understood, can be devastating to an individual, and is a drain on our financial and healthcare systems."

According to Hollis, one of the chief dangers of medical identity theft is having your medical history become entwined with that of the identity thief. "For example, let's say at some point, you were a victim of identify theft. Now you could be involved in a situation—such as a car accident—and you end up in the emergency room. A medical professional searches your records and finds a diagnosis such as diabetes. However, the medical records aren't yours, but may belong to the identify thief. If a doctor gives you insulin when you're not diabetic, the consequences can be deadly."

For individual patients, the theft of their medical identification numbers presents a very different scenario to resolve than "regular" identity theft. Hollis says, "It is much more difficult to remove false information from your medical history with Health Insurance Portability and Accountability Act regulations protecting medical records."

Hollis says that the best protection is prevention. "It is important to check your explanation of benefits [EOB] documents carefully, shred old insurance statements and cards, and be careful when giving out identity information such as your Social Security number and address," he said.

The Blue Cross and Blue Shield Association encourages everyone to follow some simple guidelines to decrease their chances of becoming a victim.

- Inspect your EOB statements issued by your insurer and contact your family physician, hospital, or pharmacy regarding any suspicious charges.
- Keep insurance cards and your insurance identity numbers somewhere safe.
- Request a free copy of your records about once a year. You have a right to a copy of your records from every health insurer (and nearly every healthcare provider) under the health privacy rule issued under the authority of the HIPAA.

More information about protecting your medical identity is available at www.bcbs.com/blueresources/anti-fraud/explanation-of-benefits.html.

## PREVENTION AND SECURITY

Ben Franklin's wise adage of "an ounce of prevention is worth a pound of cure" is just as true when applied to protecting against possible medical identity theft. Here are 14 best practices for prevention and protection for both the patient and healthcare providers to consider:

1. **Guard your medical insurance card.** In many ways it is just as valuable as your credit card. "An insurance card is like a Visa card with a $1 million spending limit," warns Hollis.[22] Safeguard the card and the information contained on it. When you check in at your doctor's office, keep an eye on the card until you get it back. If it is lost, take the same steps you would if you lost your credit card. Instruct your family members to do the same.

2. **If it sounds too good to be true, it usually is.** Be skeptical when you receive calls from telemarketers offering "free" medical care, health screenings, or discounted medical plans. Con artists often use ruses to get unsuspecting victims to provide information. The data could be used in submitting phony medical claims and identity theft in your name. Never give your medical insurance number or any other personal information to anyone who calls, and that includes anyone coming to your door soliciting products or services. If you cannot easily say no, at least require them to mail you detailed information before you provide any information. Scammers usually will not follow-up; they will just move on to another potential victim.

3. **Be Web savvy.** There are innumerable collection points for your personal information. Many are found on the Web. While Web sites may simply be collecting marketing information, think about whether you want to provide information on yourself, including illnesses and medical conditions. Be extra careful when registering on health sites or dialing toll-free numbers to ask about new drugs, treatments, or an illness.

4. **Opt out.** Do not be your own worst enemy and disclose confidential information on product registration and warranty cards or marketing surveys. Send in opt-out forms to stop information from being shared with third parties.

5. **Talk to your doctor and pharmacist about patient privacy.** Ask them about their privacy and security procedures. I would venture to guess that you have never done that, and most people probably have not either.

6. **Read your EOB statement, then read it again.** Carefully read each and every explanation of benefits letter that you receive after medical treatment. "Our No. 1 defense is the consumer himself," says Hollis. "We send our explanation-of-benefits notices, and people round-file those right off the bat. If people would look at those, a lot of theft would get caught."[23] Look for signs of unauthorized treatments performed under your name and insurance coverage. This may simply be a mistake, or it may be evidence of fraud that you will need to address immediately. Report any discrepancies to your insurance provider. Exhibit 8.1 is a resource that anyone can use in reviewing and understanding their EOB for possible identity theft.

7. **Get your medical records.** Consider requesting a copy of your medical records from your doctor or hospital. You should not have a problem getting them, but if you do, you have recourse. File a complaint with the Office of Civil Rights at the United States Department of Health and Human Services who will intervene on your behalf. Contact them at 800-368-1019 or at www.hhs.gov/ocr/privacyhow tofile.htm. Once you have your medical file, review it thoroughly.

8. **Review your medical records.** Just as you should review your credit report each year, do the same for your medical information. Ask your medical insurer to provide a disclosure history from doctors and insurers as to what information was disclosed in the past year. Look for disclosures that you are not familiar with or did not request, and promptly follow up. Look for payments in your name for treatment you did not receive. Look for address changes, as this is a common practice by identity thieves. Healthcare fraud, like identity theft, is big business for fraudsters, and being vigilant is the best medicine.

9. **Correct your medical records.** If you uncover errors or fraud, contact the medical provider and have the problematic information in your medical file corrected. If the services relate to Medicare or Medicaid, contact their local offices. You can also visit their Web site at www.cms.hhs.gov/regionaloffices. Always file a police report whenever you are a victim of any identity theft related crime.

10. **Require photo ID for medical treatment.** More and more hospitals are requiring photo identification to be presented at time of admission and/or treatment in addition to insurance cards. Obviously, this may not be possible in all cases, especially emergency conditions. "You can't get on an airplane or cash a check without ID," stated Marie Whalen, assistant vice president of ambulatory services at the University of Connecticut Health Care Center in Farmington. "Why should healthcare be any different?"[24]

11. **Shred, shred, shred.** The same rule applies to medical information as to any other personal information. Shred those EOBs and any other medical data that you no longer need. Do not toss those empty prescription bottles into the trash or recycling bin without first removing the label containing the patient's name, doctor, medication, and other information.

12. **Do not use your SSN.** Although your Social Security number has been a common identifier for medical treatment, it is generally being replaced with a specific medical identification number. Do not provide your SSN to your doctor or hospital when admitted. If that does not work, demand to know what safeguards are in place to protect you.

13. **Leave your valuables at home.** When admitted for a hospital stay or even for outpatient treatment, leave your credit cards and other important documents at home. Take as little as possible with you. Ask if the facility has a locked cabinet where you can secure your valuables, such as your wallet or purse, while being treated and ensure that you can hold the key.

14. **Speak up.** Do not be afraid to ask questions and voice your concerns. As they say, the squeaky wheel gets the grease. Inquire about who will have access to your patient files, overall security, and other related issues. Do not settle if your

concerns are not answered. Ask to speak to higher-ups. Consider appointing a family member to handle this aspect to insulate the patient from confrontations. The patient has enough on his or her mind at this time and does not need added stress.

## Exhibit 8.1   Review Your EOB Statement to Prevent Fraud

**Your Health Insurance Company**

*Explanation of Benefits (EOB)* **This is not a bill**

06/07/08

1   JOHN DOE
123 MAIN STREET
ANYTOWN, USA 54321

*Customer Service 1-800-123-4567*

*Visit your local plan Web site.*

### Claim Information

| | | |
|---|---|---|
| 2  Member Name: | | John Doe |
| 3  Group Number: | | AX1234 |
| 4  Identification No.: | | CX456789AB |
| Claim No: | | 8022200000X |
| Patient Name: 5 | | John Doe |

### Summary

6

| | |
|---|---|
| Total Billed | $65.00 |
| **Total Benefits Approved** | **$26.10** |
| Amount You May Owe Provider | $ 2.90 |

The following shows how the claim was adjusted.

### Service Information

7

| Service Description | 8 Service Date | 9 Amount Billed | Not Covered | Covered |
|---|---|---|---|---|
| **IMAGING RADIOLOGY** | | | | |
| Medical Emergency X-ray | 05/08/08 | 65.00 | 36.00 | 29.00 |
| **Totals** | | **$65.00** | **$36.00** | **$29.00** |

### Coverage Information

| | | | |
|---|---|---|---|
| **Totals** | **$65.00** | **$36.00** | **$29.00** |
| PARTICIPATING PROVIDER OPTION (PPO REDUCTION) | | -$36.00 | |
| **Deductions** | | | |
| Your 10% Coinsurance Amount | | 2.90 | |
| **Total Deductions** | | | **-$2.90** |
| **Total Benefits Approved** | | | **$26.10** |
| **Amount You May Owe Provider**    10 | | | **$2.90** |
| Total covered benefits approved for this claim $26.10 to IMAGING RADIOLOGY on 6/07/08. | | | |

## Explanation of Benefits

It is important to carefully read the Explanation of Benefits, or EOB, when you receive it. Your health insurer sends this document to you after you or a covered family member receives healthcare services. Reviewing your EOB is a big step in preventing healthcare fraud and medical identity theft. If you find inaccuracies in this form, you should contact the medical provider and your health insurer's customer service. Here is a key to some of the parts of the sample EOB that is pictured here. This is ONLY A SAMPLE REPRESENTATION and is NOT an actual EOB. The one you receive from your insurer may be different.

1.      Incorrect name/address may indicate that you have been a victim of ID theft; unapproved use of your medical identity, or that a clerical mistake has caused you to receive another person's EOB. Contact your insurer if you find that this information is incorrect.

2–4.    Incorrect group or identity number may indicate that you have been a victim of ID theft; unapproved use of your medical identity, or that a clerical mistake has caused you to receive another person's EOB. Contact your insurer if you find that this information is incorrect.

5.      The person who received the indicated services—deliberate errors in this field may indicate that someone is trying to obtain additional payment. Or it could indicate that someone else received services which are being billed to your ID number. This may indicate ID theft or other fraud. Incorrect information could result in a false diagnosis on your medical record creating a dangerous situation for you or a covered family member.

6.      Summary box, including the total billed by the provider for the services, show the benefits approved and paid by your health insurer. You may owe the remainder. If these amounts are well above what you were led to believe, this may indicate your bill is being inflated to increase payment beyond what was authorized. Report this to your insurer.

7–8.    Check descriptions and dates of services. Wrong information may indicate that services are being misrepresented to receive higher payment than authorized. Contact your insurer if you find errors in this field.

9.      Amount billed by the provider for each service. If these amounts are well above what you were led to believe, this may indicate your bill is being inflated to increase payment beyond what was authorized. Report this to your insurer. (See #10.)

10.     Amount you may be responsible for paying. If services and costs are beyond expectations then you may have paid too much. Contact your insurer to determine if you are due a refund from your provider.

## AND SO IT CONTINUES

The lack of security for our most precious personal medical information is both a sad and continuing story. In March 2008, a Salt Lake City schoolteacher was visiting a local surplus store to purchase scrap paper for her fourth-grade students. For about $20 she got what she was looking for and much more. What she received horrified her; the scrap paper was in reality the medical files of 28 Central Florida Regional Hospital patients. The files had been shipped in December 2007 via United Parcel Service (UPS) to Las Vegas for a Medicare audit and never arrived at the intended address. Assuming the package was lost, both the hospital and UPS tried to trace it without success. Apparently, the package was undeliverable and was sold off at auction by UPS. (It is common for shipping companies to sell off packages that cannot be delivered as addressed or cannot be returned to sender.)

Eventually, the missing files found their way to the surplus store. A document found when the files were purchased noted that the contents were sold because the shipper could not deliver it to the address or locate the original mailer. The files contained all the information that would be expected to be found in such medical files. To make matters worse, the hospital knew the files were missing for several months and never informed the affected patients that their files had been lost. The hospital made the disclosure only as a result of the publicity generated by the teacher's discovery. "I'm aghast," said Marcy Lippincott, a Florida attorney whose father's records were among those lost and sold. "I'm wondering who to sue. It's a complete invasion of privacy. It's appalling to think your records can be out there somewhere like that."[25]

On April 11, 2008, Dwight McPherson, a former employee in the patient admissions department at prestigious New York Presbyterian Hospital/Weill Cornell Medical Center, was arrested and charged with computer fraud, identity document fraud, transmission of stolen property, and sale of stolen property.[26] Over a two-year period, he stole and sold the information of nearly 50,000 patients using his insider access to the patient registration system. McPherson confessed to Postal Inspectors that in 2006 he was approached by an Atlanta-based identity theft ring that offered him money for access to the patients' information.[27] These coconspirators specifically requested personal information from male patients born between 1950 and 1970.[28]

McPherson first sold a group of 1,000 records for $750 followed by a second group of 1,000 for $600. The people that McPherson sold the medical information to intended to use it for criminal activity, most likely identity theft. Postal Inspectors in Atlanta learned of McPherson's involvement while conducting another investigation where they found patient records from New York Presbyterian Hospital.[29] Postal Inspectors then began a separate investigation and contacted the hospital. A review of the hospital's computer logs found that McPherson's user login was used for the unauthorized access of 49,841 patients.[30] Following the discovery, the hospital began the arduous task of contacting all patients whose files were breached, setting up a hotline for information and assistance, and offering free credit-monitoring services. The sad thing with these many breaches is that it seems that the criminals are working harder to harm us than we are in protecting ourselves.

## NOTES

1. Federal Trade Commission, *Fighting Back Against Identity Theft,* www.ftc.gov/bcp/edu/microsites/idtheft/consumers/resolving-specific-id-theft-problems.html#MedicalIdentityTheft.
2. Federal Trade Commission, "2006 Identity Theft Survey Report" (November 2007), www.ftc.gov/os/2007/11/SynovateFinalReportIDTheft2006.pdf.
3. Sid Kirchheimer, "Stealing Your Health," *AARP Bulletin* (September 2006), 22.
4. Beth Wilson, "Medical Identity Theft Is Often an 'Inside Job,'" *American Medical News*, March 3, 2008, www.ama-assn.org/amednews/2008/03/03/prsc0303.htm.
5. James Quiggle, "Medical ID Theft Spreading the Pain," *Fraud Focus* (Fall 2007), 4.
6. Ibid.
7. Kevin Helliker, "A New Medical Worry: Identity Thieves Find Ways to Target Hospital Patients," *Wall Street Journal*, February 22, 2005, D1.
8. California Attorney General Press Release, "Attorney General Bill Lockyer, State Health Director Bonta Announce New Campaign Against Medi-Cal Program,

Special Fraud Alert Warns of Physician Identity Theft for False Claims," December 29, 1999, http://ag.ca.gov/newsalerts/release.php?id=541&.

9. Ibid.

10. California Attorney General Press Release, "Attorney General Lockyer Announces Arrests of Six Suspects in Sophisticated $1.4 Million Medi-Cal Fraud and Identity Theft Scheme," July 6, 2000, http://ag.ca.gov/newsalerts/release.php?id=707&.

11. Ibid.

12. Ibid.

13. Dean Foust, "Diagnosis: Identity Theft," *BusinessWeek*, January 8, 2007, 30.

14. Kirchheimer, "Stealing Your Health."

15. U.S. Department of Health and Human Services, "Summary of the HIPAA Privacy Rule," www.hhs.gov/ocr/privacysummary.pdf.

16. Ibid.

17. Speech by Tommy G. Thompson, Secretary of Health and Human Services, at the Health IT Summit, Washington, DC, July 21, 2004, www.hhs.gov/news/speech/2004/040721.html.

18. Jay Greene, "Microsoft Wants Your Health Records," *BusinessWeek*, October 15, 2007, 44.

19. "The New Threat to Your Medical Privacy," *Consumer Reports*, March 2006, 39.

20. Ibid.

21. Ibid.

22. Max Alexander, "Your Medical Records Stolen! How to Protect Yourself," *Reader's Digest*, November 2006, www.rd.com/money/savvy-consumer/scams-frauds-rip-offs/id-thieves-stealing-medical-records/article30232.html.

23. Ibid.

24. Ibid.

25. Associated Press, "Medical Records Sold to Teacher as Scrap Paper," March 10, 2008, www.msnbc.msn.com/id/23561667/.

26. Verena Dobnick, "NYC Hospital Worker Charged with Stealing and Selling Info on Nearly 50,000 Patients," Associated Press, April 12, 2008, //ca.news.yahoo.com/s/capress/080412/world/hospital_id_theft.

27. Dave Hogarty, "Hospital Employee Admits to Selling Patient IDs," Gothamist. com, April 13, 2008, www.gothamist.com/2008/04/13/hospital_id_thi.php.

28. Rich Shapiro, "Stolen Hospital Records Sold to Identity Thieves," *New York Daily News*, April 13, 2008, www.nydailynews.com/news/ny_crime/2008/04/13/2008-04-13_stolen_hospital_records_sold_to_identity.html.

29. Ibid.

30. Douglas Montero and Kati Cornell, "'Scam' Guy Hit 50,000," *New York Post*, April 13, 2008, www.nypost.com/seven/04132008/news/regionalnews/scam_guy_hit_50_000_106316.htm.

# CHAPTER 9

# Fake IDs

"The criminal use of false identification documents represents a multibillion dollar problem in the United States."[1] This quote could easily have been ripped from today's headlines, but actually it was stated in a government report on false identification in 1976. Little has changed since that time, as phony identification (ID) documents continue to fuel many fraud and forgery schemes, and especially identity theft. Fake IDs are also closely tied to illegal immigration, drug smuggling, fugitives from justice, underage drinking, and other crimes and violations. Fraudulent identification documents are a necessary tool for committing identity theft. False identification fraud can be defined as "the intentional use by an individual of a document containing a name or personal attributes other than his own for the purpose of assisting in the commission of a crime or in avoiding the legal consequences of a previous crime."[2]

Common identification documents include birth certificates, driver's licenses, passports, visas and alien registration cards, Selective Service registration cards, voter registration cards, government IDs, privately issued IDs, and credit cards. Social Security numbers (SSNs) and cards were never meant for identification but are often used for that purpose. All of these identification documents can be easily altered or counterfeited for fraudulent purposes. Alteration involves changing significant elements of the identification document, such as replacing a photograph, changing an age or birth date, or altering physical identifiers. Counterfeiting is an "unauthorized creation of a complete document by an unauthorized source to support a false identification."[3] In many cases, alteration or counterfeiting is not necessary; the perpetrator simply obtains an identification document of another person, such as a birth certificate, and uses it as his or her own to obtain other ID documents, such as a driver's license.

Today, a driver's license has become a de facto national identity card. It is universally accepted as identification almost everywhere, whether opening a bank account, cashing a check, using a credit card, or buying alcohol. It is accepted by the Transportation Security Administration to get through airport security and board an airplane. It is also the most widely counterfeited identification document. Countless underage teenagers have used readily available and custom-made phony driver's licenses to gain access to bars and purchase liquor. Four of the five 9/11 hijackers who crashed planes into the Pentagon in 2001 obtained driver's licenses from the Virginia Department of Motor Vehicles. Although they used their real names in applying for the licenses, they provided other false information, including residence information, to obtain the IDs.

When I was a Postal Inspector in Los Angeles in the mid-1990s, I learned firsthand how easy it was to obtain fake IDs. All one had to do was go to MacArthur Park in the Westlake neighborhood of the city. It is named after the late General Douglas MacArthur, and it is a very beautiful urban park. It was also a ready source of any type of phony identification documents. On Alvarado Street bordering the park, if one drove slowly, any number of individuals would approach and offer every imaginable counterfeit ID document.

The purchaser would indicate the kind of document needed and the identification details such as name, date of birth, SSN, and so on. The seller would name the price and once the deal was agreed on, the purchaser was told to return in a few hours. If a photograph was needed, the buyer could either provide one or was referred to a nearby shop for a picture. True to their word and upon returning, the document creators would again approach and provide an unbelievably legitimate-looking ID. There were also degrees of quality. Poorer-quality work was cheaper; if one was willing to pay, the quality would be excellent. For additional costs, working magnetic stripes could be provided on particular documents.

I know this because on occasion, when law enforcement officers were doing undercover operations and were pressed for time, we used these sources to obtain IDs quickly. The trade in fake IDs still goes on today. The fake ID vendors still have a flourishing street trade. Law enforcement has attacked the problem with limited success as phony identification is constantly in demand. In fact, Los Angeles has been called "the epicenter of the fake ID trade." As one illegal immigrant who used the fake ID vendors to obtain a Social Security card and an alien registration card stated: "The people who have been here a long time tell you. Everybody knows you can buy papers in MacArthur Park."[4]

## FAKE IDS ON THE WEB

People with access to the Internet do not have to go to the trouble of driving to MacArthur Park. The Web has an unending supply of sites catering to fake ID seekers. Most specialize in driver's licenses from all 50 states but usually offer a wide range of other IDs. Some sites claim their driver's licenses are "novelty IDs" to be used for demonstration purposes and entertainment, but they are quick to add they can include an "authentic hologram" for an additional cost. Some sites specialize in college diplomas. One site promised that their diplomas use the same high-quality parchment paper as major universities. Online vendors do not ask if the purchaser actually graduated from the particular college or university.

In fact, there were so many Web sites on the Internet offering phony IDs for sale, it was inevitable that a "best of" site would be created. The site, called www.fakeidsite.com, is now closed down as a result of a criminal prosecution that is discussed later in this chapter. The premise of this creative site was that there were so many fake ID sites available but their quality and reliability were often questionable. Promising a one-stop shopping review, the "Fake ID Review Site" compiled detailed reviews of many of the popular sites, breaking them down into "both good and bad fake ID suppliers." Identity thieves did not have to waste precious time trying to find the best site to obtain their phony IDs. They went to this site, got the fake IDs they needed, and quickly got back to the important crime at hand.

I was amused at one reviewer's comment about sending money for a phony ID and then getting ripped off when the site did not provide the promised phony identification. I rather thought it was poetic justice. Another review for the now-defunct Web site www.sob-ids.com remarked, "Customers state that the holograms are flawless, and that the bar codes and magnetic stripes work. This site allows you to come to their location if you happen to be in Mexico." The "sob" part of their Web address stood for "South of the Border," where the site allegedly relocated to avoid U.S. government investigation and prosecution. Their homepage proclaimed that they had to leave the United States "due to inane and stringent U.S. laws."

## SENATE HEARING ON PHONY IDS

In response to complaints from financial institutions, law enforcement, and the public, Congress held a hearing on May 19, 2000, to look into the then-emerging problem of phony IDs and credentials available via the Internet. The hearing presented the findings of the subcommittee investigation of more than 60 Web sites that sold either fake IDs or the computer templates for customers to use in the manufacture of authentic-looking identification documents. Senator Susan M. Collins, chair of the Permanent Sub-committee on Investigations at the time, opened by stating that the hearings would explore a new and disturbing trend involving "the use of the Internet to manufacture and market counterfeit documents."[5] Here are some key points that Senator Collins made in her opening statement:

> With little difficulty, my staff was able to use Internet materials to manufacture convincing IDs that would allow me to pass as a member of our armed forces, a reporter, a student at Boston University, or as a licensed driver in Florida, Michigan, and Wyoming, to name just a few of the identities I could assume.

> These counterfeit identification documents are relatively easy to manufacture. With only a modest understanding of the Internet and $50.00 worth of supplies purchased from an arts and crafts store, one can design authentic-looking identification documents within a few hours, or even minutes.

*The Web sites investigated by the Subcommittee offer a vast and varied product line, ranging from driver's licenses to military identification cards to federal agency credentials, including those of the Federal Bureau of Investigation and the Central Intelligence Agency. Other sites offer to produce Social Security cards, birth certificates, diplomas, and press credentials.*

*For the criminal who has just stolen someone's identity, these sites offer an attractive service. For a relatively low price, the crook can get a state driver's license using the victim's name and date of birth, but showing the criminal's photograph. Or, the thief can obtain a fraudulent birth certificate using the stolen identity, fabricate some utility bills purporting to show his or her residence, and then use these documents to trick the DMV into issuing a real driver's license. These fake driver's licenses appear to serve as 'gateway documents' that allow criminals access to other bona fide identification materials.*

*While the manufacture of false identification documents by criminals is nothing new, the Internet allows those specializing in the sale of counterfeit identification to reach a broader market of potential buyers than they ever could by standing on a street corner in a shady part of town. They can sell their products with virtual anonymity through the use of e-mail services and free Web hosting services and by providing false information when registering their domain names. Similarly, the Internet allows criminals to obtain fake IDs from the seclusion of their own homes, substantially diminishing the risk of apprehension that attends purchasing counterfeit documents on the street.*[6]

## JUSTICE SERVED

In 2002, federal prosecutors charged eight defendants involved in an international conspiracy to sell fake identification documents issued by state motor vehicle departments. Two of the defendants operated Web sites that sold fake IDs, including www.fakeidsite.com and www.sob-ids.com. While the Web sites were located on computer servers in other countries, the two defendants who operated the sites were actually located in Riverside, California. Mail from purchasers of phony IDs was sent to other countries but was redirected to mail drops in California to give the false impression that the operations were based outside the country.[7]

## INTERSTATE IDENTITY THEFT AND FAKE ID RING

On June 3, 2002, Discover Card advised the Postal Inspection Service of the non-receipt and fraudulent use of dozens of credit cards apparently stolen from the mail in New Jersey and used in Connecticut for cash advances. As a result of this information, Postal Inspectors from New Jersey and Connecticut teamed up to jointly work this investigation.

Inspector Donald Landisi coordinated the New Jersey aspect of the case. His investigation determined that the cards would have been processed through a postal facility in New Jersey. Due to the large number of cards stolen, Inspector Landisi believed the cards were stolen from within the processing center, but an investigation did not identify any suspects.

Meanwhile, Postal Inspector/Team Leader Patrick Bernardo, based in New Haven, Connecticut, worked the other end of the case. He collected complaints from Connecticut banks where the credit cards were used. The credit cards had been used at banks in Mystic, New Britain, Naugatuck, New London, and other locations. Inspector Bernardo obtained bank surveillance photos of several suspects, a male and several females, receiving cash advances on the stolen cards. The job was now to identify the people in the photos.

A total of 80 Discover cards were involved and of those, 57 had been activated by the same cell phone number. As these were new cards being mailed to customers, they had to be activated by the true card holders from their home telephones. Since the cards never reached the intended customers, it was believed that the thieves had somehow activated the cards. The Card Activation Program (CAP) was instituted by the credit card industry at the suggestion of a Postal Inspector at a time in the early 1990s when card thefts and fraud were hitting the industry particularly hard. (For more information on CAP, see Chapter 11.)

Inspector Landisi subpoenaed the cell phone records for the number used to activate the cards. It was learned that the phone was a prepaid cell phone account with no name associated with it. This was a temporary dead end, but there would be more to do. Inspector Landisi discovered that 70 Capital One cards had also been stolen, and they too were processed through the same New Jersey mail processing center. More stolen cards were identified from other banks, such as First USA and HSBC. Further investigation determined that more than 200 stolen cards from Discover, Bank One, Capital One, First USA, and HSBC were involved with over $1 million in fraudulent cash advances.

As is often the case, the investigators got a lucky break early in the investigation. On June 13, 2002, a female was arrested in a Connecticut bank attempting her second cash advance of the day. She initially refused to provide her name to the police and was held in jail. In July 2002, Inspector Landisi assisted in the interview of the defendant, and she was identified. She also began to cooperate and identified her boyfriend only as Anwar. She admitted that she activated 20 to 30 credit cards using Anwar's cell phone. She did not know his full name but told the investigators that he drove a black Mercedes and received a speeding ticket that she paid for.

Inspector Landisi subpoenaed her credit union account and received the check she used to pay for the boyfriend's fine. The summons number was on the check; using it, Inspector Landisi obtained Anwar's full name and other identifying information as well as his DMV photo. Anwar's car was registered in Massachusetts and he had a listed home address there, but in reality he lived in Brooklyn, New York. Inspector Bernardo then obtained a search warrant for Anwar's apartment in Brooklyn and together with other inspectors and agents, executed the search on September 30, 2002. They arrested Anwar at the scene.

The apartment yielded a treasure trove of evidence including:

- Eight cell phones which were used to activate 57 stolen credit cards
- Counterfeit driver's licenses and resident alien identification cards corresponding to the stolen credit cards and checks

- Credit cards stolen from the mails and other sources
- Several stolen and forged credit card convenience checks
- A stolen checkbook
- Credit report headers and histories from unsuspecting victims
- Corporate invoices and checks still in their mailing envelopes

The inspectors also found a figurative smoking gun—a handwritten note—detailing how to commit identity theft. The note read:

*3 things needed for fraud:*

*1. State ID (Driv. License, Non-Driver ID, Permit)*
*2. Social Sec. Card*
*3. Copy of lease or utility bill*

While the inspectors were conducting the search in the apartment, three suspects unwittingly came to the door and were arrested. In their possession were two newly stolen corporate checks amounting to more than $160,000. As is often the case with fraudsters caught in the act, they quickly agreed to cooperate against their criminal associates. Anwar agreed to help the investigators and identified several accomplices who provided him stolen credit cards, checks, and fake IDs.

Postal Inspectors tracked down one of these suspects working with Anwar and arrested him. The suspect, Bennie, also quickly offered to cooperate against other fraudsters. He identified a major credit card and fake ID supplier for the ring by the name of Lucas. Lucas had operatives in Brooklyn and Staten Island who stole mail from mailboxes, focusing on credit cards, checks, and other financial information. Lucas also allegedly obtained stolen cards from insiders at postal facilities. He was well known to Postal Inspectors as someone they had previously arrested for mail theft in 1999 and sent to jail. Now out of prison, he was back at his old ways.

The inspectors used Bennie to make several undercover buys from Lucas, including stolen credit cards with corresponding phony IDs, handwritten lists of victim names, SSNs, birth dates, and other identifying information. Lucas was arrested in Brooklyn in July 2003. It was learned that he was mailing stolen credit cards to other states as well as overseas to be used by his associates. Lucas's cell phone records provided additional proof of his crimes and the extent of the fraud. The records revealed calls to numerous banks and credit card issuers to activate stolen cards.

The defendants employed social engineering in their calls with the call center to change the listed home telephone number for the call activation. To prevent fraud, credit card issuers typically require that a new card be activated from the true card holder's home phone. Customers can activate their new cards from other than a home phone, but to do so they have to provide additional verifying information. Knowing the ins and outs of the credit card business benefited the scammers, who easily manipulated the system.

The call center's focus is customer service. If a call center operator asked too many questions, fraudsters would say that they did not need all the hassles and were going to cancel the credit card. The call would then be referred to the Retention Department to save the customer account from cancellation. In many cases, this ploy worked, and the unwitting customer service representatives would approve the stolen cards for use. The defendants had stolen so many cards that even if one card was detected as being stolen, they had many more to use.

The fraudsters also had some inside help. The gang corrupted a Discover Card employee in Ohio who agreed to provide card holder information. He activated many of the cards for the gang and provided them with verification information so they could activate the accounts from their cell phones. The investigators had a turn of good luck that assisted the investigation. Law enforcement in Ohio arrested the corrupt Discover Card employee in June 2002. He agreed to cooperate in a sting operation to arrest one of the conspirators.

In the end, the ring involved dozens of people. The defendants were convicted and received sentences ranging from probation to five years in prison. More than $1.5 million in credit card losses were identified. Credit cards were stolen from suspected locations in New York, New Jersey, Virginia, Massachusetts, Connecticut, and elsewhere. Yet there were some unanswered questions. Inspectors knew many of the cards had been taken from postal facilities. but they could not identify any culpable employees. Unfortunately, credit card theft is addictive. Sooner or later, however, these thieves will be caught.

Like any successful investigation, the outcome was the result of good old-fashioned police work. Agents spent hundreds of hours manually reviewing telephone logs, credit reports, bank accounts, videos from banks where the defendants used the stolen cards, and other documents. The investigators tracked down every lead and interviewed dozens of bank and credit card representatives. They created a link analysis to connect the various defendants to each other and the many uses of the cards, and revealed the national and international aspects of the case. Link analysis is an investigative tool that links information to determine relationships and connections for investigative findings.

Other investigative tools included the effective interviewing of the defendants to obtain additional evidence, admissions of guilt, and eventual cooperation. The widespread use of technology was also a benefit to the investigators; cell phone records connected the fraudsters to the stolen cards via the activations and to each other. A key technique was the excellent interagency cooperation and sharing of information between the regional banks, credit card companies, Postal Inspectors in Boston, New York, and New Jersey, the Secret Service in Connecticut and New York, the New York Police Department, local police departments, and the United States Attorney's Offices in Connecticut, New York, and New Jersey. Cooperation between law enforcement and the financial services industry has always been critical for detecting and stopping identity theft.[8]

## OPERATION CATCHNET

The United States Postal Inspection Service was the driving force in creating and sponsoring the Financial Crimes Task Force covering the central Indiana area in March 2003. The task force consisted of federal, state, and local law enforcement whose goal was to reduce the impact of identity theft and related crimes in the greater Indianapolis area. The task force collected a variety of identity theft data from banks, retailers, other businesses, complainants, identity theft databases, and other sources. The task force focused on criminal activities that contributed to root causes of identity theft.

The task force found that Indiana Bureau of Motor Vehicles (BMV) identification documents were often used in the commission of identity theft crimes, especially in the Indianapolis area. It was decided that to do the most good in addressing the problem of phony driver's licenses and other BMV identification, an investigation and sting operation codenamed "Operation Catchnet" would be launched in November 2003. Numerous investigations were conducted by the Financial Crimes Task Force as a result.

One of the concerns that the task force had was that BMV employees might be compromised through bribery to provide driver's licenses to unauthorized individuals. The BMV agreed to be part of the task force cooperative effort to both clean house and arrest identity theft offenders through undercover operations. Law enforcement officers assumed undercover roles as BMV trainees to observe fraudulent documents presented by those wishing to obtain Indiana driver's licenses and identification cards. Social Security cards used as identification by suspects could be verified through telephonic contact with offsite task force members. At least one of the document reviewers included an officer with expertise in reviewing fraudulent immigration documents such as passports, visas, and Form I-94 (U.S. Customs and Border Protection nonimmigrant arrival/departure form).

Identification documents presented by customers were photocopied and hand-carried by BMV employees to a central location. Law enforcement personnel would examine the documents, determine if they were phony, and, if necessary, initiate immediate surveillance of the suspect(s). The internal document review team members rotated with the outside surveillance team. Radio contact was maintained among the internal document review team, the surveillance team, and the arrest team. Suspects were apprehended a distance away from the BMV branch so as not to arouse suspicion at the branch if other suspects were outside. In fact, it was found that other unsuspecting offenders continued their fraudulent activities with no idea that people were being arrested.

To determine how significant the document abuse problem was, approximately 20 transactions for new identification were examined at one BMV station over a six-hour period on November 20, 2003. Of the 20 transactions, eight fraudulent transactions were identified. Seven foreign nationals were arrested as a result. On November 24, 2003, three more foreign nationals were arrested. On December 11, 2003, seven additional foreign nationals were arrested for fraudulent document transactions at another BMV office. More than 70 transactions were examined at BMV sites resulting in seven arrests, or a 10% arrest ratio.

One of those arrested was found to be a leader of an identity theft ring operating in Indianapolis involved in over 200 fraudulent transactions in a two-year time span. A search of the defendant's residence revealed phony passports, $13,000 in cash, fraudulent tax ID cards, credit cards in many names, and classified internal BMV documentation. The BMV documents implicated several BMV employees in bribery schemes. This disclosure resulted in the arrests of four BMV employees.

In one investigation, five defendants were indicted by the United States Attorney's Office for the Southern District of Indiana for a fraudulent immigration document scheme. Between 2000 and 2003, the ringleaders assisted Chinese nationals, many of whom were in the United States illegally, in fraudulently acquiring driver's licenses and identification cards from the Indiana Bureau of Motor Vehicles. Knowing that the BMV had tightened security in the issuance of identification documents, the defendants obtained phony Social Security cards, fraudulent U.S. visas, I-94s, and foreign passports to assist in obtaining the licenses. They were charged with conspiracy to unlawfully produce identification documents, false use of passports, misuse of visas and other immigration documents, and fraud.

In a number of cases, identification documents were used in the commission of identity theft crimes. One case that was referred to the task force involved a suspect who committed $80,000 in identity theft with car loans. The subject used four fraudulently obtained BMV identifications for his scheme in various names. An investigation into the mailing of narcotics involved a foreign national who received a BMV identification card and was also in possession of an Ohio resident's SSN. The suspect assumed another identity and was involved in drug trafficking. He was arrested after receiving a controlled delivery of several pounds of marijuana.

An interesting development from this investigation illustrated that identity theft associated with the Indiana BMV documents did not always equate to economic crimes. Some of the people who obtained the phony documents did not use them for financial gain but so they could remain in the United States. Most of the fraudulently obtained documents, however, were used for identity theft–related crimes. Evidence was also developed that BMV employees took bribes to help the foreign nationals obtain fraudulent identification.

The United States Attorney for the Southern District of Indiana responded to the indictments of five of the defendants in Operation Catchnet by stating:

*A driver's license issued in the United States is one of the most valuable government documents produced. It provides freedom and opportunity to travel, to work, to open bank accounts, and to conduct other important activities of daily life. More importantly, a driver's license serves as a universal identification tool. State agencies rely on the validity of United States immigration documents and foreign passports, and the foundation for our identification system is put at grave risk when fraudulent documents are produced and used.*[9]

As of December 2003, as many as 12 separate identity theft gangs operated in the Indianapolis metropolitan area. Multiply that by the thousands of cities and towns in the United States, and one can easily see that identity theft is much more than just a problem, it is an epidemic. Investigation continued over the next few months resulting in additional arrests in Indiana. The publicity from the undercover operation and subsequent arrests caught the attention of potential fraudsters worldwide. A Zimbabwe Internet chat room posted warnings that those using illegal documents for identification purposes to gain residence in the United States should avoid Indiana.

The Indiana BMV used Operation Catchnet to upgrade its prevention and detection program to lessen document fraud. It instituted a new double-check procedure whereby individuals submitting documents from U.S. Customs and Border Protection will be issued a temporary 60-day driver's permit while the BMV checks the validity of the documents for a driver's license. The temporary permit cannot be used for identification purposes. In another recommendation to combat corruption and criminality, more intensive background investigations of BMV employees was considered as a best practice.

The work of the Postal Inspection Service and the Central Indiana Financial Crimes Task Force was so successful that it was recognized as a 2004 Webber Seavey Award semifinalist. The Webber Seavey Award for Quality in Law Enforcement is presented annually to law enforcement agencies and departments worldwide in recognition of their work in promoting a standard of excellence in protecting the quality of life in the communities served. The award is jointly sponsored by the International Association of Chiefs of Police and Motorola.

## MAJOR FRAUDULENT DOCUMENT MANUFACTURING RING

In December 1994, Postal Inspectors and Immigration and Naturalization Service (INS) agents dismantled a major counterfeiting ring responsible for the manufacture and distribution of fraudulent Alien Registration and Social Security cards in Southern California. The investigators seized 115,000 counterfeit INS and Social Security documents with an estimated street value of $5.75 million. These phony identification documents could have been used for a variety of identity theft crimes. Also seized were high-speed printers, photo enlargers, negatives, and metal plates of counterfeit "Green Cards" and Social Security cards. Los Angeles Postal Inspector Ralph Perez was the case agent in one of the largest seizures of phony documents.

## USING IDENTITIES OF THE DEAD

On November 13, 1999, Gregory Revson, posing as Edward Cantor, entered a Pontiac GMC car dealership in Pembroke Pines, Florida, and purchased a new 1999 Chevrolet Suburban for $32,000. He presented a Florida driver's license in the name of Cantor but with his own photograph. Revson paid for the car with a car loan check drawn on an account in Cantor's name at Peoples First Community Bank. Social Security Administration records determined that Cantor died in October 1999. Peoples First Bank advised that a loan application in the name of Cantor was received via an Internet application on November 10, 1999. The home address listed was that of the deceased man. The mailing address listed was that of a post office box in Hollywood, Florida and that is where the loan check was mailed. In June 1999, Revson opened another post office box in the name of Ralph Alfonso at the same Hollywood, Florida, post office. Revson presented a Florida driver's license in the name of Alfonso as identification to open the box. Investigation determined that Alfonso had been incarcerated in a Florida prison since March 1999.

Following an investigation by the Postal Inspection Service, Revson was arrested on September 19, 2001. A search of his apartment yielded voluminous fraudulent documents and other evidence of identity theft. Included were seven birth and 20 death certificates from Florida, New York, New Jersey, Michigan, Pennsylvania, and Vermont, phony driver's licenses in 20 different names, 18 fraudulently obtained credit cards in nine different names, and other evidence. During his interview by law enforcement, Revson admitted his involvement in identity theft. He also told the investigators that they would find additional evidence in his computer files. Internal Revenue Service criminal investigators later arrested Revson for filing false federal income tax returns in the names of other people and receiving the tax refunds. On October 25, 2002, Revson was sentenced to five years in prison for his crimes.[10]

---

## IDENTITY THEFT HALL OF INFAMY

### Richard Joseph Tagliamonte

Some fraudsters have such larceny in their hearts that when they come across an astoundingly wicked scheme, they embrace it and never let go. That was the case of Richard Joseph Tagliamonte, a career grifter who fleeced victims with identity theft for much of his life. Tagliamonte had a long history of stealing other people's identities, reaching back long before it was ever called identity theft. He started his criminal activities as a teenager in the 1960s and continued over the years until he was finally sent to prison for a very long time in 2007 at the age of 57. Thus, Tagliamonte is well suited for membership in the Identity Theft Hall of Infamy.

Tagliamonte was first arrested in 1968 by the New York Police Department for grand larceny and burglary, but it was his second arrest, a year later when he was 19, that got him started as an identity thief. Tagliamonte was arrested by the Manhattan District Attorney's Office on February 5, 1969, for falsely claiming to be R. Hartford Duke, a fabricated relative of supermarket heir Huntington Hartford and tobacco heiress Doris Duke. Using a method Tagliamonte would repeat more than 30 years later, he showed up at the New York offices of game show producer Goodson-Todman. The people in the office took a liking to the affable, clean-cut young man, and before long he was doing all sorts of odd jobs for the staff. They had no way of knowing that he was not who he claimed to be.

He made sure to let everyone know that he was related to the Hartford and Duke families, although it was a lie. Presumably the belief that Tagliamonte was somehow related to these exceedingly rich and powerful people helped curry favor with the employees. Of course, his intent was more than just being an errand boy. He soon got access to blank checks imprinted with the names of the company owners, Mark Goodson and William Todman. Tagliamonte "forged 24 checks, ranging from $6 to $2,500 and totaling $6789.37."[11] He also stole $3,000 from a dormant bank account of the real Huntington Hartford. It was believed that

*(Continued)*

Tagliamonte was able to accomplish this because he found a lost bank book belonging to the real Hartford. Of note, Tagliamonte was a "Dapper Dan" even then. At his arraignment on the criminal charges in February 1969, he was well dressed for someone his age, with a cashmere overcoat and Italian-style shoes.[12]

Like many scam artists, Tagliamonte found it hard to stay away from a life of crime. Fraud becomes a part of their lives, and they just cannot stop victimizing the naive and unprotected. Tagliamonte was in and out of trouble and jail over the next 25 years. He had several arrests in the 1970s for various crimes, including possession of a forged instrument, forgery, grand larceny, wire fraud, and criminal impersonation. In 1979, he was sentenced to seven years in prison for involvement with drugs and stealing prescription pads. He was arrested in 1991 for mail fraud, in 1993 for credit card fraud, and again he went to jail. Even after he got out, he conducted another scheme and was returned to prison. By 2000, he had spent a significant part of his adult life behind bars.[13]

November 2000 was a turning point for Tagliamonte. At that time, a well-dressed and silver-tongued Tagliamonte appeared at the door of a nunnery in Brewster, New York. The Community of the Holy Spirit operated by Episcopal nuns would become both his sanctuary and base of criminal operations. He identified himself as Richard Maldonado and boasted about all the important people he knew. He presented a letter of introduction from a high-level official at Saint Patrick's Cathedral in New York City and quickly talked his way into the confidence and hearts of the sisters. Just as he had done 30 years earlier at Goodson-Todman Productions, he did odd jobs around the nunnery, always with a smile and a pleasant word. But he also installed two telephone lines that he intended to use to victimize the rich and famous.[14]

Over the next few years, Tagliamonte defrauded jeweler Tiffany & Company, upscale department store Neiman Marcus, electronics manufacturer Toshiba, as well as banks and credit card companies, by obtaining credit lines that he criminally used. He hijacked the identity of a company once owned by the late Greek shipping magnate Aristotle Onassis and used it as his own. He tried to defraud BF Goodrich out of $325,000 by doctoring a consulting contract, putting the chief executive's name on it, and sending it to accounts payable at BF Goodrich. He defrauded the Greentree Foundation out of $35,000 by opening up a line of credit at computer manufacturer Hewlett-Packard. Greentree is a foundation set up by the widow of John Hay Whitney, the banker, diplomat, and investor. Using the line of credit, Tagliamonte had Toshiba ship him almost $15,000 in computer equipment in the name of Organon International, a pharmaceutical company. Organon is formerly the U.S. subsidiary of Akzo Nobel, a Fortune 500 company based out of the Netherlands. Organon has now been acquired by Schering-Plough.

Tagliamonte always wanted to be someone he was not. He desired fame and fortune, and while he had neither, he always portrayed himself as upper crust. In 2002, he thought he finally found his way to wealth but instead gained notoriety and a ticket to the Identity Theft Hall of Infamy. For in 2002, *Forbes* published its annual list of the 400 richest Americans. One of those profiled was Texas oil and gas billionaire Sid Richardson Bass. Tagliamonte read this issue of the magazine and saw his mark in the person of Bass.

Another identity thief profiled in this book as a charter member of the Identity Theft Hall of Infamy, Abraham Abdallah, also saw this very same issue of *Forbes* magazine. He was in Brooklyn, just across the river from Tagliamonte, and he too went on a fraud spree using the stolen identities of the richest Americans. Abdallah made front-page headlines in the *New York Post* and in newspapers across the world with the identity theft he perpetrated on the rich and famous.

Around the same time as the publication of the *Forbes* article, Tagliamonte became friendly with a loan consultant in Union City, New Jersey. She had access to credit information, and Tagliamonte gave her a story as to why he needed credit checks on several people, including Bass. She fell for his gift of gab and ran the reports. Using Bass's personal information, Tagliamonte obtained credit cards in Bass's name and set up a fictitious company named Bass Capital Holdings, Inc. He created phony identification, including a Texas driver's license in Bass's name. Using social engineering and deceit, he obtained checking account and other business and personal information about Bass and his many companies.

Tagliamonte used the fraudulently obtained credit cards in Bass's name and also tried to pass counterfeit checks drawn on Bass's checking account. Tagliamonte also got more than 20 credit cards in the names of other people. He had the names and addresses of the Who's Who of New York, from Donald Trump and Regis Philbin to Michael Bloomberg and Yoko Ono, and many, many others. It is amazing how much information is available today on everyone, but even more on people in the public eye. Whether it is a *Forbes* magazine article or any number of Internet searches, there is a world of information that can be found and fraudulently used.

Tagliamonte had two mail drop addresses, one in New York City and another one in New Jersey. The New Jersey address was a vacant home where he had the checks and credit cards sent. He eventually moved from the nunnery in upstate New York to the nuns' New York City location. Subsequently, he moved to a hotel in the city. To get a reduced room rate, he falsely claimed that he had lost his apartment due to the World Trade Center attack.[15] This was a despicable thing to do. Fraudsters have no conscience when it comes to doing something that benefits them. Later, he moved to an apartment in Union City, New Jersey, that became his new base of operations.

Tagliamonte was finally tripped up because of a parking ticket he received. He paid the ticket with a fraudulent Bass credit card, and Postal Inspectors used that to track him down in New Jersey. Inspector Walley Wang scoured the streets of Union City and Weehawken, New Jersey, until he finally located the car, a Chevy Malibu rental in Bass's name. Inspector Wang set up a surveillance of the car and

*(Continued)*

on January 14, 2004, the trap was sprung. As Tagliamonte was getting into the car, the Postal Inspectors approached him and asked his name. Hoping that one more big lie would work, he gave the name of Sid Bass. When that did not fly, he gave the name of Richard Munoz. With time running out, he then gave the name of Emilio Negron. Finally, Tagliamonte knew the game was over and he was going to jail again.

Postal Inspectors then searched Tagliamonte's apartment. In it they found a wealth of evidence. Phony identification and financial records were everywhere. Birth certificates, Social Security cards, driver's licenses, credit reports, boxes of counterfeit checks, cash, designer clothes, and of course numerous unauthorized credit cards in many different names including Sid Richardson Bass were found in the apartment. Also found was a pad with detailed notes on the many identity theft schemes he committed. Of special note, the investigators also found the *Forbes* magazine profile of Bass and the other richest Americans. Inspector Wang believed that Tagliamonte kept copious notes and all the other incriminating evidence because he was proud of his crimes and that he thought he was too smart to get caught.

Tagliamonte was indicted on October 5, 2004, on a variety of identity theft and other related charges and held in jail until his trial in early 2007. The evidence against him was overwhelming. On February 6, 2007, he was convicted by a jury on charges of identity theft, credit card fraud, mail and wire fraud, and possession of counterfeit checks. The amount of the fraud was almost $1 million in actual and intended losses. On October 24, 2007, he was sentenced to 15 years in prison for his crimes. He was also given a fine and court-ordered restitution.

This was one of the longest prison sentences ever given for identity theft and related crimes. The federal judge who sentenced Tagliamonte almost doubled the recommended sentence and stated that a longer sentence was needed to protect the public from Tagliamonte and prevent him from committing further crimes. The judge referred to him as a "liar" and a "fraud."[16] "This is a long and well-deserved sentence," said the United States Attorney for New Jersey. "Tagliamonte was cunning in his ability to defraud and is clearly someone for whom prison is the only deterrent."[17]

The Postal Inspection Service concurred. "The hard work of our Postal Inspectors paid off. We are gratified to help put this crook behind bars. He ruined the lives of innocent victims and cost legitimate and respected businesses thousands of dollars," said Newark Division Postal Inspector in Charge David Collins.[18] Inspector Collins had much more than a passing interest in a career criminal that his office had arrested and sent to prison. For the irony here was that some 15 years earlier, Collins had arrested Tagliamonte for victimizing a wealthy woman who lived on the Upper East Side of Manhattan in another identity theft and check fraud scheme.

However, the comments of the investigator who spent several years tracking Tagliamonte down and then putting him behind bars are most telling. Inspector Wang stated:

*Tagliamonte was indiscriminate in his selection of victims. He picked on everyone from a billionaire to small business owners, and everyone in between. As long as you had good credit you were a target. He was as good as it gets as an identity thief in my opinion. Tagliamonte used his intelligence and charm to disarm people and use them for his own personal gain. Whether you were a victim or a friend, he always knew what each person was going to offer and how he was going to exploit it for his benefit. As technology advanced, it improved his ability to find information and then use it to defraud individuals and companies. He passed himself off as a trust fund baby but in reality he was living one step away from homelessness. He was a self-described charming, intelligent, funny, and cunning individual who thought of himself as an upper crust individual when in fact he was a two-bit con man.*[19]

Although Tagliamonte would spend most of his remaining years in prison, he may have had the last laugh as he knew that that his imprisonment would not stop the spread and impact of identity theft. During an interview with a reporter, he claimed that the particular crimes he was convicted of were just the "tip of the iceberg" of identity theft. "The average ordinary Joe on the street would be terrified if they knew how extraordinarily vulnerable they are," he said.[20]

## NOTES

1. United States Department of Justice, *The Criminal Use of False Identification: The Report of the Federal Advisory Committee on False Identification* (November 1976), 8.
2. Ibid., 12.
3. Ibid., 13.
4. Anna Gorman, "California: Fake ID Trade Makes a Name for Itself," *Los Angeles Times*, November 30, 2005, accessed via www.officer.com/web/online/Top-News-Stories/California–Fake-ID-Trade-Makes-a-Name-for-Itself/1$27166.
5. Opening Statement of Senator Susan M. Collins, Chairman, Permanent Sub-committee on Investigations, "Phony IDs and Credentials Via the Internet—An Emerging Problem," May 19, 2000, http://hsgac.senate.gov/051900_coillins.htm.
6. Ibid.
7. U.S. Department of Justice, Office of the United States Attorney, Central District of California, News Release, "Eight Charged in Relation to Fake IDs Sold on the Internet," December 20, 2002, www.usdoj.gov/criminal/cybercrime/mclellan Indict.htm.
8. Postal Inspectors Don Landisi and Patrick Bernardo provided the author with investigative details and comments that were included in this section.
9. United States Attorney's Office, Southern District of Indiana, Press Release, "Elizabeth Lang and Four Others Federally Indicted for Fraudulent Immigration Document Scheme," June 24, 2004.
10. Postal Inspector Jack Galvin's comments to the author, November 13, 2007.

11. Morris Kaplan, "Youth Using Alias Seized in Forgery," *New York Times*, February 6, 1969, select.nytimes.com/gst/abstract.html?res=F30D11FD35541B7B93C4A91 789 D85F4D8685F9.
12. Ibid.
13. Jeff Whelan, "The Con Man and the Convent: A Convoluted Tale," *Star Ledger* (Newark), November 11, 2007, www.nj.com/news/ledger/jersey/index.ssf?/base/news-8/119330229526.
14. Ibid.
15. Ibid.
16. United States Attorney's Office, District of New Jersey, Press Release, "Union City Man Sentenced to 15 Years for Identity Theft and Credit Card Frauds," October 24, 2007, www.usdoj.gov/usao/nj/press/files/pdffiles/tagl1024rel.pdf.
17. Ibid.
18. "Con Man Uses Nunnery as Home Base, Lands in Jail," *Postal Inspection Service News* 2, no. 1 (January 2008), 6.
19. Postal Inspector Walley Wang's comments to the author, February 13, 2008.
20. Jeff Whelan, "The Con Man and the Convent."

# CHAPTER 10

# Legislation and Criminal Statutes

In speeches, testimony, and the media, we continually hear about the need for tougher laws to combat identity theft. The fact is that a number of excellent federal statutes and acts have been in existence for many years. Both new legislation and enhanced versions of prior laws are always being enacted to add to the arsenal of government weapons. Statutes, or laws, are passed by legislatures or, in the case of federal statutes, by the United States Congress. These statutes include the old stalwarts of mail fraud, wire fraud, unauthorized use of a Social Security number (SSN), and access device fraud as well the newer aggravated identity theft statute. The states have also taken action by passing identity theft statutes mimicking federal criminal laws. The United States Congress has enacted legislation covering consumer credit, healthcare accounts, privacy, identification documents, money laundering, terrorism, and other important individual and business issues. All of these issues are impacted by identity theft, and these legislative acts and criminal statutes are intended to provide greater protections to individuals and businesses.

A detailed summary of the significant federal criminal statutes and legislative acts related to the prevention and prosecution of identity theft–related crimes as well as protections afforded consumers and businesses follows.

## CRIMINAL STATUTES

### Mail Fraud

The Mail Fraud Statute is America's oldest federal fraud statute. Enacted in 1872, it has been used to protect the public from every imaginable fraud and scam, including credit card fraud and identity theft. It defines fraud as "any scheme or artifice to defraud, or for obtaining money or property by means of false or fraudulent pretenses, representations, or promises."[1] The word "artifice" was included in the original statute, meaning "trickery or guile," both of which are very descriptive of fraud. There are two important elements of mail fraud: fraud or attempted fraud *and* the use of the United States Mail or other private or commercial interstate carrier in furtherance of the fraud.

The Mail Fraud Statute reads:

*Whoever, having devised or intending to devise any scheme or artifice to defraud, or for obtaining money or property by means of false or fraudulent pretenses, representations, or promises, or to sell, dispose of, loan, exchange, alter, give away, distribute, supply, or furnish or procure for unlawful use any counterfeit or spurious coin, obligation, security, or other article, or anything represented to be or intimated or held out to be such counterfeit or spurious article, for the purpose of executing such scheme or artifice or attempting so to do, places in any post office or authorized depository for mail matter, any matter or thing whatever to be sent or delivered by the Postal Service, or deposits or causes to be deposited any matter or thing whatever to be sent or delivered by any private or commercial interstate carrier, or takes or receives therefrom, any such matter or thing, or knowingly causes to be delivered by mail or such carrier according to the direction thereon, or at the place at which it is directed to be delivered by the person to whom it is addressed, any such matter or thing, shall be fined under this title or imprisoned not more than 20 years, or both. If the violation affects a financial institution, such person shall be fined not more than $1,000,000 or imprisoned not more than 30 years, or both.[2]*

The statute has been effective in prosecuting fraudsters who steal personal information, complete fraudulent credit card applications using that stolen information, and then mail the completed applications to banks and credit card issuers. From the early days of fraudulent credit card applications, the Mail Fraud Statute was and has been used as a weapon of choice in punishing criminals who steal the identities of others for financial gain. The statute is also used for other related identity theft crimes where the mail is an essential element in facilitating the fraud.

### *Maze* Decision

Something happened in 1974 that changed the way credit card fraud cases were prosecuted. At the time, many of the cases involved the theft of credit cards by pickpockets and prostitutes who obtained the cards directly from the victims. The government based federal Mail Fraud Statute prosecutions on normal business mailings, including the mailing of credit card statements to the victim card holders. These statements detailed the unauthorized charges made by fraudsters.

These thefts had nothing to do with the U.S. Mails. The Mail Fraud Statute requires that both elements be present: (1) a scheme to defraud and (2) the use of the mails in furtherance of that scheme. The government's theory for use of the mail was based on "the passage of the sales slips by mail to the issuing agency and thence to the card holder, and the delay inherent in this procedure which permitted the fraud to remain undetected for a period of time, as a use of the mails in the continuation and therefore the furtherance of the scheme to defraud."[3] Unfortunately, they were legally wrong.

Eventually, convicted defendants argued that the use of the Mail Fraud Statute was inappropriate and legally wrong in these types of cases. In the landmark case of *United States v. Maze*, the Supreme Court ruled on January 8, 1974, that a credit card mailing must be directly linked to the fraudulent scheme in order to be a chargeable offense. As a result, these cases were no longer prosecuted with the Mail Fraud Statute. In reality, the *Maze* decision was of little consequence, as credit card fraud was evolving and about to take on far more dire manifestations. Law enforcement would look back on these simple credit thefts as the "good ole days" and wish that was the extent of the problem. But it was not to be.

*Maze* examined whether a mailing that the defendant knowingly "caused" was sufficiently related to the underlying fraud to fall within the mail fraud statute. The defendant in *Maze* took his roommate's credit card and car without permission and went on an extended trip. He used the card and signed the roommate's name to charge food and lodging. Therein was the fraud. Each merchant who furnished goods and services to the defendant mailed the invoice to a bank in Louisville, Kentucky, forming the basis for the mail fraud counts. The subsequent federal indictment charged four counts of mail fraud and one count of transporting a stolen car across state lines.[4]

However, the court rejected the argument that the mailings were designed to permit the scheme to continue and that the defendant's "scheme reached fruition when he checked out of the motel and there is no indication that the success of his scheme depended in any way on which of his victims ultimately bore the loss." The court stated that mailing the invoices to Kentucky was not meant to "lull" the victims in any way as distinguished from mailings in other cases.[5]

Chief Justice Warren Burger, commenting on the *Maze* decision, said the Mail Fraud Statute was a "stopgap device to deal on a temporary basis with the new phenomenon [referring to credit card fraud] until particularized legislation can be developed and passed to deal directly with this evil."[6] As a result of the *Maze* decision, Congress enacted Title 15, United States Code, Section 1644, Interstate Transportation and Use of a Credit Card in a Fraudulent Manner. Years later, Congress enacted Title 18, United States Code, Section 1029, Access Device Fraud, to use in prosecuting credit card fraud, and identity theft by inference. Subsequently, Title 18, United States Code, Section 1028(a)(7), a separate criminal statute, was enacted. It is interesting to note that then Chief Justice Burger recognized credit card fraud, and the yet to be named but related identity theft, as "this evil."

## Wire Fraud

In 1952, federal law enforcement gained a new tool to fight fraud with the enactment of the Wire Fraud Statute. It is the sister statute to the Mail Fraud Statute, after which it was patterned. Wire fraud covers the use of interstate wire, radio, or telephone communications for the purpose of executing a scheme or artifice to defraud, or obtaining money or property by means of false or fraudulent pretenses, representations, or promises. The penalty for wire fraud is a fine or imprisonment of not more than 20 years, or both. If the violation affects a financial institution, the defendant shall be fined not more than $1 million or imprisoned not more than 30 years, or both.[7]

The Wire Fraud Statute has been used in conjunction with the Mail Fraud Statute when prosecuting fraudsters, since telephone conversations and interstate wire communications, including Internet and email usage, often serve to further fraud schemes. It is important to note that the statute requires that wire communications must be *interstate* rather than *intrastate* in order to charge the statute in a prosecution. That is usually not a problem as so much commerce is done both interstate and internationally. For example, if a fraudster located in California calls a financial institution in New York and uses the identity of an account holder to order unauthorized credit cards or request a credit increase, wire fraud could be charged along with other crimes.

## Bank Fraud

Bank fraud is a federal criminal violation that occurs when a person knowingly executes, or attempts to execute, a scheme or artifice to defraud a financial institution, or to obtain any of the monies, funds, credits, assets, securities, or other property owned by, or under the control of, a financial institution, by means of false or fraudulent pretenses, representations, or promises. The penalties for bank fraud include a fine of not more than $1 million or imprisonment of not more than 30 years, or both.[8]

The Bank Fraud Statute was enacted in 1984 and is similar in wording to both the Mail and Wire Fraud statutes without the requirement for use of the mails or interstate wire communications. The statute was enacted to modernize older federal banking statutes for better prosecution of financial crimes. In applying the statute, the government must show that the victim of the fraud is a financial institution. The perpetrators can be bank insiders, customers, or other third parties.

The Bank Fraud Statute is used for a variety of financial crimes including fraudulent credit and loan applications, check kiting, check forgery, credit card fraud, automatic teller machine (ATM) fraud, and other related offenses. Identity thieves will often use stolen personal information to open credit card accounts and apply for loans under fraudulent pretenses.

## False Statements in Loan and Credit Application

False Statements in Loan and Credit Applications is the federal statute that applies to making false statements to financial institutions on loan and credit applications. The statute reads: "Whoever knowingly makes any false statement or report, or willfully overvalues any land, property, or security, for the purpose of influencing in any way the action of a financial institution, shall be fined not more than $1,000,000 or imprisoned not more 30 years, or both."[9] This statute has also been used to prosecute identity thieves who submit fraudulent credit card and loan applications to financial institutions.

## Mail Theft

Mail theft is often the source of personal and financial information used for identity theft. Several federal statutes apply to the theft of mail, both by postal employees and by those external to the postal system. Title 18, United States Code, Section 1708, Theft or Receipt of Stolen Mail Matter Generally, is used to prosecute external parties who steal or possess stolen mail of any kind from mailboxes, collection boxes, postal vehicles, carrier carts, or other authorized mail receptacles or depositories. Title 18, United States Code, Section 1709, the Theft of Mail Matter by an Officer or Employee, is used to prosecute United States Postal Service employees who steal or possess stolen mail. The penalty for both statutes is a fine or imprisonment of not more than five years, or both.

## Misuse of a Social Security Number

Misuse of a Social Security Number is used to prosecute individuals for the fraudulent use of an SSN. The statute reads:

> *Whoever, for the purpose of obtaining (for himself or any other person) any payment or any other benefit to which he (or such other person) is not entitled, or for the purpose of obtaining anything of value from any person, or for any other purpose, with intent to deceive, falsely represents a number to be the social security account number assigned by the Commissioner of Social Security to him or to another person, when in fact such number is not the social security account number assigned by the Commissioner of Social Security to him or to such other person, shall be guilty of a felony and upon conviction thereof shall be fined or imprisoned for not more than five years, or both.[10]*

## Student Loan Fraud

Student Loan Fraud is used to prosecute student loan fraud, including the use of stolen identity information to apply for and receive such loans. The statute reads:

> *[A]ny person who knowingly and willfully makes any false statement, furnishes any false information, or conceals any material information in connection with the assignment of a loan which is made or insured, or attempts to so make any false statement, furnish any false information, or conceal any material information in connection with such assignment shall, upon conviction thereof, be fined not more than $10,000 or imprisoned for not more than one year, or both.[11]*

The statute also covers attempted student loan fraud, where the defendant submitted a fraudulent student loan application but was not successful in receiving any funds.

## Conspiracy

Conspiracy to Commit an Offense or to Defraud the United States is a very useful statute when two or more defendants are involved in federal crimes. The statute reads:

> *If two or more persons conspire either to commit any offense against the United States, or to defraud the United States, or any agency thereof in any manner or for any purpose, and one*

*or more of such persons do any act to effect the object of the conspiracy, each shall be fined under this title or imprisoned not more than five years, or both. If, however, the offense, the commission of which is the object of the conspiracy, is a misdemeanor only, the punishment for such conspiracy shall not exceed the maximum punishment provided for such misdemeanor.*[12]

Conspiracy can be used with any of the above-mentioned statutes or any other applicable statute.

## Access Device Fraud

The striking growth of identity theft and credit card fraud in the early 1980s caused Congress to focus on the need for improved legislation. As a result, several new statutes were enacted. The Credit Card Fraud Act of 1984 added access device fraud provisions as part of the Comprehensive Crime Control Act of 1984. Title 18, United States Code, Section 1029, Access Device Fraud, expanded the older, limited provisions of Title 15, United States Code, Section 1644 (Fraudulent Use of Credit Cards). The new statute broadened the existing definitions of credit card and debit instruments to include access devices, including account numbers, as well as increasing maximum penalties for fines and imprisonment, and providing significant repeat-offender penalties.[13]

Congress enacted this legislation to provide federal prosecutors broad jurisdiction to prosecute a variety of credit card fraud schemes.

> *Congress intended that Federal prosecutions for the use of "unauthorized access devices" be directed particularly to activity involving a criminal or an organized crime ring that traffics in fraudulent access devices. Situations in which a valid card owner knowingly uses an expired or revoked card should remain under the jurisdiction of state and local authorities or be handled through the civil actions available to the credit card companies.*[14]

Title 18, United States Code, Section 1029 is formally designated as Fraud and Related Activity in Connection with Access Devices but is commonly called the Credit Card Statute. It applies to a variety of crimes involving access devices. The term "access device" means any card, plate, code, account number, electronic serial number, mobile identification number, personal identification number, or other telecommunications service, equipment, or instrument identifier, or other means of account access that can be used, alone or in conjunction with another access device, to obtain money, goods, services, or any other thing of value, or that can be used to initiate a transfer of funds (other than a transfer originated solely by paper instrument).[15] Access devices can include "debit cards, automated teller machine (ATM) cards, computer passwords, personal identification numbers, credit card or debit card account numbers, long-distance access codes, and the Subscriber Identity Module (SIM) contained within cellular telephones that assign billing."[16]

## Fraud and Related Activity in Connection with Computers

The Counterfeit Access Device and Computer Fraud and Abuse Act was enacted on October 12, 1984. It was the first federal legislation to address computer fraud and abuse.

Computer crime has grown tremendously since the 1980s and is an element in many identity theft schemes. As part of the act, the criminal statute of Fraud and Related Activity in Connection with Computers was created. Over the years, this statute was enhanced and broadened in scope to criminalize seven different types of computer abuse as well as to allow for civil actions arising out of computer crime. Although Congress has enacted other criminal statutes related to computers, this is the one most often used by federal prosecutors in prosecuting computer crime.

The statute reads in part:

*Whoever intentionally accesses a computer without authorization or exceeds authorized access, and thereby obtains information contained in a financial record of a financial institution, or of a card issuer, or contained in a file of a consumer reporting agency on a consumer, as defined in the Fair Credit Reporting Act; or information from any department or agency of the United States; or information from any protected computer if the conduct involved an interstate or foreign communication. Penalties for violations of this statute include fines and imprisonment from five years to life. The extreme penalty of life imprisonment applies if the offender knowingly or recklessly causes or attempts to cause death from violations of this statute.*[17]

## Identity Theft

Title 18, United States Code, Section 1028 is officially called Fraud and Related Activity in Connection with Identification Documents, Authentication Features, and Information but is commonly called the Identity Theft Statute. The various elements of the statute read:

*Whoever . . .*

1. *knowingly and without lawful authority produces an identification document, authentication feature, or a false identification document; or*

2. *knowingly transfers an identification document, authentication feature, or a false identification document knowing that such document or feature was stolen or produced without lawful authority; or*

3. *knowingly possesses with intent to use unlawfully or transfer unlawfully five or more identification documents (other than those issued lawfully for the use of the possessor), authentication features, or false identification documents; or*

4. *knowingly possesses an identification document (other than one issued lawfully for the use of the possessor), authentication feature, or a false identification document, with the intent such document or feature be used to defraud the United States; or*

5. *knowingly produces, transfers, or possesses a document-making implement or authentication feature with the intent such document-making implement or authentication feature will be used in the production of a false identification document or another document-making implement or authentication feature which will be so used; or*

6. *knowingly possesses an identification document or authentication feature that is or appears to be an identification document or authentication feature of the United States which is stolen or produced without lawful authority knowing that such document or feature was stolen or produced without such authority; or*

7. *knowingly transfers, possesses, or uses, without lawful authority, a means of identification of another person with the intent to commit, or to aid or abet, or in connection with, any unlawful activity that constitutes a violation of Federal law, or that constitutes a felony under any applicable State or local law; or*

8. *knowingly traffics in false or actual authentication features for use in false identification documents, document-making implements, or means of identification; shall be punished as provided in subsection (b) of this section [next paragraph].*

Penalties include fines and imprisonment for up to 20 years. If the crime is committed to facilitate an act of domestic or international terrorism, imprisonment can be as much as 30 years.[18]

## Aggravated Identity Theft

Aggravated Identity Theft is codified in Title 18, United States Code, Section 1028A, and reads:

> *Whoever, during and in relation to any felony violation enumerated in subsection (c), knowingly transfers, possesses, or uses, without lawful authority, a means of identification of another person (including name, date of birth, Social Security number, driver's license, employer or taxpayer identification number, electronic identification number or access device of any kind) shall, in addition to the punishment provided for such felony, be sentenced to a term of imprisonment of two years.[19]*

The mandatory two-year prison term is consecutive to any other imprisonment imposed. The predicate felonies used for enhancement include theft of public money, embezzlement, mail fraud, wire fraud, bank fraud, passport and visa fraud, immigration offenses, and Social Security fraud and false statements. Predicate felonies are those crimes that are committed in conjunction with the instant offense of identity theft.

## LEGISLATIVE ACTS

### Fair Credit Reporting Act

Congress enacted the Fair Credit Reporting Act (FCRA) in 1970, and it has undergone a number of amendments over the years. The FCRA ensures the privacy of information in consumer credit reports and protects consumers from the disclosure of inaccurate information maintained by credit reporting agencies. The FCRA limits the uses for consumer reports and provides both access to these reports by consumers and the ability to correct mistakes that are discovered. There are restrictions on businesses that provide information about consumers to credit reporting agencies and those that use this information. The FCRA covers organizations that collect consumer reports and those that use consumer reports, especially for employment purposes.

The FCRA does not limit the amount or type of information that can be collected, but consumer reporting agencies must disclose personal information to third parties only under certain circumstances. Generally, consumer information may be released only with the written consent of the subject of the consumer credit report. Consumer credit reports may include information on creditworthiness, credit standing, credit capacity, character, general reputation, personal characteristics, or mode of living of consumers. The conditions for release and use include employment, credit or insurance determinations, licensing, government benefits, or other appropriate "legitimate business need." The FCRA was amended by the Fair and Accurate Credit Transaction Act in 2003 and is discussed in a section with that name later in the chapter.

## Fair Credit Billing Act

The Fair Credit Billing Act (FCBA) was enacted in 1974 and amended 1968's Truth in Lending Act. This legislation protects consumers from unfair billing practices and establishes procedures for resolving errors on credit accounts, including credit cards and other revolving charge accounts. It does not cover installment contracts, such as loans or credit extensions paid on a fixed repayment schedule. The FCBA covers billing errors and those errors resulting from fraudulent charges made on consumers' credit accounts. This act limits the liability for unauthorized credit card charges to no more than $50 per card for credit card account holders. Although this fraud protection was legislated, in actuality many credit card issuers generally do not hold victimized account holders responsible for any amount of fraudulent charges.

Under the FCBA, consumers have the right to dispute billing errors through a settlement process. These types of billing disputes are covered:

- Unauthorized charges
- Charges that list wrong dates or amounts
- Charges for goods and services that were not received or delivered as agreed
- Errors in math
- Failure to post payments and credits, such as returns
- Failure to send bills to a current address of the consumer
- Charges for which the consumer has requested an explanation or clarification[20]

Upon discovery of a billing dispute, consumers should immediately send a certified letter to the merchant or organization detailing the complaint in writing. The complaint letter should be sent as soon as possible after the error is noticed. Credit card companies and other service providers often have time limits under which to file a dispute so be aware of these deadlines. Keep copies of everything that is submitted, and never send original documents. Make sure to follow-up with a telephone call and additional letters if you do not receive a timely response. FCBA violations including fraudulent, deceptive, and unfair business practices can be reported to the Federal Trade Commission (FTC). Contact the FTC at 1-877-FTC-HELP or at www.ftc.gov/sentinel.

## Privacy Act of 1974

The Privacy Act of 1974 was enacted after revelations of government intrusion into citizens' private lives by the administration of President Richard Nixon. It limits the collection of personal information by government agencies and prohibits secret government files with certain limitations as described. The act states:

*No agency shall disclose any record which is contained in a system of records by any means of communication to any person, or to another agency, except pursuant to a written request by, or with the prior written consent of, the individual to whom the record pertains, unless disclosure of the record would be for various, lawful government purposes.*

The exceptions allowing for use of personal records include:

- Use by the Bureau of the Census for statistical research or planning and carrying out a census or survey
- Routine use by a government agency
- Use by the National Archives and Records Administration as a record which has sufficient historical or other value to warrant its continued preservation by the government
- For civil or criminal law enforcement purposes
- To protect the health or safety of an individual
- For congressional investigations and other administrative purposes[21]

The Privacy Act requires that each government agency maintain a system of records so upon request by an individual to gain access to his or her record, or to any information pertaining to him or her which is contained in the system, that person can review the record and receive a copy of all or any portion thereof. The act also requires that each government agency have an administrative and physical security system to prevent unauthorized release of personal records.[22]

## Family Educational Rights and Privacy Act of 1974

The Family Educational Rights and Privacy Act (FERPA) protects the privacy of student education records. Educational records are defined as any records that are maintained by an educational institution and contain personal information particular to an individual student.

*The law applies to all schools that receive funds under an applicable program of the U.S. Department of Education. FERPA gives parents certain rights with respect to their children's education records. These rights transfer to the student when he or she reaches the age of 18 or attends a school beyond the high school level. Students to whom the rights have transferred are considered "eligible students."[23]*

Parents or eligible students have the right to inspect and review the student's education records maintained by the school or institution. They also have the right to correct any records found to contain factual inaccuracies. Generally, schools must have written permission from the parent or eligible student in order to release any information from a student's education record. There are exceptions where

FERPA allows schools to disclose those records, without consent, to certain parties including:

- School officials with legitimate educational interest
- Other schools to which a student is transferring
- Specified officials for audit or evaluation purposes
- Appropriate parties in connection with financial aid to a student
- Organizations conducting certain studies for or on behalf of the school
- Accrediting organizations
- To comply with a judicial order or lawfully issued subpoena
- Appropriate officials in cases of health and safety emergencies
- State and local authorities, within a juvenile justice system, pursuant to specific state law[24]

FERPA also states that educational institutions:

*[M]ay disclose, without consent, "directory" information such as a student's name, address, telephone number, date and place of birth, honors and awards, and dates of attendance. However, schools must tell parents and eligible students about directory information and allow parents and eligible students a reasonable amount of time to request that the school not disclose directory information about them. Schools must notify parents and eligible students annually of their rights under FERPA. The actual means of notification (special letter, inclusion in a PTA bulletin, student handbook, or newspaper article) is left to the discretion of each school.[25]*

This disclosure of student's personal information for inclusion in directories is extremely problematic. Any disclosure allows for potential identity theft, and the amount and kind of information that can be released to directories is exactly the information that identity thieves crave. In addition, most people never read the disclosure statements they receive let alone respond to them. I find that even with the disclosure notifications under FERPA and the ability for parents and students to prohibit disclosure, there is no good reason to disclose this information, period. In today's climate of diminished privacy and increased risk of identity theft, why disclose any personal information to directories?

## Drivers Privacy Protection Act of 1994

In response to a number of high-profile cases in which criminals obtained the victims' addresses through accessing Department of Motor Vehicle (DMV) records, including the stalking murder of actress Rebecca Schaeffer in 1989, Congress passed the Drivers Privacy Protection Act in 1994.[26] The act prohibits any state DMV, its employees, or any contractors from knowingly disclosing an individual's personal information to a third party and from disclosing certain types of information without the individual's consent. A newer amendment prohibits a state from selling or releasing DMV records to marketers without express permission.[27]

Personal information is defined as "information that identifies an individual, including an individual's photograph, social security number, driver identification number, name, address (but not the 5-digit zip code), telephone number, and medical or disability information."[28] Subject to exceptions, this information cannot be disclosed. However, an individual's photograph or image, SSN, and medical or disability information can be shared if the DMV obtains express, signed consent from the person.[29]

The act lists a number of circumstances in which personal information may be legally shared, regardless of consent. Many of the exceptions cover public safety matters, such as usage by law enforcement, courts and government agencies, investigating accidents and other insurance matters, and motor vehicle manufacturing recalls and notices.[30] Information may also be disclosed to businesses, but only for the purpose of verifying information submitted by the individual to the business. This exception allows the DMV to release the correct information, but only if the business has incorrect information and is used to prevent some sort of malfeasance by the individual. This would apply in situations where a person is attempting to perpetrate some sort of fraud, hide from creditors, or evade a legal claim against him or her.[31]

Violating the act subjects a person to a criminal fine and a state DMV to a civil monetary penalty. Any person who violates the act by obtaining, disclosing, or using personal information can be sued by the affected individual. The state of South Carolina challenged the act, because South Carolina law permitted the state to sell its drivers' records for marketing purposes. In 2000, the controversy reached the Supreme Court as *Reno v. Condon*, with the Court unanimously upholding the act's constitutionality.[32]

### Health Insurance Portability and Accountability Act

The Health Insurance Portability and Accountability Act (HIPAA) aims to ensure that providers secure electronic papers in the same way they secure physical paper records, improving overall informational security. Congress passed the law in 1996 in response to the growing use of the Internet and electronic communication of medical records. Its stated goal was to assure individuals that their health information is properly protected while at the same time allowing important uses of the information to protect the health and well-being of the individual and the public at large. The act covers health plans, healthcare providers, and clearinghouses that transmit health information in electronic form.

Protected health information is defined as individually identifiable health information created or received in any form. The Privacy Rule, enacted to carry out HIPAA's requirements, protects consumers from having their personal health information exploited, disclosed, or otherwise misused, whether by insurance companies, employers, or anyone else. In many cases, consent from the patient must be obtained before information can be disclosed, and when it is disclosed, it often must be limited to the minimum amount of protected health information needed. The Security Rule defines how to protect personally identifiable health information in electronic form.

When HIPAA was first enacted, it focused on the portability aspect of medical coverage. Now it focuses mostly on privacy and security issues of medical records.

Health information maintained by an employer such as in a personnel file is not covered by HIPAA. It additionally does not apply to worker's compensation plans.

## Identity Theft and Assumption Deterrence Act of 1998

The Identity Theft and Assumption Deterrence Act of 1998 created the new federal crime of identity theft. Although identity theft had been prosecuted previously under a number of other statutes, this was the first time that a specifically named law was enacted. The act makes it a crime for a defendant who "knowingly transfers or uses, without lawful authority, a means of identification of another person with the intent to commit, or to aid or abet, any unlawful activity that constitutes a violation of federal law, or that constitutes a felony under any applicable state or local law." The act expanded the definition of a "means of identification" to include names, Social Security numbers, credit cards, cellular telephones, electronic serial numbers, or other pieces of information that may be used alone or in conjunction with other information.

The act increased criminal penalties based on the number of victims, made interstate identity theft a crime, required the Federal Trade Commission to create a complaint and reporting center for identity theft victims, required mandatory restitution for identity theft victims, forfeiture of personal property used to commit identity theft, and other enhancements. The Senate bill was introduced by Arizona Senator Jon Kyl and was signed into law on October 30, 1998.

## Gramm-Leach-Bliley Act

The Gramm-Leach-Bliley Act, known as the Financial Modernization Act of 1999, includes provisions to protect consumers' personal financial information held by financial institutions, defined as companies that offer financial products or services to individuals. It aims to prevent companies from selling personal financial information without the customer's knowledge or approval. The Gramm-Leach-Bliley Act has three principal parts: the Financial Privacy Rule, the Safeguard Rule, and pretexting provisions.

The Financial Privacy Rule governs the collection and disclosure of customers' personal financial information. The rule also applies to companies that receive the information, regardless of whether they are considered financial institutions. This rule covers both consumers and customers. Consumers are individuals who obtain or have obtained a financial product or service from a financial institution for personal reasons. Customers are consumers with continuing relationships with the financial institutions; these relationships must be significant and/or long term. Customers get privacy notices automatically, while consumers get them only if the company shares the customer's information with another nonaffiliated company. The privacy notice must be a clear, conspicuous, and accurate statement of the company's privacy practices. The notice should include what information the company collects about its customers and consumers, with whom it shares the information, and how it protects or safeguards the information.

The Safeguard Rule requires all financial institutions to design, implement, and maintain safeguards to protect customer information. The rule applies not only to financial institutions that collect information from their own customers but to financial institutions such as credit reporting agencies that receive customer information from other financial institutions. Gramm-Leach-Bliley requires that a company have a security plan to protect the confidentiality and integrity of personal customer information.

The pretexting provisions protect consumers from individuals and companies, or those acting under their direction, from obtaining their personal financial information under false pretenses, a practice known as pretexting.[33]

## USA PATRIOT Act

The USA PATRIOT Act was enacted in November 2001 in the wake of the September 11 terrorist attacks and subsequently amended in following years. It gave the government new powers to utilize in the war on terrorism. USA PATRIOT is an acronym that stands for *U*niting and *S*trengthening *A*merica by *P*roviding *A*ppropriate *T*ools *R*equired to *I*ntercept and *O*bstruct *T*errorism. It greatly increased the power of the executive branch by broadening the definition of "terrorist" and simultaneously broadening the government's powers of surveillance and ability to share information between departments. Among other powers, the government may track suspects by roving wiretaps; issue "sneak and peek" warrants, which allow searches without the suspect's knowledge; monitor communications; and obtain access to sensitive personal records. Relevant to corporate compliance, the act includes mandatory anti–money-laundering provisions intended to combat the ability of terrorists to finance their operations.

The express authority given to the federal government to combat money laundering with new regulations also allowed the government to institute additional rules in conjunction with the provisions. The rules require all financial institutions to establish anti-money-laundering programs. At a minimum, the programs have to include: the development of internal policies, procedures, and controls; the designation of a compliance officer; an ongoing employee training program; and an independent audit function to test programs. Financial institutions are also obligated by rules covering the verification of the identity of customers. In addition, they must: verify the identity of any person seeking to open an account to the extent reasonable and practicable; maintain records of the information used to verify a person's identity, including name, address, and other identifying information; and consult lists of known or suspected terrorists or terrorist organizations provided to the financial institution by any government agency to determine whether a person seeking to open an account appears on any such list. Finally, in order to effectuate better information gathering, securities dealers and brokers are required to report suspicious activity to the government.

## CAN-SPAM Act

The Controlling the Assault of Non-Solicited Pornography and Marketing Act, known as the CAN-SPAM Act of 2003, "establishes requirements for those who send commercial email, spells out penalties for spammers and companies whose products are advertised in spam if they violate the law, and gives consumers the right to ask emailers to stop spamming them."[34] The law bans false or misleading header information, prohibits deceptive subject lines, and requires that the email be identified as an advertisement, include the sender's physical postal address, and give recipients an opt-out method. Violations of this act can lead to fines of up to $11,000 per violation; the Department of Justice can also seek criminal penalties when appropriate.[35]

## COPPA

The Children's Online Privacy Protection Act (COPPA) covers "the online collection of personal information from children under 13" and requires parental consent before any such information is collected or shared.[36] COPPA also sets outs the responsibilities operators have to protect children's privacy and safety online. Operators of Web sites directed at children under the age of 13 must post a privacy and information policy, outlining, among other things, what kinds of personal information are collected from children, how it will be used, to whom it will be disclosed, and how parents can review the information collected and how they can ask for such information to be deleted.[37]

## Fair and Accurate Credit Transactions Act of 2003

The Fair Credit Reporting Act (FCRA) was amended by the Fair and Accurate Credit Transactions Act (FACTA) of 2003 and took effect on June 1, 2005. FACTA provides much good news to consumers in the war against identity theft. It also gives consumers much-needed improvements to privacy, accuracy of consumer credit reports, limits on information sharing, and disclosure rights. FACTA requires the establishment of a fraud alert system for consumers who may be the victims of identity theft, credit card account number truncation on electronic receipts, account blocking by consumer credit reporting agencies after a police report is filed by victims, the creation of red-flag indicators for financial institutions and creditors to use in spotting identity theft, free credit reports on an annual basis from the three major credit bureaus, and other enhancements.

### *Free Credit Reports*

One of the best aspects of FACTA is that all individuals can receive copies of their credit reports once a year at no charge from each of the three major credit bureaus, Experian, Equifax, and TransUnion. Previously, there was a cost incurred to receive credit reports. This free service increases the ability of consumers to receive and review their credit reports for errors and possible identity theft. All consumers should avail themselves of this opportunity to scrutinize their credit reports.

Credit reports are available either through a dedicated Web site (www.annual creditreport.com), by telephone (877-322-8228), or by mail. The Privacy Rights Clearinghouse recommends that consumers order their free reports by telephone or mail rather than via the Internet. "A World Privacy Forum report released in July 2005 exposed hundreds of imposter Web sites. Some sites lure you in with free offers, but just want to sell you products like credit monitoring services. Others are outright frauds that aim to steal your personal information."[38] It is safe to order credit reports online as long as you are sure that you have correctly spelled the legitimate site, www.annual creditreport.com. Imposter sites use similar-sounding names and make use of common spelling errors to misdirect consumers. The FTC advises consumers who want to be extra careful to link to the official annualcreditreport.com site from the FTC's Web site (www.ftc.gov/bcp/menus/consumer/credit/rights.shtm).

### *Fraud Alerts*

FACTA provides victims, or those who believe they are about to be victims of identity theft or other frauds or crimes, with the right to contact the credit bureaus to flag their accounts. These fraud alerts are effective for a period of 90 days but may be extended up to seven years as long as a police report has been submitted detailing the victimization of the requestor. This flagging process alerts third parties who may use the credit history information from credit reporting services that the named individual's credit information may be compromised.

The act also creates a new category of alert called an active duty alert specifically for active duty military personnel. This special alert in the credit report of military personnel stationed outside the United States advises creditors that the subject is out of the country and does not have immediate access to credit. This alert can be useful in protecting military personnel who lack the ability to adequately monitor their credit activity. Active duty alerts can be in effect a minimum of 12 months.

Once a fraud alert has been placed on a consumer's credit report, no new or increase of credit can be approved without the credit issuer contacting the consumer at a telephone number previously provided. The consumer must then approve the credit issuance. This process allows individuals to discover unauthorized attempts to commit identity theft and other crimes using their names and personal information.

### *Truncation*

In a further attempt to reduce opportunities for identity thieves to obtain credit and debit account numbers, related expiration dates, and other personal information, whether by Dumpster diving or other sources, FACTA prohibits the printing of full account information on receipts and other documents. This information must now be shortened by only including the last five digits of an account. This truncation requirement only applies to electronically printed receipts and not to handwritten or imprinted receipts if that is the sole means of recording a credit or debit card transaction. This truncation also applies to Social Security numbers.

### *Red-Flag Guidelines*

FACTA requires federal regulators to establish and maintain guidelines to identify possible risks and red flags that both financial institutions and consumers can use to detect identity theft and other frauds. In creating the red flags, regulators must identify patterns, practices, and specific forms of activity that would be indicative of identity theft. Financial institutions and creditors must then use these red flags to adopt procedures to mitigate the risk of identity theft and other financial crimes.

Specifically noted in the act is the risk of account takeovers by identity thieves using fraudulent changes of address. The act states that

> *if a card issuer receives notification of a change of address for an existing account, and within a short period of time (during at least the first 30 days after such notification is received) receives a request for an additional or replacement card for the same account, the card issuer may not issue the additional or replacement card, unless the card issuer, in accordance with reasonable policies and procedures, notifies the cardholder of the request at the former address of the cardholder and provides to the cardholder a means of promptly reporting incorrect address changes.*[39]

The Appendix, *Designing an Effective Identity Theft Red Flags Rule Compliance Program*, provides an overview of the FACT A Red Flags Rule requirements, the 26 Red Flags of identity theft described in the act, and action steps to achieve effective compliance with the program requirements.

## *Disposal of Consumer Report Information and Records*

The act requires businesses and individuals to destroy records containing personal information, by shredding, burning, or pulverizing. Paper records must be destroyed in such a fashion that they cannot be read or reconstructed. Electronic records must be destroyed or erased so they cannot be read or reconstructed. This requirement applies to consumer reports such as credit reports, medical files, and employee background checks that are gathered. Unfortunately, the regulation applies only to third-party prepared reports but not information that consumers complete themselves. Disposal requirements apply to:

- Consumer reporting agencies
- Lenders
- Insurers
- Employers
- Landlords
- Government agencies
- Mortgage brokers
- Automobile dealers
- Attorneys and private investigators
- Debt collectors
- Individuals who obtain a credit report on prospective nannies, contractors, or tenants
- Entities that maintain information in consumer reports as part of their role as service providers to other organizations covered by this rule[40]

There are many other provisions of FACTA, including disputing inaccurate information in a consumer credit report, protection of medical information in the financial system, confidentiality of medical contact information in consumer reports, improving financial literacy, employee misconduct investigations conducted by a third party or an employer, and what may or may not be disclosed. For more detailed information, please refer to Fair and Accurate Credit Transaction Act of 2003.

## Identity Theft Penalty Enhancement Act

The Identity Theft Penalty Enhancement Act was signed into law by President George W. Bush on July 15, 2004. The act enhances prison sentences for identity thieves who commit other crimes, including terrorism. "For example, when someone is convicted of mail fraud in a case involving stolen personal information, judges will now impose two sentences, one for mail fraud, and one for aggravated identity theft. Those convicted of aggravated identity theft must serve an additional mandatory two-year prison term."[41] Defendants who commit other financial and document crimes in connection with a terrorism case would receive an additional prison term of five years. There are also increased penalties for trusted insiders who abuse their positions of trust, including people who work at banks, government agencies, insurance companies, and others who maintain financial data.[42]

## Real ID Act of 2005

Criticism of a national identification card has been a familiar refrain for years, with many people opposing any measures that would institute such a card. However, the Real ID Act, passed on May 11, 2005, took major steps toward such an outcome, with the act mandating that all states meet federally established standards for driver's licenses. It should be noted that the act did not pass on its own merits but rather was attached to an appropriations bill for Iraq war spending and relief for victims of the 2005 Southeast Asia tsunami disaster.[43]

The intent of the act is to introduce tough, uniform standards on identification, with stringent verification that applicants for new driver's licenses and renewals must meet, including checking birth certificates and national immigration databases to ensure that they are American citizens or legal residents. The idea is to prevent terrorists and illegal immigrants from obtaining driver's licenses, such as the licenses illicitly obtained by several 9/11 hijackers. The new IDs would have high-tech security features and would include special data encoded, such as on a bar code. States would also link their databases of driver's license data together, forming a national driver's license database.[44]

The act set a May 11, 2008, deadline for states to comply with the regulation or to have received extensions. All 50 states received compliance extensions even though six states, New Hampshire, Maine, South Carolina, Oklahoma, Washington, and Montana, passed laws rejecting the Real ID Act and its requirements. The next major deadline is December 31, 2009, where all states must have complied with act's requirements or else sought an additional extension.[45] Effectively, the law will require that all existing licenses be replaced between 2014, for people under 50, and 2017, for those 50 and over. By those dates, all 245 million driver's license and state ID holders must apply for a Real ID, with each applicant bringing a photo ID, birth certificate, proof of Social Security number and proof of residence.[46]

If a state does not comply with the Real ID requirements, federal agencies will not accept that state's licenses as proper identification. This means that citizens of those states will need a passport or some other approved form to serve as proof of identification at an airport or federal building, or when applying for federal benefits.[47]

Even though many of the physical features of the license requirement are already commonplace across the country, criticism of the act has been steady. Critics decry the law's "unfunded mandate": The act will cost states billions of dollars to implement, but the federal government will provide only approximately $40 million to all states to cover expenses.[48] The law does not provide any minimum encryption or safety standards to ensure that the information in the national databases will not be compromised. This is important because this national database would be 51 different linked databases (all states in addition to the District of Columbia), rather than one very large database. If hackers were able to infiltrate just one database, they could very well have access to the entire thing. It is also unknown what restrictions, if any, will be placed on the use of a national license database by third parties.[49]

Real ID does address some very important issues, namely the patchwork system of identification issuance in this country. It is not particularly difficult for a person to obtain a legitimate identification under a false name or with false information. Although no system would completely eliminate improper issuance, the more stringent controls could be very beneficial in keeping driver's licenses and identification cards out of the hands of terrorists and criminals. However, Real IDs or the underlying documents could be falsified, or DMV workers could be bribed to issue fake IDs. The database could also be a major problem for two reasons. First, as soon as it is instituted, it will become a "holy grail" for hackers. Second, how can the information in the database be verified and how can mistakes be corrected, particularly since limitations on the database's use have not been clearly defined?[50] These questions and more will continue to stir debate at least until Real ID's provisions are fully executed, if that day ever comes.

### Financial Data Protection Act of 2006

The Financial Data Protection Act of 2006, also known as the Data Accountability and Trust Act, was introduced in Congress as a measure to combat identity theft and streamline a multitude of differing state laws regarding credit freezes. A credit freeze functions as a check on identity theft because it blocks the release of a credit report, preventing the issuance of credit and hobbling identity thieves from opening new accounts using stolen data.

The measure would have preempted state laws that allow consumers to authorize a credit freeze of their credit records and instead reserve that power solely for victims of identity theft. However, before instituting a credit freeze, a victim must first file a police report noting the unlawful use of personal information by another individual.[51] Merely having data stolen or lost would not be enough to allow a credit freeze under this law.

147

According to the bill's coauthor, Representative Steven LaTourette, the bill would have protected the nation's financial system by streamlining a "patchwork of competing and conflicting state laws" and thus preventing frequent credit freezes from undermining it.[52] It also would have preempted state laws dealing with consumer notification after data breaches. The bill, backed by the major credit unions, came under intense criticism by consumers' groups, state attorneys general, and privacy advocates, among many others.[53]

Thankfully for the American public, the bill died without ever reaching the floor of the House. This bill would have placed the financial interests of the credit bureaus ahead of those of the public and other businesses. Since credit bureaus make money by selling credit information, anything that potentially interferes with accessing the reports hurts them. However, credit freezes prevent the issuance of credit to identity thieves, thus preventing fraud and theft.

By nationalizing identity theft legislation, the bill would have stripped states of the power to institute tough identity theft laws. Without a comparably strong federal standard to take its place, many of the gains made in fighting identity theft would have been lost.

## IMPACT OF LEGISLATION

Most states have laws similar to existing federal legislation on identity theft, credit card fraud, privacy, consumer credit issues, and other related individual and business issues. Many are patterned on existing federal laws. Some states, such as California, are ahead of the curve in the areas of data breach notification and restricting the use of SSNs to reduce identity crimes. Although this chapter has not discussed every existing federal and state law or regulation related to identity theft issues, the information provided is a good compilation of existing legislation. More important, it provides an overview of the issues and the government's response to the threat of identity theft crimes and the need for even greater protections.

If success is judged by the number of prosecutions for identity theft–related crime, then there is no doubt that law enforcement has been doing its job. But if success is determined by a decrease in this crime, a lessening of its overall impact, and greater personal protections for our citizens and businesses, then the reality is that much more needs to be done.

## NOTES

1. Mail Fraud Statute, Title 18, United States Code, Section 1341.
2. Ibid.
3. Charles A. Miller, *Economic Crime: A Prosecutor's Hornbook*, National District Attorney's Association (March 1975), 36.
4. Martin T. Biegelman, *Protecting with Distinction: A Postal Inspection Service History of the Mail Fraud Statute,* United States Postal Inspection Service (June 1999), 14.

5. Ibid.
6. Ibid.
7. Wire Fraud Statute, Title 18, United States Code, Section 1343.
8. Bank Fraud Statute, Title 18, United States Code, Section 1344.
9. False Statements in Loan and Credit Application, Title 18, United States Code, Section 1014.
10. Misuse of a Social Security Number, Title 42, United States Code, Section 408(a)(7)(B).
11. Student Loan Fraud, Title 20, United States Code, Section 1097.
12. Conspiracy, Title 18, United States Code, Section 371.
13. Criminal Resource Manual, Title 9, United States Attorney's Manual, www .usdoj.gov/usao/eousa/foia_reading_room/usam/title9/crm01024.htm.
14. Ibid.
15. Access Device Fraud, Title 18, United States Code, Section 1029.
16. United States Secret Service, "Criminal Investigations: Access Device Fraud," www.secretservice.gov/criminal.shtml.
17. Fraud and Related Activity in Connection with Computers, Title 18, United States Code, Section 1030.
18. Identity Theft Statute, Title 18, United States Code, Section 1029.
19. Aggravated Identity Theft, Title 18, United States Code, Section 1028A.
20. Federal Trade Commission, "Facts for Consumers: Fair Credit Billing," www.ftc.gov/bcp/edu/pubs/consumer/credit/cre16.shtm.
21. Privacy Act of 1974, www.usdoj.gov/oip/privstat.htm.
22. Ibid.
23. Family Educational Rights and Privacy Act of 1974, www.ed.gov/policy/gen/guid/ fpco/ferpa/index.html.
24. Ibid.
25. Ibid.
26. See "The Drivers Privacy Protection Act (DPPA) and the Privacy of Your State Motor Vehicle Record," Electronic Privacy Information Center, http://epic.org/ privacy/drivers.
27. Ibid.
28. Drivers Privacy Protection Act, United States Code Title 18, Part I, Chapter 123, Section 2725(3).
29. Ibid., Section 2721(a)(2), 2725 (4).
30. Ibid., Section 2721(b).
31. Ibid.
32. See *Reno v. Condon*, 528 U.S. 141 (2000).
33. Gramm-Leach-Bliley Act, //frwebgate.access.gpo.gov/cgi-bin/getdoc.cgi?dbname= 106_cong_public_laws&docid=f:publ102.106.pdf.
34. Federal Trade Commission, "The CAN-SPAM Act: Requirements for Commercial E-mailers," www.ftc.gov/bcp/conline/pubs/buspubs/canspam.shtm.
35. Ibid.
36. Federal Trade Commission, "How to Comply with the Children's Online Privacy Protection Rule," www.ftc.gov/bcp/conline/pubs/buspubs/coppa.shtm.

37. Ibid.
38. Privacy Rights Clearinghouse, www.privacyrights.org/fs/fs6a-facta.htm.
39. Fair and Accurate Credit Transactions Act of 2003, frwebgate.access.gpo.gov/cgi-bin/getdoc.cgi?dbname=108_cong_public_laws&docid=f:publ159.108.pdf
40. Federal Trade Commission, "Disposing of Consumer Report Information? New Rule Tells How," www.ftc.gov/bcp/edu/pubs/consumer/alerts/alt152.shtm.
41. "President Bush Signs Identity Theft Penalty Enhancement Act," July 15, 2004, www.whitehouse.gov/news/releases/2004/07/20040715-3.html.
42. Ibid.
43. National Conference of State Legislatures, Real ID Act of 2005: Driver's License Summary, www.ncsl.org/standcomm/sctran/RealIDSummary05.htm.
44. Real ID Act of 2005, HR 418, 109th Congress, May 11, 2005, www.govtrack.us/congress/billtext.xpd?bill=h109-418.
45. Declan McCullagh, "Homeland Security Blinks on Real ID: No Hassles on May 11," News.Com, April 2, 2008, news.cnet.com/8301-13578_3-9909928-38.html?from=rss.
46. Elliot C. McLaughlin, "Federal ID Plan Raises Privacy Concerns," CNN.com, August 16, 2007, www.cnn.com/2007/POLITICS/08/16/real.id/index.html.
47. Eric Lipton, "Rebellion Growing as States Challenged a Federal Law to Standardize Driver's Licenses," *New York Times*, February 5, 2007, www.nytimes.com/2007/02/05/washington/05real.html.
48. McLaughlin, "Federal ID Plan Raises Privacy Concerns."
49. Erik Larkin, "Coming Soon: National ID Cards?" *PC World*, May 31, 2005, www.pcworld.com/article/id,121077-page,1/article.html; Jaikumar Vijayan, "Privacy Groups Renew Push Against Real ID Bill," *Computer World*, May 4, 2007, available at: www.networkworld.com/news/2007/050407-privacy-groups-renew-push-against.html.
50. See Bruce Schneier, "Real ID: Costs and Benefits," Schneier on Security, January 30, 2007, www.schneier.com/blog/archives/2007/01/realid_costs_an.html.
51. Data Accountability and Trust Act, H.R. 3997, 109th Congress, introduced October 6, 2005, www.govtrack.us/congress/billtext.xpd?bill=h109-3997.
52. Byron Acohido, "Bill Would Limit Consumers' Credit Rights," *USA Today*, June 15, 2006, www.usatoday.com/money/perfi/credit/2006-06-14-credit-freeze-usat_x.htm.
53. See, e.g., Martin H. Bosworth, "Congress Considers 'Worst Data Bill Ever,'" ConsumerAffairs.com, www.consumeraffairs.com/news04/2006/03/congress_data_bill.html. See also Acohido, "Bill Would Limit Consumers' Credit Rights."

# CHAPTER 11

# Law Enforcement Efforts

Law enforcement has done more than just fight identity theft through criminal investigations and prosecutions. It has also been at the forefront of promoting best practices in detection and prevention, instituting education and awareness campaigns, developing strong partnerships with the financial services and business communities, and recommending legislation to lessen identity theft. These are just some examples of the many law enforcement efforts over the years to fight identity theft and its related crimes.

## METRO RICHMOND IDENTITY THEFT TASK FORCE

The use of law enforcement task forces has been a productive detection and prevention approach in combating identity theft. Combining the resources of several law enforcement agencies and prosecutors' offices has worked to bring identity thieves to justice while publicizing the impact of identity theft and offering prevention information. The work of the Metro Richmond (Virginia) Identity Theft Task Force is an excellent example of a successful task force implementation.

The Metro Richmond Identity Theft Task Force was created in October 2004 to develop a cooperative effort among various federal, state, and local law enforcement agencies in the Richmond, Virginia, area to investigate the growing problem of identity theft as well as other financial crimes. The working definition of identity theft used by the task force is "unlawfully obtaining, possessing, transferring, or using identifying information of another person without the other person's consent and with the intent to harm or defraud another."[1] Among the crimes investigated are classic identity theft schemes, counterfeit checks, stolen government checks, Internet fraud schemes, and other criminal offenses related to fraud and forgery. The emphasis has been on organized crime and other gang activity that has a high impact on the public and the financial services industry.

The task force is comprised of full-time members from the Postal Inspection Service, United States Secret Service, Federal Bureau of Investigation, Richmond Police Department, Henrico County Police Department, and Chesterfield County Police Department. Part-time members include the Social Security Administration, Office of the Inspector General (OIG), Housing & Urban Development OIG, Defense Criminal Investigative Service, Diplomatic Security Service, and Immigration and Customs Enforcement. Prosecutions are handled by the United States Attorney's Office, Eastern District of Virginia, and the Virginia Attorney General, who aggressively prosecute offenders in federal and state courts. The task force also has two industry partners, the Better Business Bureau and the National White Collar Crime Center.

The task force operation is housed at the offices of the Postal Inspection Service in Richmond, where office space and equipment are provided including computers, Internet access, desks, and telephones. The central location for a base of operations promotes a close interaction and beneficial interchange of information. Local law enforcement officers are deputized as Special U.S. Marshals so they can investigate and make arrests on the related federal crimes used to prosecute the defendants. Prosecutors are assigned to the task force to speed cases through the system. The investigators hold weekly meetings to share intelligence and status of cases. There are also formal monthly meetings of the combined task force. A strong relationship with prosecutors and a commitment to delivering results for the community have been elements for success.

The overall focus of the task force is on organized groups, fraud recidivists as well as education and crime deterrence. It has set up an informative Web site that provides detailed information on the task force; on the many federal, state, and local agencies involved in investigating and prosecuting identity theft; on identity theft–related scams; on how to report if one is a victim of identity theft; press releases on cases; wanted posters, federal and state laws related to identity theft; prevention tips; and links to other informative sites. The site can be viewed at www.richmondIDtheft.com.

Besides the proactive investigative approach, the task force also employs a strong prevention message through a steady stream of press releases after each arrest and prosecution. These press releases detail the cases and publicize prevention methods as well as the work of the Metro Richmond Identity Theft Task Force. The public outreach includes presentations made by task force members to educate the public and raise awareness of the problem of identity theft. Presentations are made to groups and organizations throughout the Richmond area and are tailored to the particular audience.[2]

## OPERATION RECONCILE

One of the major cases investigated and prosecuted by the task force was "Operation Reconcile." The investigation started in the fall of 2004 and became public in November 2006 with multiple indictments and arrests. "Reconcile" was used as a code name because of its implied dual meaning. Since most of the criminal activity involved banks being defrauded, the operation was a way of "reconciling" their losses. The second meaning pertained to the criminals and the concept of "reconciling" their criminal behavior, like a "day of reckoning."

According to Postal Inspector/Team Leader Dave McGinnis, a key member of the task force, the Operation Reconcile cases were meant to send a message, via a mass roundup, to would-be identity thieves that they had better think twice before engaging in this particular crime. Since law enforcement has now banded together in the Metro Richmond area, cases are prosecuted jointly on the federal level utilizing the Aggravated Identity Theft statute.

Operation Reconcile had three main objectives: (1) target fraud recidivists and ongoing identity theft schemes by individuals; (2) create public awareness of the penalties associated with identity theft; and (3) deter future identity theft crimes. The prosecution strategy was to indict each target on one count of identity theft or bank fraud. The task force also used all related criminal activity as relevant conduct at sentencing. That included any counterfeit, stolen, and altered checks, credit card fraud, and misuse of Social Security numbers (SSNs) and other identification.

The operation targeted identity theft recidivists, abuse-of-trust cases, illegal aliens, and bank insiders involved in fraud. There were 65 investigators and prosecutors involved in the operation during the two-year investigation. When the case became public on November 14, 2006, 51 defendants were charged in 45 indictments. There was a coordinated roundup of defendants over a two-day period. Twenty-six defendants were charged with Aggravated Identity Theft, a federal crime. The law on Aggravated Identity Theft was enacted in July 2004 and carries a mandatory minimum term of imprisonment of two years. Aggravated identity theft applies when a defendant commits other predicate felonies during the commission of identity theft. In addition, a sentence under this statute must run consecutively to any other prison term imposed. There were 106 victims identified in Operation Reconcile.

Six of the defendants who pleaded guilty in January 2007 provide a snapshot of how identity theft can be perpetrated. Three were bank employees who fraudulently obtained credit cards that they personally used. A fourth defendant obtained a bank account in the name of a victim and deposited stolen checks into that account. A fifth defendant received stolen checks that he had others cash at various area banks for him. The sixth defendant obtained a stolen check, altered it to make himself the payee, and then negotiated the check at a local credit union. The more involved the defendants were in criminal activity, the longer the jail terms they received, with sentences of between two and four years in prison.

The task force used the publicity around these 51 indictments to announce the kick-off of a campaign to educate the public on the enhanced penalties for Aggravated Identity Theft. The "Think Before You Do IT" campaign was started in November 2006. The "IT" refers to identity theft. The centerpiece of the campaign was signs that proclaimed "ID THEFT = 2 Years in Federal Prison" placed on area buses. The campaign emphasized consumer awareness to let people know that committing identity theft equals two years in federal prison. The awareness campaign included a press conference, "Think Before You Do IT" advertisements on buses run by the Greater Richmond

Transit Company, and ongoing public service announcements on identity theft prevention.

The outcome of the campaign included increased hits on the task force Web site, an increase in crime tips and victim inquiries, and further dedication of the member agencies to fight identity theft. The Postal Inspector in Charge in Richmond praised the cooperation of the task force participants by stating: "The Metro Richmond Identity Theft Task Force is a fine example of what can be achieved when the law enforcement community comes together to address a specific problem in the community." He added, "The member agencies of the task force are dedicated to fighting identity crime and will continue to vigorously protect the good names and identities of the citizens of metro Richmond."[3]

## FELONY LANE GANG

The Metro Richmond Identity Theft Task Force also teamed with a task force in another state to break up another identity theft ring. The task force investigators in Virginia became aware of the Felony Lane Gang (FLG) due to their criminal activity in Chesterfield and Henrico counties, Virginia, in February 2007. The basic scheme involved the theft of checkbooks and driver's licenses from unattended cars, especially those cars parked at sports fields and gyms. Transients were recruited and transported to other areas by the gang members so they could cash the stolen checks. The task force began compiling and sharing information on numerous vehicle break-ins, related fraud losses, reviewing bank photos of the suspects and descriptions of the vehicles used by them.

As the task force continued its investigation, members learned that another task force had been investigating the FLG for several years. Since November 2004, the U.S. Secret Service's South Florida Organized Fraud Task Force had been investigating an organized criminal group operating in Broward, Palm Beach, and Miami-Dade counties who were engaged in identity theft and other crimes. The South Florida Organized Fraud Task Force found that the gang members targeted vehicles parked at day care centers, gyms, cemeteries, and other locations, where unsuspecting victims left wallets, purses, and other property in plain view in vehicles. The defendants also used robberies and physical violence, often against women, to obtain personal information including driver's licenses, Social Security cards and numbers, debit cards, credit cards, and checks. The FLG used the victims' identification and other personal information to commit a variety of crimes, including identity theft, bank fraud, credit card fraud, and other crimes.

This investigation was code-named "Operation Felony Lane" due to the use of drive-through teller lanes at banks to cash or deposit forged checks using the identity of one victim to cash a forged check from another victim.

*Armed with stolen identification (Florida Driver's Licenses, ID's, Social Security Cards, credit cards), and with stolen checks, the defendants would go to the farthest lane of the drive-in teller at local banks, which is the most difficult place for bank surveillance to view their activity (hence, the name 'Felony Lane'). Once at the drive-in teller, the suspects* *produced a check written to one of the stolen identities (an identity for which they had false identification) and cashed the check. The payee on the check and the false identification was often in the name of an individual who was a previous victim of a home burglary, vehicle break-in, purse snatching or strong armed robbery, where their identities were stolen. The bank account was often a business account that had suffered a theft and had sufficient funds in their accounts to process the checks. These checks are normally written for amounts from $1,500 to $5,000 each and multiple checks are written on each victim's identity. The suspects were well organized, usually traveled in groups and used counter-surveillance tactics, communicated by cell phone, and used disguises such as wigs, glasses or hair dye when perpetrating their frauds.*[4]

Female gang members generally would be the ones to negotiate the stolen checks. The "blocking vehicle," usually a rental car, was used to distract tellers in the first drive-through lane, the lane closest to the teller window. Often a sports utility vehicle would be used as its larger size provided greater blocking of the second vehicle and suspect in the outside lane. The blocking vehicle's occupants would try to engage the teller in conversation to further distract the teller's attention from being too focused on the other transaction taking place in the outside lane. The female defendants made sure to wear wigs to match the hair color of the photo on the stolen identification documents. The defendants also did account takeovers where they impersonated the true account holder either in person or by telephone. They would change the home address on the victim's account and also use stolen credit cards at merchants in the area.

The scheme began in Florida in 2004 and moved to Virginia, where it continued from September 2006 into 2007. Losses in Florida were in the millions of dollars. Losses to financial institutions in the Eastern District of Virginia exceeded $350,000. On November 1, 2006, 20 defendants were indicted in the Southern District of Florida on various charges of conspiracy to commit bank fraud, aggravated identity theft, and identity theft. In April 2007, the leader of the conspiracy was sentenced to nine years in prison. Other members of the gang received jail sentences between one and three years with lesser-involved participants receiving probation. In December 2007, six members of the gang pleaded guilty in the Eastern District of Virginia to charges of conspiracy to commit bank fraud and aggravated identity theft.

## THOUGHT LEADER IN IDENTITY THEFT PREVENTION

### Henry Herrera

Henry Herrera is a Postal Inspector assigned to Washington, DC, as program manager for the Postal Inspection Service's Financial Crimes Group. As program manager, he has the responsibility of overseeing the national identity theft program for the Postal Inspection Service. Herrera became a Postal Inspector in

*(Continued)*

1986 and throughout his career has worked numerous identity theft investigations. He is a subject matter expert in identity theft and provides in-service training and guidance to field inspectors. Herrera works closely with the President's Identity Theft Task Force, which was established by an executive order signed by President George W. Bush in May 2006.

Inspector Herrera led the Identity Theft Working Group, which was part of the Financial Industry Mail Security Initiative sponsored by Inspection Service Headquarters. This group produced identity theft awareness guides and training videos. Inspector Herrera was also a driving force behind the publication of a report entitled *Fighting Identity Theft,* which contained best business practices for law enforcement and the financial industry, improving exchange of intelligence between private and public sectors and developing a comprehensive awareness program. He also served as a technical advisor in the filming of the Showtime movie *The Inspectors II* on the subject of identity theft.

Inspector Herrera believes that in order to attack the identity theft problem to the fullest extent possible, the focus needs to be in three major areas; prevention, detection, and detention. In Philadelphia in 1991, Inspector Herrera was tasked with a special credit card crime prevention assignment. This request was an attempt to shift the focus from not just making more arrests but stopping identity theft crime from happening in the first place. "My goal was to identify all the major credit issuing banks in the Philadelphia Division and customize service and crime prevention procedures in each bank to protect both the banks and their customers," he says.

Early on, Inspector Herrera learned that each bank had its own unique problems as well as problems similar to the others. In the early 1990s, banks hesitated to share information with each other. As a neutral participant and as a representative of the Postal Inspection Service, Inspector Herrera created an environment in which he could bring the representatives from the various financial institutions together to share the "best practices" in addressing financial fraud. One key element was to fully understand the extent of the problem and identify the weaknesses in the system. Another main ingredient was to identity the "experts" in the field and all the key players who could develop solutions to the flaws in the system.

Over the years, a number of training and best practice materials were produced with recommendations for implementing security strategies to minimize the risk of financial fraud. Inspector Herrera was instrumental in the creation of these educational materials. These materials included *Identity Theft Awareness and Victim Guide*; *Identity Theft: Safeguard Your Personal Information*; *Detecting and Preventing Account Takeover Fraud*; *Detecting and Preventing Credit Application Fraud*; two training videos entitled *The Game of the Name* and *Identity Crisis*; and the report already described, *Fighting Identity Theft.*

During his 22 years investigating financial crimes and working with financial institutions in their prevention, Inspector Herrera learned that everyone has a small piece of the puzzle and a role to play to combat and prevent identity theft. He reinforces the notion that access to the pertinent information must be kept to a minimum. "When the suspect obtains personal data, then the mechanisms must be in place to make it very difficult to use that information for financial gain," he advises. "When these systems fail, then it becomes very important to identify and apprehend those 'financial termites' who are responsible for perpetrating the identity theft."

Inspector Herrera also strongly believes law enforcement must be properly trained in the most current fraud trends as they relate to the advances in technology and have the resources to combat identity theft. "In looking at how the criminal is using more sophisticated means to commit fraud, it has become very clear that we must unite our efforts to be better prepared to face the challenges of tomorrow," he says. "Through communication and cooperation we can more effectively protect our financial and computer infrastructure."

Inspector Herrera acknowledges that identity theft will never be completely eliminated. "The best thing anyone could hope for is to minimize their exposure to reduce the likelihood of becoming a victim. When an individual becomes a victim, then early detection is needed to minimize the damage."[5]

## LAW ENFORCEMENT EFFORTS TO ENACT ANTIFRAUD LEGISLATION

Law enforcement has done more than just investigate and prosecute identity theft cases. It has also been instrumental in promoting legislation to combat the crime. This was the case in Connecticut, where dedicated professionals saw their efforts to enact a state credit card statute become reality. Connecticut became one of the first states to enact a credit card fraud law allowing state prosecution of violations occurring in several locations within the state to be consolidated for prosecution in one jurisdiction. This legislation came to fruition as a result of the hard work of many people, and especially two dedicated federal agents.

Veteran Postal Inspectors Al Dockus and Paul Hinman worked on the idea that was initially conceived by Hinman in early 1996, for a specific state statute to prosecute credit card fraudsters and identity thieves. Both inspectors, assigned to Connecticut at the time, were very active in credit card fraud investigations. They saw the impact of these crimes on individuals and the financial services industry as well as difficulties in bringing criminals to justice. Dockus and Hinman knew that law enforcement needed every possible weapon in the fight against fraud.

Because many of the credit card frauds committed by the same individuals or gangs were small losses that occurred in various locations, it was necessary to prosecute violations separately in each of the county jurisdictions where the actual fraud occurred. The new law would enable the prosecutors to consolidate the defendant's offenses in various counties into a single criminal prosecution in one geographical court jurisdiction.

From the beginning, there was support for the proposed law, as it was believed that the state legislature would embrace it. With the expected strong support from the banking lobby, law enforcement, and the public, the law had a good chance of passing. Still, the inspectors knew that enacting legislation is a time-consuming process that is never easy with all the elements of politics, government, and special interests colliding. They soon learned that the timing for presenting a new bill to the Connecticut judicial committee was less than ideal as the committee had a full agenda and would not be able to get to any new bill introduced in 1996.

Dockus and Hinman began to lobby a state representative for his support. They continued to work with the Connecticut Chief State's Attorney and enlisted the United States Attorney's Office, numerous banks and credit card companies, and the International Association of Financial Crimes Investigators, among others. It took a year of effort but in March 1997, a proposed bill entitled "An Act Concerning a Study of Credit Card Fraud" was discussed at a Banking Committee hearing. Dockus and Hinman made a brief presentation in support of the legislation.

The Chief State's Attorney sent a letter to the committee that stated:

> Credit card fraud has reached epidemic proportions in Connecticut as in many states. It will take a concerted effort by all levels of agencies to deal with the complex nature of this crime. . . . H.B. 6852 is an important step in gaining an understanding of the issues involved and developing a strategy for dealing with the problem in the next legislative session.[6]

This support was critical.

On March 3, 1998, a public hearing was scheduled at the State Capitol to discuss the merits of the legislation. Dockus and Hinman testified in their capacity as officers of the Connecticut chapter of the International Association of Financial Crimes Investigators. Dockus detailed the growing threat of credit card fraud and identity theft and the many international criminals who exploit the financial system for their personal gain. He explained at the time that credit card fraud was being prosecuted using existing statutes, but they were inadequate for effective prosecution. He testified:

> Internationally, nationally and locally within the State of Connecticut credit card fraud is reaching epidemic proportions. Even with various loss prevention and security systems consistently being initiated, the volume of credit card fraud continues to increase.

> An increasing threat in recent years has been from organized gangs and is international in scope. Organized crime gangs, particularly Nigerian, Asian, Russian and others dealing in counterfeit cards, fraudulent applications, cards stolen from the mail and merchant fraud has given rise to increased credit card fraud throughout the world. Many of these gangs migrate into Connecticut.

> These statutes are generally prosecuted as misdemeanors when the value of a fraudulent transaction is $500 or below. Amounts in excess of $500 may be prosecuted as felonies. The reality of credit card fraud investigations conducted in Connecticut is that fraud activity exceeds $500 in a high percentage of cases.

> However, it is most common that the fraudulent activity is spread throughout a number of the localities, throughout the state, each having a different geographical area. In many cases, the illegal activity in any geographical area is often below the $500 amount, making the act in that area a misdemeanor. This is done by design, rather than coincidence, by the perpetrator.

*The passing of this legislation will have many benefits. Among these—and not only these—but among these it would increase the likelihood of arresting and convicting a perpetrator as a felon. It would cause budget reductions for the state by litigating in one area instead of numerous areas.*

*Credit card fraud is a relatively simple and extremely mobile crime. The number of individuals involved in this illegal activity is increasing. This legislation will go far towards letting those perpetrators know that we will now be able to pursue them more effectively.*[7]

The hearings were successful and got the bill moving forward through the legislative process. The Connecticut General Assembly passed Public Act 98-45, "An Act Concerning the Prosecution of Certain Credit Card and Automated Teller Machine Fraud Offenses." The bill was signed into law by the governor on May 19, 1998 and took effect on October 1, 1998. Dockus, now retired, commented at the time that the presentation of fraud loss statistics helped win support of a state senator who usually opposed new legislation.[8] Unfortunately, those fraud losses would continue to grow in the years to come.

## M.I.A.M.I. PROGRAM

The M.I.A.M.I. Program (*M*ail *I*nitiative *A*gainst *M*isappropriated *I*dentities) that Postal Inspectors developed in the late 1990s in South Florida is an example of a strategic approach to preventing identity theft. This initiative recovered significant amounts of stolen mail and credit cards before they were fraudulently used. The program also helped law enforcement educate area banks regarding new schemes and the scope of the identity theft problem. The goal of the M.I.A.M.I. Program was twofold: (1) the timely notification to law enforcement of false addresses used for fraud, and (2) to quantify the results of this prevention initiative.

### Background

In the 1990s, Miami and much of South Florida had become one of the leading areas of identity takeover and credit/debit card fraud. Much of the criminal activity was conducted by members of highly organized groups, but suspects ran the gamut from small-time credit card thieves to full-scale operations employing confederates within the banking system supplying victim information on a wholesale level.

Traditionally, criminals used victims' information to request replacement credit cards sent to post office boxes and commercial mail receiving agencies (CMRAs) that had been established to harvest the cards. With the new initiatives proposed by the Inspection Service to make CMRA's more easily identifiable to the mailers, the criminals were using a new trend of redirecting the credit cards to vacant houses.

The vacant houses were used for a short period of time but received the mail of multiple victims, usually with the same surname. By the time inspectors became aware of a suspect address, the criminals abandoned it and established new addresses. The timely notification when suspect addresses were being used and active aided inspectors in pinpointing investigative focus.

Similarly, when inspectors became aware of a reported fraud address, they often were able to recover abandoned mail. Frequently this mail included replacement credit and debit cards, bank statements, and the true account holders' canceled checks. Inspectors recovered this mail for safeguarding and contacted the issuing bank to notify them of the recovery. Often this was the first notification to the bank of a problem with the accounts; a check of the bank's system usually indicated some fraud had already occurred. The notification by the Postal Inspector allowed the bank to suspend and/or monitor the account to prevent and minimize the bank's potential exposure to continued fraud.

The inspector usually directed the mail back to the issuing sender bank with little regard for the potential savings the investigation produced. It was determined there should be some established process to quantify the potential monetary savings the bank experienced due to the inspector's preventive intervention in the safeguarding of the financial mail.

### Awareness and Response

The M.I.A.M.I. Program succeeded by establishing a partnership with Postal Service management on this initiative. Postal Inspectors addressed station managers, carrier supervisors, and the carriers themselves on the problem of identity theft and the newly established reporting system. The importance of timely reporting to the Postal Inspectors of any suspect address was stressed. As a result, carriers would report whenever they suspected a vacant house was being used to receive large volumes of financial mail.

Postal Inspectors recruited local and national banking and credit card fraud investigators to supply a written authorization form to the Inspection Service. The form permitted inspectors and their designees (Postal Supervisors) to withhold, photocopy, and/or record information on the envelope of suspected mail. The letters were maintained on file with the Postal Inspection Division coordinator. When the mail was no longer necessary for evidentiary purposes, it was returned to sender. A master list of various bank investigators was compiled into a database used to return the mail. A form letter was attached indicating where the mail had been recovered and listing each piece. A quantification form was maintained so that the investigator could document the potential loss to the financial institution had the mail not been intercepted. Overall, the M.I.A.M.I. Program was an important initiative in reducing the incidence of identity theft.[9]

### FINANCIAL INDUSTRY MAIL SECURITY INITIATIVE

The Financial Industry Mail Security Initiative (FIMSI) is the brainchild of the United States Postal Inspection Service. FIMSI was created in 1992 and in November 2007 celebrated its fifteenth anniversary of serving the interest of Postal Service customers and businesses. FIMSI's goal has been to improve partnerships and communications between the Postal Inspection Service, other law enforcement agencies, credit card and retail industries, financial institutions, and the airlines. FIMSI meetings provide a forum for sharing trend data and developing strategies to address fraud and theft. FIMSI has helped the financial and retail industries reduce and—even better—prevent nonreceipt losses due to identity theft, credit card fraud, bank fraud, mail theft, check schemes, and Internet fraud.

FIMSI organizes working groups to focus on specific industry and law enforcement problems. The working groups were created during the regular FIMSI meetings via members volunteering on specific projects to develop working solutions. The working groups would then meet separately from the regular meetings to work on the goals at hand; they would then report back to the general meeting their specific ideas to push forward as potential new countermeasures. Successful collaborations resulted from the working relationship between the industry and law enforcement, which was considered a unique partnership at the time.

The working groups have helped develop a variety of fraud prevention publications as well as two identity theft training videos. The industry has adopted many of the Postal Inspection Service's suggestions, resulting in reduced fraud losses. Group activities have resulted in new and innovative prevention initiatives, including:

- **Card Activation Program (CAP)** was an innovative idea developed by a Postal Inspector that was presented to the credit card industry and adopted. Formerly "live" credit cards mailed to the cardholders were now "dead" until the consumer called the issuer to provide certain identifying information, such as an SSN to activate the card. A sticker on front of card had a toll-free number for the cardholder to call. While there was initial reluctance by some issuers to implement CAP, it soon became the norm for the entire industry. CAP opened the door to other ideas. Eventually, cardholders could call in from their home telephones and the cards would be activated without speaking to a live operator. Initiating a credit card activation program has significantly reduced fraud losses on cards mailed to consumers.

- **Address Verification System (AVS)** was developed to curtail mail order/telephone order (MO/TO) fraud using stolen account numbers, where the address of the order would be sent to an alternate address, often a CMRA. AVS worked when the mail order company receiving the order contacted the issuer if the "order address" did not match the "account address." AVS was usually used for orders above $300, and it quickly began to reduce the number of complaints in MO/TO fraud. Identifying CMRA addresses and other mail drop sites as potential locations for fraud is an excellent fraud prevention tool.

- **Automated Number Information (ANI)** was implemented to help stem the threat to the CAP as suspects began to gain SSNs to activate cards, getting around CAP completely. ANI worked similar to CAP except that the phone number the cardholder called from had to match what was on file with the issuer, either the home or the work phone. This activated the card. CAP soon became CAP/ANI, especially in higher-risk locations.

- **Neural networks** were developed as large fraud losses were realized, especially on high credit line accounts. The "neural" network was like a "lock" surrounding the account that measured regular spending patterns and sent "alerts" when these regular patterns were disrupted, such as the amount spent (numerous cash advances), location of charges (out of state or country), and type of charges (jewelry, rental cars, etc.) that may not be typical of the card holder pattern. The neural network can be adjusted accordingly, depending on issuer security decisions.

- **National Change Of Address Information System (NCOAIS)** relates to the United States Postal Service Change of Address (USPS COA) system whereby the issuer can "run" its address list (which can be in the millions) against the USPS COA system for a small fee in an attempt to eliminate "old" or bad addresses to clean up their lists. FIMSI encouraged the credit card industry to use the USPS COA. Doing this reduces chances of preapproved applications getting into the hands of nonintended addressees and thus reduces the fraud exposure.[10]

These are just a sampling of the many successful countermeasures developed since the formation of FIMSI in 1992. The success of FIMSI is due to the Postal Inspectors' ongoing interactions and sharing of information with the financial services industry and the resulting development of new fraud prevention measures. The countermeasures were developed by the strong partnerships of industry representatives and Postal Inspectors. These innovative concepts would not have been accomplished without both sides working together to get them pushed through to the executive level at the companies involved.

## NOTES

1. Postal Inspector Dave McGinnis's comments to the author, November 12, 2007.
2. Ibid.
3. United States Attorney's Office, Eastern District of Virginia, Press Release, "Fifty-One Defendants Indicted in Federal Identity Theft Round-Up Known as 'Operation Reconcile,'" November 14, 2006, www.usdoj.gov/usao/vae/Pressreleases/11-NovemberPDFArchive/06/20061114operationreconcile.pdf.
4. United States Attorney's Office, Southern District of Florida, Press Release, "Operation Felony Lane Defendants Sentenced in Bank Fraud and Identity Theft Conspiracy," April 20, 2007, www.usdoj.gov/usao/fls/PressReleases/070420-06.html.
5. Postal Inspector Henry Herrera's comments to the author, March 21, 2008.
6. Letter dated March 11, 1997 from John F. Cronan, Executive Assistant State's Attorney, Office of the Chief State's Attorney, State of Connecticut to the Banking Committee of the Connecticut General Assembly.
7. Transcript of Public Hearing before the Banks Committee for Proposed Legislation (Bill No. 5279), Connecticut General Assembly, March 3, 1998, www.cga.ct.gov/ps98/chr/ba-0303-1530.htm.
8. "IAFCI Efforts Empower Fraud Prosecution in Connecticut," *IAFCI News* 147 (Fall 1998), 1.
9. Postal Inspector Jack Galvin's comments to the author, November 14, 2007.
10. Postal Inspector Randy DeGasperin's comments to the author, January 15, 2008.

# CHAPTER 12

# Teens and Young Adults as Victims and Perpetrators

Every age group is affected by identity theft, especially teenagers and young adults. A 2007 Federal Trade Commission (FTC) study on identity theft found that teenagers and young adults are the fastest-growing population targeted by identity thieves. The age group of 18- to 29-year-olds made up 28% of identity theft complainants. Identity thieves like teens because they usually have an unblemished credit history, and it can take years before the crime is discovered. Teenagers may not regularly use their Social Security numbers (SSNs) until late in their teen years or even into their early 20s. Thus, the crime may not be detected until teens try to obtain credit. If they have not obtained credit cards or loans, they will not have a credit rating.

Unfortunately, teenagers are also perpetrators of identity theft. In April 2001, a 17-year-old California girl was charged as an adult in a long-running identity theft scheme. The teen used stolen identities to apply for bank loans, attempted to wire cash transactions, and purchased computers and other merchandise over the Internet. She was also charged with grand theft auto and possession of a firearm.[1]

A teenage college student at St. John's University in Jamaica, New York, was the victim of identity theft allegedly by her former boyfriend and his jealous new girlfriend. The jealous girlfriend extracted revenge by using the victim's SSN to drop classes that the victim had registered for. This occurred several times, and St. John's Information Technology Department was able to identity the perpetrator when she logged in as the victim. Both the ex-boyfriend and the jealous girlfriend were suspended from the college, and the New York Police Department and the Queens, New York, District Attorney began a criminal investigation of identity theft.[2] While this may have started as a simple prank without a financial motive, the potential damage and impact is evident. Identity theft can be much more than simply stealing money.

## TEENAGE HACKERS

In October 2003, the Securities and Exchange Commission (SEC) charged Van T. Dinh, a 19-year-old from Pennsylvania, with hacking into an investor's online account and making unauthorized trades on the account. The teenager concealed his true identity by using "various online aliases, multiple e-mail accounts, and employing foreign Internet service providers and several anonymizing websites."[3] This was the first ever identity theft case litigated by the SEC. The defendant was also investigated by the Federal Bureau of Investigation (FBI) and prosecuted by the United States Attorney's Office in Massachusetts.

The SEC's detailed October 9, 2003 complaint against Dinh alleged:

*Between June 18 and 27, 2003, the defendant purchased over 9,100 Cisco Systems, Inc. put option contracts with a July 19, 2003 expiration date for $10 per contract. These options gave Dinh the right to sell Cisco common stock at a price of $15 per share, but would expire worthless if the price of Cisco stock stayed above $15 per share. As July 19 approached, it became increasingly likely that the Cisco options would expire worthless.*

*On July 7, Dinh contacted several members of www.stockcharts.com, an investment analysis website, in order to obtain their e-mail addresses. Using an alias, Dinh filled out e-mail-based web forms inquiring about the members' personal websites; those who replied revealed their e-mail addresses to Dinh.*

*The next day, using a second alias, Dinh e-mailed the members who had responded to his earlier inquiry and invited them to test a new stock-charting tool. The e-mail invitation from Dinh directed the recipients to a website featuring a downloadable version of the purported stock-charting tool. In reality, the program was a disguised version of "The Beast," a keystroke-logging program[4] that allowed Dinh to remotely monitor the computer activity of those who downloaded it.*

*At least one recipient of Dinh's July 8 e-mail, a TD Waterhouse online brokerage customer, unwittingly downloaded and installed The Beast on his home computer, thereby enabling Dinh to monitor his computer activities, identify his online brokerage account, and steal his log-in and password information.*

*On the morning of July 11, eight days before their expiration, Dinh's Cisco options were more than $3 'out of the money.' Nevertheless, Dinh accessed his personal online brokerage account and placed a series of orders to sell his Cisco options at $5 per contract. These sell orders went unfilled until Dinh infiltrated the TD Waterhouse account and placed corresponding orders to buy Cisco options at the $5 contract price. Each of these buy orders was executed against sell orders from Dinh's own account, until Dinh had sold 7,200 of his Cisco option contracts and depleted virtually all of the available cash in the TD Waterhouse account. On July 19, the Cisco options expired worthless.[5]*

Dinh settled the case with the SEC on May 5, 2004, by consenting to the final judgment that permanently enjoined him from violating the antifraud provisions of federal securities law. Dinh previously pleaded guilty to the federal charges of securities fraud, wire fraud, and unauthorized computer access in furtherance of a fraud and on May 5 was sentenced to 13 months in prison, three years of supervised release, and a fine. Prior to his sentencing, Dinh paid restitution in the amount of $46,986 to the victim investor.[6]

## TEEN DÉJÀ VU

In 1985, Postal Inspectors found teenagers in Long Island, New York, involved in credit card fraud after the teens came across a primer on a computer bulletin board. The very detailed how-to guide provided instructions on how to commit credit card fraud. Using this information, the teens found credit card numbers on other computer sites and through Dumpster diving in garbage bins, as described in the online manual. Before they were caught, they had ordered thousands of dollars of computer equipment and had the merchandise mailed to a nearby home while the occupants were on vacation.

In April 1997 in Los Angeles, California, five teenagers were arrested for essentially the same scheme as their Long Island counterparts. They used their computer expertise to acquire victims' credit card numbers and other information from subscribers to an online service. They then purchased merchandise over the Internet with the stolen card numbers. They had the merchandise delivered to a vacant house in their neighborhood. A search of the teens' homes found the illegally obtained merchandise, lists of stolen credit card numbers and personal information, invoices, computer equipment, and orders from other high school students who wanted to share in the fraud.

Although separated by 12 years and considerable advances in technology, the two scams were essentially the same.[7] And both involved teens.

---

### IDENTITY THEFT HALL OF INFAMY

---

#### Abraham Abdallah

Identity theft can become an addictive crime for many perpetrators, and it can start at an early age. This is true in the case of recidivist identity thief Abraham Abdallah who learned how easy and lucrative the crime was when he was just a teenager. Prior to 2001, most people had never heard of this fraudster unless they were investigating identity theft in New York City or were one of his many victims. Abdallah had been very active as an identity thief since the mid-1980s, when he was a teenager in Brooklyn. Arrest after arrest for identity theft–related

*(Continued)*

---

crimes did not deter him from further criminal activity. More important, he continually adapted to changing times by embracing technology to expand his identity theft crimes. In 2001, he hit the big time and a worldwide media spotlight when he stole the identities of the rich and famous. As a result, Abdallah is as close as one can come to being the poster child for identity theft.

### BEGINNING OF A SERIAL IDENTITY THIEF

Law enforcement first met Abdallah in 1985 after an arrest for attempting to obtain an individual's credit report to use for fraudulent credit card applications. After his arrest, he agreed to assist in the preparation of a training video on preventing identity theft. TransUnion Credit Bureau produced this video, called *Crime of the '80s*. The training video helped to educate law enforcement, the credit card and banking industries, and the public about identity theft and credit card fraud. Abdallah appeared on the video discussing his criminal behavior in general and his involvement in credit card fraud and identity theft in particular.

Abdallah stated on the video that he started doing credit card fraud when he was 16. He described how easy it was to obtain personal information on his victims and then to steal money from financial institutions. He also stated, "I just need your name" in order to do credit card fraud and it "all depends on how good your credit is" as to whether he would be successful. That was true then and it is true now. When asked how much money he could make doing this fraud, he stated "a lot." Although he claimed that he had learned from his first arrest and was now reformed, his promise of going straight was short-lived. Abdallah continued his criminal behavior over the years. His name became well known to federal agents and detectives as a result of his numerous arrests for identity theft and related crimes. At an early age, he saw how easy it was to perpetrate identity theft, and it became his criminal career.

I was a Postal Inspector in those years and worked mail theft, credit card fraud, and identity theft cases in Brooklyn, New York. As a result of my work in this area, I was asked by TransUnion to also appear on the video to discuss my perspective on the growing problem of identity theft. From my many cases and even more arrests, I could see it was becoming a major problem throughout the country. Our concern back then was that the Abdallahs of the world would embrace this crime and overwhelm law enforcement agencies making the "Crime of the '80s" the crime wave of the future. I did not actually meet him at the time but after seeing him in the video, I knew I would never forget him.

About three or four years later, I was walking through my office in Brooklyn, New York, when I passed the processing area for arrestees. There I saw Abdallah in the custody of two other Postal Inspectors. I immediately recognized him. The other inspectors told me that he was under arrest for credit card fraud. Abdallah obtained bank and credit card statements stolen from the mail and then opened mail drops in the victims' names. He then fraudulently applied for credit cards in the names of people whose mail was stolen. I asked him about his promise of leaving a life of crime behind. All he could do was look at me with a sheepish grin and say, "I guess I forgot about that." After that chance meeting, I knew we would be hearing much more from Abraham Abdallah.

Abdallah continued in his career of crime. In 1994, he did an account takeover of a credit card belonging to the president and chief executive officer (CEO) of a large electronics and appliance retailer in the New York metropolitan area. Posing as the executive, Abdallah submitted a change of address request to the credit card issuer. The address was changed to a Mail Boxes, Etc. location in New York City that Abdallah rented. After the change of address, Abdallah then requested and received a credit line increase. Thanks to the diligent fraud control department at the bank, losses on the card were minimal, and this criminal activity was reported to Postal Inspectors. Abdallah was subsequently located and arrested in December 1995 in the U.S. Virgin Islands. He was eventually extradited to New York City, where he pleaded guilty in February 1998 to federal charges of bank fraud, credit card fraud, and wire fraud. Abdallah was sentenced to 32 months in prison followed by three years of supervised release. The few years in prison kept Abdallah out of circulation, but the wheels of fraud were hard at work in his brain.

Sadly, An Accurate Prediction

Beginning in September 2000 and continuing into early March 2001, Abdallah, now aided by his brother and others, embarked on the most ambitious scheme of his criminal career. It would land him in the media's crosshairs for masterminding the largest theft of identities at the time. According to federal authorities, Abdallah devised a scheme to steal approximately $22 million from a variety of wealthy individuals, corporations, and financial institutions. He picked some of his victims from the *Forbes* magazine list of "The 400 Richest People in America." Abdallah's scheme was successful as he conned banks and brokerage firms to transfer the true account holders' funds to accounts that he controlled.

Never one to forget his roots in identity theft, Abdallah duped the major credit bureaus, including Experian and Equifax, into providing him the credit reports on the country's wealthiest people using the names of investment banking firms Goldman Sachs and Bear Stearns as if they were the ones requesting the credit reports. Once he had this personal information, he cloned his victims' identities to gain access to their brokerage accounts at Merrill Lynch, Fidelity Investments, and elsewhere. He opened accounts at investment firms using the identities of his rich victims. He posed as a chief executive of a major corporation and attempted to liquidate a large amount of money from a U.S. account and transfer it out of the country. As part of the scheme, he altered a $30 check to $6.5 million for deposit in an account fraudulently opened in the name of a president of a large corporation.

During the time of this scheme, he held his day job as an unobtrusive busboy. That was just a cover for his move to the big time. He used sophisticated

*(Continued)*

167

Web-enabled cell phones, virtual voicemail, email accounts, and computers at public libraries to avoid detection. He rented a mail drop in Manhattan in the name of Microsoft cofounder Paul Allen. "What this guy was doing was setting up mailboxes all over the place," said a U.S. Postal Inspector involved in the investigation.[8] He also returned to the tried-and-true method of identity theft by stealing mail with personal information.

The crime spree was detected when Siebel Systems reported to the New York Police Department that someone had sent an email requesting a wire transfer of $10 million from Siebel founder Thomas Siebel's Merrill Lynch account to an account that Abdallah had set up. Law enforcement was on his trail for six months before arresting him in a sting operation in Brooklyn. He had ordered equipment to clone credit cards with stolen account information. The police and federal agents were waiting for Abdallah to pick up the package at a mail drop, and when his accomplice showed up, they followed him. The accomplice eventually led them to Abdallah, who was arrested on March 7, 2001. This high school dropout had finally gained infamy but not fortune.

In his possession at the time of his arrest was a copy of the October 5, 2000 issue of *Forbes* with the article entitled "The 400 Richest People in America." He had handwritten notes including the SSNs, addresses, investment accounts, and other personal information on many of the individuals in the article including Steven Spielberg, Ted Turner, Warren Buffett, Oprah Winfrey, Paul Allen, Sumner Redstone, Michael Eisner, and scores of others. He had over 800 fraudulent credit cards and tens of thousands of blank credit cards, all waiting to be cloned for identity theft. He also had lists containing credit card numbers and other data on hundreds of individuals as well as seven handwritten steps on how to commit identity theft.

On October 3, 2002, Abdallah pleaded guilty in federal court to numerous counts of mail and wire fraud. He was subsequently sentenced to 10 years and 10 months in prison. Abdallah's criminal career included 11 arrests by the New York Police Department and another 14 by federal law enforcement for credit card fraud, bank fraud, mail fraud, and other crimes. Postal Inspectors alone arrested him four times since 1986 for mail fraud and related crimes alone. "I wish I could say that this was all about money—then I'd have a reason to explain why I've ruined my life," stated Abdallah at his sentencing.[9]

Abdallah has been a con artist his entire adult life. He conned victims and he also conned judges. At his February 1998 sentencing for stealing almost $100,000 using fraudulent credit cards, he begged for mercy. "I won't let you down by reappearing before you in the future," he promised the federal judge.[10] His silver tongue obviously worked its magic as the judge sentenced Abdallah to a very lenient 2.5-year prison sentence. As soon as he got out of jail in 2000, he went right back to what he did best—stealing identities. This is why Abdallah is a charter member of the Identity Theft Hall of Infamy.

A HISTORY LESSON

We cannot forget how identity theft has grown and the serious impact it has had. Yet I am not sure we all learn the lesson that history teaches. A few years ago I attended a fraud seminar in California. One of the speakers was a respected and experienced professional involved in the detection of healthcare fraud. He was extremely knowledgeable about the various healthcare frauds and the problem of fraud. You can imagine my surprise when he provided the attendees a detailed resume that listed his date of birth, SSN, employment history, his wife's name, date of marriage, and children's names. Imagine what a fraudster such as Abdallah would do with this information!

## IT IS SO EASY, EVEN A CHILD CAN DO IT

Identity theft is so prevalent and so easy to commit that one can argue that anyone criminally minded can do it, even a child. While I say that somewhat facetiously, in reality teenagers and young adults, mere children, have been the perpetrators. That was the case in San Diego in March 2005 when 34 defendants, all between the ages of 18 and 22, were indicted in one of the largest identity theft rings ever prosecuted in the state of California. "This was a sophisticated crime ring that involved account holders, recruiters, lieutenants, and the top bosses."[11]

Mail was stolen from homes in the San Diego area with the ring targeting outgoing mail containing checks. The thieves then chemically washed the checks to remove the inked writing, entered new information, and cashed them through bank accounts of the various accomplices they recruited. Between 2002 and 2005, the gang recruited young adults with bank accounts into which the stolen and altered checks were deposited. Once deposited, large withdrawals were made from the accounts. All account holders then filed affidavits with the financial institutions claiming they were victims of fraud and forgery so they would not be suspected of the crime.

The case first came to light when individual homeowners in San Diego started complaining that checks they had mailed had not been received by the addressees. The outgoing mail was generally for payment of mortgages, utilities, credit cards, and other service payments, and had been placed in Postal Service collection boxes or in their home mailboxes for carrier pickup. Many of the complainants provided copies of their altered and deposited checks. Postal Inspectors noticed that many of the checks had similar handwriting styles and eventually identified three distinct handwriting styles. They also determined that most of the account holders were teenagers or young adults and that most shared the same story of how their accounts were breached.

The account holders stated that they had lost or misplaced their automated teller machine (ATM) cards, their personal identification numbers (PIN), their bank account numbers, and sometimes their California driver's licenses and Social Security cards. Many also filed police reports claiming thefts of their purses or wallets and stating that the stolen personal information was contained therein. This explanation and variations of it were provided over and over again by the account holders. Some of the accounts had five or six stolen checks deposited, and the amounts were generally between $3,000 and $7,000.

In reality, these account holders were willing participants in the fraud. They were recruited by members of the gang and offered approximately $1,000 to $2,000 for each check deposited into their accounts. In some cases, they received less than the promised amounts. These "walkers" would deposit the stolen checks that other gang members, the "runners," had stolen and washed. Two main gang leaders came up with this fraud, then it took on a life of its own because it was so easy to do.

The United States Postal Inspection Service was the investigative agency on the case. Postal Inspector Robert Diaz was one of the case agents. Inspector Diaz is a highly experienced federal agent who has investigated identity theft, credit card fraud, mail theft, counterfeiting, forgery, and the manufacture of phony identification. In interview after interview in this case, he and other investigators were told the same story by the account holders who willingly participated in the identity theft scheme for money. Here is one of the confessions:

*On May 1, 2003, Postal Inspectors interviewed Johanne Puntanilla regarding the $7,500 check which had been negotiated through her account. She stated that she was approached by her cousin, Jeffree Albano Punzal, and asked if she needed any money. Puntanilla stated that she did and Punzal subsequently got her in contact with an unnamed "friend" who would explain what she needed to do. This friend contacted Puntanilla via Punzal's cell phone. The friend explained that she would need to provide him with her ATM card, PIN number and Washington Mutual account number. She was told that several checks would be deposited into her checking account and funds would be subsequently withdrawn. She stated she was told by the friend not to report her "missing" information until after she was contacted.*

*Once the fraudulent checks were deposited and withdrawn through her account, she was contacted by the friend and was told to contact her bank to report that her cards were missing. She stated she was told to fill out an affidavit of fraud and forgery with the bank. She stated that the friend told her to "play dumb" and act as though she didn't know anything if approached by the police or the bank. Puntanilla stated that she has never seen the friend and has only spoken to him via her cousin's cell phone. She stated that shortly after she spoke with the bank, she received $2,000 from her cousin. She stated the money was payment for providing the friend with her account information.*[12]

Most of the defendants had no prior criminal records. Inspector Diaz's investigation used interviews of the mail theft victims, document analysis, and handwriting comparisons to gather the initial evidence. Interviews of the account holders provided admissions of guilt that resulted in their "flipping" and providing evidence against the other gang members. Inspector Diaz also used electronic surveillance to record incriminating conversations between the cooperating subjects and other targets. Search warrants provided additional evidence of wrongdoing.

The fraud loss in this case totaled approximately $1 million. Twenty-nine defendants received felony convictions for their crimes. The two gang leaders received sentences of between two and three years in state prison and $145,000 in court-ordered restitution. The runners received minimal jail terms, generally between three months and

16 months. The account holders received probation and were ordered to pay restitution equivalent to the amount of the stolen checks deposited into their accounts. Clearly, the defendants were very lucky to have received such minimal jail time for their crimes. Their ages and lack of criminal histories benefited them but only so much.

In reflecting on the case, Inspector Diaz commented:

> *The unfortunate aspect to the case is that all these account holders were young adults just starting off with no real criminal backgrounds. They thought what they were doing by selling their account information was a victimless crime not hurting anyone. In fact, the person they really hurt was themselves. They now have to deal with paying restitution to the banks in the thousands of dollars in addition to the associated problems they will face in the future with having a felony conviction on their record.*[13]

## EVIL MENTOR

A California woman exploited the college students who worked for her by stealing their identities. Christina Kyeonghee Kim owned a restaurant in Arcata, California, and employed students attending a nearby university. She fraudulently used the students' SSNs, driver's licenses, and dates of birth that they provided for employment for identity theft. She used this stolen personal information to create new identities as well as to alter her own identity with some of the purloined information. Kim opened 49 bank accounts and credit cards under the stolen identities and used the various lines of credit. Among the many things she purchased with these defrauded funds were a new home, designer clothes, and jewelry.

In all, she obtained more than $1 million through this identity theft scheme. But it did not stop there. Proving my Potato Chip Theory of Fraud, as previously detailed in Chapter 4, Kim also engaged in insurance fraud by falsely claiming a burglary at her home. She claimed that personal items, including valuable artwork, were stolen in the burglary, and she provided false documentation to the insurance company claiming the value of the items stolen was between $800,000 and $1 million. In April 2006, the United States Attorney in San Francisco charged Kim with 51 counts of bank fraud, mail fraud, and aggravated identity theft.[14]

Kim's scheme lasted seven years. Making matters even worse, she acted as an

> *informal "mentor" to Korean foreign exchange students attending Humboldt State University. Kim used her position of trust as an employer and mentor to steal the personal identifying information of her family members, employees, and young foreign exchange students attending Humboldt State University.*[15]

She took advantage of the very young people she was entrusted with mentoring and watching over as their employer. She violated that trust when she stole their identities and forged their signatures on bank and credit card applications, checks, and other line of credit documents. She eventually pleaded guilty to 47 counts of the indictment in March 2007. On December 12, 2007, Kim was sentenced to 54 months imprisonment.[16]

## CHILD ID THEFT

As vigilant as adults are about safeguarding their identities, they must be aware that children can also be victims of identity theft. That is because they have SSNs and birth certificates that can be easily compromised. As a result, identity thieves are targeting children more and more. Children as victims of identity theft present a unique set of problems, and special steps must be taken to protect them. Children can be easy targets for identity thieves, since often no one is monitoring their credit. Thus, thieves can use the identity for years, leaving an unsuspecting minor with a shattered credit history.

Thieves will acquire children's SSNs, often selling them to illegal immigrants who use them to obtain driver's licenses or open bank accounts. The stolen SSNs can also be used by criminals to start a new life, confident that they will have years before the fraud is detected.[17]

Although the numbers of identity theft complaints involving children are increasing, they still remain small. As of 2005, only about 5% of the complaints received by the FTC involved minors. However, the true number may well be much higher, since the crime can remain undetected for years.[18] Many times a child's identity is not stolen by a complete stranger but rather a family member or friend. Unscrupulous relatives will latch onto a child's unblemished credit history and exploit it for their own ends.[19]

Often it is the parent who is the culprit in stealing the child's identity. Parents have access to a child's birth certificate and SSN. After damaging their own credit through unpaid debt and bankruptcy, their children's untouched credit is a tempting resource. In 2002, a father in Billings, Montana, was sentenced to five years in prison for obtaining credit cards in his daughter's name and then running up $12,000 in unpaid charges. In another case, a father discovered that his ex-wife opened credit cards in their young daughter's name. Again proving that the Potato Chip Theory of Fraud applies to identity thieves, the ex-wife was working in a nursing home and also stole $125,000 from an Alzheimer's patient. She was arrested and convicted.[20]

In a study conducted by the Identity Theft Resource Center on the subject of child identity theft, more than half the victims had their identities stolen between the year of birth and age five. In most cases, the culprit was a parent, and the stolen identity was used for work and/or credit.[21] Yet there are many others who have access to a child's personal information. A three-month-old baby had his identity stolen by a nurse in the hospital where he was born. The parents determined that the identity theft occurred in the hospital when the child "was mailed a bill for extensive back-injury treatments" that clearly was for an adult patient.[22]

There are things parents can do to protect their children from identity theft and its devastating effects. If an organization asks for the child's SSN number or a copy of a birth certificate, ask if the information is really necessary. Except for government-related requests, the SSN is often unnecessary. A child's credit report should be checked from time to time; if a credit report exists for a child who should not have one, that is a red flag that fraud is being committed. Credit bureaus do not create credit reports until a person begins to apply for credit. Another red flag is the receipt of credit card solicitations when the child had never applied for credit, unless a parent had already added the child's name to an existing credit card or opened an account.[23]

## PREVENTION AND SECURITY FOR TEENAGERS AND YOUNG ADULTS

Just as for all age groups, teens and young adults need to check their credit reports annually. If teens do not have credit cards or loans, they should not have credit histories. If they do find an active credit report, it might be an indicator of potential fraud and the need for further inquiry. The same prevention rules apply for teens as for adults.

Qwest Communications has rolled out a unique education and awareness program for teenagers to protect them from becoming victims of identity theft. The showcase of the initiative is an interactive Web site[24] that provides excellent prevention resources. The site provides videos, lesson plans, tips, and warning signs of identity theft for teens as well as the top five ways that teens can become victims including:

1. Sharing too much personal information on social networking sites
2. Trusting and talking to strangers they meet on these sites
3. Posting SSNs, dates of birth, and other personal information at online job sites
4. Falling victim to phishing scams
5. Storing SSNs and other personal information on cell phones that can easily be lost or stolen[25]

The site provides a number of red-flag indicators of identity theft that are specific to teens but can be useful for others as well. They include:

- Applying for your first driver's license and learning that one has previously been issued
- Finding out about outstanding tickets for traffic infractions that you did not incur and that have not been paid
- Submitting credit card and student loan applications that are being denied
- Receiving collection statements for unknown debt[26]

Teen identity theft prevention recommendations from Qwest include:

- Be careful to whom you provide your SSN and other personal information.
- Do not carry your Social Security card or birth certificate, and keep them in a secure location.
- Do not give your driver's license to anyone, even a friend.
- Keep your credit cards, checkbook, and cellular phone in a safe place.
- Do not give personal information to anyone unless you are absolutely sure of who they are and why they need the information.
- Order a copy of your credit report. This is especially important when applying for student loans.
- Insist that your college or university not use your SSN as your college identification number.[27]

**NOTES**

1. "Teen Pleads Innocent to Identity Theft Charges," MSNBC.com. August 6, 2001, www.msnbc.com/local/knbc/nbc0kz982qc.asp.

2. John Cody, "Two Students under Investigation in Identity Theft Case," *The Torch* (St. John's University), December 1, 2004, 3.

3. U.S. Securities and Exchange Commission, Litigation Release No. 18696, "SEC Settles Case Against Hacker Charged with Breaking into Investor's Online Account, Making Unauthorized Trades," May 6, 2004, www.sec.gov/litigation/litreleases/lr18696.htm.

4. A keystroke-logging program is a hacking tool that allows someone to remotely monitor the actual computer keystrokes of another Internet user without their knowledge via a surreptitiously installed program on the unsuspecting person's computer. A "Trojan horse" is another hacking program in which malicious or harmful code is secretly inserted into the victim's computer but disguised as seemingly harmless files or data. The unwitting victim is deceived into thinking that the program is something other than what it is purported to be. This allows the hacker to gain control of the breached computer.

5. U.S. Securities and Exchange Commission, Litigation Release No. 18401, "SEC Charges Hacker with Breaking Into Investor's Online Account, Placing Unauthorized Buy Order," October 9, 2003, www.sec.gov/litigation/litreleases/lr18401.htm.

6. U.S. Securities and Exchange Commission, Litigation Release No. 18696, "SEC Settles Case Against Hacker."

7. Martin T. Biegelman, "Fraud on the Internet: Postal Inspectors Confront a New Challenge," *Law Enforcement Report*, United States Postal Inspection Service (Summer 1998), 2.

8. Greg Farrell, "Hacker Stole Identities of Richest Americans," *USA Today*, April 13, 2001, www.usatoday.com/life/cyber/tech/2001-03-20-hacker.htm.

9. Bob Sullivan, *Your Evil Twin: Behind the Identity Theft Epidemic* (Hoboken, NJ: John Wiley & Sons, 2004), 27.

10. Mike Claffey, Robert Gearty, and Dave Goldiner, "Celeb Hack Had Knack," *Daily News*, March 21, 2001, 9.

11. Office of the District Attorney, County of San Diego, News Release, "San Diego County's Largest Identity Theft Ring Broken Up, 34 Indicted on 66 Felony charges," March 18, 2005.

12. Affidavit for Search Warrant, Superior Court of San Diego, Central Division, sworn to by Postal Inspector Robert Diaz, August 8, 2003.

13. Postal Inspector Robert Diaz's comments to the author on January 23, 2008.

14. U.S. Department of Justice, Office of the United States Attorney, Northern District of California, News Release, "Humboldt Woman Arraigned on Charges of Stealing Student Identities to Make More than $1 Million," April 12, 2006, sanfrancisco.fbi.gov/dojpressrel/2006/sf041206a.htm.

15. U.S. Department of Justice, Office of the United States Attorney, Northern District of California, News Release, "Arcata Business Woman Sentenced to $4^1/_2$ Years in

Million Dollar Identity Theft Scheme," December 13, 2007, www.usdoj.gov/usao/can/press/2007/2007_12_13_kim.sentenced.press.html.

16. Ibid.

17. Barbara Whitaker, "Never Too Young to Have Your Identity Stolen," *New York Times*, July 21, 2007.

18. Brigitte Yuille, "Stolen Innocence: Child Identity Theft," Bankrate.com, www.bankrate.com/nltrack/news/debt/20070103_child_identity_theft_a1.asp.

19. John Leland, "Identity Thief Often Found in Family Photo," *New York Times*, November 13, 2006; Janet Shamlian, "Main Culprits in Kids' ID Theft? Family Members," MSNBC.com, March 3, 2005, www.msnbc.msn.com/id/7045490.

20. Abigail Goldman, "Kid's Identity Theft Prevalent—Often by a Family Member," *Arizona Daily Star*, December 17, 2006, A7.

21. Julian Mincer, "Identity Theft Targets Children," *Wall Street Journal*, November 21, 2007, D2.

22. Goldman, "Kid's Identity Theft Prevalent."

23. Brigitte Yuille, "7 Steps to Protect Your Child from Identity Theft." Bankrate.com, www.bankrate.com/nltrack/news/debt/20070103_child_identity_theft_b1.asp?caret=3.

24. www.incredibleinternet.com/identity-theft.

25. Teens and Identity Theft, Qwest Communications, www.incredibleinternet.com/identity-theft/protect-your-identity.

26. Tips for Teens, Qwest Communications, www.incredibleinternet.com/related/tips-for-teens.

27. Ibid.

# CHAPTER 13

# Victims and Victimization

"I keep telling them I didn't do it and I have to keep proving it. The banks and the police just don't believe me that I'm the victim here." That is something I have heard from victims of identity theft for three decades. In case after case, they have been frustrated trying to convince financial institutions and law enforcement of their victimization. Even when they can clearly demonstrate the crimes levied against them, they are often at a loss to restore their credit history and reputation.

Survey after survey finds that this is the case. Identity theft is the evil gift that just keeps on giving. A June 2005 Nationwide Mutual Insurance Company survey of 1,097 identity theft victims found that most spend an average of 81 hours cleaning up their damaged credit. Even more disturbing, the survey found that 28% of victims were unable to restore their identities and clean up their credit even after a year of trying. "The survey shows that recovering from identity theft can be difficult, costly and stressful, but what is most alarming is that despite the time, money, and personal duress victims go through, resolution is not always achieved," said Kirk Herath, associate general counsel for Nationwide.[1] Although many victims face minimal financial impact, some are not as lucky, as indicated by the results of this study. Debit card holders for one are usually not reimbursed for their losses. Still, the monetary impact can be eclipsed by the reputational and emotional toll.

There has been story after story of victims who tried to report their victimization to the police but were rebuffed. Either the police claimed they did not have jurisdiction to investigate identity theft or did not believe the victim. Cleaning up one's credit report can take time and effort. Credit reports are used for much more than opening credit card accounts and obtaining loans. They are necessary for employment decisions, renting apartments, and obtaining utility services, for instance. Fraudsters can keep using stolen identities for years and share the information with other criminals who use it for their scams. The stolen identity can live on for years, continuing to damage the victim.

"With ID theft, you have to keep proving you are innocent," said an identity theft victim in Washington State. "If your house is robbed, you call the police, you fill out the insurance forms—you don't have to constantly be on the defensive to show you didn't rob it yourself."[2]

## AN IDENTITY THEFT NIGHTMARE

The frightening story of a Southern California man who had his credit and his life ruined for 13 years by an identity thief in Florida is the ultimate victimization. Imagine being negatively affected year after year and unable to stop it. That is what happened to Clay Henderson, who lost his wallet while vacationing in Daytona Beach, Florida, in 1987. Douglas Staus was on the run from law enforcement in New Jersey for fraud charges. He found the wallet and quickly took over Henderson's identity. Over the years, Staus purchased cars, obtained credit cards and loans, and got married twice, all under Henderson's name, Social Security number (SSN), and date of birth. He started a business, but complaints started when he failed to deliver what he promised.

While Staus was living a lie, Henderson's life was deteriorating. The identity theft damaged Henderson's credit and impacted his employment. He was unable to get credit cards or apartment leases. His federal job required a security clearance, but due to Staus's criminal record, Henderson received a limited clearance. Henderson protested, but no one would listen. The limited security clearance resulted in poor career opportunities. Eventually he spent a week in jail when police picked him up on an arrest warrant out of Florida thinking he was Staus.

Henderson tried desperately to get someone's attention. He reached out to law enforcement all over Florida to help him. At last, police in Hernando County, Florida, heard his anguish. Justice finally arrived in August 2001, when law enforcement arrested Staus for a multitude of fraud and identity theft crimes. Staus even gave police a phony name when he was arrested.[3] Justice was served, but it took 13 years to end Henderson's nightmare. "Justice delayed is justice denied," as British statesman and prime minister William E. Gladstone famously said.

## GETTING A NEW SSN IF ALL ELSE FAILS

Even when all instances of identity theft have stopped, credit bureaus may not have corrected victims' credit files. Victims must continually check their credit reports for fraudulent accounts, phony addresses, and fraud losses in their names. In extreme cases of identity theft, where there was such extensive use of one's stolen SSN and identity that there was little chance of repairing the credit history, victims have requested and received new SSNs. It is not an easy or common practice but it can be done. Here is what the Social Security Administration has to say about this:

### Should you get a new Social Security number?

*If you have done all you can to fix the problems resulting from misuse of your Social Security number and someone still is using your number, we may assign you a new number.*

*You cannot get a new Social Security number:*

- *To avoid the consequences of filing for bankruptcy;*
- *If you intend to avoid the law or your legal responsibility; or*
- *If your Social Security card is lost or stolen, but there is no evidence that someone is using your number.*

*If you decide to apply for a new number, you will need to prove your age, U.S. citizenship or lawful immigration status and identity. For more information, ask for Your Social Security Number And Card (Publication Number 05-10002).*

*You also will need to provide evidence that you still are being disadvantaged by the misuse.*

*Keep in mind that a new number probably will not solve all your problems. This is because other governmental agencies (such as the Internal Revenue Service and state motor vehicle agencies) and private businesses (such as banks and credit reporting companies) likely will have records under your old number. Also, because credit reporting companies use the number, along with other personal information, to identify your credit record, using a new number will not guarantee you a fresh start. This is especially true if your other personal information, such as your name and address, remains the same.*

*If you receive a new Social Security number, you will not be able use the old number anymore.*

*For some victims of identity theft, a new number actually creates new problems. If the old credit information is not associated with the new number, the absence of any credit history under the new number may make it more difficult for you to get credit.*[4]

## OPERATION GAFFLE

A highly sophisticated, multijurisdictional, organized identity theft, counterfeit credit and debit card fraud, and fencing ring was crippled on December 8, 2005, when 13 of the group's major participants were arrested by agents from the United States Postal Inspection Service in Newark, New Jersey, and detectives from the Hudson County, New Jersey, Prosecutor's Office. The law enforcement officers dubbed this investigation Operation Gaffle after the self-proclaimed name of the gang, the "Gaffle Kings." It was a most appropriate name. "Gaffle" is an urban slang term meaning to steal, rip-off, and scam, which was exactly what this group of criminals was doing.

In a series of early morning raids, Postal Inspectors and Hudson County Detectives, in cooperation with the New York County District Attorney's Office, the Manhattan and Bronx District Attorneys, the New York City Police Department, and the Secret Service, executed a series of coordinated search and arrest warrants in New Jersey and throughout New York City. Simultaneous search and arrest warrants were also executed in Massachusetts, Florida, South Carolina, and Georgia. Postal Inspectors from the Newark Division and detectives from the Hudson County Prosecutors Office were assisted by Postal Inspectors and local authorities in those jurisdictions.

The investigation began in June 2005, as a spin-off from an earlier investigation by Newark Postal Inspectors and the Hudson County Prosecutors Office. In this earlier case, subsequent to the arrest of Frank "TK" Robertson, a forensic examination of his computer uncovered over 2,000 victim names, addresses, and credit card account numbers. Robertson was a career criminal with 18 arrests over the years for credit card and identity theft–crimes. The accounts on Robertson's computer were found to have over $1.3 million worth of fraudulent transactions. In this case, an informant was utilized and a subsequent wiretap was authorized on the cell phones of four of the main players. Following a trail of fraud and deception, Postal Inspectors and detectives uncovered an additional $1 million in fraudulent credit card purchases in more than 30 different states as well as fraudulent withdrawals from automated teller machines (ATMs).

The leaders of the organization, Robertson of Union City, New Jersey, and Christopher Mack of Manhattan, were involved in the mass production of counterfeit credit and debit cards, fraudulently encoded with the legitimate account numbers of unsuspecting victims, as well as the making of false identification. Robertson and Mack purchased the compromised account information from computer hackers from outside of the United States who were able to penetrate corporate databases to obtain the individual account information of the victims. The two made payments to these sources through the use of e-money, an anonymous form of digital currency.

This highly sophisticated operation conducted much of its business on the Internet, with the targets sharing their stolen information via email. The group illegally obtained cash and merchandise in several ways. Using counterfeit credit cards, the criminals targeted large electronic retailers and warehouse stores. Coconspirators, many from New Jersey, and others who were friends or relatives of the main players, would travel to different states, from Maine to Florida, to use the fraudulent cards. High-end electronics were routinely purchased in these states, transported back to the New Jersey/New York area and then resold, either to fences in New York City or on eBay. Robertson and Mack also routinely mailed counterfeit cards to their associates in various other states, who would also make fraudulent retail purchases, then ship a portion of the items to them as payment for the cards.

Investigators also seized recently mailed items, meant for sale on eBay, while in transit. In another aspect of the conspiracy, the suspects used counterfeit bank debit cards, encoded with legitimate account numbers belonging to unsuspecting victims, to make fraudulent withdrawals of hundreds of thousands of dollars from ATM machines in the New Jersey/New York area and other states. The victims of this organized enterprise included hundreds of members of the State Employees Credit Union of North Carolina, whose account numbers and related PIN codes were compromised by hackers located in Estonia and Italy.

Postal Inspectors, Hudson County detectives, and other law enforcement agents recovered hundreds of counterfeit credit cards and hundreds of counterfeit Bank of America ATM cards as well as the computers and machines to make these cards.

Approximately $60,000 in cash was also recovered. Search warrants were executed at a number of storage facilities in New Jersey, New York, and Georgia, where the defendants stored stolen merchandise. Additional search warrants were executed at two New York stores involved in the fencing process. A total of five postal trailer trucks were filled with seized merchandise. Additional seizures were made including property belonging to Robertson and Mack. Postal Inspectors in Atlanta, Boston, Charlotte, Miami, and New York assisted in this excellent investigative effort.

Subsequently, all the defendants in Operation Gaffle pleaded guilty to state charges of conspiracy before Judge Kevin Callahan in Hudson County Superior Court and were sentenced to prison terms. Frank "TK" Robertson and Christopher "C-Mack" Mack each received 12 years in prison. Other key conspirators received between five and 10 years in prison. In addition to pleading guilty to the state charges, extra federal prison time was imposed on several of the defendants as a result of federal probation violations.

The computer expertise of identity theft thieves continues to grow, as do the criminal histories of the suspects. In this case, the main players had previous arrests ranging from murder to drug dealing, armed robbery, assault, and fraud. This group was able to enlist people with various jobs (bank employees, gas station attendants, business owners, car dealership and healthcare employees, along with the unemployed) to assist in their criminal activity. In addition, this case highlighted the fact that state and federal law enforcement working together is a must in order to stop identity thieves who use jurisdictional issues to advance their criminal activity. "You can steal more money with a pen and a computer than with a gun, and because of this, identity theft numbers will continue to rise," said Postal Inspector Scott Mathews, the case agent in this investigation. "All companies and law enforcement agencies must take an aggressive and relentless approach to combating this epidemic with the understanding security will increase revenue while removing the 'cost of doing business' attitude."[5]

## VICTIM AND WITNESS RIGHTS

Law enforcement has placed a particular emphasis on protecting the rights of victims and witnesses of crime. This book is focused on the evils of identity theft and ensuring the rights of those impacted by this or any crime is paramount. Content from an excellent brochure on victim and witness rights published by the U.S. Postal Inspection Service that is germane to all victims and witnesses follows.

*Know Your Rights: A Guide for Victims and Witnesses of Crime*

*Publication 308, August 2005*

**Your Rights**

*As a victim or witness of a crime, you have these rights:*

1. *The right to be reasonably protected from the accused.*
2. *The right to reasonable, accurate, and timely notice of any public court proceeding, or any parole proceeding, involving the crime or of any release or escape of the accused.*

181

3. *The right not to be excluded from any such public court proceeding, unless the court, after receiving clear and convincing evidence, determines that testimony by the victim would be materially altered if the victim heard other testimony at that proceeding.*

4. *The right to be reasonably heard at any public proceeding in the district court involving release, plea, sentencing, or any parole proceeding.*

5. *The reasonable right to confer with the attorney for the government in the case.*

6. *The right to full and timely restitution as provided in the law.*

7. *The right to proceedings free from unreasonable delay.*

8. *The right to be treated with fairness and with respect for the victim's dignity and privacy.*

*As an agency of federal law enforcement professionals, the U.S. Postal Inspection Service is concerned about problems that may be experienced by victims and witnesses of crime. We know that, as a victim or witness, you may feel anger, confusion, frustration, or fear as a result of your experience.*

*We have prepared this information to help you deal with problems and questions that may surface during an investigation and to provide you with a better understanding of the criminal justice system. We have included information and services available to you as a victim or witness.*

*We hope this information will be helpful. We encourage you to contact the Postal Inspector handling your case or your Victim/Witness Coordinator if you have further questions.*

### Investigating the Case

*Although the days and months ahead may be difficult for you and your family, your assistance is important to ensure that justice is served.*

*During the investigation, you will be informed of the status of the case. Throughout the investigation, a Postal Inspector or Victim/Witness Coordinator will remain your primary contact. If you have questions, be sure to contact one of these individuals as soon as possible. A criminal investigation can be complex and lengthy. It may involve several federal and local agencies.*

*Remember, your interests are important to us. We are here to help answer any questions you may have.*

*If your case is accepted for prosecution, you will be contacted by the attorney's office assigned to handle your case. Most prosecutors' offices have a Victim/Witness Coordinator to help answer your questions and assist with your concerns during the pretrial and court phases of the case.*

### If You Are Threatened or Harassed

*If anyone threatens you, or you feel you are being harassed because of your cooperation with authorities, report it to your Postal Inspector. There are penalties for harassment and other threats. The Inspector may discuss protective measures with you. If you feel you are in immediate danger, dial 911.*

### If You Were Physically Injured

*If you were injured or threatened with physical injury as a result of the crime, and lack insurance or other means to pay for medical bills, check your state's crime victim compensation program. In many states, the cost of counseling, lost wages, and certain funeral expenses may be covered.*

*The law varies by state, but your Victim/Witness Coordinator can provide you with the necessary information.*

### If You Had Property Stolen

*As part of its investigation, the Postal Inspection Service hopes to recover any property or money stolen from you. If we recover it, we will notify you and make every effort to have it returned as quickly as possible. Restitution may be available for property not recovered or for the cost of any necessary repairs.*

### Assisting with Your Employer

*Upon request, during the investigation and court processing, we can call your employer to discuss the importance of your role as a victim or witness to the government's case and to explain any absences you may need to take from your workplace.*

### Restitution

*If a person is arrested and successfully prosecuted in your case, you may be eligible for restitution. This is a court-ordered payment made to you as a victim of a crime. Upon conviction, the offender pays out-of-pocket expenses resulting from your victimization.*

*If the court orders restitution at sentencing, it may consider the offender's present and future ability to pay. If the defendant has assets, the court may order restitution to be paid immediately or in scheduled payments. In many cases, however, the proceeds of the crime are no longer available and the defendant does not have sufficient assets to pay restitution. It is possible, therefore, that a victim may not receive restitution.*

*Other remedies may include a civil suit or small claims court action. Restitution cannot be avoided through bankruptcy.*

### Assisting with Your Recovery

*Victims and witnesses are emotionally affected by crime. Although everyone reacts differently, victims and witnesses commonly report some of these behaviors:*

- *Increased concern for your personal safety and that of family members. You may naturally be more cautious.*
- *Trouble concentrating on the job.*
- *Difficulty handling everyday problems or feeling overwhelmed.*
- *Going over the circumstances of the crime again and again, and thinking about what might have gone differently.*
- *Difficulties from financial loss.*

*These problems are normal, and they may decrease with time. Talking with the Postal Inspector handling your case or a Victim/Witness Coordinator may assist in your recovery.*

*If the defendant either pleads guilty or is found guilty, you have the opportunity, before sentencing to submit an "Impact Statement" describing the emotional, physical, and financial effects of the crime on your life and that of your family. A Victim/Witness Coordinator can help prepare the statement, if needed.*

### For Assistance

*Call the Victim/Witness Coordinator at your local Postal Inspection Service office for information on the status of your case. If the case is prosecuted federally, you should receive information on how to access the Department of Justice's Victim Notification System (VNS). VNS is a computer-based system that provides updated information on your case. You can access it at no cost via a toll-free number.*

### Other Programs

*U.S. Department of Justice
Office for Victims of Crime
202-307-5983
www.ojp.usdoj.gov/ovc*

*National Organization for Victim Assistance
1-800-879-6682
www.trynova.org*

*National Center for Victims of Crime
1-800-394-2255
www.ncvc.org*

*U.S. Postal Inspection Service
475 L'Enfant Plaza SW, Room 3100
Washington, DC 20260-3100
http://postalinspectors.uspis.gov/*

*Federal Trade Commission
1-877-FTC-HELP (toll free)
www.ftc.gov*[6]

## VICTIM NOTIFICATION SYSTEM

The Department of Justice's Victim Notification System (VNS) is a cooperative effort between the U.S. Postal Inspection Service, the Federal Bureau of Investigation, the U.S. Attorney's Offices, the Federal Bureau of Prisons, and the Department of Justice's Criminal Division.

*This free, computer-based system provides federal crime victims with information on scheduled court events, as well as the outcome of those court events. It also provides victims with information on the offender's custody status and release. In addition to the written notifications generated through VNS, victims can obtain automated status information by calling the VNS Call Center at 1-866-365-4968 (1-866-DOJ-4YOU) or by accessing the VNS Internet site at www.notify.usdoj.gov. A Victim ID# and PIN# are required to access the VNS Call Center or VNS Internet site.*[7]

# THOUGHT LEADERS IN VICTIM AND WITNESS RIGHTS

## Georgia Hanif and Julie Werner-Simon

Georgia Hanif is the Victim/Witness Coordinator for the United States Attorney's Office in Los Angeles. She is a recognized expert in victim and witness rights and has worked tirelessly on their behalf for many years. Hanif developed and implemented a victim notification process for the U.S. Postal Inspection Service and developed a wide variety of programs focused on protecting victims of crime including training law enforcement officers in victim/witness rights and seizing assets for restitution. She has helped build an exceptional Victim/Witness Assistance Center in the U.S. Attorney's Office that is a model for other federal, state, and local programs. Ms. Hanif speaks to nonprofit groups, such as the American Association of Retired Persons (AARP), Daughters of the American Revolution (DAR), and local schools on fraud and identity theft prevention measures. She was recognized by the Royal Canadian Mounted Police for her victim advocacy and assistance involving an international telemarketing scheme. Her efforts on behalf of victim rights under the Crime Victims Rights Act of 2004 have set case law precedent in *Kenna v. United States District Court*.

Julie Werner-Simon is an Assistant United States Attorney for the Central District of California, based in Los Angeles, where she prosecutes white-collar crime cases as senior litigation counsel of the Major Frauds Section. During her tenure in the U.S. Attorney's Office (USAO), Werner-Simon has received numerous awards and recognition including the Director's Award for Superior Performance for her successes in investigating and prosecuting complex financial fraud crimes as well as for her work in training federal prosecutors on ethical considerations in investigating and prosecuting federal offenses. In April 2002, she was honored with the USAO's Victim Recognition Award for her efforts on behalf of crime victims. Werner-Simon has also produced legal education films including the excellent awareness and prevention DVD entitled *Stop Identity Theft Now* that is available through the United States Department of Justice.

Here Hanif and Werner-Simon provide their insightful comments, creative ideas, and recommendations on the prosecution perspective and protection of the rights of identity theft victims and witnesses. The views expressed are those of the individuals only and do not necessarily reflect the position of the United States Attorney's Office for the Central District of California, the United States Department of Justice, or any other government agency:

*All U.S. Attorney's Offices have Victim/Witness Units and they are governed by the Executive Office for United States Attorneys. Our role is to assist victims at the time charges are filed. Prior to that, the responsibility belongs to the federal investigative*

*(Continued)*

*agencies. Many times we work closely with our victim/witness counterparts and federal agents in those agencies to ensure a seamless transition for victims. We liaison with law enforcement, probation, clerk of courts, financial litigation units charged with postjudgment debt collection from defendants, banks, credit card companies, and of course victims and witnesses.*

*During the constitutionally mandated criminal discovery process, prosecutors should take extra care in disclosing victim's personal information. When such materials are given to defense counsel, all personal information should be redacted. While prosecutors typically file Rule 6(e) disclosure orders, which permit them to give grand jury materials to the defense and which limit the defense's ability to provide the 6(e) material to parties not involved in the preparation of the defense, prosecutors have not been doing the same thing for non–grand jury information.*

*Assistant United States Attorneys (AUSA) should routinely seek protective orders from the court that permit the government to give the materials to the defense (these include witness statements, bank records, etc.) but that require that the defense only use them in preparation of the case. Additionally, the order should also prevent any replication and dissemination of those materials by anyone including defendant to third parties who are not part of the defense attorney's staff (i.e., paralegals and investigators). There should be a specific bar to disseminating the information in any form including posting the information on a Web site. The aim here is to prevent identity theft and the reloading of fraud victims or the making of new victims by the release of discovery "on the street."*

*AUSAs should attempt to invite defense counsel to prosecutor's office to review victim bank account loss information rather than release hard copies to defendant's counsel. AUSAs should help victims notify credit reporting agencies and credit card companies about the victim/witness status. Each U.S. Attorney's Office should have such a form letter personalized by the case AUSA in conjunction with the Victim/Witness Unit. Always make sure this letter is turned over in discovery, as it is* Giglio *material.*[8]

*We constantly train law enforcement in understanding and enforcing victim/witness rights along with asset forfeiture and seizing assets for restitution. In some cases, this has caused a change of mind-set for many federal agents. The forefeiture program in its infancy was promoted as a way for law enforcement to both punish the offender and to lessen their operating budgets by obtaining seized assets their agency may need. Consequently, agents are accustomed to seizing assets as part of the forfeiture program. The practice of seizing assets to be sold for victim restitution is now promoted vigorously in this district as part of the mandated requirement of timely restitution per the Criminal Victims's Rights Act.*

*We are also involved in rewriting the language in plea agreements and criminal judgments to make enforcement easier. We have implemented training for court clerks and probation officers to ensure that all parties assist victims. Several years ago, we created a DVD entitled* Stop Identity Theft Now *that is aimed at the general public. The DVD emphasizes steps individuals can take to clear up any credit issues that developed as a result of identity theft as well as prevention measures. The DVD can be requested by individuals as well as state and local law enforcement agencies by calling*

*1-888-228-0315 and providing a mailing address. There are no copyright restrictions on the DVD, which enables duplication.*

*Over the years, we have seen many things change for the better for victims. The Crime Victims' Rights Act of 2004 provides enforcement mechanisms to ensure better compliance and protections for victims. Since the passage of this act, internal procedures have been implemented and these provide additional safeguards for victims. One important aspect of our role as advocates is providing court support to the victims. Depending on the length of the trial, victim support can become time challenging while trying to maintain a heavy workload. Nevertheless, victims are entitled to be treated with dignity and respect throughout the judicial process. To accomplish this element, victim units in all the U.S. Attorney Offices are mandated to provide a waiting area in the court for victims and witnesses and their advocates. In many cases, the coordinators accompany victims into court and explain the court events as they occur.*

*While these best practices and procedures are for federal use, they would also apply at state and local levels. Most state and local prosecutors have victim/witness programs. In some cases, the programs are domiciled in local police stations, thus ensuring faster response to victim needs.*

*Identity theft has become the fastest-growing crime in the United States and around the world. Tougher legislation for white-collar and cybercrime along with additional investigators are needed. Credit card companies and banks could benefit from a victim advocacy program that would liaison with law enforcement toward more efficiency in dealing with fraud victims. Communication and cooperation among local, state, and federal law enforcement agencies are crucial to ensure that victims are assisted and criminals brought to justice.*

## RECENT MILESTONES IN VICTIMS' RIGHTS

President George W. Bush has said that "[w]hen our criminal justice system treats victims as irrelevant bystanders, they are victimized for a second time."[9] In recent years, the government has taken this compelling statement to heart and has enacted key legislation and court decisions as well as policy enhancements, all focused on protecting the rights of victims of crime, and especially those of identity theft victims. Here are some of the recent milestones in victims' rights:

*2003*

*In November, President Bush signs the Fair and Accurate Credit Transactions Act, providing new protections against identity theft, as well as provisions to help victims of identity theft recover from their financial losses. . . .*

*2004*

*Legislation is signed by President Bush that defines aggravated identity theft and establishes penalty enhancements for such crimes. For instance, under the law, offenders who steal another person's identity information in connection with the commission of other specified felonies (such as crimes relating to immigration, nationality, citizenship, and various forms of fraud) would be sentenced to an additional two years in prison. The legislation also prohibits the court from ordering an offender's sentence for identity theft to run concurrently with a sentence imposed on the same offender for any other crime. . . .*

### 2005

*In May, the updated* Attorney General Guidelines for Victim and Witness Assistance *is published. The guidelines incorporate provisions for crime victims' rights and remedies, including the Crime Victims' Rights Act, which have been enacted since the publication of the last edition. . . .*

### 2006

*In late January, the United States Court of Appeals for the Ninth Circuit decided* Kenna v. U.S. District Court *for the Central District of California, in which the court considered whether the Crime Victims' Rights Act (CVRA), 18 U.S.C., Section 3771, gave victims the right to speak at sentencing hearings. The case involved a father and son who swindled dozens of victims. The defendants pled guilty to wire fraud and money laundering. More than 60 victims submitted victim impact statements. At the father's sentencing, several victims spoke about the effects of the crimes, but at the son's sentencing, the judge refused to allow the victims to speak. The Court of Appeals relied heavily on statements made by U.S. Senators Jon Kyl and Dianne Feinstein, sponsors of the CVRA, and held that the district court judge had made a mistake. In its decision, the appeals court made the following three important points: (1) in passing the CVRA, it was the intent of Congress to allow victims to speak at sentencing hearings, not just to submit impact statements; (2) victims have a right to speak even if there is more than one criminal sentencing; and (3) the remedy for a crime victim denied the right to speak at a sentencing hearing is to have the sentence vacated and a new sentencing hearing held in which the victims are allowed to speak. This decision is an important step in securing the rights of crime victims.*[10]

## "THE BEST-LAID PLANS OF MICE AND MEN OFTEN GO AWRY"

One identity theft victim's nightmare should be a wake-up call to everyone that even employing several levels of protection may not be enough to fully protect against this crime. Frank Hernandez of Phoenix, Arizona, dutifully shredded any documents that might contain his name or personal information. He even obtained a credit protection monitoring service that he thought would give him an added level of security. But his plans for protection were not enough. An undocumented immigrant was able to pay $500 for Hernandez's SSN and Arizona driver's license number. It was never determined how Hernandez's personal identifiers were compromised, but they were nonetheless.

Hernandez eventually learned of the identity theft when he received notification that his driver's license had been suspended for unpaid speeding tickets in New Mexico. That was November 2005. Imagine Hernandez's surprise and consternation when he remembered that the last time he had set foot in New Mexico was 10 years earlier. As is often the case, few would listen to his claims of being a victim of identity theft. It took him two years to finally get his suspended license back. His insurance company did not believe him either. "It was painful to get rid of because of the bureaucratic hassles.

You have to prove who you are. It was really horrible," Hernandez said.[11] Interestingly enough, the identity thief was finally located not by the police but by the detective work of Hernandez himself. He started to check his credit report regularly and "in March 2006, he discovered someone was using his identity and Social Security number to rent an apartment in Mesa."[12] He quickly alerted the Mesa, Arizona, Police Department who conducted surveillance at the apartment complex and arrested the fraudster. The bad news is that this is but one of the 40 to 50 new cases of identity theft the Mesa Police Department receive each month.[13]

## FOREVER VIGILANT

A few years ago I was in an airport shuttle van heading to SeaTac Airport in Seattle, Washington. En route, we stopped at a house to pick up a passenger. Just before getting into the van, this woman stopped at the mailbox in front of her house, placed several outgoing letters inside, and raised the red flag to indicate to the mail carrier that mail was ready for pickup. I got to talking with this passenger and remarked that it was not a good idea to place outgoing mail into an unlocked mailbox. I explained that the raised red flag signaled to mail thieves that inviting mail possibly containing checks and other personal information was inside. "You could become a victim of identity theft," I said. "Oh, that's just what I need considering my bad luck," she uttered.

She explained that a few months earlier, she had left her pocketbook in her car parked in her driveway. She did not think about it until she went to her car the following morning and saw that someone had broken the car window and stolen her purse. Inside was her wallet with multiple forms of identification and several credit cards. She did not report the theft to the police but did call her credit card issuers to close the accounts. I asked if she had done anything else such as check her credit reports for possible unauthorized use of her name and credit. She had not. After telling her of the many bad things that could happen as a result of identity theft, I have no doubt she left the shuttle far more concerned than when she had entered. I also hope that she was motivated to do more to protect her good name in the future and not become a victim. Chapter 20 contains numerous steps to follow if one should be the unfortunate victim of identity theft.

## NOTES

1. Nationwide Mutual Insurance Company Survey of Identity Theft Victims, "ID Theft Victims Struggle to Achieve Resolution" (July 2005), www.prnewswire .com/cgi-bin/stories.pl?ACCT=104&STORY=/www/story/07-26-2005/ 0004074946&EDATE=.
2. Jolayne Houtz, "ID Theft: You Have to Keep Proving You Are Innocent," *Seattle Times*, June 13, 2006, A1.
3. "Identity Theft Led to 13-Year Nightmare," MSNBC.com, August 9, 2001, www.msnbc.com/local/wfla/mgacx58y5qc.asp.
4. Social Security Administration, "Should You Get a New Social Security Number?" www.ssa.gov/pubs/10064.html#new.

5. The content for the Operation Gaffle section was provided by Postal Inspector Scott Mathews and from the U.S. Postal Inspection Service Media Advisory, "New Jersey 'Gaffle' King Pleads Guilty to Identity Theft" (December 2005).

6. United States Postal Inspection Service, "Know Your Rights: A Guide for Victims and Witnesses of Crime," Publication 308 (August 2005), www.usps.com/cpim/ftp/pubs/pub308.pdf.

7. U.S. Department of Justice's Automated Victim Notification System, www.usdoj.gov/criminal/vns/.

8. "Milestones in the New Millennium," Special Supplement to the 2006 National Crime Victims' Rights Week Resource Guide, www.ojp.usdoj.gov/ovc/ncvrw/2006/pdf/special_supplement.pdf.

9. Ibid.

10. Senta Scarborough, "Man's ID Theft Nightmare Takes 2 Years to Iron Out," *Arizona Republic*, February 13, 2008, www.azcentral.com/community/mesa/articles/0213mr-idtheft0214.html.

11. Ibid.

12. Ibid.

13. Under United States federal law, the term "Giglio," or Giglio Material as it is commonly called, refers to material that tends to impeach the character or testimony of a government witness in a federal criminal trial. The government, in the form of the prosecutor's office, is required to turn over all relevant Giglio material to the defense. See *Giglio v. United States*, 405 U.S. 150 (1972).

# CHAPTER 14

# The San Diego Experience

This is the story of the city of San Diego's experience with identity theft and the interrelated crimes of mail theft, check fraud, forgery, and methamphetamine abuse as seen through the eyes of a criminal investigator charged with investigating these violations and protecting businesses and the public. Although this particular criminal activity has impacted many cities in America over the last three decades, San Diego, California, has been particularly hard hit. A number of factors came together to create a perfect storm that fostered a very bad experience for the inhabitants of this city.

Postal Inspector Phil Garn was at the epicenter of the identity theft explosion in San Diego during the early 1990s. He has seen firsthand how methamphetamine fueled and then transformed fraud and forgery into identity theft. When he started his career in law enforcement in 1990, identity crimes were referred to as "mail theft," "check forgery," or "credit card fraud." It was not until around 1993 that the term "identity theft" came up routinely. Inspector Garn took me through the roots and evolution of the "San Diego Experience" from his vantage point in the trenches. He provided the majority of the content for this chapter, and his insight and experiences are greatly appreciated.

## DESTINATION OF CHOICE

Separated from the vast sprawl of Los Angeles and Orange counties by the huge Marine reservation of Camp Pendleton, San Diego was long considered a sleepy little Navy town, known mostly for its proximity to Tijuana, Mexico. This began to change as servicemen returning from the World War II and later Vietnam discovered its temperate

Mediterranean climate and charm. The local economy began a subtle change in the 1970s, shifting away from the aircraft plants of Convair and General Dynamics, the shipyards of San Diego Bay, and the home of the tuna fleet. New businesses and industries began to develop, including high-tech Qualcomm, biotech, consumer, and service industries such as Petco, and of course tourism with Sea World, Wild Animal Park, the San Diego Zoo, and miles of exquisite beaches. Attracting people from all over the nation and the world, the economy and superb weather spurred a vast building expansion through the surrounding desert chaparral north and east into the dry mountains. Water from the Colorado River made this newly reclaimed desert green.

## RISE OF THE NDCBU

By the 1980s, San Diego, Imperial, Riverside, and San Bernardino counties experienced a tremendous building boom. To service the growing homeowner and business community, the United States Postal Service focused on centralized mail delivery, particularly for all of the new construction of high-density housing. This included houses, condominiums, and apartments. One of the principal innovations was the neighborhood delivery and collection box unit (NDCBU). The NDCBU combined the features of a Post Office box, rural mailbox, and a collection box to service multiple residences. This curb mounted unit was similar to the apartment "gang box" in that a letter carrier could open a single panel to deposit mail into individual compartments in a close grouping for a number of separate residences.

Centralized delivery represented a tremendous savings for the Postal Service. Rather than individually delivering from house to house, the letter carrier could simply open the back of the NDCBU, remove the outgoing mail from an attached compartment, and place incoming mail in the individual boxes for many houses right at the curb. As the Postal Service's biggest expense was manpower, these small savings of time turned out to be huge dollar savings of hourly rates, especially over the course of a fiscal year. Remember, mail is delivered six days a week, 52 weeks a year, so even a savings of an hour a day for a single route would add up quickly. There were literally hundreds of routes in San Diego proper and thousands of new deliveries being added yearly.

To tap the potential cost savings, the Postal Service established centralized delivery in new housing and business projects. Likewise, when areas were redeveloped or converted, centralized delivery soon followed. A typical pattern of development involved the demolition of a small beach cottage and its replacement with a multiunit condominium complex. After the completion of construction, the Postal Service followed with the NDCBU. Again, this centralized delivery was a huge savings for business areas as well as residential communities; and postal managers received both recognition and financial bonuses for implementing these savings.

This new delivery pattern was so efficient that it spread throughout new developments in San Diego County then to a postal district that included gigantic developments in Riverside and San Bernardino counties (San Bernardino is the largest county geographically in the continental United States). This model was also adopted in Phoenix, Arizona, which was rapidly growing to become the fifth largest city in the nation. With the success of centralized delivery in the West, the East took notice, especially as suburbs were rapidly expanding into what had been rural areas. Eastern developers also copied their western counterparts, placing houses extremely close together and building large apartment/condominium complexes in new suburban areas.

## UNFORESEEN ACHILLES' HEEL

But a critical oversight in San Diego would severely compromise centralized delivery and fuel identity theft. In order to protect mail in collection boxes and apartment complexes, the Postal Service developed an all-purpose lock that could be installed in a wide variety of frames and mountings to secure collection boxes, apartment gang boxes, key keepers, and electronic locks for businesses and apartment complexes to allow letter carriers access, as well as in NDCBUs. This lock was produced exclusively by the Postal Service. As it was stamped with an "arrow" symbol, it became known as an Arrow lock. The keys were unique and issued as accountable property to employees.

What that meant was letter carriers or collectors had to sign the key out at the beginning of their shifts and return it at the end of the day, where it was locked in a cabinet before they left to go home. These keys were also supposed to be attached to the belt by a brass chain to reduce the chance of loss through accidental misplacement or theft. To further enhance security and limit losses, the Postal Service developed dozens of combinations each with a different key pattern for each Arrow lock series. The idea was to have a different key series for offices or zones that bordered each other (one for each zip code).

It was believed that if a criminal got a key through robbery or burglary, or made a counterfeit copy, the losses would be localized. As few people knew the boundaries of the different zip codes, a stolen key or counterfeit might work on one street but not on another street a few blocks away. Additionally, because the locks' serial numbers were not externally visible, a criminal would not know that that Arrow key or counterfeit might also work in another state or city. There were severe federal criminal penalties for misuse of postal keys and locks including up to 10 years in prison and a $250,000 fine as well as administrative penalties for postal employees that included termination even for the accidental loss of an arrow key. There were also some corresponding state statutes for fraud and forgery including possession of a burglary tool. However, as San Diego expanded, the Arrow lock series X, as it was called, never varied. What this meant was that by the early 1990s, a single X series Arrow key would open more than 68,000 locks in an area stretching from the Mexican border north past La Jolla and from the Pacific Ocean east to La Mesa 13 miles away.

Criminals found that the Arrow lock mechanisms could easily be pried from rickety apartment gang boxes in old complexes and used to make counterfeit keys that would open the locking mechanism. The attraction of the counterfeit key for the criminal was that the criminal could open a gang box or NDCBU panel, remove items of value including checks and credit cards (although they typically stole everything inside), then close the panel, leaving no signs of forced entry. Typically the theft was not discovered until the victims received their bank or credit card statements weeks later. This unavoidable delay resulted in an investigative trail that went cold.

These keys were also not easily recognizable; apart from postal employees, no one had an idea what the key was. When confronted by local police and sheriffs, criminals often told officers it was something innocuous like a key to a storage locker or a piece of equipment like a refrigerator part. The same went for the stolen locks; once broken down into components, they were even harder to identify. However, whereas the postal Arrow key was very durable, the counterfeit copies, typically machined with a Dremel tool from scrap metal, can openers, or common table knives, were brittle and had very short operational lives. Large numbers of broken keys were recovered both by inspectors and postal maintenance personnel.

Counterfeit keys first began to appear in San Diego with the infamous Ezell gang in the late 1980s. But it was not until 1992 that the Postal Service began to change out the locks and vary Arrow keys in San Diego at the behest of Postal Inspectors and the U.S. Attorney's office. This critical delay allowed mail theft to become firmly entrenched in the methamphetamine-using community as it expanded east across the United States. Meth's spread is discussed in further detail later in the chapter.

## THEFTS AND FRAUDS OF THE 1980s AND 1990s

The theft of replacement checks for those previously stolen, and new and reissued credit cards stolen from the mail were initially the most common frauds encountered by Postal Inspectors in San Diego during the late 1980s and early 1990s. Alteration, forgery, split deposits, washing or bleaching checks, false changes of address, and other variations occurred but with much less frequency. However, as more individuals became involved with what was to become identity theft, the industry and governments realized the seriousness of the problem and began to adopt some protective measures.

The most common fraud was simply forging stolen replacement checks. Criminals would pass these at merchants or for take-out food or cash a check made out to themselves or an assumed identity at a branch of the account holder's bank, or conduct a split deposit scheme. In the split deposit scheme, a criminal would deposit a stolen check into an account and request a portion of the total amount back in cash. For a $500 check, the criminal might ask for and receive $250 back. Fraudsters were so bold as to order pizzas and pay the delivery driver with a stolen check. Postal Inspectors caught a number of crooks who paid for pizzas with these stolen checks.

In the early 1990s, Postal Inspectors began to encounter groups that enlisted college students. The criminals would give $100 to the students to open a bank account and obtain a debit card and personal identification number (PIN). The students would turn over the debit card and PIN to the gang leaders, receive another $100, and be told to report the card stolen in a couple of days. The leaders would then run a split deposit on the account and fraudulently withdraw hundreds or even thousands of dollars at various ATMs.

Although counterfeit IDs were not hard to obtain, most criminals were able to use social engineering at banks and merchants to pass stolen checks. "Oh, I left my ID in my wallet at home" or "My purse was stolen and all I have is my bank statement or my electric bill [also stolen from the mail]" were the common excuses used by scammers. Counterfeit IDs ranged from original documents issued by the Division of Motor

Vehicles (DMV) to conform to a fictitious identity or stolen ID, to totally phony identification such as "Official Tax Payer ID Card." Any alert teller or experienced sales clerk should never accept these poor-quality IDs, but they were used routinely.

Some forgers made up large boards with changeable lettering that looked like a giant driver's license. The criminal would stand or sit in the lower right portion of the ID background and the forger would take a photograph of the criminal. The developed photo appeared to be two-dimensional, was in color, and was cut to size. It could also be laminated or placed on a blank plastic card (California driver's licenses were not supposed to be laminated, so lamination was usually a big tip-off).

The "buildup" was the most common counterfeit driver's license encountered during the early 1990s. Meth users would use a blue background like a towel or sheet and have their picture taken, usually in an apartment or house, with a Polaroid camera. Then they would type the desired identifying information on a particular typewriter with a font similar to that used by DMV. They then would go to a photocopy shop and have it reduced to 77% or 75%. Then the criminal would glue the documentary part to a plastic card, add the photo, and finally laminate the card. One could easily tell a buildup because one could feel the layers. By the time the State of California had instituted holograms for security, criminals had access to computers and were able to counterfeit holograms.

Military IDs made from stolen blank ID forms were frequently encountered by law enforcement in San Diego. Typically a sailor or Marine working at the military pass office would steal a single form or a stack of blank ID forms, which would be sold on the underground market. Details were typed in and a picture of the criminal was affixed. This was in the days before today's modern graphics programs, not to mention color copiers and printers. Street criminals were just starting to use computers in 1993 and 1994 in San Diego.

Fraudsters would also overwrite stolen checks. As an example, a check payable to AT&T for $25 would be scratched out and made payable to John Smith for $500, and would usually be accepted by untrained tellers. Instances of criminals painstakingly forging the victim's signature were extremely rare. Washing checks, using common chemicals to remove the handwritten inked writing but leaving the printed portions of the check, would not become commonplace until the mid- to late 1990s, although meth users were doing check washing as early as 1992 or 1993.

Criminals would often test stolen credit cards at gas stations to see if they were active. If there was a problem they could drive away quickly, particularly as gas pumps became automated. Gas station attendants were supposed to get license plate numbers from questionable transactions, but this again was a rare occurrence. Criminals would also make routine purchases, such as Q-tips and diapers, at a convenience store as opposed to far more valuable high-ticket clothing such as expensive leather jackets at a department store. Fraud investigators working for retailers were well aware that thieves would purchase clothing and other items with stolen cards and then fence the merchandise, and they closely monitored purchases of particularly expensive items with suspicious cards.

Criminals would also purchase an item at one store then return the item at another branch of the same store and get either a cash refund or a gift certificate. The gift certificate could be sold to other criminals or redeemed at another location. Fraudulently purchasing gift certificates with stolen credit cards was also a popular scam. Again, clerks rarely asked for identification, particularly at higher-end establishments, such as Nordstrom and Neiman Marcus.

One criminal used a homemade tool to manipulate and open the locks securing Post Office boxes. He would sweep banks of boxes from the outside in broad daylight looking for replacement credit cards. This would take place just after the postal clerks had put up the mail and before customers arrived to retrieve it. He would then request personal identification numbers from the issuing banks, which were sent to the boxes he had just burgled. He would collect the letters containing the PINs, leaving the rest of the mail undisturbed, and close the box. The fraudster would then go to ATM machines that did not appear to have surveillance cameras and make cash withdrawals using the stolen cards and PINs. Postal Inspectors identified over $1 million in losses, and this was in the early 1990s.

As stolen credit cards and checks became harder to negotiate, criminals turned to washing checks and using personal information gained from mail theft, Dumpster diving, and banking sources to divert existing accounts or fraudulently open new accounts in victims' names. These schemes were developing concurrently with straight theft and being passed throughout the meth-using community. However, while these new protection features closed off or limited certain schemes, criminals latched on to other well-tested frauds.

The Postal Buddy was an experimental electronic kiosk that dispensed stamps and other products as well as allowed customers to change addresses. It was tested in the San Diego area in the early 1990s. These kiosks were extremely vulnerable as criminals could use stolen cards to fraudulently purchase the machine's inventory of stamps. The stamps and other products were worth thousands of dollars, and the fraudsters acted with near impunity. In addition, they could also input fraudulent changes of addresses to further aid their criminal schemes.

Because these machines had a direct link to the Postal Service's Computer Forwarding System (CFS), address changes were made almost overnight. So, by the time a confirmation letter was sent to the old address, the system relabeled the confirmation letter, which was then directed to the new fraudulent address. Victims had no idea their addresses had been changed and they were being victimized until their mail delivery stopped. This allowed the investigative trail to grow cold. Postal Buddies were eventually removed. Almost a decade later, the Postal Service piloted new electronic kiosks with improved security features and fewer products and services.

## IMPACT OF METH IN SAN DIEGO

During the cocaine boom in the mid-1980s, outlaw bikers in San Diego learned that another more potent stimulant, methamphetamine, could be easily produced in the home for a fraction of the cost of imported cocaine. Initially they learned about the ephedrine reduction method for synthesizing methamphetamine from readily available and unregulated ephedrine, a common ingredient in cold medicines. Needless to say, methamphetamine use and production took off like a rocket. As San Diego Sheriff's Department Detective Steve Reed related, "When I left the [San Diego Narcotics] Task Force [NTF] in 1982, aside from cocaine, the only stimulants we would see were cross-tabs and black beauties [amphetamines] that were coming across the border from Mexico. When I came back to NTF in 1987, meth and meth labs were everywhere."

Not only was methamphetamine cheaper than cocaine, but the drug's effects lasted significantly longer. It quickly supplanted cocaine as the drug of choice in San Diego. In an area such as San Diego, which is near to the U.S.–Mexican border and a principal smuggling route, where cocaine should be more readily available, meth is by far the more dominant drug. The initial appeal was simply economic, a longer-lasting, cheaper product that could essentially be made at home or in the backyard.

Meth use expanded east and north into Riverside, San Bernardino, and Imperial counties then into Arizona. It initially bypassed Los Angeles and San Francisco, jumping into Oregon and Washington States via outlaw bikers and other criminal communities, then rapidly expanded into the mainstream populations of those states. Although local law enforcement attacked labs and California placed restrictions on precursor chemicals, putting the smaller chemists or "cooks" in jail, there was a huge and profitable market for the drug. Mexican drug-trafficking organizations stepped in to fill the void with superlaboratories south of the border and established smuggling routes for marijuana, heroin, and cocaine. Unfortunately during the time it has taken for methamphetamine to march east, the expanding communities on the East Coast have adopted the same centralized mail delivery that made the vast tracks of housing in Southern California and Arizona so vulnerable.

However, a unique set of circumstances developed in San Diego during the late 1980s: (1) poorly protected high-value banking and merchant products (credit cards and replacement checks); (2) vulnerable high-density housing with centralized mail delivery using a single lock combination; and (3) methamphetamine, which touched off a devastating crime wave that would sweep east across the United States.

This epidemic began with a gypsy crime family who had learned how to make counterfeit postal Arrow keys, which secured collection and apartment boxes as well as the relatively new NDCBUs to steal credit cards and checks.

During the late 1980s and early 1990s in San Diego, meth users quickly discovered those unique vulnerabilities of the banking system. Addicts could make much more money more quickly exploiting stolen credit cards or checks, particularly replacement items sent through the mail, with far less personal risk than prostitution, auto theft, or burglary. They also realized that the courts viewed these "paper crimes" as victimless because the banking industry made the individual victim whole and passed off the losses to customers. Punishment was far less severe than for robberies or burglaries, although time behind bars allowed criminals to pass on and refine techniques.

The banking industry was very cooperative with individual investigations, but it often resisted prevention suggestions. At first, banks resisted modifying their products, such as sending out "dead" credit cards that needed to be activated upon receipt, claiming they would lose business. The banks were concerned about customer service and how this added step prior to use would be perceived. Once losses cut into their bottom-line profits, institutions began to react by implementing stronger prevention tools and technology. However, these significant delays allowed identity theft to become part of the meth-amphetamine culture. As the drug spread, so did this prime source of illicit financing.

Additionally, banking and financial insiders who were drug users began passing inside techniques and tips in exchange for meth.

Initially, investigation of meth-related identity theft did not appeal to law enforcement either, as they were considered "paper crimes" versus more dangerous robberies, burglaries, or narcotics cases. It spread through loosely knit criminal networks, leaving law enforcement without central figures to target or to garner media notoriety. Meth was still not yet perceived as a major component, as there were other organized gangs, particularly Nigerian Criminal Enterprises, perpetrating similar scams in the big cities of the East and West.

One telling indicator of how methamphetamine and identity theft transformed the criminal landscape in San Diego was the near disappearance of postal armed robberies in the area. After a series of hijack robberies of letter carriers in 1992 and a brief series of Post Office robberies in 1995 (both series were meth-related), San Diego experienced almost no robberies of postal personnel or facilities for many years. Fraudsters realized that committing economic crime was far safer than perpetrating violent crime. Yet just 100 miles north, in Los Angeles, Postal Inspectors formed a major crimes team to deal with the rash of armed robberies they were experiencing.

## THOUGHT LEADER IN IDENTITY THEFT PREVENTION

### Phil Garn

Postal Inspector Phil Garn has seen the impact of identity theft and other related crimes on the citizens of San Diego and surrounding areas. As a federal agent, he has been involved in hundreds of cases of identity theft, mail theft, credit card fraud, and narcotics over his career. As a result of his experiences, he has come to embrace strong law enforcement in order to deter the problem and protect the public.

A graduate of the University of Virginia and former Naval Reserve officer, Garn began his postal career in 1985 as a letter carrier and became a Postal Inspector in 1990. Investigations with the Inspection Service ranging from external crimes, internal crimes, fraud, terrorism, child exploitation, and prohibited mailings have taken him from Anchorage to Acapulco and from Buffalo to Buenos Aires. He was the case agent for the international child exploitation investigation Operation Special Delivery and a founding member of the San Diego Internet Crimes Against Children Task Force and is currently assigned to the San Diego Narcotics Task Force.

Garn has also been instrumental in developing and implementing prevention strategies. In the early 1990s, Postal Inspectors in San Diego recognized that unique conditions in the area contributed to the growing problem of identity theft. "The unique conditions in San Diego primed the identity theft explosion," Garn stated. "Centralized delivery and a single Arrow key combination for a city of over

1 million [68,000 locks], the banking and credit card industry, and meth-amphetamine all contributed to this perfect storm." Through the combination of these factors, a rash of mail theft rapidly turned into an epidemic.

In addition to enforcement, San Diego Postal Inspectors instituted several prevention strategies. They set out to educate local law enforcement, the banking industry, and the public. They lobbied to enhance federal sentencing guidelines for mail theft. The Postal Service began to vary key combinations in San Diego and developed more secure locking mechanisms to secure collection boxes and NDCBUs. Finally, a coordinated appeal to the credit card industry began, in order to enhance security of their products.

Inspectors developed a training and awareness program on the extent of the problem for area law enforcement. They showed police officers the difference between real and counterfeit Arrow keys and provided them with flyers and law enforcement notices listing federal violations and depicting slightly altered copies of counterfeit keys. Most important, they asked the police officers to call the inspectors if they encountered subjects of interest during their investigations or patrol work. Patrol officers responded enthusiastically as they frequently arrested subjects for "under the influence of methamphetamine" violations who also had counterfeit keys and/or stolen mail. The inspectors typically responded to the field or the station at all hours of the day and night and took the cases federally, or assisted with investigation of state violations. Additionally, they wrote letters of appreciation to officers who assisted them with investigations.

The Inspection Service began setting up informal law enforcement task forces to focus on mail theft and become more proactive. They partnered with the U.S. Secret Service, Department of State Diplomatic Security Special Agents, and the San Diego Police Department Fraud Forgery and Narcotic Street Team Detectives, especially on gang investigations, as well as with other state and local police.

In 1991 and 1992, inspectors would collect broken-off counterfeit keys for local postal locks recovered by maintenance personnel from the San Diego collection box maintenance section. As Inspector Garn picked up one particular batch of broken metal bits, he told a postal supervisor, "They [the criminals] are killing us with these counterfeit keys." Not long after, San Diego Inspectors Diana Torpey and Thomas Hofius, among others, found an answer to the problem with a significantly strength-ened locking mechanism that was almost impossible to defeat or counterfeit.

The Inspection Service also focused on educating the public about protecting their mail and their identities. This grassroots effort directly reached homeowners' groups, including apartment renters and condominium associations, through speeches and circulating flyers in local neighborhoods. The message was fairly simple: Collect your mail every day; do not leave mail in your mailbox overnight; if you are on vacation, complete a vacation hold for the duration of your trip; report any instances of box tampering or fraudulent credit card charges. They encouraged witnesses to report descriptions of suspicious people and cars, especially license plate numbers, and to call the police immediately and notify the Inspection Service.

*(Continued)*

Furthermore, the inspectors worked with the media to publicize the problem. They gave interviews to local television reporters who would become great advocates for the Postal Inspection Service and champions for the public combating what would come to be known as identity theft. Tips from the public started coming in that resulted in the arrests of mail thieves.

## EMERGENCE OF ORGANIZED GANGS

Postal Inspectors first began to encounter the Ezell Gang in 1987 in mail theft investigations. By 1990, they had arrested the principal family members as well as a number of their associates. Many of these associates were auto thieves, burglars, and prostitutes. It was these seemingly subordinate and peripheral members of the Ezell Gang who would have the most significant impact on check fraud and identity theft for several reasons. They were members of very tight, mobile networks that freely exchanged schemes and techniques. Most street criminals stay not only on the street but on the same streets for most of their criminal lives; however, these individuals, many of whom were male and transsexual prostitutes, were part of tight underground communities that traveled extensively committing their crimes. These crimes were much more lucrative than more violent crimes with far fewer physical risks and less severe punishments.

In November 1993, Postal Inspector Garn was debriefing a source who was describing the Ewain Starke Gang, an offshoot of the Ezells, and their criminal relationships, when he made a startling discovery: this gang was led by an ex-police officer and his wife, an ex–letter carrier. Months earlier, methamphetamine users whom the inspectors had arrested for mail theft were telling them that a current or former police officer was making counterfeit Arrow keys. One morning, another inspector told Garn she had arrested a suspect who told her some more about this mystery cop, including his first name and that he was married to a letter carrier.

"I can't believe this," said Inspector Garn, as he immediately knew the names of both the cop and his wife. "I knew because I had carried mail with the wife when I was a letter carrier in the 1980s prior to becoming a Postal Inspector." This investigation underscores how quickly methamphetamine took over, as once-productive members of society became linked to the Ezells. It also demonstrated how identity theft and networking became part of the meth culture.

## THE WAY IT IS TODAY

I wanted to find out what Postal Inspectors were encountering in the field today and how they were approaching investigations and prevention of identity theft. The answers came from two team leaders who are responsible for investigating identity theft in the San Diego Field Office, Postal Inspectors Melisa Llosa and Jody Kowahl. Inspector Kowahl began her Inspection Service career in 1990 and was on the external crimes team from 1994 through 2001, where she was a founding member of the San Diego Regional Fraud Task Force (SDRFTF). She had additional experience investigating mail fraud and in management as an assistant inspector in charge for the Los Angeles Division. In 2007, she returned to San Diego as the team leader for the multifunctional team that investigates mail theft. Inspector Llosa began her career in New York on the Manhattan External Crimes Team in 1998, moved to San Diego in 2002 where she was a member of the CATCH Team (Computer and Technology Crime High Tech Response Team, a multiagency team involved with the investigation of identity theft) for four years, then became the team leader in 2006 for the other multifunctional team that investigates mail theft.

The most obvious change from the early 1990s is there are now two teams of Postal Inspectors in San Diego that investigate identity theft as well as two formal multiagency task forces, SDRFTF and CATCH. Most of the inspectors are also cross sworn as Special San Diego Sheriff's Deputies. The vast majority of the identity theft cases are prosecuted in state court (local versus federal prosecutions). Further measures to reduce attacks, such as the adoption of highly resistant Medeco brand locks with a variety of key combinations, unfortunately did not produce the expected results. In response to the new locks, offenders developed a low-tech, if criminally ingenious, device to get around these measures.

With the introduction of the Medeco locks and various key combinations, criminals were no longer able to access the locks surreptitiously with counterfeit keys. The strengthened locking mechanism and frame made them much harder to pry open, and numerous key combinations made the more sophisticated lock even harder to duplicate and reduced access. Criminals then began to steal the entire boxes, both the NDCBU and the typical blue mail drop box, by pulling them off the concrete mountings. After transporting the stolen boxes to remote locations, they would break into them and steal the mail, leading to the striking sight of discarded big blue mailboxes in canyons around San Diego County.

Inspectors then came across a very novel, low-tech device to literally fish mail out of the boxes. The criminals would wrap layers of duct tape or other sticky substances on a piece of wood or other object, secure this sticky "hook" with a line or string, and drop it into the snorkel of the collection box or down the drawer into the mail that had been deposited. Letters would stick to the hook, and criminals would reel these in to remove items of value, particularly bill payments with associated checks. Inspectors countered with a two-pronged approach: publicly through newspaper articles, radio and television interviews wherein they encouraged customers not to deposit mail in collection boxes after the last posted pickup time, so it would not be vulnerable to an after-hours attack; privately inspectors worked with the Postal Service to develop antifishing devices that would not allow criminals to withdraw the fishing devices. As Inspector Kowahl said, "San Diego inspectors lead the nation in prevention projects designed to protect mail." Of course, as these antifishing devices were installed, criminals refined devices to defeat these new deterrents.

Washing checks stolen from collection boxes using common household products to remove the endorsements on personal checks (as detailed in Chapter 6) became the primary scheme in the mid-1990s through the turn of the century. Criminals also went high tech using computers and commercial business programs to capitalize on victims' identity information they were able to steal from banking documents, known in law enforcement circles as profiling. In the past, criminals were stealing items of value to fraudulently use such as credit cards, blank replacement checks, or completed checks, which were washed and fraudulently reendorsed; criminals were now using these documents and account statements to build "profiles" and perpetrate a variety of schemes.

One of the principal profiling schemes is to use the victim's account number and bank routing numbers from canceled or stolen checks to create new checks using commercially available check printing programs. For about $50, criminals can buy a check program, such as TurboCheck or VersaCheck, which not only has the software but also blank check stock from which they can create negotiable items. Criminals input fraudulent information into the program and use the stolen account number and bank routing number to create a new document. This new check may appear to be the account of John Doe, although the actual account and routing number are for Jane Smith's checking account at the Acme Bank. Fraudsters then use these checks to purchase items and get cash back. Electronic cash registers process these checks and debit the victim's account regardless of what is printed on the checks. Although the check may be printed with the Bank of America logo, the account and routing number may be for a Wells Fargo account.

Often criminals utilize the tried-and-true scheme of purchase and return in order to get cash. They particularly target home stores such as The Home Depot or Lowe's, where they purchase an expensive but common tool with a counterfeit check, then return the item the following day to obtain cash. Culprits also network and exchange information as to which stores are particularity vulnerable and what limits and countermeasures are in place.

Criminals continue to use computers to create fraudulent identification cards, which they began to do back in the early 1990s. Although graphic programs have improved significantly, the quality of fake IDs still ranges from exceptional to very bad counterfeits. Another dodge criminals use is to keep their fake ID behind the plastic of a wallet so that the merchant or teller cannot see the flaws, such as printed holograms or poor or blank card stock.

Scammers have also developed many new ways to fraudulently use credit cards and personal information. They often order merchandise over the telephone or via the Internet. Crooks have found that they do not even need the correct expiration date or security code. They often order the merchandise using the stolen account number and just make up an expiration date. They fence these items but also order gift cards, which are even harder to trace and are more anonymous particularly if ordered from the Internet, where certificates are printed on-site versus sent to a physical address. Criminals also use houses and residences in their neighborhood that are vacant or where the true residents are away at work to receive gift cards and merchandise, victimizing the residents as well as the account holders.

Although the teams of both Inspector Kowahl and Inspector Llosa have encountered organized groups, such as Nigerian Criminal Enterprises, in San Diego, the vast majority of subjects are still street-level criminals. As Inspector Kowahl said, it is almost "a cottage industry" of networked individuals versus more structured gangs like the Nigerians. Inspector Llosa said there appear to be several classes of criminals: those at the bottom who are stealing and Dumpster diving for account and personal history information and a higher class at the top of this food chain that is perpetrating most of the fraud with ID counterfeiters. Both inspectors agreed about the high number of recidivists encountered by their teams, often arresting subjects multiple times while out on pretrial release for the same crimes. Inspector Llosa said about nine out of 10 cases are methamphetamine related, a fact that is hardly surprising, as meth is still the most prevalent drug aside from marijuana in the region.

Although some things have changed, much has not. The scourge of identity theft lives on in San Diego and throughout the world.

# CHAPTER 15

# The Rich, the Famous, and the Dead Get No Peace

Oprah Winfrey, Tiger Woods, Steven Spielberg, Paris Hilton, Will Smith, Michael Jordan, Ross Perot, Brett Favre, Robert DeNiro, and Ted Turner—this reads like a Who's Who of the Rich and Famous, but it is just a partial list of the many celebrities who have become victims of identity theft. It is not surprising that these stars are being victimized. They are rich, very rich in many cases, and are high profile. Their personal lives are very public, and they live the good life for the world to see each and every day on our televisions and computer monitors. Fraudsters know these celebs have good credit and fortunes to steal. Plus, their personal information is easy to obtain from a multitude of sources. Insiders such as assistants, nannies, chauffeurs, and the many people in their entourages are all potential identity thieves. Yet external criminals are just as much a threat.

Career con man and identity thief Abraham Abdallah, profiled in Chapter 12, realized that targeting the rich and famous was a ticket to fame and fortune. Although he never met any of these celebrities, he did not need to in order to steal their identities. He did it through reading about them in *Forbes* magazine's profiles of "The 400 Richest People in America" as well as social engineering, technology, greed, and lots of chutzpah.[1]

At the Web site of the Internet Movie Database (www.imdb.com), visitors can find extensive data on movies and television shows as well as personal information on actors and actresses. The biographical details of almost every movie or television star imaginable can be easily viewed. Dates and places of birth, names of spouses, dates of marriage, names of children, and amazing amounts of other personal information are posted for these stars. The biographies of producers, directors, newscasters, and other celebrities who have been involved with television or the movies are also readily available. The only identifiers missing are Social Security numbers (SSNs).

Basketball legend Michael Jordan's credit card account number was obtained by an identity theft ring in Chicago that bribed bank employees to turn over customers' names and account information. The gang stole information belonging to more than 70 people and defrauded their accounts of more than $1 million. The gang leader wanted to find someone who looked like the basketball superstar in order to pose as him and steal his fortune. Finding the right impersonator was a tough task, and Jordan was lucky he was not fleeced. An informant told police what the scammers were up to, and they were arrested before they could use Jordan's card. More than 20 conspirators were eventually arrested.

In 2003, Postal Inspectors and the Financial Crimes Task Force of Southwestern Pennsylvania arrested convicted felon Carlos Lomax for stealing the identity of actor Will Smith. Smith had no clue that Lomax had stolen his life. It was not until Smith attempted to buy a new home and found that his credit was damaged did he realize he was an identity theft victim. Lomax pleaded guilty to opening 14 fraudulent accounts in Smith's name in the Pittsburgh area and was sentenced to 37 months in prison. But it did not end there. Lomax was already on probation for an earlier identity theft conviction involving former Atlanta Hawks basketball player Steve Smith. Lomax was released after 30 months but was unable to adjust to life outside prison. He violated probation by not making restitution to his victims and in December 2005 was ordered back to jail for two more years.[2]

A career criminal with 20 misdemeanor and felony convictions over a 17-year period stole the identity of golf superstar Tiger Woods in 1998 and 1999. Anthony Taylor of Sacramento, California, obtained Woods's personal information and then applied for credit cards in Woods's name. Taylor also obtained a driver's license in Woods's real name of Eldrick T. Woods. Although the defendant received only $20,000 from the scheme, he was sentenced to a life sentence under California's three-strikes legislation due to his career criminal status.[3]

## DUMPSTER DIVING HITS A HOME RUN

Identity thieves do not need to be high-tech when low-tech is more than adequate to find personally identifiable information (PII). This was the case for a Dumpster-diving identity thief who, in Chicago in 2006, hit the mother lode when he went through the garbage of SFX Baseball in Northbrook, Illinois, a leading sports agency serving Major League baseball players. There David Dright found financial records and other personal information belonging to 91 Major League players including Pedro Martinez, Moises Alou, Jim Thome, and Miguel Tejada.

When Postal Inspectors and other law enforcement officers searched Dright's Chicago apartment in December 2006, they found SSNs, dates of birth, loan applications, canceled paychecks, tax returns, and other documents belonging to the major leaguers.[4] None of the documents had been shredded before being discarded by SFX. Investigators also found numerous credit card applications, birth notices, and death announcements in the apartment.

To make matters worse, investigators later developed evidence that Dright had stolen the identities of deceased children in order to apply for credit cards in their names. He was using "birth announcements and death notices of infants to try to create fictitious financial accounts."[5] A detective involved in the investigation at the time stated, "I'll be getting hold of different parents and I have the job of notifying them that their child's identity, their deceased child's identity, may have been compromised."[6] Dright later pleaded guilty to aggravated identity theft and related charges but was sentenced only to probation.

## NO REST FOR THE DEAD

The preceding case illustrates that identity thieves will exploit any opportunity to commit fraud. It is not just celebrities who are identity theft targets. Sadly, the dead are also victimized by the lowest-of-the-low fraudsters. People can spend their entire lives working hard, growing a good reputation, and leaving a sound legacy when they depart this world. Unfortunately, due to the good life they left behind, their identities are subject to theft and abuse by identity thieves. We see this in case after case where the deceased have their names, SSNs, and other PII stolen from the grave.

Identity theft has given rise to many new terms used to describe the variations of the crime and the ploys used to collect personal information. "Tombstoning" is but one of these new terms. Tombstoning is the collection of names, dates of birth, and other information by walking through cemeteries and recording the information for later fraudulent use. One brazen and heartless fraudster used this approach to violate the dead and enrich himself.

Larry Steve Albert was always able to blend in and never stand out. As the federal agent who eventually tracked him down and arrested him said, "He was remarkably unremarkable. There were no clues, public records, work history, vehicle purchases, to his whereabouts since 1986. . . . He just disappeared."[7] He was just so average that no one would ever think he could be a scammer. This allowed him to commit identity theft for many years and not get caught. Along the way, he stole the identities of more than 200 deceased persons from at least eight states.

Albert had a simple but time-tested method: He focused on deceased people, many of them children, for the identity thefts. Albert would target small towns and small banks. He would claim to be a newly arrived resident of the town and was opening a bank account. He presented fake drivers licenses, Social Security cards, rental agreements, and other documents as identification proof. Deposits of $100 were the norm, and once he received his checks, he would paper the town with bad checks. Wal-Mart, Staples, JCPenney, Target, Lowe's, and other stores were among his favorites for fraud. Albert also violated the trust of his family. He altered the SSNs of five of his sons and used them for phony identification.[8]

Albert would repeat this identity theft again and again in numerous states over the years. New Mexico, Washington, Nevada, Oregon, Colorado, Utah, North Carolina, and

Montana were all venues for his crimes. When he was first arrested in Albuquerque in February 2004, he provided a phony name and identification that allowed him to make bail and then flee. Unfortunately for Albert, he left his car behind, and that was his undoing. Inside the pickup truck was a three-ring binder detailing his identity theft activities since 1986. Included was a list of all the identities he had used over the years. This and other information in the truck helped special agents from the Federal Bureau of Investigation (FBI) and Social Security Administration track Albert down in Washington State in October 2005, where they arrested him.[9]

In December 2005, Albert pleaded guilty to mail fraud and using a false Social Security card. He had no choice; the evidence against him was overwhelming. In Washington State alone, he used the identities of 40 deceased children. He wrote thousands of bad checks. Prosecutors charged him with at least $183,000 in bad checks that he passed. He was 62 years old when he was sentenced on May 5, 2006, in Seattle to three years in prison. He had no prior history of arrests and under federal sentencing guidelines, this was the recommended sentence. And that was unfortunate.

Larry Steve Albert was a serial identity thief and did far more harm that just financial crime. He desecrated the good names and reputations of those whose names he stole. "Committing crimes in the names of deceased children is incredibly callous and quite painful to the relatives of those who have died," the federal prosecutors told the sentencing judge. "Indeed, one victim compared this crime to the desecration of their son's grave," they added.[10]

## GENEALOGY AND THE RISK OF IDENTITY THEFT

Family history and roots are of deep interest to many of us. Whoever would have thought that something as seemingly innocent and nonthreatening as genealogy would open millions of people to potential identity theft? The increasing interest in one's family tree and the growth of the Internet has resulted in another criminal opportunity for identity thieves to steal personal information.

In a quest for learning more about one's family, genealogy sites have proliferated. More and more families have home pages that detail their descendants and everything about them. Names, relationships, birth dates, birthplaces, addresses, occupations, and more can be found at these sites. A mother's maiden name, a common password for credit card accounts, is often found on home pages. While people would not give this information to someone they met on the street, they openly list it in their family trees online for the world to see, and use. People have called this "privacy suicide."

It reminds me of my lectures about the need for fraud prevention on the Internet. I said that educated consumers learned to be leery of door-to-door salespeople who tried to sell them snake oil and the moon. We taught consumers to be equally suspicious of telephone or mailed-in offers that were "too good to be true." Now we need to continually enlighten the American public about the potential for fraud on the Internet. Just because something appears on your computer monitor does not make it necessarily true. The same rules of common sense and caution apply when online. Do not forget, "If it sounds too good to be true—even if it's on the Internet—it probably is." When did I first say this?—1998.

People may not know that their relatives have listed them and their personal information on family tree sites. If they knew, they may or may not approve of having their personal data available for the world to view. But they should be told in advance and have the choice. "If a family member is going to put up the genealogy, I think they should notify all the living members of that family tree," said Beth Givens, of the Privacy Rights Clearinghouse.[11]

In 2001, California started to address how it sold the birth and death records of its citizens after the information started showing up on the Internet. These records, which contained other information such as mothers' maiden names, could be used for identity theft. The issue came to light for the state when it learned that these vital records were posted on various genealogy Web sites such as RootsWeb.com, which is owned by Myfamily.com. As a result, birth, marriage, and divorce records were removed. "I think what people are concerned about is the possibility that someone might find a mother's maiden name in those records and sometimes that information is used as a password on a bank account and things like that," commented a chief executive of Myfamily.com at the time.[12]

Death records are still readily available at RootsWeb.com and many other online sites as well as through traditional public records at federal, state, and local venues. One major source of death records is the readily available Social Security Death Index. While this information has always been available, it was much harder to obtain this personal information before the ease of online search. In a typical online site, one can find death information that includes name, date of birth, date of death, SSN, and last residence.

Some people supportive of genealogy have downplayed the risks of identity theft. They claim that in the various identity theft surveys, none of the common sources of the fraud is from records obtained from vital records departments. They ask for proof that identity thieves use vital records such as birth and death certificates for their crimes. I read a blog where a noted genealogist lamented that there was too much emphasis on the possibility of identity theft using readily available information at online genealogy sites. He felt this was much ado about nothing as he was unaware of any actual identity theft cases resulting from information obtained from family trees and genealogy sites. In fact, he claims to have challenged anyone to show him that genealogical information was the root cause of any identity theft case.

Although I understand this person's passion for genealogy, he is asking to prove a negative. In criminal investigations of identity theft, it can be very hard to determine just where the purloined PII came from. I liken this genealogist's reasoning to an analogy. Just because your home has never been burglarized, does that eliminate the need to have locks on your doors and to use them? It always comes down to eliminating risk through prevention. Why take the chance that your PII can be stolen and fraudulently used? Always consider that the greater the availability of personal information on the Web, the greater the opportunity for possible misuse. And this longtime genealogist may be splitting hairs when he claims that there are no documented cases of identity theft from genealogy sites.

The devastating combination of identity theft and methamphetamine use was depicted in Chapters 6 and 14. Unfortunately, the two evils had an equally damaging end result for a genealogy business. In 2005, the son of a respected genealogist was found to have stolen "invoices from his father's business to forge passports, credit cards, and check-books to support his meth addiction."[13] Heritage Creations was a genealogy business in the Salt Lake City area that provided research on family histories and other services. The business owner's world and family were rocked when local newspaper headlines disclosed "an operation that involved swapping methamphetamines for the identities of people who purchased products for genealogy research."[14] The damaging reputational impact of this case most probably was a factor in the business filing Chapter 7 bankruptcy in 2006.

On another genealogy blog, the blogger included some questions and answers on whether there was an identity theft risk from genealogy sites publishing SSNs of deceased family members. He stated that just the opposite: the publishing of names of deceased people and their SSNs allows businesses and others to verify whether a particular SSN was active or not and whether the person is deceased. He actually stated that this helps prevent identity theft. This well-intentioned but misinformed blogger has obviously never met identity thief William Kinnaird. There have been numerous cases where identity thieves have used death records to commit their frauds. Kinnaird did just that and got his information from a genealogy site. The next case study further illustrates his modus operandi.

---

### IDENTITY THEFT HALL OF INFAMY

#### William M. Kinnaird Jr.

William M. Kinnaird Jr. was one of the smartest criminals that one veteran Postal Inspector ever encountered. But he was not smart enough to avoid becoming a recidivist and long-term resident of a federal penitentiary. Inspector Brian Huenefeld has been a Postal Inspector for almost 20 years and has worked identity theft cases for the last 10 years. Although he has investigated sophisticated criminal gangs involved in identity theft, this particular defendant was involved in a different aspect of the crime that Inspector Huenefeld had not previously seen. That was because Kinnaird was using the identities of people who were either deceased or nonexistent. Many of the deceased were children.

Kinnaird was arrested in the early 1990s by the United States Secret Service and charged with counterfeiting checks in Dayton, Ohio. He was sentenced to three years in prison for his crimes. When Kinnaird got out of prison in 1995, he was required to pay restitution of approximately $75,000. Due to his criminal record, he had a hard time finding employment and needed to make money. He then made the wrong decision of returning to a life of crime with another fraudulent scheme, identity theft.

He initially used the identities of deceased older individuals to obtain credit cards. As time went on, he realized that doing fraud in this manner could cause problems for him. The credit bureaus generally had the victims' names listed as deceased in their databases, and survivors could learn of the fraud. Kinnaird decided to use another approach for the identity theft. Sometime in the late 1990s, he was able to obtain a list of deceased children, either through the Social Security Administration or from the states of Ohio and North Carolina, as the majority of the victims died in those states.

Kinnaird used the names and identifiers of these victims to apply for credit card accounts when they would have turned 18 through 23 years of age. This activity grew over time, and Kinnaird actually established credit in the deceased victims' names. He used post office boxes, commercial mail receiving agency (CMRA) boxes, and even rented an office to use as a mail drop for the addresses of the victims. He would make regular payments on the accounts because he knew that if a person has good credit, that would generate additional credit card solicitations.

This fraud was brought to Inspector Huenefeld's attention in late 2005. His office in Cincinnati received a call from a UPS Store employee who reported that one of their boxes was receiving mail in numerous names and the mail was mostly from banks and credit card companies. Inspector Huenefeld discovered a total of five mail drops in Ohio and Kentucky used by Kinnaird. He was able to identify over 160 victims with over 700 credit card accounts issued in their names. The balances on these accounts exceeded $1.8 million. When Inspector Huenefeld initially contacted the banks that issued the suspect credit cards, they insisted there was not any fraud as the accounts were current and payments were being made on a regular basis. The inspector showed them they were wrong.

The personal information that Kinnaird obtained and used for fraudulent credit cards included victims' names, dates of birth, and SSNs. In several cases, he created fictitious names and associated these names with the deceased victims' SSNs and dates of birth. The victims died between 1977 and 1998. Twelve were more than 70 years of age when they died. The great majority of the other victims had died before reaching the age of majority.

Kinnaird was able to steal money through automated teller machine (ATM) withdrawals and through a credit card merchant account that funneled funds to an account he controlled. Kinnaird used the money to maintain a comfortable lifestyle and to build a very nice suburban home. He obtained an MBA from the University of Cincinnati during this period and also appeared on the game show *Jeopardy* in 2004.

To gather additional evidence, Inspector Huenefeld employed reverse Dumpster diving on Kinnaird's household garbage. A common law enforcement tool is to go through the garbage of a suspect when allowed by law. This can be as useful a technique for investigators as it is for fraudsters who steal personal information for criminal use. Inspector Huenefeld hit a home run with this garbage run as he found:

*Fifty credit card statements that corresponded to the fraudulent credit card accounts that were previously identified.*

*Over 20 credit card solicitations (mailed) to the victim names and addresses.*

(*Continued*)

*Credit card accounts addressed to all five of the fraud addresses controlled by Kinnaird.*

*Three spreadsheets that contained specific information regarding the fraudulent credit card accounts. Some of the information on these spreadsheets included the name of the credit card company, account number, credit limit, and balance.*

*Also included on the spreadsheets were columns entitled Pending Transfers, Balance, Available, User ID, and Password.*[15]

Executing a search warrant at Kinnaird's residence in January 2006, Postal Inspectors found over 700 credit cards and hundreds of pieces of mail in the victim names addressed to the various addresses Kinnaird controlled. Inspectors found credit card statements and cash that were going to be used to make payments on the fraudulent accounts. Kinnaird maintained a spreadsheet for his fraud accounts that contained passwords, phone numbers, e-mail addresses, mothers' maiden names, and other key information. Also found was information on new post office boxes and CMRAs that Kinnaird had recently opened in St. Louis, Chicago, Indianapolis, and other cities to expand his fraud scheme. He was in the process of changing the addresses on the existing accounts to these new addresses.

Inspector Huenefeld had a federal arrest warrant for Kinnaird at the time of the search. Kinnaird was arrested and agreed to speak with the federal agents after waiving his Miranda Rights against self-incrimination. Kinnaird said he was surprised that it had taken so long to catch him. He thought that he would have been arrested years earlier for stealing the identities of the dead. He explained how he first used the identities of elderly deceased people and then later dead children. Kinnaird detailed how he obtained information from Ancestry.com, an online genealogy site that contained SSNs and dates of birth. Once he had this personal information, he would make up the rest of the necessary information, such as the mother's maiden name. He would cross reference the SSN with the Social Security index to find ones that were not reported as being deceased. All the stolen identity information and fraudulently obtained credit card details were maintained on his computer that was seized. There were over 1,000 names listed but luckily not all had been used for fraud.

In the face of overwhelming evidence, Kinnaird pleaded guilty in June 2006. The detailed description of Kinnaird's criminal activity that follows comes from the Statement of Facts signed on May 31, 2006 by Kinnaird and submitted to the court pursuant to his guilty plea in June 2006:

*From January 1995 to January 2006, William Kinnaird defrauded several financial institutions by using the identities of deceased individuals to apply for and open credit card accounts and other loans. In other cases, Kinnaird created fictitious names and dates of birth and used that information to open credit card accounts.*

*During the course of this scheme, Kinnaird opened over 700 fraudulent credit card accounts using over 160 victim names. The total losses to the various financial* *institutions exceeded $1.7 million. Kinnaird used multiple addresses in this scheme, but as of January 2006, the five main addresses he used to receive mail were in West Chester and Cincinnati, Ohio, and Crestwood, Kentucky.*

*Kinnaird was able to convert funds to his own use from these fraudulent credit card accounts in three ways. One was through Automated Teller Machine (ATM) withdrawals. Kinnaird obtained Personal Identification Numbers (PIN) for most of these fraudulent credit cards and was able to withdraw cash using ATMs.*

*Another way Kinnaird was able to convert funds from these fraudulent credit card accounts was through credit card checks. An examination of deposit records for Kinnaird's U.S. Bank checking account was conducted from October 1998 through October 2005. This analysis showed that 104 credit card checks drawn against various fraudulent credit card accounts were deposited into Kinnaird's U.S. Bank account. The total value of these credit card checks was $193,282.*

*Another way Kinnaird was able to convert funds from these fraudulent credit cards was through a fraudulent credit card merchant account. A credit card merchant account is set up by businesses in order for that business to be able to accept credit cards as payment for products or services. In October 2002, a credit card merchant account was established through Key Bank in the name of 'Rent an MBA.' This account was opened by Kinnaird. On the application, Kinnaird was listed as Owner/ President.*

*This merchant account was serviced by Payment Resources International. Payment Resources International provided an updated application that was completed by Kinnaird on December 9, 2005. Kinnaird listed his business address in Cincinnati, Ohio. Kinnaird listed his home address in Cincinnati, Ohio. [Due to privacy concerns, the actual addresses are not listed here.]*

*This application listed Kinnaird's U.S. Bank account number as the account for funds to be wired from the various charges. Records from the 'Rent an MBA' merchant account show that between October 2002 and November 2005, there were $820,000 Visa and MasterCard charges toward his merchant account. These funds minus fees were electronically deposited into Kinnaird's U.S. Bank account. Every charge to the merchant account was from one of the fraudulent credit cards opened by Kinnaird.*

*As part of the scheme, Kinnaird made regular payments on all of these fraudulent credit card accounts. Payments were generally made with money orders. This was done so that the accounts remained current and it reduced suspicion by the credit card companies. This also assisted in establishing 'good credit' for the fraud victims. Once the account was approved and payments were made on a regular basis, the credit card companies often raised the credit limit of the account. This also made it easier for Kinnaird to obtain approval for additional credit cards on these fraudulent accounts.*

*Kinnaird was able to keep track of this through various spreadsheets and files. Kinnaird tracked every active credit card on his computer at his residence in Crestwood, Ohio. Kinnaird used these spreadsheets and files to track balances, payment due dates, available credit, and other pertinent information.*

*(Continued)*

> *One example of this fraud involves a credit card account opened in the name of Victim A with a Social Security number of \*\*\*-\*\*-\*\*\*\*. [Out of respect and privacy concerns for the victim, the name and SSN are not included here.] The home address listed on the application was in West Chester, Ohio. The SSN was issued to Victim A on or about May 18, 1982. Victim A was reported in Social Security records as being deceased on November 30, 1995. [Both the date of birth and date of death listed here have been changed.] The address used on the application was in reality a UPS Store mailbox opened by Kinnaird. Kinnaird mailed this credit card application to Chase Bank in Wilmington, Delaware.*
>
> *On or about March 30, 2001, Chase opened a MasterCard credit card account in the name of Victim A and sent a credit card from Omaha, Nebraska to the UPS Store mailbox via the U.S. Mails. From the date this account was opened to on or about January 26, 2006, Kinnaird made numerous charges and payments toward this account. The charges consisted of balance transfers, ATM cash withdrawals, and charges to Kinnaird's fraudulent merchant account, Rent an MBA.[16]*

On October 20, 2006, Kinnaird was sentenced to 140 months imprisonment. The federal sentencing guidelines recommended a prison sentence of 120 to 150 months and the government recommended 130 months. The almost 12-year sentence that the federal district court judge handed out to Kinnaird was no doubt due to the egregious nature of the crimes.

## WHO IS JOHN DOE?

Not everyone who steals an identity does it to commit credit card fraud or similar financial mischief. Now and then someone steals an identity to become that person and to obscure his or her original identity. Sometimes a person does this so often that it becomes almost impossible to tell who he or she is. This was the case of a man arrested in 2008 in Seattle, Washington, who was the living embodiment of a true "John Doe."

The tale begins when the Royal Canadian Mounted Police contacted the FBI in November 2007, looking for information on a man claiming to be Dwayne Spill, who had requested a copy of his birth certificate. However, the real Spill had been dead for 26 years. This tip led the FBI to a small windowless room in a rundown Seattle office building, occupied by a man identifying himself as Robert Lowe, though the name "D.A. Spill" appeared on the mailbox. As the FBI would later discover, the real Robert Lowe died 30 years earlier at the age of 17.[17] Dogged investigation by the FBI led to more aliases and multiple driver's licenses issued in other names, all listing the same address. All told, the man has used at least 32 identities since the 1980s. At the time authorities arrested him in March 2008, they were unable to determine his real identity, charging him as "John Doe."[18]

The tangled trail of multiple identities, fake identification, and deception almost resembled super-spy Jason Bourne, of the popular *Bourne Identity* movie franchise, starring Matt Damon. To further the intrigue, Doe had altered his fingerprints by burning his fingertips with acid to prevent identification.[19] According to a federal agent investigating the case, Doe's talent for disappearing into someone else's identity has made untangling his true identity all the more difficult. Over the course of months of investigation, authorities learned Doe had assumed the identities of at least five dead people and was in the process of assuming two more, both from Canada. His modus operandi was to steal the identities of men who had died young many years earlier. This minimized his chance of detection as the age of the identity would correspond with his own.

For each name, he then assumed multiple aliases and had dozens of pieces of identification, including driver's licenses and Social Security cards. He has lived in six different states and has multiple criminal convictions under a variety of names.[20] Further complicating the situation, "it appears Doe would sometimes adopt an identity . . . only to go to court and have that name legally changed."[21]

Despite all these difficulties, the mystery of John Doe finally began to clear after five months of investigation. Federal agents positively identified the mystery man through Air Force records, which then led to a positive identification by his parents. Doe, whose real name is Scott Andrew Shain, was a former Air Force officer from Boston who flunked out of flight school and then, according to his parents, fell off the face of the earth.[22] Although Shain faces numerous felony charges including mail fraud and aggravated identity theft, as well as outstanding warrants in Seattle for forgery and in Colorado for passing bad checks, impersonation, and menacing with a handgun, the case continues to vex investigators.[23]

Why would he assume so many identities over the years, especially because there was no evidence that he tried to use the identities for profit? Was he hiding from something? Many of his behaviors also baffle investigators. Shain was always considered very intelligent, with plans to fly jets in the Air Force, yet when he was arrested he was living in what a federal agent aptly described as a "hovel": a filthy, windowless 10-by-12-foot office without a kitchen or bathroom.[24] Another investigator called Shain a "bit of a savant," due to the complexity and intricacies of the fraud, which was unlike anything he had seen before.[25] Agents also learned that Shain, under another identity, had been interviewed by Secret Service agents after making threats against then-President Clinton; the agents took from him a homemade flamethrower.[26] Was Shain a criminal mastermind, mentally disturbed, or a mix of both? Even though authorities know his name, the former John Doe is still a mystery.

## WHAT IS A GENEALOGIST TO DO?

There is an even more recent criminal case where a scam artist used a popular genealogy research site to commit identity theft. Tracy June Kirkland, using numerous aliases, was charged with Mail Fraud, Aggravated Identity Theft, Unauthorized Use of an Access Device, Misuse of a Social Security Number, and other crimes in a federal indictment filed in Los Angeles in April 2008. According to the indictment, Kirkland carried out the fraudulent scheme between October 2005 and March 2008 in part, as follows:

- *Defendant searched the website www.rootsweb.com for identifying information for deceased individuals, such as name, date of birth, social security number, and zip code.*

- *Once defendant obtained a deceased individual's identifying information, she would search other websites to obtain a recent address for the deceased individual.*

- *After obtaining as much information as possible about a deceased individual, defendant would randomly call various credit card companies to determine if the deceased individual had an access-device[27] account with the credit card company.*

- *When defendant discovered a deceased individual's access-device account with a particular credit card company, she would take over the account by requesting that the address on the account be changed to one of several rented mail boxes that she controlled or to another address connected to the defendant. On some of these access-device accounts, defendant would add her name as an authorized user.*

- *Defendant used the access devices she had taken over to make purchases for her personal benefit.*

- *In this manner, defendant took over more than 100 access-device accounts issued by credit card companies, including Nordstrom Federal Savings Bank, Macy's, and GE Money Bank.[28]*

Contrary to the opinion of some genealogists, there is a significant risk of identity theft from fraudsters using genealogy sites. Given the popularity of genealogy sites, what is the answer? Many genealogists recommend not posting information on living relatives. Err on the side of caution. When placing family trees online, make sure that the family line stops at the last generation where all members are deceased. That may not stop an identity thief who targets the dead, but going back a few generations may make it a lot harder. Do not include personal identifiers such as SSNs, dates of birth, marriage dates, or other confidential information for any living relative. In any case, permission should be obtained from any person whose personal information will be placed on an online family tree.

Genealogy research site Ancestry.com offers a number of tips to protect family data and prevent identity theft that are summarized next.

1. **Change your secret question and answer.** Stop using your mother's maiden name as account verifiers. Many financial institutions have already ceased this practice. Use alternative questions such as "What was your first pet's name?" or other questions that are not generally known or that can be determined.

2. **Privatize the genealogy files shared with others.** Many family researchers share computer files with others. "If you create GEDCOM files and upload them to websites for inclusion in a place like the Ancestry World Tree, WorldConnect, and other locations, you are urged to use your program's 'privatize' facility to prevent inclusion of information about living people." According to the Web site www.familysearch.org, "GEDCOM stands for **Ge**nealogical **D**ata **Com**munications and is a file format specification that allows different genealogical software programs to share data with each other. It was developed by the Family and Church History Department of The Church of Jesus Christ of Latter-day Saints to provide a flexible, uniform format for exchanging computerized genealogical data."[29]

3. **Maintain two separate databases or consider excluding any living people from the database.** With two separate files, you can have one with both living relatives and deceased ancestors, and the other with only deceased ancestors. Files can be

combined as necessary to produce reports, but make sure to create backup versions of each file with different names and then merge them. If there is a need to "share information with others or upload a GEDCOM to a website database," share only the one with the deceased relatives, not the living ones. Make sure you really know the people you are communicating with online.

4. **Do not share information on a living person without first obtaining a signed authorization.** Ensure that you gain approval "from the intended recipient agreeing not to share the data in any way with anyone without your prior written permission." This may not be legally binding, but it may deter inappropriate use of information.[30]

## IDENTITY THIEVES ARE EQUAL OPPORTUNITY ABUSERS

It is ironic that both celebrities and the dead are linked by their connection to identity thieves. Both offer financial gain to these criminals. The public's fascination with celebrities will unfortunately not abate. For many people, it is a way to live through these personalities with their wealth, fame, beauty, gossip, and daily headlines in the tabloids. The lives of the rich and the famous are an open book that is easily read by fans and identity thieves alike. There needs to be an even higher level of vigilance to protect them from internal and external identity risk. Criminals will continue to target them as well as the dead, who are even easier targets. The deceased have no way of fighting back. Their personal information is completely exposed and unprotected. Only their relatives and friends can help them, and that is if, by chance, they learn of the victimization of the departed. The stories in this chapter foretell a much bigger problem. Prevention techniques and strong laws can do only so much in protecting against an unstoppable crime unless we fundamentally change how we disclose our personal information.

## NOTES

1. *Chutzpah* is a Yiddish term meaning unbelievable gall, audacity, arrogance, or utter nerve.
2. Associated Press, "Jail for Will Smith Identity Thief," December 28, 2005, www.cbsnews.com/stories/2005/12/28/entertainment/main1168894.shtml.
3. Ramon Coronado, "Jury Say Woods Imposter Should Get '3 Strikes' Term," *Sacramento Bee*, January 10, 2001, www.threestrikes.org/sactobee2.html.
4. Dave Wischnowsky, "ID Theft Hits Big League, Cops Say," *Chicago Tribune*, December 21, 2006, //lists.jammed.com/ISN/2006/12/0099.html.
5. Art Peterson, "Man Charged in Major League Identity Theft," *Suburban Chicago News*, December 20, 2006.
6. Mike Parker, "ID Theft Suspect Targeted Dead Children, Athletes," CBS Channel 2, December 21, 2006, cbs2chicago.com/local/david.dright.identity.2.334103.html/.
7. Peter Lewis, "Thief Stole More than 200 IDs, Some from Graveyards," *Seattle Times*, April 3, 2006, A1.

8. Ibid.

9. Ibid.

10. U.S. Department of Justice, Office of the United States Attorney, Western District of Washington, News Release, "Man Who Used the Identities of Hundreds of Deceased Children Sentenced to Prison for Mail Fraud and Production of False ID," May 5, 2006, www.usdoj.gov/usao/waw/press/2006/may/albert.htm.

11. Margaret Mannix, "Home-Page Snoops." *U.S. News Online*, May 11, 1998, www.usnews.com/usnews/issue/980511/11mone.htm.

12. Katie Hafner, "California Stops Selling Personal Data," *New York Times*, December 13, 2001, http://query.nytimes.com/gst/fullpage.html?res=9B0CE0D9153F F930A25751C1A9679C8B63.

13. Kimberly Powell, "Genealogist's Son Implicated in Possible Identity Theft," Kimberly Powell's Genealogy Blog, January 8, 2005, genealogy.about.com/b/ 2005/01/08/genealogists-son-implicated-in-possible-identity-theft.htm.

14. Laura Hancock, "Arrests Link Meth, Genealogy," *Deseret Morning News*, January 4, 2005, deseretnews.com/dn/view/1%2C1249%2C600102659%2C00.html.

15. Application and Affidavit for Search Warrant for the residence of William J. Kinnaird, Jr. in Crestwood, Kentucky, subscribed and sworn to by Postal Inspector Brian L. Huenefeld on January 25, 2006, before United States Magistrate Judge Dave Whalin, Western District of Kentucky.

16. Statement of Facts signed by defendant William M. Kinnaird, Jr. on May 31, 2006 and included in his federal plea agreement filed in United States District Court for the Southern District of Ohio pursuant to his guilty plea in June 2006.

17. Paul Shukovsky, "FBI Takes Man of Many Aliases into Custody," *Seattle Post-Intelligencer*, March 21, 2008, http://seattlepi.nwsource.com/local/355869_john doe21.html.

18. Mike Carter, "Who Is This Guy?" *Seattle Times*, March 21, 2008, A1.

19. Mike Carter, "John Doe: Mastermind or Troubled Mind," *Seattle Times*, March 22, 2008, A8.

20. Ibid.

21. Ibid.

22. Mike Carter, "Who Is He? Now They Know," *Seattle Times*, March 25, 2008, B1.

23. Carter, "Who Is This Guy?"; Paul Shukovsky and Kathy Mulady, "Authorities Finally Put Correct Name to Man Who Used 32 Aliases," *Seattle Post-Intelligencer*, March 24, 2008, http://seattlepi.nwsource.com/local/356226_johndoe25.html? source=rss.

24. Carter, "John Doe: Mastermind or Troubled Mind"; Shukovsky, "FBI Takes Man of Many Aliases into Custody."

25. Carter, "John Doe."

26. Carter, "Who Is He?"

27. Title 18, United State Code, Section 1029, Fraud and Related Activity in Connection with Access Devices, defines an "access device" as any card, plate, code, account number, electronic serial number, mobile identification number, personal identification number, or other telecommunications service, equipment, or instrument identifier, or other means of account access that can be used, alone or in

conjunction with another access device, to obtain money, goods, services, or any other thing of value, or that can be used to initiate a transfer of funds (other than a transfer originated solely by paper instrument), www4.law.cornell.edu/uscode/uscode18/usc_sec_18_00001029----000-.html.

28. *United States v. Tracy June Kirkland*, defendant, Indictment filed April 15, 2008, Cr. No. 08-00448, United States District Court for the Central District of California, 1–3, blog.wired.com/27bstroke6/files/tracy_june_kirkland.pdf.

29. FamilySearch.org Questions—GEDCOM, www.familysearch.org/Eng/Home/FAQ/frameset_faq.asp?FAQ=faq_gedcom.asp.

30. Avoiding the Theft of Your Identity, www.ancestry.com/learn/library/article.aspx?article=5828&o_iid=1644&o_lid=1644&offerid=0%3a7858%3a0.

# CHAPTER 16

# Identity Theft Goes Global

Identity theft is far too financially advantageous not to garner the attention of fraudsters worldwide. It was evident that sooner or later the world's economic criminals would also see the vast insidious value of this crime and want a piece of the action. While identity theft has taken a strong foothold in the United States over the last 30 years, scammers the world over now are focusing on identity theft and related crimes. Over the past few years, law enforcement in the United States has seen an increasing level of activity from foreign organized criminal groups through computer and Internet schemes. The President's Identity Theft Task Force report addressed this growing problem by stating:

*In Asia and Eastern Europe, for example, organized crime groups are increasingly sophisticated both in the techniques they use to deceive Internet users into disclosing personal data, and in the complexity of tools they use, such as keyloggers (programs that record every keystroke as an Internet user logs onto his computer or a banking Web site), spyware (software that covertly gathers user information through the user's Internet connection, without the user's knowledge), botnets (networks of computers that criminals have compromised and taken control of for some other purpose, ranging from distribution of spam and malicious computer code to attacks on other computers.)*[1]

Almost every country in the world is seeing an increase in identity theft activity. Those that did not previously experience the problem are now seeing it firsthand. Unfortunately, most did not learn from the lessons that the United States faced as the crime grew and evolved. The citizens and businesses of these countries are being hit with a double-barreled blast of both low- and high-tech identity crimes.

## AUSTRALIA

Identity crime, as identity theft is called in Australia, is one of a number of issues and trends shaping crime in that country. Identity crime includes production of fraudulent documents, fraudulent applications for identification documents, and identity theft. Like many other countries, Australia has been hit hard by identity theft and incidents continue to increase.

> *Instances of identity crime have been growing for some years and it is now fundamental to many organized crime activities. While concerted and coordinated efforts are being made to prevent and reduce identity crime, organized crime groups continue to commit identity crime to further their criminal activities and produce profit.*[2]

In 2004, the New South Wales Parliament issued a briefing paper reporting that identity theft losses amounted to $3.5 billion for Australia. Other statistics indicated that yearly losses for identity theft were between $1.1 and $3.5 billion.[3] In a 2006 survey in Australia, 8% of respondents indicated that they had been victims of identity theft.

## JAPAN

Although Japan has experienced data breaches of personal information including confidential financial and health data, Japanese business leaders typically respond in a much different fashion from their western counterparts. Executives publicly apologize to those victimized as well as to all customers. This humbling experience is done both in writing and at very public press conferences. Although quite representative of Japanese culture, this process may not stop the growth of identity theft. Japan has seen huge growth in public acceptance of credit cards, and the link between these cards and identity theft poses potential problems. In 2000, fraudsters used skimming devices "to steal the credit card details of approximately 80,000 customers of the department store Takashimaya."[4] As more and more consumers and businesses use credit cards, the number and variety of identity theft crimes will increase.

In an unprecedented act of corporate identity theft, organized crime members in Japan falsely claimed they were affiliated with Japan's NEC Corporation and conned dozens of companies in China and Taiwan "to manufacture pirated products under the NEC brand."[5] The criminals hijacked NEC's good name and were able to exploit it to their advantage. The scheme operated for almost two years. At some point, NEC learned of the fraud using its name. The company subsequently conducted its own investigation using private investigators. The investigation resulted in the arrests of the gang leaders but did not end the threat of this crime.

Japan's Personal Information Protection Act went into effect on April 1, 2005, and provides enhanced standards and protections for the personal information handled by financial, medical, and telecommunications companies. It was enacted as a result of widespread availability of personal data, especially in digital form. Among its many requirements is for companies to ensure that data is secure from loss, unauthorized access, and disclosure. People who violate the act are subject to fines and imprisonment.

## UNITED KINGDOM

In the United Kingdom, it is estimated that identity theft costs the economy $3.4 billion each year. In 2007, it was named as the country's fastest-growing crime. Eighty-six percent of citizens polled in 2008 reported that identity theft and information theft from cellular telephones topped their list of security concerns.[6] Although identity theft is a long-entrenched crime in the United States, it is a relatively new phenomenon in the United Kingdom. Many citizens are not aware of how best to protect themselves from identity theft or even how to react if victimized. A study found that 25% of the public would not notice if their passports were missing, and 80% did not know what to do if they lost their birth certificate. Identity thieves are often insiders in financial institutions or neighbors and friends with access to personal information. The stolen information is used to open credit card accounts, obtain loans, and order merchandise online. The average identity theft loss in the United Kingdom is $16,000.[7]

The Fraud Act of 2006 and the Identity Cards Act of 2006 are important pieces of legislation for targeting identity theft in the United Kingdom. The Fraud Act defined identity fraud and established specific offenses to fight the growing problem. The offenses include possessing and creating access devices for use in fraud and obtaining related services dishonestly. The Identity Cards Act created specific criminal offenses related to the possession and use of fraudulent and unauthorized identity documents. The government also created a Home Office Identity Fraud Steering Committee that is an ongoing collaboration between U.K. financial institutions, government, and law enforcement to combat the threat of identity theft. The committee has created a Web site available at www.identity-theft.org.uk.

The risk of data breaches is just as serious in the United Kingdom as in the United States. The pharmacy chain Alliance Boots, Ltd. announced in April 2008 that the bank accounts of 27,000 customers were stolen. Companies in all industries and of all sizes are not doing enough to protect sensitive personal information, whether by limiting what is maintained on employee laptops or encrypting those laptops. "Despite increased public awareness of the impact that identity theft can have on customers, many firms are still not taking this risk seriously," said the director of Financial Crime and Intelligence for the Financial Services Advisory (FSA).[8] The FSA investigated 56 cases of lost or stolen customer data from financial services firms in 2007. To make matters worse, phishing schemes have targeted customers of most U.K. financial institutions. The tried-and-true techniques of identity thieves are catching on, although in the United Kingdom Dumpster diving is referred to as bin raiding.

## MOROCCO

In February 2008, Moroccan authorities arrested a 26-year-old engineer who allegedly stole the identity of a member of the governing royal family. The defendant created a false profile of the king's younger brother and prince on a popular social networking site.[9] Although the man admitted that he created the account in the prince's name, he said that he did it only because he admired the prince. He claimed to do what many others do each and every day: "Create a profile of a celebrity or a star on Facebook."[10]

There was no indication that the suspect profited from this identity theft; nonetheless, he was quickly prosecuted and sentenced to three years in prison and a small fine. After "local protests and international criticism" about the harsh punishment and physical abuse while in jail, the suspect was granted a royal pardon and released from prison in March 2008.[11]

## BRAZIL

The BRICS—the emerging economies of Brazil, Russia, India, and China—are expected to be dominant forces in the global economy in the years ahead. As much as they are attracting the attention of the world's leading businesses, they are also a magnet for identity thieves. "The Brazilian cybercrime landscape is even more treacherous than North America's. Fraud is one of the main concerns of financial institutions in Latin America," said an executive of a technology company that sells products and services to detect and prevent identity theft. In August 2005, Brazilian police arrested 85 people who allegedly stole more than $33 million from online bank accounts of unsuspecting victims. In February 2006, 55 fraudsters were arrested for taking $4.7 million from 200 bank accounts using stolen account numbers and passwords obtained through an e-mail virus. In the first quarter of 2008, the Brazilian National Computer Emergency Response Team (CERT) reported 30,000 cybercrime incidents.

There are several reasons for the growth of identity theft and related frauds. Many organized crime groups are seeing the significant financial value of both traditional and online scams. The easy availability of technology and those who can use it for criminal activity are other factors. In addition, there is always the need for better laws and more trained law enforcement personnel to attack the problem. Yet there is some good news on the horizon. The publicity around identity theft has increased awareness and prevention in Brazil. Since 2006, when CERT reported 198,000 cybercrime incidents, its largest number ever, the number of incidents has dramatically decreased.

## RUSSIA

The Russian economy is booming. Russian citizens are seeing the trickle-down effect of this wealth generation. Their standard of living is improving, and they are using credit cards like never before. One in seven Russian consumers used credit to purchase big-ticket items in 2007, a number that is is rapidly increasing. That also makes Russian citizens a huge target for fraudsters. Much of the identity theft schemes are of the typical fraudulent credit card application or identity takeover variety. In one instance, a phony passport was used to open three different credit accounts as well as a cellular telephone account in the victim's name. It is believed that Russian banks are losing as much as $4 billion a year to identity theft schemes.[12] It also is believed that in many of the identity theft schemes, bank insiders are involved.

The Anti-Phishing Working Group (APWG) is a global association of technology and financial business leaders along with law enforcement that is focused on eliminating identity theft, phishing, and other Internet frauds and scams. According to the APWG, as of December 2007, Russia was number three in the world of countries that host sites that are launching pads for phishing attacks. The United States was number one. Also according to the APWG, Russia was number six in the world for Web sites that host malicious code in the form of either phishing-based key-loggers or a Trojan downloader that downloads a keylogger.

## INDIA

India got its first taste of how identity theft can have both a financial and reputational impact on business with a very public fraud in 2005. Employees of a call center in Pune, India, doing work for a bank in the United States were implicated in stealing account information and funds of bank customers. Call centers are the fastest-growing segment of India's outsourcing industry. They are often the focal point of controversy for the siphoning of jobs from western countries as well as concerns over data theft and misuse of that information. Although studies have shown that data theft and misuse in India is no greater than in other countries, including the United States, this case raised questions about data-security procedures. It also brought to the surface the growing risk of identity theft in India.

MphasiS, a business process outsourcing company doing call center work for Citibank, was at the center of this firestorm over identity theft. MphasiS employees were accused of "tricking four Citibank customers during routine calls into divulging their Social Security numbers (SSNs), personal identification numbers, and other sensitive data and later transferring money from their accounts by wire into new bank accounts set up" in the western India city of Pune.[13] The employees and their criminal associates ultimately stole $350,000 by raiding the victims' accounts from cybercafés. The victimized Citibank customers noticed suspicious transactions and alerted the bank, and an investigation ensued. Indian authorities later arrested three MphasiS employees and nine other individuals. Sadly, MphasiS decided to blame the victims for not being better at protecting themselves from identity theft. The company issued a statement defending its security procedures by stating "The initial investigations reveal that MphasiS' security procedures in fact worked and the fraud could not have been prevented as some gullible customers have parted with their passwords/pass-codes carelessly. The accused individuals had no prior criminal record and passed all reference checks."[14]

This episode highlighted potential security and compliance problems at some call centers in India that can increase the possibility of data breaches and identity theft. High employee turnover rates—as much as 100% in some instances—contribute to this problem. Such high turnover makes it hard to train and monitor employees. Compounding the problem is a high turnover of managers who are needed to provide oversight and accountability for employees. There is often poor employee background screening. The best indicator of future performance is past performance. Without thorough background checks, there is no telling whether people who are ethically challenged are being hired. Corporate cultures that focus on financial gain at any cost are also to blame for this problem as employees emulate their leaders' practices, both the good and the bad.[15]

## CHINA

China's powerhouse prosperity has paved the way for a burgeoning middle class with the means and desires to live well. That means homes, cars, and the trappings of wealth. China and its citizens have also embraced technology. With 220 million Internet users, China leads the world in Web surfers. There are also some citizens who use technology for evil. According to the APWG, as of December 2007, China was first in the world for Web sites that host malicious code in the form of phishing-based key-loggers or Trojan downloaders. It was also second in the world of countries that host phishing sites, which serve as launching pads for phishing attacks.

In January 2008, police in Shenzchen arrested 18 members of an Internet identity theft ring. The defendants defrauded hundreds of victims throughout China with losses of almost $13.7 million. The fraudsters opened a phony company promising interest-free and quickly approved loans. This was the bait to lure in the victims. People who fell for the scammers' pitch provided personal information, such as bank account numbers and passwords, in order to obtain the loans. They were told to register their financial information on the company's Web site in order so their credit history could be checked. The criminals then transferred the victims' money to their own bank accounts using fake identification. In another variation of the scheme, the defendants would pose as Citibank employees and conduct telephone marketing surveys to obtain personal information.[16]

## GLOBAL PHISHING SCHEME

Phishing schemes are the ideal mechanism for global criminals. They can plan and implement large-scale attacks on victims in numerous countries while operating from the implied safety of another country. That was the case in May 2008 when federal authorities in the United States charged 38 people with stealing names, SSNs, credit card information, and other personal and financial information from thousands of consumers and hundreds of financial institutions.[17] Most of the defendants were based in Romania, but the scheme also operated in the United States, Canada, Portugal, and Pakistan. The fraudsters based in Romania "snagged information about thousands of credit and debit card accounts and other personal data from people who answered spam e-mail."[18] Once the financial information was received, it was "sent to the U.S. and encoded on magnetic cards" that could be used to withdraw money from bank accounts.[19]

In a related aspect of the investigation, seven Romanians were indicted in January 2008 for spamming people with false information, convincing them to visit hacked Web sites that appeared to be the legitimate sites of Citibank, Wells Fargo, PayPal, and others. In announcing the arrests, a Department of Justice official commented, "Criminals who exploit the power and convenience of the Internet do not recognize national borders; therefore our efforts to prevent their attacks cannot end at our borders either."[20]

## TERRORISM AND IDENTITY THEFT

Terrorists also know the importance of stolen identities and fraudulent identification documents for carrying out their fanatical agendas. Identity crimes provide both cover for infiltration as well as a financial means to fund their terrorist activities. The use of stolen identities has become an even greater concern since the devastating September 11, 2001, attacks as we have learned how terrorists have embraced identity theft. Dennis M. Lormel, former Federal Bureau of Investigation Chief of the Terrorism Financial Review Group, testified before Congress in July 2002 about this threat. Here are but a few of his particularly alarming comments about how terrorists are adopting identity theft:

> *The stolen identity provides a cloak of anonymity for the subject while the groundwork is laid to carry out the crime. This includes the rental of mail drops, post office boxes, apartments, office space, vehicles, and storage lockers as well as the activation of pagers, cellular telephones, and various utility services.*

> *The threat is made graver by the fact that terrorists have long utilized identity theft as well as Social Security number fraud to enable them to obtain such things as cover employment and access to secure locations. These and similar means can be utilized by terrorists to obtain Driver's Licenses, and bank and credit card accounts through which terrorism financing is facilitated. Terrorists and terrorist groups require funding to perpetrate their terrorist agendas. The methods used to finance terrorism range from the highly sophisticated to the most basic. There is virtually no financing method that has not at some level been exploited by these groups. Identity theft is a key catalyst fueling many of these methods.*

> *For example, an al-Qaeda terrorist cell in Spain used stolen credit cards in fictitious sales scams and for numerous other purchases for the cell. They kept purchases below amounts where identification would be presented. They also used stolen telephone and credit cards for communications back to Pakistan, Afghanistan, Lebanon, etc. Extensive use of false passports and travel documents were used to open bank accounts where money for the mujahadin movement was sent to and from countries such as Pakistan, Afghanistan, etc.[21]*

The al Qaeda terrorist network has documented the importance of identity theft as a facilitation tool to be used in their terrorist jihad. An al Qaeda training manual found in a computer file in the Manchester, England, home of a member of the terrorist organization has specific sections and references to forged documents, identity theft, setting up safe locations for staging operations, and methods of avoiding detection.[22] These terrorists have done their homework and understand the value of identification documents and the theft of identity. Some of the chilling instructions to terrorists in training from the section entitled "Counterfeit Currency and Forged Documents" include:

- *All documents of the undercover brother, such as identity cards and passport, should be falsified.*
- *When the undercover brother is traveling with a certain identity card or passport, he should know all pertinent information such as the name, profession, and place of residence.*
- *The brother who has a special work status (commander, communication link, etc.) should have more than one identity card and passport. He should learn the contents of each, the nature of the [indicated] profession, and the dialect of the residence area listed in the document.*

- *When using an identity document in different names, no more than one such document should be carried at one time.*
- *The validity of the falsified travel documents should always be confirmed.*
- *When a brother is carrying the forged passport of a certain country, he should not travel to that country. It is easy to detect forgery at the airport, and the dialect of the brother is different from that of the people from their country.*[23]

In the section entitled "Apartments—Hiding Places," these instructions are provided for obtaining and using apartments for covert activities:

- *It is preferable to rent these apartments using false names.*
- *Under no circumstances should anyone know about the apartment except those who use it.*
- *A single brother should not rent more than one apartment in the same area, from the same agent, or using the same rental office.*
- *Avoiding police stations and government buildings. Apartments should not be rented near these places.*
- *It is preferable to rent apartments in newly developed areas where people do not know one another.*
- *Ensuring that there has been no surveillance prior to the members entering the apartment.*
- *It is necessary to have at hand documents supporting the undercover (member). In the case of a physician, there should be an actual medical diploma, membership in the (medical) union, the government permit, and the rest of the routine procedures known in that country.*[24]

Al Qaeda is committed to a perverted form of holy war against anyone who does not believe in its radical fanaticism. Its members' desire is to destroy any way of life that is different than their own. They do this through suicide bombings, kidnappings, assassinations, and intimidation as well as massively coordinated attacks involving large-scale death and destruction. Yet they also employ other damaging tactics. Economic warfare is also in their terrorist tool kit. Al Qaeda is determined to undermine the financial infrastructure of the United States and other countries in any way possible. These terrorists have embraced technology in their pursuit of electronic information to create economic destruction and mayhem. "Al Qaeda could use run-of-the-mill hacker techniques to build a large botnet to steal identities. It could then use those machines that they have taken over to process fake transactions in the name of that consumer."[25] If they were successful in launching hundreds of thousands of these attacks, there is always the possibility that confidence in online commerce could be impacted. The viability of this economic warfare strategy is problematic but one thing is certain: Al Qaeda will use every possible weapon against us.

The 9/11 Commission Report also looked at how the terrorists used identification documents. The report found that:

*For terrorists, travel documents are as important as weapons. Terrorists must travel clandestinely to meet, train, plan, case targets, and gain access to attack. . . . In their travels, terrorists use evasive methods, such as altered and counterfeit passports . . . and identity theft. . . . Targeting travel is at least as powerful a weapon against terrorists as targeting their money. . . . The federal government should set standards for the issuance of birth certificates and sources of identification, such as driver's licenses. Fraud in identification documents is no longer just a problem of theft. At many entry points to vulnerable facilities, including gates for boarding aircraft, sources of identification are the last opportunity to ensure that people are who they say they are and to check whether they are terrorists.[26]*

## GLOBAL IDENTITY THEFT AND MONEY LAUNDERING RING

Identity theft is fast becoming a global problem. Technology, worldwide criminal networks, and greed all contribute to this fact. Other troubling aspects combine to making identity theft deadly at times. As we have seen earlier in this book, identity theft and credit card fraud are white-collar crimes, and there is often the mistaken perception that violent crimes are not associated with them. That is not necessarily the case; crime knows no restrictions. In addition, it is quite common that a major investigation starts down one path but ends up going in many different directions as additional crimes are discovered. That was what happened in an investigation that started in Maryland in the mid-1990s but soon spread to many other states and countries around the world. The case study that follows tells volumes about how credit card fraud and identity theft can intertwine with drug trafficking, money laundering, and murder, all with an international twist.

The investigation started when a keen-eyed NationsBank fraud investigator discovered unusual transactions in a customer's account that indicated possible money laundering. The investigator reached out to the Financial Crimes Task Force in Baltimore, Maryland. The Task Force consisted of Postal Inspectors, the IRS Criminal Investigation Division, and the Customs Service. Although the case started out as a drug and money laundering investigation involving a ring of Nigerian nationals, by the end it was primarily an identity theft case. Arrests were made in Florida, Maryland, Illinois, California, New York, and London.

The scheme was international in scope and was directed by defendant Adeniyi Allison from London and Nigeria. Allison fled the United States after being convicted on credit card fraud charges in the state of Virginia in 1993. Allison masterminded a money laundering operation to assist friends and associates in moving money obtained from various frauds to their home country of Nigeria. Some of the subjects were building large homes in Nigeria using the proceeds of their criminal activities. Allison directed activities of associate Beverly Mitchell and others via fax machine from overseas. He directed them to deposit funds from his associates who were engaged in credit card fraud and drug trafficking. Allison then directed Mitchell and others to wire transfer these funds to businesses outside the United States.

## Identity Theft Aspect

In the identity theft aspect of the case, mail containing credit cards and other personal information was stolen from victims' residences and businesses. The ring obtained SSNs, dates of birth, and other confidential information from a variety of sources to obtain credit cards, open bank accounts, and defraud financial institutions. Money was sent to Nigeria, Korea, London, Belgium, Taiwan, and Italy.

Allison had friends working at an American Express customer service office and at their personal identification number (PIN) center. They provided account numbers and PIN numbers that were used on white plastic to make cash advances. As mentioned earlier, "white plastic" is a term used by fraudsters and law enforcement. White plastic cards are credit card–size pieces of plastic of any color that are meant to be used as a credit card with collusive merchants. They are sometimes called blue plastic. The plastic card is embossed with valid but stolen information, such as a card holder's name, account number, and expiration date.

There were many twists and turns in this case including two brutal murders that remain unsolved. Approximately $1 million in fraudulent credit card charges were associated with this scheme, and more than $2 million in laundered proceeds were eventually identified. Several suspects received 14-year sentences under the money laundering guidelines, and a total of 14 defendants were convicted. The case included a wiretap and an international arrest and extradition from England.

During searches, federal agents recovered credit reports and other personal information that was obtained from car dealers, hospitals, the Social Security Administration, and a real estate office. The investigators were initially unsure of the source of the credit reports from the real estate office. Then two appraisals containing the same company and individual names from the report header were on letters of appraisal for property presented to a criminal court judge on behalf of a suspect being held in jail for serious crimes. The defendant tried to use this stolen information as his own to show his roots to the community in order to obtain bail for release from jail. Needless to say, the magistrate was not amused and the defendant remained behind bars.

## Involvement of Nigerian Organized Criminal Groups

The description of Nigerian organized criminal groups that follows comes from the application and affidavit of Postal Inspector Kenyon Male, Jr. for a search warrant on April 9, 1996. Inspector Male was assigned to the Washington Division of the Postal Inspection Service at the time. Based on his training, experience, and participation in other investigations involving the violations of the structuring statutes and the money laundering statutes, Inspector Male affirmed under oath:

1. *That there are organized criminal groups operating in the United States which are made up of individuals from the West African country of Nigeria.*

2. *That these Nigerian organized criminal groups are primarily involved in the illegal activities of heroin smuggling and distribution, credit card fraud, advance fee schemes, bank and credit card account take-overs, and money laundering of the*

*proceeds derived from these illegal activities. There is no strict segmentation of activities among these groups; and many of these groups are usually involved in more than one of these illegal activities.*

3. *That these Nigerian organized criminal groups are often regional or national in scope. The activities of these groups are usually directed by one or more individuals who remain in the country of Nigeria, and one or more individuals in the United States. In order to direct the activities of the members of their organizations, these leaders rely on various forms of communications such as papers, facsimile machines, cellular telephones, voice-mail boxes, as well as conventional telephonic communications.*

4. *That in order to facilitate their illegal activities in the United States and throughout the world the individuals who are members of these Nigerian organized criminal groups utilize many forms of false identification, such as false birth certificates, passports, and driver's licenses that are used to fraudulently obtain visas and travel under false pretenses, open numerous bank and credit card accounts, and rent drop boxes, apartments, and storage locations. These individuals often utilize many false identities which make it extremely difficult for law enforcement to track their activities and locate their assets.*

5. *That due to their well-documented activities in heroin smuggling and various fraud schemes, Nigerian nationals have come under increased scrutiny from Customs, banking, and other financial industry officials worldwide. In order to circumvent this increased scrutiny, Nigerian nationals involved in these illegal activities often attempt to recruit individuals of other nationalities, who are usually females, to carry out their smuggling and banking activities.*

6. *That Nigerian organized criminal groups operating in the United States utilize a number of schemes to place their illegal profits into the banking system and/or transport or transmit their illegal profits outside of the United States. These schemes include the "structured" purchase of monetary instruments (i.e. money orders and cashier's checks) with cash to evade the federal currency reporting requirements, opening numerous bank accounts in nominee or false names with subsequent use of the bank's access to the international electronic funds transfer services, the use of front companies, currency smuggling, the purchase and subsequent export of commodities, the use of express mail services, the exchange of U.S. dollars domestically for Nigerian naira, and the sale of U.S. dollars held domestically in the U.S. on the Nigerian black market in foreign exchange.*

7. *That Nigerian organized criminal groups involved in credit card and other types of bank fraud often maintain within their premises, in their vehicles, on their persons, in safe deposit boxes, storage lockers, and other locations, over which they maintain dominion and control: notes; correspondence; bank account information; credit cards and associated account information; monetary instruments and receipts relating to their purchase; storage locker, safe deposit and post office box rental agreements and keys; Express Mail labels and receipts; identification and travel documents; phone and address books; and other documents relating to their fraudulent schemes*

8. *That Nigerian organized criminal groups involved in credit card and other types of bank fraud purchase and maintain assets and investments in their own names, aliases, front company, and nominee names. Records relating to the acquisition, maintenance and disposition of these assets and investments as well as other*

*expenditures of illegal proceeds are often maintained within their premises, in their vehicles, on their persons, in safe deposit boxes, storage lockers and other locations, over which they maintain dominion and control.*[27]

## Detailed Account of the Investigation

This detailed account of the origins of the investigation and the subsequent twists and turns comes from United States Customs Service Agent Christopher J. Buzzeo's sworn affidavit in support of a search warrant authorized by a Magistrate Judge in the Eastern District of New York on May 9, 1996:

*The investigation, to date, identified Adeniyi Momodu Allison and Christopher Olusegun Omotunde as the leaders of an international Nigerian organized criminal group that is involved in credit card fraud and the laundering of both drugs and fraud monies generated in the United States. The fraud activities of the Allison/Omotunde group in the U.S. are being directed by Christopher Omotunde from his residence in Upper Marlboro, MD. Adeniyi "Ade" Allison is directing the group's international money movements from Nigeria where he is a fugitive from a conviction for credit card fraud in the Eastern District of Virginia.*

*The group utilized a store front located at 1506 Wisconsin Avenue, NW, in Washington, DC, called Designers Collective, Inc. nee Vogue International Designers, Inc. One of Designers Collective's employees, Helen Olopade, a United Kingdom national of Nigerian descent conducted the group's banking activities at the direction of Allison utilizing the business checking accounts of Vogue International Designers (now closed) and Designers Collective, as well as two personal checking accounts.*

*In the Spring of 1994, IRS-CID Special Agent Donald L. Temple of the Maryland Financial Investigative Task Force received a criminal referral from Linda Parker, Fraud Investigator for NationsBank of Maryland, reporting that Beverly R. Mitchell had recently opened an account at NationsBank. Shortly after she opened the account, a pattern of suspicious deposits into and wire transfers out of the account began to occur. In researching Mitchell's account activity, Ms. Parker discovered that Mitchell had a second account in which the same activity was occurring. Based on this information, Special Agent Barry Lewis of the U.S. Customs Service began a criminal investigation into the apparent laundering of large sums of monies by Mitchell. In November of 1994, the IRS-CID and the Postal Inspection Service joined the investigation.*

*On March 23, 1995, Beverly Mitchell's body was discovered in a field in LaPlata, MD, where she had been left after a brutal murder. The homicide remains unsolved. Shortly after her body was discovered, the investigating agents gained access to Beverly Mitchell's residence through the consent of her parents. Investigators found in the bedroom very detailed records concerning her laundering of over $1 million for the Allison/Omotunde organization. The investigation, to date, has documented in excess of $1.5 million laundered internationally by the organization.*

*Within a day or two of the death of Beverly Mitchell, the body of Temitayo Ikudayisi was found in a van in Washington, DC. The coroner's report estimated that Ikudayisi had been dead 1-2 weeks prior to the discovery of his body. Ikudayisi had recently been released from prison resulting from a fraud conviction in Chicago. Ikudayisi allegedly was an associate of Christopher Omotunde in his fraud activities. Ikudayisi had been tortured and then executed. This homicide also remains unsolved.*

*Your affiant has been advised by Special Agent Donald Semesky, IRS CID, Baltimore, that Postal Inspector Phillip Bartlett had been involved in the execution of a Maryland State Search Warrant and the arrest on August 14, 1995 of a Nigerian national named Adewale Abdebesin Kasal, for credit card fraud. The search warrant was executed at Mr. Kasal's residence in Columbia, Maryland.*

*Inspector Bartlett stated that after Mr. Kasal was advised of his Constitutional rights, he agreed to cooperate with the government. During the course of the search of Mr. Kasal's residence, a business card from U-Store, 6120 Livingston Road, Oxon Hill, Maryland was recovered. Mr. Kasal admitted that he currently rents storage bin number G4F at this location under the alias of William Miller. He then signed a consent to search form to permit the search of this location.*

*Inspector Bartlett has further advised on August 15, 1995 storage locker G4F was searched by members of the Washington, DC Fraud Task Force. Recovered during the search were numerous stolen checks, credit cards, U.S. Mail, fraudulent identification and numerous documents with names and account numbers. Inspector Bartlett advised that during the course of the debriefing of Mr. Kasal, he (Kasal) stated that many of the items found in the storage bin were the property of Christopher Omotunde. Mr. Kasal advised the debriefing agents that Christopher Omotunde would provide him with stolen checks and fraudulent identification in various names. Mr. Kasal also stated that he would receive a percentage of the proceeds for his participation in the various frauds from Christopher Omotunde. Mr. Kasal further stated that Christopher Omotunde also engages in bank fraud schemes.*

*During his debriefing Kasal stated that Christopher Omotunde paid for and attended the funeral of Temitayo Ikudayisi in April 1995. According to Kasal, Omotunde issued a warning to the others at the funeral that anyone who cooperates with the police and testifies against other Nigerians will be "killed" like Temitayo.*

*In March 1996, your affiant debriefed a confidential source of information (CSI) who has worked operationally for the DEA from 1993 to 1995. CSI has never supplied false information during his/her cooperation. CSI's information and an introduction that he/ she arranged has resulted in the arrest and successful prosecution of one person for drug trafficking. CSI informed your affiant that an individual named "Rilwan," who is currently in Nigeria, is presently moving large amounts of money for Nigerians involved in drugs and credit card fraud in the Washington, DC metropolitan area. CSI also identified Christopher Omotunde as an associate of Rilwan.*

*Your affiant has reviewed the deposited items for two accounts at the First Union National Bank which were opened in the name of Adeniyi Allison with an address in London, England. This address is recorded in Beverly Mitchell's records. The deposited items to these accounts are similar in nature to the items which were deposited to the accounts of Mitchell and Omotunde, i.e. structured money orders purchased in Chicago and New York. Many of these money orders list the name, Rilwan Allison, as the payee. During the debriefing of the CSI, it stated that it did not want its name revealed as a cooperator, because it feared for its life. CSI referred to Temitayo Ikudayisi and how he went to a party one night with people he thought were his friends, and was abducted.*

*Analysis of Mitchell's records, as well as subpoenaed bank records of her's, Allison's, Omotunde's and other organization members' bank accounts, reveals a pattern to the group's method of operation in moving their funds, i.e. the funds that were being laundered by Mitchell, and now Olopade, are first being converted to money orders and bank checks, with an occasional third party check (all of which appear to have been purchased in a structured manner, i.e. under $10,000, consecutively numbered on the same day, with the vast majority being under $3,000), by members of the organization in the cities where they are located.*

*These monetary instruments are then express mailed to "drop boxes" or Designers Collective from these co-conspirators in Illinois, New York, New Jersey, Georgia, and Florida. These monetary instruments are then deposited into checking accounts, often through deposits made after normal banking hours at ATM machines. Once these funds are deposited, instructions are received via facsimile from Ade Allison in Nigeria directing which bank, country, and beneficiary account they are to be wired to.*

*Analysis of the applications for transfer of funds associated with these wire transfers indicates that the funds are being used for payment on apparent commercial transactions. The records of Dun & Bradstreet were obtained for many of the international recipients of these wire transfers. Your affiant has reviewed these Dun & Bradstreet reports, which confirm that these companies sell commodities such as electrical appliances, writing and printing supplies, automotive parts, and earring piercing equipment.*

*Listed as the senders on these wire transfers are various Nigerian companies. The Nigerian company listed as the primary sender of these wire transfers is Atinuke Allison and Sons, Ltd. Another Nigerian company, Premier Standard Industrial, Ltd., is the beneficiary of many of these wire transfers. Recovered from the residence of Beverly Mitchell, after her death were facsimile messages from Allison to Mitchell directing her as to the amount, destination, and for whose benefit funds should be wired.*

*These messages were sent on Premier Standard's letterhead. The telephone numbers listed on this letterhead are the same as the numbers reflected in Beverly Mitchell's phone books as Allison's work numbers. Your affiant is aware of the means and methods utilized by Nigerian criminal organizations to launder illicit proceeds. Based on your affiants' review of the above records it appears as if Allison is laundering the group's money and bringing it into Nigeria in two manners: a) he is purchasing commodities which he is then importing into Nigeria and re-selling, and b) he is entering into contracts with various narcotics and fraud groups to launder and/or purchase their U.S. dollars, which he is then reselling in the foreign exchange black market.*[28]

## Evidence of Identity Theft

The federal agents in this case conducted numerous search warrants and obtained significant amounts of important evidence. In one very telling example, Postal Inspector Male and other federal agents conducted a search warrant at a residence in Wyandanch, New York, on May 10, 1996. They found this evidence hidden in the attic:

1. *More than 15 credit cards in the names of numerous individuals, both male and female, none of which were in the name of the defendant.*
2. *Driver's licenses for the individuals whose names appeared on the above credit cards.*

3. *Several blank, unembossed credit cards.*

4. *Over 30 credit cards in the defendant's own name drawn on all different banks.*

5. *Equipment designed to print personal bank checks, including transparencies which contained master copies of the checks, without names but with bank names.*

6. *A book containing names, social security numbers, mother's maiden names, occupations, and other credit information.*

7. *Credit reports for numerous different individuals.*

8. *Approximately 30 Macy's credit card applications in numerous and different names.*

9. *Boxes of blank checks in numerous different names.*

10. *Approximately $6,000 in structured postal money orders.*

11. *Blank Postal change of address forms.*[29]

This is typical of the evidence usually found in identity theft cases. It is similar to what other federal agents and I found during searches in the 1980s. It is also no different from what law enforcement is finding today in search warrants.

## Aftermath

Of the 14 defendants in this case, most pleaded guilty. Ringleader Omotunde pleaded guilty to money laundering charges on January 10, 1997, and agreed to cooperate against his codefendants. He testified as a government witness on January 21, 1997. He told how he and other members of his fraud ring developed contacts in car dealerships, financial institutions, mortgage companies, and credit-reporting agencies to obtain the victims' personal information. He detailed to the jury how he rented an apartment in Allentown, Pennsylvania, and installed a telephone there in case credit card issuers called to confirm information on applications. Omotunde had the calls automatically forwarded to his cell phone so that he could answer and provide false information.[30] He detailed how he and his ring made millions of dollars in the easy-to-do crime of credit card fraud. Omotunde's cooperation against the other defendants resulted in a reduced prison term of only 51 months.

One of the defendants who pleaded guilty during his trial to money laundering and heroin-trafficking charges threatened to cast a spell on anyone who would testify against him. He reportedly placed a curse on the agents, judges, and prosecutors in this case. The defendant claimed to be a practitioner of witchcraft, called "juju" in Nigeria.[31] His threat of voodoo was not powerful enough, however, as he was sentenced to almost 13 years in prison.

The investigation disclosed more than $1.5 million in credit card fraud resulting from the criminal misuse of personal financial information and mail theft from more than 1,000 victims. The conspirators utilized insiders from American Express, the Social Security Administration, car dealerships, and other businesses and organizations to obtain personally identifiable information.

Two other defendants who went to trial were convicted and sentenced to lengthy prison terms. Another twist in this unusual case was a foot chase in London that netted a key conspirator and fugitive, Allison. Allison had gotten into an argument with an employee at a rental car agency, and the police were called. Allison tried to flee but an alert Scotland Yard "bobby" ran him down and tackled him. In Allison's possession were documents linking him to the other defendants.[32]

## NOTES

1. The President's Identity Theft Task Force, *Combating Identity Theft: A Strategic Plan*, April 2007, 13, www.idtheft.gov/reports/StrategicPlan.pdf.
2. Australian Crime Commission, *Organised Crime in Australia* (2007), www.crime-commission.gov.au/content/publications/Other_Publications/080117_Organised_Crime_In_Australia.pdf.
3. Written comments from a presentation made by Detective Sergeant Rodney Mills, Victoria Police, Heidelberg, Victoria, Australia, at the Association of Certified Fraud Examiners' 18th Annual Fraud Conference, Orlando, FL, July 16, 2007.
4. Dr. Alan F. Westin, "Data Leakage and Harm," www.privacyexchange.org/japan/dataleakEd.html.
5. Evan Blass, "NEC Falls Victims to Sophisticated 'Corporate Identity Theft,'" April 27, 2006, www.engadget.com/2006/04/27/nec-falls-victim-to-sophisticated-corporate-identity-theft/.
6. Nick Heath, "Brits Living in Fear of Identity Theft," May 20, 2008, www.silicon.com/research/specialreports/fulldisclosure/0,3800014102,39225528,00.htm.
7. "ID Burglary Risk Ignored," April 22, 2008, www.myfinances.co.uk/news/bank-accounts/bank-account-fraud/id-burglary-risk-ignored-$1219804.htm.
8. Caroline Binham, "Banks, Lenders Must Protect Data from Fraud, U.K.'s FSA Says," April 24, 2008, www.bloomberg.com/apps/news?pid=20601102&sid=alPccpflbvUI&refer=uk.
9. Chris Williams, "Moroccan IT Manager Arrested Over Fake Facebook Account," *The Register*, February 18, 2008, www.theregister.co.uk/2008/02/18/morocco_fb_fake_prince/.
10. "The Fouad Mourtada Affair," Wikipedia.org, accessed May 26, 2008, //en.wikipedia.org/wiki/Fouad_Mourtada.
11. Ibid.
12. "Living to Pay Off Another Man's Debt," *Russia Today*, May 3, 2008, www.russiatoday.ru/features/news/24270.
13. Saritha Rai, "Indian Outsourcers Move to Fix Security," *International Herald Tribune*, June 17, 2005, www.iht.com/articles/2005/06/16/business/security.php.
14. Andy McCue, "$350,000 Citibank Theft Victims 'Gullible and Careless,' Indian Call Center Firm Says the Fraud Could Not Have Been Prevented," April 12, 2005, www.silicon.com/research/specialreports/offshoring/0,3800003026,39129475,00.htm.
15. Anthony Mitchell, "Indian Call Center Fraud Case Highlights Need for Change," *E-Commerce Times*, April 12, 2005, www.ecommercetimes.com/story/42112.html.
16. Wu Nanlan, "Police Crack Down on Internet Identity Theft," January 11, 2008, www.china.org.cn/english/China/239068.htm.

17. Lara Jakes Jordan, "38 Charged in Global Phishing Scheme," *Associated Press*, May 19, 2008, www.time.com/time/world/article/0,8599,1807712,00.html?xid=rss-topstories.
18. Ibid.
19. Ibid.
20. Ibid.
21. Testimony of Dennis M. Lormel, Chief, Terrorist Financial Review Group, Federal Bureau of Investigations, Before the Senate Judiciary Committee Subcommittee on Technology, Terrorism and Government Information, July 9, 2002, in support of the Identity Theft Penalty Enhancement Act, www.fbi.gov/congress/congress02/idtheft.htm.
22. The al Qaeda Training Manual was found by the Manchester, England Metropolitan Police Department during a search of a residence occupied by a member of al Qaeda. The manual was described as a "military series" related to the "Declaration of Jihad." The manual was translated into English and subsequently introduced as evidence at a terrorist bombing trial in New York City, www.usdoj.gov/ag/manualpart1_1.pdf.
23. Al Qaeda Training Manual, 23–24, www.usdoj.gov/ag/manualpart1_1.pdf.
24. Ibid., 26–28.
25. John Bambenek, "Al Qaeda's Economic War and Online Identity Theft: A Perfect Storm," *Men's News Daily*, December 22, 2006, http://mensnewsdaily.com/2006/12/22/al-qaedas-economic-war-and-online-identity-theft-a-perfect-storm/.
26. The 9/11 Commission Report: Final Report of the National Commission on Terrorist Attacks Upon the United States (New York: W.W. Norton & Company, 2004), 384–390.
27. Application and Affidavit in Support of Search Warrant to search a Postal Express Mail package, sworn to and signed by Postal Inspector Kenyon Male, Jr. and IRS-CID Special Agent Donald C. Semesky, Jr., United States District Court, District of Maryland, April 9, 1996, 3–4.
28. Application and Affidavit in Support of Search Warrant to search a residence in Wyandanch, New York, sworn to and signed by Special Agent Christopher J. Bruzzeo, United States Customs Service, United States District Court, Eastern District of New York, May 9, 1996, 4–7.
29. *United States against Tony K. Oderinde, Defendant*, Criminal Complaint, sworn to and signed by Postal Inspector Kenyon Male, Jr., United States District Court, Eastern District of New York, May 10, 1996, 3.
30. Scott Higham, "Figure in Fraud Ring Describes Maze of Schemes," *Baltimore Sun*, January 22, 1997, 5B.
31. Scott Higham, "How Nigerian Criminal Cast Spells to Control Enemies," *Baltimore Sun*, February 3, 1997, 1A.
32. Scott Higham, "Fraud Victim Testifies about Illegal Buys on Credit Cards," *Baltimore Sun*, January 28, 1997, 1B.

# CHAPTER 17

# Privacy and Data Breaches

Our privacy is under attack like never before. We live in a digital world where life is literally an open book. With a click of a mouse, anyone anywhere in the world can learn who we are and what we have done, both good and bad. Much of our personal information is being collected in huge databases. Our consumer profiles are shared and sold to data brokers and marketing firms for a wide variety of purposes. Social networking sites are proliferating, and people are willingly posting every imaginable detail of their lives. Identity thieves and sexual predators are seizing on this information for criminal purposes. Young people who proudly display photos of their drinking binges on social networking sites are not thinking of the photos' impact on possible future employers who may check the sites for background screening purposes.

## LOSS OF PRIVACY

In an event launch on January 25, 1999, former Sun Microsystems chief executive officer (CEO) Scott McNealy stated, "You have zero privacy anyway. . . . Get over it."[1] McNealy made the comment when asked about what privacy safeguards he was including in a new technology he was promoting. Unfortunately, at the time he was right about the state of privacy in the wired world. But the growth of the Internet and identity theft requires a greater focus on protecting people and data. After having had several years to reflect on this comment, McNealy in a speech in February 2006 stated: "It's going to get scarier if we don't come up with technology and rules to protect appropriately privacy and secure data, and the most important asset we have is obviously the data on people—our customers and employees and partners." He added, "And if we can't protect that, people are not going to go online."[2]

Yet people are going online, and in even greater numbers each and every day. Facebook, MySpace, and LinkedIn are but some of the many very popular social networking sites. They are great people interaction tools and quite effective in connecting people. Social networking "is the chosen mode of communication of everyone they know. So if you're not in it, you're just not in the loop."[3] We will not be able to stop the onrushing technology revolution or resulting dangers. Fraudsters have learned the value of the Internet for criminal activity in a big way. We knew it would happen. In a speech on March 15, 1999, then Attorney General Janet Reno said, "We cannot allow cyberspace to become the wild west of the information age." Unfortunately, that is exactly what has happened. Identity theft and other fraud schemes are proliferating in the online world.

Ensuring privacy and protections in the Internet age is quite a challenge. In many cases we are our own worst enemy. Most of the data breaches that have occurred in recent years have been the result of security lapses that could have been avoided. Whether it is carrying a laptop laden with far too much sensitive information and failing to encrypt the hard drive, to simple security procedures such as shredding confidential files before discarding them, we all can do better in ensuring privacy.

## DEFINING "PRIVACY"

Microsoft defines "privacy" as allowing individuals to determine how and to what extent their personal information will be collected, used, and shared with others. We must all care about privacy protections and how our personal information is used. Personally identifiable information (PII) is unique information that identifies a particular person. PII includes name, date of birth, Social Security number (SSN), email address, telephone number, and financial and medical information. This information has become a commodity, a very valuable commodity. Expanding business models want and need more and more information on people. These personal data are critical to business growth, but at the same time consumers want accountability. Although the legal requirements for privacy are critical, privacy is also about earning customer trust.

Identity theft is a serious threat to our privacy, but there are many other factors that intrude into our privacy. London has ringed its central district with surveillance cameras to provide an "eye in the sky" to increase personal protection and decrease crime. This constant surveillance helped identify and capture terrorists who attempted to set off car bombs in the city in 2007. New York City is planning a similar video surveillance network to protect the city and its citizens. E-Z Pass and other electronic transmitters that allow motorists to speed through toll booths can also be used to track their movements. These monitoring examples are just a few of the many privacy challenges facing people today. The Privacy Rights Clearinghouse, a nonprofit consumer information and advocacy organization, believes the top privacy issues include:

- Identity theft
- Online privacy and e-commerce
- Video surveillance
- Biometrics technologies
- Wireless communications and location tracking
- Data profiling
- Background checks
- Information broker industry
- Public records on the Internet
- Financial privacy
- Medical records confidentiality
- Wiretapping and electronic communications
- Youth privacy issues
- Digital rights management
- Radio Frequency Identification (RFID)[4]

## DATA BREACHES

Data breaches and identity theft were the main topics at the RSA Conference on Information Security in San Francisco, California, in February 2007. "Data are the currency of the Internet age for legitimate—and illegitimate—businesses," said Howard Schmidt, former chief information officer at eBay.[5] "It's a stupid system," commented Microsoft chairman Bill Gates on the current credit card issuing system. "It's a weak system when someone with your Social Security number or mother's maiden name can apply for credit without you knowing it."[6] Gates's solution is a combination of biometrics and a system that requires a consumer's approval when any financial transaction occurs.

There is no question that data breaches are a significant risk to privacy. A 2005 study by security software provider Credant Technologies found that 90% of people who had their laptops stolen had sensitive business and personal information on the hard drives. A 2003 Pepperdine University study found that data losses cost businesses in the United States more than $18 billion a year and is significantly more today. A Ponemon Institute study on data breaches found that 20% of data breach victims cut their ties with the organization after the breach. Data breaches are bad for business.

Many of the data breaches in recent years have been the result of lost or stolen laptops. It is shocking how much sensitive PII can be found on laptops. In December 2005, financial services company Ameriprise Financial learned that a laptop containing the names and SSNs of hundreds of thousands of employees and customers was stolen from an employee's car. Although the laptop was password protected, it was not encrypted as required by the company. In May 2006, a laptop used by a data analyst with the United States Department of Veterans Affairs was stolen from the employee's home. The laptop contained personal information on more than 28 million veterans, military personnel, and their spouses.

Data breaches are not just a U.S. problem. In 2007, government workers in the United Kingdom lost two computer disks with the personal information of 25 million residents of that country. The disks contained names, addresses, dates of birth, insurance identifiers, and other financial information. Sent through regular interoffice delivery channels, they disappeared. Although the disks were password protected, they were not encrypted. Skilled computer forensic specialists could easily break those passwords and access the information.

The Privacy Rights Clearinghouse has been maintaining a running chronology of data breaches since January 2005. Since that time, more than 227 million records containing sensitive personal information has been breached from financial institutions, healthcare providers and hospitals, universities, government agencies, and other types of businesses. The PII was compromised through both low-tech and high-tech means. Breaches resulted from theft of unencrypted laptops from cars, homes, and hotel rooms; compromised passwords; insider thefts; hacking; lost backup tapes; thefts of packages of files and computer tapes being shipped; and generally careless exposure of PII. Exhibit 17.1 is a sampling of the many data breaches that have occurred between 2005 and 2008.

Billions of dollars can be spent on information security systems, but just one weak link can compromise the entire system. Laptops are that weak link. Companies have hardened their defenses to limit what comes into their networks, laptops, and the data on them, but that is not enough. Sensitive information freely leaves work sites each and every day with employees who carry their laptops home and during travel. Sales of laptop computers far outpace those of desktop systems. With the convenience of mobile computing, people carry their laptops everywhere. The big question is why such sensitive data are kept on unprotected laptops despite the huge risk. Removing all but the most necessary information is a start. A best practice is conducting audits to ensure compliance by checking for unsecured files, sensitive files that do not belong on laptops, and the use of encryption technology.

Although not an absolute solution to the risk of data breach, encryption of data is a great start. Encryption encodes data so that it can be accessed only with special passwords and keys. That is not to say that encryption is foolproof. Highly skilled forensic experts can break encryption, but encryption will eliminate most of the threat of data theft. Encryption, however, works only if employees use it once it is installed.

Portable digital devices present another risk for lost data. Some companies are disabling USB ports on computers to ensure that these devices cannot be used. Flash drives are easy to use to extract sensitive information and small enough to hide and remove from the premises. The digital age provides numerous avenues to store PII and other sensitive information that needs to be protected.

Although more and more companies are holding their employees accountable for lost computers containing sensitive PII, that will not fix the problem. Disciplining employees who violate this policy is akin to closing the barn doors after the horses have run away. One Fortune 500 company requires employees to use a cable lock to secure laptops to stationary objects at all times. This is a good policy, but most cable locks can be defeated with a simple screwdriver. That is not to say that using a cable lock when in the office or hotel room is a bad idea. It is not. Any deterrent is good, and such locks may very well deter opportunity theft. But they will not stop hard core criminals.

**Exhibit 17.1   Sampling of Data Breaches, 2005 to 2008**

| Date | Company or Organization | Type of Breach | Number of Records Breached |
|------|------------------------|----------------|---------------------------|
| February 2005 | ChoicePoint | Bogus accounts established by identity thieves | 163,000 |
| February 2005 | Bank of America | Lost backup tape | 1,200,000 |
| March 2005 | DSW/Retail Ventures | Hacking | 100,000 |
| December 2005 | Ameriprise Financial | Stolen laptop from employee's car | 260,000 |
| March 2006 | Fidelity Investments | Stolen laptop | 196,000 |
| May 2006 | American Institute of Certified Public Accountants | Unencrypted hard drive lost | 330,000 |
| May 2006 | U.S. Department of Veteran's Affairs | Theft of laptop and computer storage device from employee's home | 28,600,000 |
| December 2006 | University of California, Los Angeles | Hacking | 800,000 |
| December 2006 | Boeing | Laptop stolen from employee's car | 382,000 |
| January 2007 | TJX | Hacking | 100,000,000 |
| April 2007 | Georgia Department of Community Health | Lost computer disk | 2,900,000 |
| August 2007 | California Public Employees' Retirement System | All or portion of retirees' SSN appeared on address panel in mass mailing | 445,000 |
| March 2008 | Hannaford Brothers | Hacking | 4,200,000 |
| April 2008 | New York-Presbyterian Hospital/Weill Cornell Medical Center | Admissions employee stole patients' data in an identity theft scheme | 50,000 |
| April 2008 | University of Miami | Theft of computer tapes | 2,100,000 |

Source: Privacy Rights Clearinghouse, A Chronology of Data Breaches, www.privacyrights.org/ar/ChronData Breaches.htm#Total

## INSIDER THREATS

Although there is the general public's fear that multitudes of foreign-based hackers and criminals are breaking into our networks and personal computers and stealing our personal information, the truth is something different. Studies over the last few years have found that the greatest threat for identity theft is from trusted insiders within organizations.[7]

In 2003, a manager at H&R Block in White Plains, New York, was charged with identity theft–related crimes for stealing the personal information of 27 customers of the tax preparation service. The PII was used to open credit cards in the names of the victims, make purchases on those cards, and withdraw money from automated teller machines (ATMs). The manager was assisted in the crime by three of her friends who were also charged. The defendants used Postal Service change-of-address orders to divert credit cards from the victims' residences to that of mail drops the criminals opened. In addition, the H&R Block employee also stole tax refund checks due customers.

Two Bellevue, Washington, businesses were attacked by insiders who stole financial information from dozens of customers. A fraudster approached employees of a mortgage company and an escrow service and recruited them to obtain information from victims' mortgage applications. Other conspirators created phony driver's licenses and documents to perpetrate the fraud. The personal and financial information was used to apply for fraudulent credit cards and withdraw money from bank accounts. The scheme continued from 2002 to 2005 before it was discovered.

## YOUR HOME IS THEIR CASTLE

The enemy within may be located under your own roof. Identity thieves know that a significant source of personal information is maintained within our residences. They may not need to actually break into the house to get what they need. Any number of people walk in through the front door on a regular basis for legitimate purposes. Nannies, caregivers, cleaning people, and repair and other service providers are just some. Nannies and caregivers may reside in the homes on a long-term basis and could very well know where personal and financial information is located. Background checks are a must for any live-in workers. Locking up key information and financial documents is also a must.

Owners of home-based businesses may employ staff. If any of these people are criminally minded, there is valuable information to be had when no is looking. Again, background checks are also highly recommended for all employees.

Vacation homes are also vulnerable. They may be vacant for long stretches of time. The owners may leave information in those locales that could be stolen by people who watch the home or come into the residence to do maintenance work. Vacation homes are also vulnerable to break-ins by opportunistic thieves who may steal PII and the computer along with the flat-screen television and DVD player.

## CARELESSNESS AS A CONTRIBUTING FACTOR

Mortgage files are particularly attractive to identity thieves. Lenders require detailed financial information on borrowers in order to assess loan risk. Mortgage applications are used to approve or deny mortgages that can range to the hundreds of thousands of dollars. The problem is what happens to those paper applications when they are no longer needed or companies go out of business. In 2007, a reporter in Indianapolis did his own investigation to determine the seriousness of this issue. Over a period of several days, he checked 40 Dumpsters behind mortgage and title companies looking for discarded mortgage files. Almost half of the companies had thrown out applications and other documents containing personal and financial information of borrowers. "You could see their complete financial lives on paper, dating back 20, 30, 40 years," said the reporter who broke the story.[8] You can imagine the borrowers' outrage upon learning about the failure to safeguard their financial histories.

## WIRELESS (IN)FIDELITY

Wireless networks (or Wi-Fi) are an increasingly popular way to connect to the Internet. Wireless networks allow users the freedom to access the Internet anywhere they get a signal, whether at home through their own wireless router or in public at a Wi-Fi hot spot. Although Wi-Fi is very convenient for users, it presents many unique dangers beyond the ones otherwise encountered by wired Internet users. Special measures need to be taken to prevent unauthorized data access, hacking, and identity theft.

Home wireless networks are very common. As many laptop users who have searched for wireless networks at home can attest, there are numerous wireless networks available for access. Only a small percentage of home wireless users bother to secure their networks by enabling encryption, even though nearly all wireless routers have this capability. Of course, as the author can attest, setting up an encrypted wireless network and configuring multiple computers to access it can be a major annoyance, even for someone familiar with computers. Rather than dealing with the hassle, many households simply do not bother. The danger of not encrypting is that all data sent over the network, including passwords, bank account information, and credit card numbers, could potentially be seen by others.

By not securing a wireless network, a person has no idea who else is accessing it or what they are doing. There have been several cases of arrests made based on unauthorized use of wireless signals.[9] One particularly strange case involved a man driving the wrong way down a one-way residential street, naked from the waist down, searching for open wireless networks from which to download child pornography. Luckily police arrested him.[10]

On the flip side, for a person without Internet access, using open wireless can be very tempting. Although the law is unsettled, people have been arrested and punished for illegally using someone else's wireless network. Furthermore, open wireless networks can be traps to catch sensitive data. Like the "evil twins" networks to be discussed shortly, with the use of programs readily available on the Internet, it would be simple for a person to set up an open wireless network, wait for someone to log on, and then capture all the data sent over the network.

The ability of people to do all of the above is unquestioned, but the likelihood of it happening is another story. A home wireless network connection can be accessed only by those in the immediate vicinity of the house. If someone lives in a neighborhood with multiple wireless connections, the likelihood that their neighbors are piggybacking on their signal lessens, as their neighbors may well have their own wireless connections. The situation also differs in an apartment building, where the signal can bleed into many more residences, and it is more difficult to determine who else might be accessing the network.

Overall, hackers and fraudsters are far more likely to focus on places where they can retrieve large amounts of data from multiple sources, such as public wireless hot spots. Hot spots, which offer open Internet access, can be a fraudster's dream. For instance, in a survey of 14 United States and three Asian airports, 57% of the networks had no encryption, 28% used the easily breakable Wired Equivalent Privacy (WEP) encryption, and only 15% used the more secure Wi-Fi Protected Access (WPA) encryption. This survey included both publicly accessible Internet and the private systems used for airport functions such as baggage handling and ticketing.[11]

Hackers have multiple methods of collecting data from public Internet users. An "evil twin" is a wireless network that appears to offer a Wi-Fi connection like those available at coffee shops, hotels, and airports, and looks just like the real network. All communications over this network can be monitored, including passwords and credit card numbers.[12] To entice users into giving up information, hackers can create fake log-in pages that look identical to legitimate ones; for instance, a user could see a screen prompting him or her to input credit information to purchase Wi-Fi access.[13] A "man-in-the-middle" attack is similar, in that the hacker sets up a deceptive Wi-Fi signal but then routes the connection into the legitimate network.[14] This attack "can make it appear that a user has a secure 'SSL' connection,"[15] indicated by a small padlock in the corner of the browser. However, "the hacker sets up one secure SSL connection with the Web surfer, and a second secure connection with the bank or other destination site. Information looks encrypted at either end, but it is decoded and viewed by the hacker in the middle."[16]

Getting access to a user's email can also be a gold mine, as it will give access to saved emails, which may contain passwords and access information for bank accounts, financial institutions, and the like.

Fraudsters also seek user names and passwords from people logging on to company networks from Wi-Fi hot spots. For instance, in one case, a financial institution traced a data breach back to an employee working on a laptop in Manhattan's Bryant Park. The employee thought he was using a public signal; in fact, it had been set up by a hacker. When the employee logged on to the company network, the hacker stole his user name and password.[17] In September 2007, the federal government indicted another hacker, Max Butler, on charges of wire fraud and identity theft. In addition to selling stolen credit cards on the Internet, Butler would rent hotel rooms and apartments using the stolen cards and false identities, then use a high-powered antenna to intercept wireless traffic. He used this technique to hack into financial institutions and data processing centers to obtain even more personal information.[18]

## T.J. MAXX ATTACK

Perhaps the most prominent wireless hack took place at TJX, the parent company of clothing retailers T.J. Maxx and Marshalls. Hackers stole at least 45.7 million credit card and debit card numbers over a period of a year and a half. The true amount of card numbers stolen may never be known, but some estimates have placed it as high as 200 million. The hackers also nabbed driver's license numbers, military identification, and SSNs.[19] Banks have claimed that tens of millions of dollars in fraudulent charges have been made and millions of cards have been canceled and reissued.[20] TJX-related fraud has been uncovered in at least seven states and seven countries, from Mexico to China.[21]

The initial attack occurred in 2005 outside a Marshalls discount clothing store in Miami, Florida. Hackers used a special antenna to intercept wireless communications between the store's handheld price-checking devices, cash registers, and store computers. They then used that decoded information to enable them to hack into TJX's main database in Massachusetts and access the company's customer records.[22] They installed a "sniffer" program which collected account numbers and information. The hackers left behind few clues in their precise and methodical attack, but a similar sniffer program used in another hack eventually lead to the criminals' downfall.[23]

As law enforcement dug deeper into the intrusion, what stood out was not the sophistication of the criminal activity but rather the lax attitude toward security demonstrated by TJX. Not only did the multibillion-dollar company fail to meet industry standards, its network was less secure than that of many home users. According to one report, TJX had met just three of the 12 requirements that credit card companies impose on merchants to protect consumer data.[24] TJX had used WEP encryption, which is arguably insufficient for home use and extremely dangerous for a major retailer, particularly since a report issued in 2001 noted that security experts were able to crack the WEP encryption of several major retailers.[25] TJX did not upgrade its network security or even install firewalls on many of its computers.

Diligent investigation and some luck eventually led authorities to the culprits, an international online crime syndicate, following leads from Ukraine to Turkey to China. Federal prosecutors indicted 11 members of the hacking ring, from five different countries. When the full details of the syndicate's activities came to light, authorities were struck by the size, scope, and complexity of the plot. It went far beyond just TJX. Starting in 2003 the hackers infiltrated via wireless access the networks of other major business including Barnes & Noble, the Sports Authority, B.J.'s Wholesale Club, as well as hacking directly into the system of the restaurant chain Dave & Busters.[26] As Attorney General Michael Mukasey said, "As far as we know, this is the single largest and most complex identity theft case that's ever been charged in this country."[27]

The indictment alleges the hacking ring stole and sold over 40 million credit and debit card numbers.[28] The ring's operations reflect the international challenges confronting those fighting identity theft, as seen in the previous chapter. The hackers in the United States infiltrated the wireless networks, an accomplice in the Ukraine brokered sales and purchases of the stolen numbers, they purchased blank credit debit and credit cards from confederates in China and stored the stolen data on servers in Eastern Europe. If the syndicate did not sell a hacked number, its members would imprint the numbers on a blank card, withdrawing hundreds of thousand in cash.[29]

This attack has proven to be very costly to the company. It faced substantial public embarrassment, lawsuits from customers and other companies, expensive security upgrades, and had to reach a settlement agreement with the Federal Trade Commission. The settlement agreement is very revealing in highlighting TJX's security deficiencies. TJX "failed to use reasonable and appropriate security measures to prevent unauthorized access to personal information on its computers networks."[30] "The agency chastised the retailer for not encrypting the data, establishing firewalls, using complex passwords or regularly updating antivirus software to make it difficult for hackers to steal customers' financial data."[31]

Despite the dangers of Wi-Fi, steps can be taken to significantly reduce risk. Home users should always enable WPA encryption on their routers as well as change both the default network name and the default access password. Businesses need to learn the lesson of the T.J. Maxx case and recognize that hackers do target insecure networks. They must establish adequate security to protect their data and ensure their customers' privacy.

When using public hot spots, always act as if someone is watching your every move. Do not access sensitive information over a public Wi-Fi network. While in public, consider turning off the computer's wireless function when not in use so as to not inadvertently connect to an evil twin network. The Federal Bureau of Investigation (FBI) also has recognized the dangers of public Wi-Fi. It counsels to not connect to an unknown Wi-Fi network, certainly a sensible precaution. The FBI also offers some further recommendation regarding public Wi-Fi usage:

- Make sure your laptop security is up to date, with current versions of your operating system, Web browser, firewalls, and antivirus and antispyware software.
- Do not conduct financial transactions or use applications like email and instant messaging.
- Change the default setting on your laptop so you have to manually select the Wi-Fi network you are connecting to.
- Turn off your laptop's Wi-Fi capabilities when you are not using them.[32]

## P2P NETWORKS

Peer-to-peer networks (known as P2P) facilitate sharing of many kinds of information. The technology facilitates many legitimate uses, such as the sharing of medical records or facilitating access to government documents.[33] However, the technology is best known and most frequently used for illegal purposes, specifically the unauthorized sharing of copyrighted music, movies, and software. The Recording Industry of America has cracked down hard on violators, suing universities (which host the networks used by the most frequent violators, college students) and individual users alike for the illegal downloading of music.[34] Beyond getting sued for sharing music, P2P also poses other, less well known dangers: allowing criminals to access sensitive data and possibly commit identity theft.

According to a recent study by Dartmouth Business School researchers, P2P networks are "an increasingly dangerous means of transmitting confidential information."[35] Use of such networks has risen steadily, reaching over 10 million users in 2006.[36] The Dartmouth researchers, focusing only on the top 30 U.S. banks, were able to access numerous sensitive documents using P2P networks. They found 1,708 documents containing sensitive bank information.[37]

This danger is not simply academic. Several incidents of data theft have been traced back to P2P intrusions. "A Pfizer worker has been blamed for leaking personal financial information on more than 17,000 current and former Pfizer employees. The information breach came after the employee installed unauthorized file-sharing software on a company laptop. The sensitive files were then accessed by one or more third parties."[38] In another incident, the names and SSNs of 5,200 Citibank customers were also leaked inadvertently onto the Internet by a Citibank employee using LimeWire, a popular P2P program.[39] Businesses may have policies prohibiting P2P programs at work, but they also need clear policies for laptop usage and access of business files on home computers in regard to P2P programs. For instance, businesses need to clearly prohibit the use of P2P programs on take-home laptops or home computers if employees will be accessing work files on those computers.

This possibility of data loss comes from the installation process. Upon installation, the user is asked to choose a folder for downloads and to share the contents of that folder. Many times users choose the My Documents folder, which often contains sensitive personal information. Depending on the program's settings, this information may be shared inadvertently. Furthering the problem is the tendency to clearly name personal files: for example, "Student Financial Aid Application," "Jones Family Tax Return," "Bank of America Account Info," and so on. Finally, many P2P programs circumvent firewall protections, diluting user protection.

Makers of the most popular file-sharing programs, including LimeWire and Bear-Share, have taken steps to help prevent users from inadvertently sharing sensitive material by restricting sharing to media files, such as music and video only.[40] Even though a user may restrict sharing to a limited section of the hard drive, viruses can expand access to other parts of the drive, giving fraudsters freer access.[41] This brings up another danger common to P2P networks beyond identity theft. P2P networks are rife with viruses, spyware, and other forms of malware. Unsurprisingly, free pornography, music, and movies are an effective form of distribution, enticing users to download what appear to be legitimate files but are in fact Trojan horses or other equally insidious type of malware.

The access and anonymity provided by P2P programs has proven to be an irresistible lure for criminals. Gregory Kopiloff of Seattle used LimeWire "to infiltrate hundreds of people's hard drives and steal tax returns, student financial aid forms and other sensitive personal data."[42] He did this not by hacking into personal computers or creating sophisticated malware but rather simply by trolling P2P networks looking for sensitive data. "Kopiloff then used that information to create bogus credit-card and bank accounts and illegally purchase thousands of dollars in merchandise."[43] Using false identities to make online purchases shipped to rented mailboxes, he obtained high-end computers, cell phones, and audio players, all of which he then resold for about half price.

After a joint investigation involving Seattle police, the Secret Service, the Postal Inspection Service, and the U.S. Attorney's Office for Western Washington, authorities exposed Kopiloff and arrested him. "Authorities said they have at least 83 victims—most of whom have teenage children and did not know the file-sharing software was on the computer."[44] The true number of people affected may well be in the hundreds. This case also emphasizes that computer users need to be aware of what is installed on their computers; something downloaded by one member of the family could severely impact everyone else.

After a September 2007 indictment, Kopiloff pleaded guilty in November 2007, admitting he used file sharing programs to get access to victims' personal information including tax returns, credit reports, bank statements, and student financial aid applications. He pleaded guilty to Mail Fraud, Accessing a Protected Computer without Authorization to Further Fraud, and Aggravated Identity Theft. He was sentenced to 51 months in prison and three years supervised release, including monitoring of his computer usage when he gets out. This was the first federal prosecution of its type.[45]

Kopiloff's prosecution is likely not to be the last of its kind. According to estimates, tens of thousands of fraudsters troll P2P networks looking for unsecured data and finding new ways to defeat users' protection. At the news conference announcing Kopiloff's indictment, the U.S. Attorney's Office in Seattle presented a demonstration by Robert Boback, the CEO of Tiversa, a computer-security firm specializing in P2P issues. Boback showed, in real time, searches being conducted on P2P networks. The vast majority of users searched for music and pornography, but many also searched for terms like "password" and "medical billing."[46] This trend of illicit searching has continued. A cursory P2P search by the author, using just one file-sharing program, revealed tax returns, billing information, bank account lists, and passwords—all found in less than a minute's worth of searching. There is far more to be done to combat this growing identity theft threat.

## BOTNETS: ZOMBIE ARMIES OF THE INTERNET

Botnets are at the forefront of the growth of cybercrime. They have been called an imminent national security threat[47] and cybercriminals' weapon of choice,[48] yet most Americans have never heard of them. In fact, millions of Americans could be part of a botnet and not be aware of it.

Botnets are responsible for nearly all spam email and, increasingly, credit card fraud and identity theft. "They can also be used to direct floods of fake traffic at a targeted website in order to bring down a rival, extract protection money, or less frequently, used to make a political point, such as the attacks on Estonia and the Church of Scientology."[49] On any given day, 40% of the computers connected to the Internet are bots, and approximately 90% of the world's email is botnet-distributed spam.[50]

The process of creating a botnet is relatively simple. Malware infects a remote computer and takes control of it, allowing it to be used as a robot; hence these infected computers are known as bots. A network of infected bots is a "botnet," operating under the control of a "botherder." The malware is designed to operate secretly without openly interfering with the computer's use. Since they operate in the background and do not affect users' day-to-day activities, individual infected computers can operate as part of the botnet without detection or even awareness by the user. By linking thousands of infected computers together, the combined computing power of these botnets rivals the world's fastest supercomputers, although instead of decoding the human genome, the power is used to hawk replica watches and set up phishing operations.

The FBI has called this one of the most serious cyberthreats, defining "botnets" as "armies of personal computers taken over by cybercriminals and used on the sly to commit all kinds of mischief, from identity theft to denial of service attacks to massive spam campaigns."[51] Note that botnets should be distinguished from "grid computing," where the processing power of numerous computers linked through the Internet form a virtual supercomputer. Users voluntarily and knowingly donate their computers' resources for grid computing application such as protein mapping or space exploration, unlike a botnet which surreptitiously commandeers a computer for illegal activities.[52]

A striking example of the power and growth of botnets is the Srizbi botnet. Although it first appeared in June 2007, it began to grow exponentially starting in February 2008. By May of that year, Srizbi comprised at least 300,000 infected computers sending 60 billion spam messages a day, accounting for half the world's spam.[53] Other botnets have used their power to harvest credit card numbers, as in the case of Owen Walker.

## PLUNDER DOWN UNDER

Owen Thor Walker, an 18-year-old New Zealander, was a member of an international hacking group that infected at least 1.3 million computers and caused losses upward of $20 million. His cybercrime ring used programs of his own design to access personal data, including user names and passwords, distribute viruses, and steal credit card information, among other crimes. Other cybercriminals used his software to commit their own misdeeds.

Walker, known as "Akill," "Snow Walker," and "Snow Whyte," taught himself computer programming; by experimenting with virus programs, he was able to create his own, and continually refined and enhanced them. He designed "an encrypted virus that was undetectable by anti-virus software." Although he was self-taught, "international investigators considered Walker's programming to 'be among the most advanced' they had encountered."[54] The code "automatically disabled any anti-virus software on an infected computer and prevented the software from being updated. The computer owner could not tell the anti-virus software was not working."[55]

Walker's network was uncovered by the efforts of New Zealand police in conjunction with the FBI and Dutch authorities. The investigation began after a distributed denial of service attack caused by Walker and University of Pennsylvania student Ryan Goldstein, apparently unintentionally, crashed the university's servers in 2006.[56]

*A distributed denial of service attack (DDoS) is a form of attack on another computer on the Internet that overloads the victim computer. A person attempting a DDoS attack enlists other computers, without the knowledge of the owners, to assist in the attack by causing other computers to bombard the target computer with requests or commands at the same time. This increases the number of messages that can be directed to the victim computer and increases the chances of slowing the victim computer and crashing it.[57]*

Walker and Goldstein attempted to covertly use the university's servers to upgrade the botnet, by uploading updated software onto the server and then having the infected botnet computers connect to the server to receive the update. However, this wave of server traffic crashed the server and disabled access.[58] The FBI's investigation into the crash led them to Walker, while New Zealand police, working with Dutch authorities, traced payments from a company in the Netherlands to Walker. The company in question, ECS International, has been prosecuted for paying hackers to use their botnets to covertly install adware on unsuspecting users' computers. Walker earned around $36,000 for his work.[59] This "DollarRevenue" scam earned Walker and others a fee for each computer they infected.

Walker lived with his parents when he committed the crimes, but they thought he was just doing legal computer programming.[60] Walker told them the money he made was from computer programming work. His parents got a rude awakening when the FBI arrested Walker in November 2007 as part of its "Operation Bot Roast II." Walker later pleaded guilty to six computer crime charges, which carried penalties of up to seven years in jail on each charge.

Unfortunately for law enforcement, the judge at sentencing dismissed all charges against Walker and let him go without a conviction, despite his guilty plea. He had to pay approximately $10,000 in damages plus around $5000 in other costs. The judge, reasoning that a conviction could hurt Walker's future prospects and considering his age, remorse, lack of criminal intent, and his suffering from Asperger's syndrome, a mild form of autism, led her to the dismissal.[61] The judge also specifically cited the possibility of Walker's employment by police or government agencies as a mitigating factor.[62]

While some of the factors the judge mentioned may lean towards sentence mitigation, they do not excuse what Walker did. The mere possibility that he might use his abilities for "good" should not excuse what he did nor overlook the fact that his involvement with the cybercrime ring was neither accidental nor infrequent. He worked with them for two years developing software to steal personal information, and knew full well what he was doing. Ultimately, Walker not did have to accept any responsibility for the millions of dollars in damage he caused or the crimes he committed. This decision sets a terrible precedent and does nothing to deter future crimes of a similar nature by others.

It also seems as though the judge did not fully understand the implications of Walker's actions, seemingly believing hacking is solely the province of bored teenagers looking for an innocent thrill. Walker, his accomplices, and those like them are profit-driven individuals who can cause tremendous damage to people all over the world. Education is needed to help judges and other lawmakers fully appreciate the severity of this problem.

Despite the rampant growth of botnets, no consensus has emerged on how to best combat them. Some experts have argued for stepped-up infection detection, to alert users that their computer is infected and for Internet service providers to block access to machines until the infection is removed. ISPs have shied away from any such proposals, fearful of alienating and confusing customers. Another proposal is to punish and shut down domain sellers or Internet service providers (ISPs) that serve as known havens for cybercriminals. Bills have been introduced in Congress that would make it easier for federal prosecutors to charge cybercriminals and to significantly enhance penalties. Unfortunately, far more needs to be done to adequately combat botnets.

# IDENTITY THEFT HALL OF INFAMY

## Philip Cummings

The sad reality about identity theft is that a trusted insider can have a major impact on individuals and business by criminally instigating a massive data breach. That was the role of the previously unknown Philip Cummings, who in 2002 was the focal point for what was then called the largest identity theft case in American history. Cummings was a low-level customer service employee at a company that dealt in consumer credit information. Through his access to this sensitive and confidential information, Cummings set in motion an identity theft scheme that involved more than 30,000 victims. The resulting criminal investigation made headlines around the world, and led to arrests and convictions and the realization that data breaches would have more of an impact on our privacy in the years to come. For all these reasons, Cummings is a deserving member of the Identity Theft Hall of Infamy.

### BACKGROUND

Teledata Communications, Inc. (TCI) has been in business since 1982. As stated on its Web site, it "connect[s] leaders in consumer and commercial finance with the credit information they need to make critical business decisions."[63] TCI is based on Long Island, New York. It provides software, hardware, and services to client companies to enable them to access credit histories from the various credit bureaus, including Experian, Equifax, and TransUnion. TCI's software, through its customized devices, links a client company to these credit bureaus via telephone lines. TCI clients use unique subscriber codes and passwords along with TCI software to access the credit bureaus and credit reports.[64]

Philip Cummings was a TCI help desk employee from mid-1999 through March 2000. As a client assistance representative, Cummings had "access to confidential passwords and subscriber codes of TCI client companies that would have enabled that employee to download credit reports from all three credit bureaus."[65] Cummings joined the conspiracy while still employed at TCI. He continued his involvement after leaving TCI in 2000 and relocating to Georgia, where he owned a small business. At this point, the life of this 35-year old English immigrant, divorced with a young daughter, was about to take a serious turn for the worse.

### THE SCHEME

In early 2000, Linus Baptiste, Cummings's former brother-in-law, approached Cummings with a lucrative scheme. Baptiste was the proverbial jack-of-all-trades who even took a turn as a music producer. This time, he came up with a get-rich-quick scheme. Baptiste would pay Cummings money for access to consumers'

*(Continued)*

253

credit reports. Baptiste knew other scammers who would pay $60 per credit report received. These scammers were a group of Nigerian nationals who already had personal information of many potential victims, including names, addresses, and SSNs, but wanted to know their creditworthiness before doing account takeovers or applying for new credit cards in their names. Cummings and Baptiste would split the money for each credit report delivered. Cummings saw the financial benefit in this fraud and readily agreed.

Shortly thereafter, Baptiste began providing Cummings with lists of names and personal information of potential victims so as to obtain their credit reports. Baptiste received these lists from as many as 20 other conspirators who had access to stolen personal information for which they intended to commit identity theft. At first Cummings would meet Baptiste in New Rochelle, New York, "with a laptop and download the requested credit reports via use of telephone lines."[66]

Cummings then left the employ of TCI and relocated to Georgia, where he continued his involvement in the identity theft scheme. At some point, Cummings provided his laptop with the TCI and client codes to Baptiste so he could continue to access credit bureaus and download credit reports on consumers. Baptiste obtained tens of thousands of credit reports, which he sold to the many street criminals he was dealing with. Using the stolen credit reports to determine their creditworthiness, these fraudsters obtained loans in the names of their victims, applied for credit cards in their names, purchased merchandise, and depleted bank accounts all over the country. More than 30,000 victims had their identities stolen with losses calculated at $2.7 million.

THE DISCOVERY

In early 2002, Ford Motor Credit Company learned that the unique subscriber code and password for its Grand Rapids, Michigan, branch had been compromised. The company determined the breach began in approximately the spring of 2001, resulting in the unauthorized downloading of approximately 15,000 credit reports. Ford utilized TCI's software and credit prompter boxes to access credit reports from the credit reporting agencies. "Ford discovered the scheme after reviewing bills sent by Experian for those credit histories and receiving numerous complaints from consumers who had been the subject of identity theft and fraud."[67] Experian searched its databases and found that the passwords and subscriber codes of other financial institutions and firms were also affected by this data breach. This discovery of an additional 6,000 credit reports that had been compromised pointed to many more potential victims and losses.[68]

Ford reported this to the FBI in Detroit, which initially investigated the case. The credit reporting agencies first told the Detroit agents that it was impossible to link a local telephone number to the unauthorized accesses to the system, because literally hundreds of 800 numbers fed into the credit reporting agency's databases; although the system linked subscriber codes and passwords to a particular credit report request, the incoming telephone numbers were not so linked. Because the

Detroit office was at an impasse with the investigation, and because mail for several of the stolen identities was being diverted to post office boxes throughout all five New York City boroughs, the matter was transferred to the New York Office of the FBI.

THOUGHT LEADER IN IDENTITY THEFT INVESTIGATION: KEVIN BARROWS

Kevin Barrows is a principal in Renaissance Associates, an investigative firm in New York that specializes in corporate investigations and litigation support services. From 1997 to 2003, he was a Special Agent with the FBI's New York Division, assigned to investigate white-collar crime. During his six years as an FBI agent, Barrows directed major investigations involving financial institution fraud, identity theft, and international money laundering, which required intensive document analysis and in-depth interviews of persons with relevant knowledge to uncover complex illegal schemes. He was also the lead case agent in the investigation and criminal prosecution of a group of individuals who stole 30,000 identities through the unauthorized computer-based accessing of personal credit information that is profiled herein.

Barrows was assigned the case because he had previous success in other large, complex, and high-profile investigations. After being assigned, he met with the Assistant United States Attorney (AUSA) handling this matter who was the Chief of General Crimes for the Southern District of New York. After reviewing the voluminous documents and records, Barrows was convinced that the way to solve this case was not to follow the traditional approach. That would be to conduct surveillance at mail drops and arrest individuals retrieving mail in the name of victims. He knew this would not be successful because these individuals were typically unable to provide information about someone above them in the criminal chain.

These lower-level subjects often were simply paid a nominal fee by an unknown person to retrieve the mail. In addition, because they had no knowledge of the fact that they were assisting in a crime, they often could not be charged with any offense and thus had no impetus to cooperate. Barrows determined that the only way to stop the continuing fraud was to find the person or persons who stole the subscriber codes and passwords.

Because Ford Motor Credit was not the only financial institution victimized, Barrows was able to eliminate employees of the financial institutions as possible suspects. Eventually, he concluded that it must be a TCI employee, past or present, and that it was likely to be a help desk representative. He turned his attention to reviewing all available records for help desk employees and interviews, looking for someone reprimanded in the past or someone who was fired and disgruntled. At the same time, he began working closely with the major credit reporting agencies, particularly Equifax, in an effort to link a local telephone number to the unauthorized reports.

*(Continued)*

After countless hours learning how the credit reporting system worked, Barrows and other investigators identified that all of the fraudulent inquiries followed a distinct pattern: They were made in large batches. The investigators isolated inquiries that followed the pattern and worked with a representative of Equifax to attempt to link even one local telephone number to an unauthorized inquiry. It was the proverbial needle in the haystack, but eventually, after countless hours, days, and weeks, Barrows and his team were able to link a specific telephone number in New Rochelle, New York, to the unlawful inquiries.

Immediately thereafter, Barrows identified the subscriber and address associated with the telephone number, and applied for, and obtained, a search warrant for the premises located in New Rochelle. The residence belonged to Baptiste. On October 29, 2002, Barrows and a team of agents executed the search warrant. They split up into various sections of what was quite a large house. Barrows was primarily downstairs interviewing the occupants and assisting in the search of the lower level. At some point, he went upstairs to see how the other members of the team were doing. He noticed that the master bedroom was very large and messy, and had a giant oversize wooden canopy bed. After several hours of searching the entire house and reviewing the contents of all of the desktop computers, it appeared that what he hoped to find was not there. Barrows called the AUSA at approximately one o'clock p.m. and told her the bad news: They failed to find documents or computerized evidence containing subscriber codes, passwords, or fraudulently downloaded credit reports.

As the agents were carrying the boxes of seized evidence out to their cars to leave, Barrows, wanting to make sure that every nook and cranny had been searched, turned to one of his fellow agents and asked him to come up to the master bedroom to take one last look. As Barrows stood in the doorway of the bedroom looking at the bed, he noticed a slight bulge in the canopy. He stepped onto the bed frame, reached onto the top of the canopy, and began tapping around with his fingers. Lo and behold, he felt papers. It was a manila folder containing dozens of credit reports and lists of names and SSNs. Barrows immediately called for the search team to join him, and they began to pull apart the bed and move furniture in the hopes of finding additional evidence.

When Barrows looked behind a dresser in an adjacent bedroom, a laptop computer, in its case, fell to the floor. He unzipped the case and, sitting right on top of the laptop was a document bearing the name Philip Cummings. Barrows then spent the remainder of the day interviewing the occupants of the home, obtaining their cooperation, and putting together the remaining pieces of the puzzle. The laptop contained the stolen subscriber codes and passwords; it was the smoking gun that he had hoped to find. Within days, Cummings was arrested in Atlanta. In less than five months, the case was solved. Following Cummings's arrest, Barrows used an informant to record telephone conversations with the street criminals who were the most heavily involved in the scheme, resulting in numerous additional arrests.

The street criminals were an incredibly large, organized, and sophisticated group of thieves. In the end, there were more than 30,000 victims and losses exceeded $100 million. Besides Ford Motor Credit, other TCI clients victimized by this scheme included the former Washington Mutual Bank, Washington Mutual Finance Company, Dollar Bank, and Central Texas Energy Supply. Baptiste pleaded guilty to the charges, followed by Cummings in September of 2004. Cummings was sentenced to 14 years in prison in January 2005.

RED FLAGS

The case implicated the biggest identity theft ring at the time. "With a few keystrokes, these men essentially picked the pockets of tens of thousands of Americans and, in the process, took their identities, stole their money and wiped out their security," said former federal prosecutor James Comey, whose office oversaw the prosecution.[69] This case and others since then have exposed weaknesses in how businesses and organizations handle personal and financial information. Yet the many red flags would have been evident if only anyone had been looking for them.

There are many questions that should have been asked and answered. How much background screening did Cummings undergo prior to hire? Why did he have unrestricted access to so much confidential information? How was he able to download the personal information of over 30,000 people over a three-year period with no one at TCI ever detecting it or stopping him? How was it that passwords were not changed and his access stopped after leaving the company? Had the company ever had similar problems in the past that did not make the headlines or receive government scrutiny?

Some experts suspected that relatively small firms with limited resources to spend on security might contribute to data breaches and privacy protection. "Teledata's relative mom-and-pop status and its easily accessed Web-based services are red flags," said a director of the Electronic Privacy Information Center at the time.[70]

Barrows recalled that he was shocked at how confidential information was written on Post-it notes and displayed in plain view in the cubicles at TCI. There was no restriction of access or accountability for passwords and other sensitive information. While TCI faced a very public scrutiny for its practices, how many companies today did not learn from this damaging event and are susceptible to data breaches?

DISHONORABLE MENTION

There is a dishonorable mention for the Identity Theft Hall of Fame for his involvement in this case: Linus Baptiste, a Cummings co-conspirator.

## PROTECTING PII

Security breach laws have either been introduced and/or enacted in most states in the United States. California set the standard with a 2003 law requiring companies to notify customers when data breaches involve PII. California and Texas allow consumers to sue companies that fail to safeguard their personal data. The European Union has had tough privacy laws for years. It bars member countries and their citizens from buying and selling personal data including data that are collected in business transactions.

The FTC is focused on privacy and privacy initiatives. Its publication for businesses to use in protecting personal information, *Protecting Personal Information: A Guide for Business,* is highly recommended and is available at www.ftc.gov/infosecurity/.

The Guide is built on five key principles:

- **Take stock.** Know what personal information you have in your files and on your computers.
- **Scale down.** Keep only what you need for your business.
- **Lock it.** Protect the information that you keep.
- **Pitch it.** Properly dispose of what you no longer need.
- **Plan ahead.** Create a plan to respond to security incidents.

It is astonishing how much of our personal and professional lives is publicly available. Go online and do a keyword search on your name. Most readers will be surprised what they find about themselves. Even more information will be found online in the future. The risk transcends identity theft as every aspect of our lives is under scrutiny. Take for example the very bitter divorce of a Broadway theater operator and his actress wife that made its way to YouTube in April 2008. The wife took to airing her grievances and anger in a very public forum by uploading a video rant on her husband to the YouTube site. The video and the resulting media stories circulated for months. The message is clear: Your private matters are no longer private. Do what you can to protect your privacy, but always remember there is much that is beyond your control in the world of today.

## NOTES

1. Polly Sprenger, "Sun on Privacy: 'Get Over It,'" Wired, January 26, 1999, www.wired.com/politics/law/news/1999/01/17538.
2. Robert Lemos, "Private Identities Become a Corporate Focus," SecurityFocus .com, February 20, 2006, www.securityfocus.com/news/11377.
3. Martha Irvine, "Social Networkers Beware: Applications Pose Risk," *Seattle Times*, April 28, 2008, E3.
4. "Privacy Today: A Review of Current Issues," Privacy Rights Clearinghouse, www.privacyrights.org/ar/Privacy-IssuesList.htm.
5. Jon Swartz, "Tech experts plot to catch identity thieves," *USA Today*, February 9, 2007, 7B.

6. Ibid.

7. Bob Sullivan, "Study: ID Theft Usually an Inside Job," MSNBC, May 21, 2004, www.msnbc.com/id/5015565.

8. Michael Hudson, "Dumped Mortgage Files Invite Identity Theft," *Wall Street Journal*, October 27, 2007, http://biz.yahoo.com/wallstreet/071023/sb119309606 825767724_id.html.

9. See, e.g., Alex Leary, "Wi-Fi Cloaks a New Breed of Intruder," *St. Petersburg Times*, July 4, 2005, www.sptimes.com/2005/07/04/State/Wi_Fi_cloaks_a_ new_br .shtml. See also Jamie Stockwell, "Wi-Fi Turns Internet into Hideout for Criminals," *Washington Post*, February 11, 2007, C1. This article mentions a case where police arrived at an apartment to arrest an offender for downloading child pornography only to discover that the real culprit was a neighbor who had committed the crime while using someone else's wireless network. Similar stories have popped up on the Internet, but the author has been unable to verify the provenance of this or any similar case. Thus, at this point they should be considered urban legends, plausible yet ultimately unverifiable.

10. "Police Warn of Wi-Fi Theft by Porn Downloaders," CTV.ca, November 23, 2003, www.ctv.ca/servlet/ArticleNews/story/CTVNews/1069439746264_64848946.

11. Stephen H. Wildstrom, "Public Wi-Fi: Be Very Paranoid," *Business Week*, March 24, 2008, 85.

12. Kevin J. Delaney, "'Evil Twins' and 'Pharming,'" *Wall Street Journal*, May 17, 2005, B1.

13. Joseph De Avila, "Wi-Fi Users, Beware: Hot Spots are Weak Spots," *Wall Street Journal*, January 16, 2008, D1.

14. Ibid.

15. Jonathan Sidener, "Using Unprotected Public Wi-Fi Poses Major Security Risk," *San Diego Union Tribune*, May 11, 2008, www.signonsandiego.com/news/ business/20080511-9999-mz1b11wifi.html.

16. Ibid.

17. Joseph De Avila, "Wi-Fi Users, Beware: Hot Spots are Weak Spots," *Wall Street Journal*, January 16, 2008, D1.

18. Kimberly Kiefer Peretti, "Data Breaches: What the Underground World of 'Carding' Reveals," to be published in *Santa Clara Computer and High Technology Journal* 25, available at www.usdoj.gov/criminal/cybercrime/DataBreachesArticle.pdf, at 24.

19. Joseph Pereira, "How Credit-Card Data Went Out Wireless Door," *Wall Street Journal*, May 4, 2007, A1.

20. "Agency Announces Settlement of Separate Actions Against Retailer TJX, and Data Brokers Reed Elsevier and Seisint for Failing to Provide Adequate Security For Consumers' Data," Federal Trade Commission, March 27, 2008, www.ftc.gov/ opa/2008/03/datasec.shtm.

21. Pereira, "How Credit-Card Data Went Out Wireless Door."

22. Ibid.

23. Ibid.

24. Ross Kerber, "Details Emerge on TJX Breach," *Boston Globe*, October 25, 2007, www.boston.com/business/globe/articles/2007/10/25/details_emerge_on_tjx_ breach.
25. Pereira, "How Credit-Card Data Went Out Wireless Door."
26. Theresa Cook, "Feds Announce 'Largest' ID Theft Case," ABC News, August 5, 2008, http://abcnews.go.com/TheLaw/story?id=5520147&page=1.
27. Ibid.
28. Ibid.
29. Brad Stone, "Global Trail of an Online Crime Ring," *New York Times*, August 12, 2008.
30. "Agency Announces Settlement of Separate Actions Against Retailer TJX."
31. Joseph Pereira, "TJX Assents to Audits of Data-Security System," *Wall Street Journal*, March 28, 2008, B4.
32. "Wi-Fi Security: Some Advice from the FBI," Federal Bureau of Investigation, May 6, 2008, www.fbi.gov/page2/may08/wifi_050608.html.
33. In a concurring opinion to the Supreme Court Case *MGM v. Grokster,* Justice Breyer listed a number of legitimate, noninfringing uses for P2P software. See *MGM v. Grokster,* 545 U.S. 913, 2005 (Breyer, J. concurring).
34. See, e.g., Wendy Leonard, "U. Campus Targeted in Music Piracy," *Deseret News*, May 24, 2008, www.deseretnews.com/article/1,5143,700228738,00.html.
35. "P2P Dangers Growing," *BusinessWeek*, October 2007, 50.
36. Ibid.
37. Ibid.
38. Ibid.
39. Joseph De Avila, "The Hidden Risk of File-Sharing," *Wall Street Journal*, November 7, 2007, D1.
40. Ibid.
41. David Bowermaster, "Indictment Marks 'New Age' of ID Theft," *Seattle Times*, September 7, 2007, A1.
42. Ibid.
43. Ibid.
44. Ibid.
45. United States Attorney's Office, Western District of Washington, "Seattle Man Sentenced to 51 Months in Prison for ID Theft Scheme That Used Computer File Sharing Programs," March 17, 2008, www.usdoj.gov/usao/waw/press/2008/mar/ kopiloff.html.
46. Bowermaster, "Indictment Marks 'New Age' of ID Theft."
47. Ryan Singel, "Zombie Computers Decried as Imminent National Threat," *Wired,* April 9, 2008, http://blog.wired.com/27bstroke6/2008/04/zombie-computer.html.
48. Federal Bureau of Investigation, Press Release, "'Bot Roast II' Nets 8 Individuals," November 29, 2007, www.fbi.gov/pressrel/pressrel07/botroast112907.htm.
49. Singel, "Zombie Computers Decried as Imminent National Threat."
50. Byron Acohida and Jon Swartz, "Botnet Scams are Exploding," *USA Today*, March 16, 2008, www.usatoday.com/tech/news/computersecurity/2008-03-16-computer-botnets_N.htm.

51. "'Bot Roast II': Cracking Down on Cyber Crime," Federal Bureau of Investigation, November 29, 2007, www.fbi.gov/page2/nov07/botnet112907.html.

52. "Grid Computing," Wikipedia, http://en.wikipedia.org/wiki/Grid_computing.

53. Press Release, "Marshal Says Srizbi Botnet Accounts for Half of All Spam," *Marshal*, May 8, 2008, www.marshal.com/pages/newsitem.asp?article=646&the section=news.

54. "New Zealand Teen Convicted Over Global Cyber-Crime Ring," *AFP* (Agencie France-Presse), April 1, 2008, accessed via www.news.com.au/technology/story/ 0,25642,23466456-5014239,00.html.

55. Shenagh Gleeson, "Superhacker Convicted of International Cyber Crime," *New Zealand Herald*, April 2, 2008, www.nzherald.co.nz/category/story.cfm?c_id= 30&objectid=10501518.

56. Ibid.

57. *United States of America v. Ryan Goldstein*, (E. Dist. Penn.), www.usdoj.gov/usao/ pae/News/Pr/2007/nov/goldsteinind.pdf, 2–3.

58. Phil Taylor, "Bot-Boy Caught in His Own Net," *New Zealand Herald*, December 8, 2007, www.nzherald.co.nz/topic/story.cfm?c_id=199&objectid=10481058&pnum =2. According to "Maarten Kleintjes, manager of the New Zealand Police national electronic crime laboratory, [bot herders] are unlikely to have powerful enough computer systems themselves to control a million other computers and so control their botnet by sending commands via hijacked 'motherships,' usually powerful machines belonging to big businesses or universities that can handle thousands of simultaneous connections."

59. Gleeson, "Superhacker Convicted of International Cyber Crime."

60. "New Zealand Teen Convicted over Global Cyber-Crime Ring," *AFP*.

61. "NZ teenage hacker charges dropped," BBC News, July 16, 2008, http://news.- bbc.co.uk/2/hi/asia-pacific/7509052.stm; "Autistic hacker's talents to be used for good," Stuff.Co.NZ, July 16, 2008, http://www.stuff.co.nz/4619629a10.html.

62. "Autistic hacker's talents to be used for good," Stuff.Co.NZ, July 16, 2008, http:// www.stuff.co.nz/4619629a10.html.

63. Teledata Communications, Inc., www.tcicredit.com.

64. *United States of America v. Philip Cummings*, Defendant, Criminal Complaint, United States District Court, Southern District of New York, sworn to on November 22, 2002 by Kevin Barrows, Special Agent, Federal Bureau of Investigation, 3.

65. Ibid.

66. Ibid., 4.

67. U.S. Department of Justice, Office of the United States Attorney, Southern District of New York News Release, "U.S. Announces What Is Believed the Largest Identity Theft Case in American History; Losses Are in the Millions," November 25, 2002.

68. Ibid.

69. Brooke A. Masters, "Huge ID-Theft Ring Broken: 30,000 Consumers at Risk," *Seattle Times*, November 26, 2002, A1.

70. Anthony M. DeStefano, "ID-Theft Nightmare," *Newsday*, November 26, 2002, A7.

# CHAPTER 18

# Identity Theft Research

Numerous research studies have examined identity theft in recent years. A 2003 *Privacy & American Business* survey found that 33.4 million Americans were victims of identity theft since 1990, including 13 million since 2001. A Gartner survey from 2003 stated that identity theft was up almost 80% from 2002. A 2005 Javelin Strategy & Research/Better Business Bureau survey reported that 9.3 million Americans were victimized in 2004 and the total U.S. annual identity theft cost was $52.6 billion. Another Javelin survey from February 2007 found that the number of U.S. victims decreased from 10.1 million in 2003 and 9.3 million in 2005 to 8.4 million in 2007 while fraud from identity theft losses decreased from $55.7 billion in 2006 to $49.3 billion in 2007. Yet a Federal Trade Commission (FTC) study released in November 2007 reported that 8.3 Americans were victims of identity theft in 2005 and total losses were down to $15.6 billion, far lower than the FTC's 2003 estimate of $47.6 billion and that of Javelin.[1]

What do these findings tell us? They tell us that no one really knows the actual scope and impact of identity theft on consumers and businesses. The studies are estimates, and the survey methodologies change from study to study. Do we really feel any safer if someone tells us that identity theft was down to only $49.3 billion in 2007? None of the studies includes anyone outside the United States, where identity theft is growing by leaps and bounds. Not one study documents the emotional toll of victimization and the utter feeling of personal violation when one's identity is stolen. Bob Dylan in his classic recording "Subterranean Homesick Blues" sings that "You don't need a weatherman to know which way the wind blows." That sums it up pretty well for surveys and research. We know we have a big problem. We see stories about identity theft almost daily in the papers and on television. Quite simply, identity theft continues to be a major problem that is not going away anytime soon.

Although we do not know how accurate research and surveys are, there are benefits from reading and understanding the findings. We gain a general understanding of the enormity of the problem and the causal factors. Research can provide insights into specific problems that can be used to understand what does and does not work in preventing identity theft. The Saint Xavier University study of identity theft incidents points out how some of the most common recommendations to detect and prevent identity theft are not always followed. The President's Task Force on Identity Theft in its *Combating Identity Theft: A Strategic Plan* provided some very sound recommendations to fight this crime. The recurring FTC studies provide context around prevalence, financial losses, and costs to victims. All of these studies are discussed in this chapter.

## SAINT XAVIER UNIVERSITY STUDY OF IDENTITY THEFT INCIDENTS

In 2006, the Institute for Fraud Prevention (IFP) awarded a research grant to the Graham School of Management of Saint Xavier University of Chicago to study identity theft occurring in Chicago, Illinois. IFP is dedicated to multidisciplinary research, education, and prevention of fraud and corruption. IFP's primary goal is to improve the ability of businesses and government to combat these crimes and to educate the general public on effective methods of recognizing and deterring them. The study, entitled *Identity Theft: Findings and Public Policy Recommendations From the Saint Xavier University Study of Identity Theft Incidents Reported to the Chicago Police Department, 2000–2006*, was issued on May 22, 2007.

Saint Xavier University (SXU) studied identity theft incidents reported to the Chicago Police Department (CPD) between 2000 and 2006. The study is based on data collected from 28,891 identity theft reports made to the police by victims. Specific data was pulled from 1,322 files randomly selected from the total case reports. Gaining this kind of unprecedented access to case files of actual identity theft incidents is remarkable, and the CPD is to be applauded for granting SXU the access rights.

In order to protect the privacy rights of the victims, protocols were put into place and thoroughly enforced throughout the study. The case files were never removed from CPD locations, and researchers did not handle any documents that contained victim-identifying information. Documents from the case files were handled only by off-duty CPD personnel working with the researchers.

The principal researcher for the study was William J. Kresse, assistant professor in Saint Xavier University's Graham School of Management and director of its graduate program in financial fraud examination and management. "This has been a fascinating view into the mind of the identity thief," Kresse said. "While some results were expected, many were quite surprising."[2] Kathleen Hanold Watland, assistant professor and director of Chicago Police Department graduate programs, Graham School of Management, SXU, and John Lucki, Detective Sergeant, Financial Crimes Investigation Section, Detective Division, CPD, and Adjunct Faculty, Graham School of Management, were the other two researchers for this study.

The executive summary and other content that follows in this section includes material reproduced from the *Identity Theft: Findings and Public Policy Recommendations* document.[3] Material in brackets is information I have added to relate the findings to this book. The study focused on the means by which identities were stolen, the manner in which the perpetrators used the stolen identity information, and the demographics of identity theft victims.

---

## Executive Summary

Among the finding[s]:
- After adjusting the figures for changes in policy, it appears that the incidents of identity theft in Chicago peaked in 2004 with a subsequent slow downward trend.
- Women are slightly over-represented as victims of identity theft.
- In line with other crimes, African-Americans are over-represented as victims of identity theft, while Hispanics are under-represented as victims of identity theft.
- Senior citizens, children, and teenagers are under-represented as victims of identity theft.
- Younger adults, especially those between the ages of 20–44, are over-represented as victims of identity theft.
- With regards to the manner in which identity theft victims became aware of the theft:
  - Most victims became aware of the theft only after being notified by credit card companies. [This reinforces the point that consumers are not reviewing their credit reports on an ongoing basis.]
  - Fewer than 10% of identity theft victims discovered the theft by reviewing a credit report. [Reviewing one's credit report is the single best thing a consumer can do to discover identity theft.]
  - Almost one in five identity theft victims first learned of the theft when they were served with legal process or received a collection notice.
- Where the means by which the identity was stolen was known:
  - In over 60% of the cases, the victim's identity was stolen by a friend, relative, or person otherwise known to the victim.
  - In one in six cases of identity theft, the victim's identity was stolen by means of a purse snatching, pick-pocketing, burglary, or robbery.
  - In less than 5% of the cases the identity was stolen as a result of stolen mail. [In the FTC study described later in this chapter, 2% thought their identity theft was related to mail theft.]

- Despite identity theft's reputation for being a "high-tech" crime, in less than 5% of the cases was a computer or the Internet used to steal the victim's identity.
- In the cases where the identity theft victim knew the perpetrator:
  - In over one third of the cases, the perpetrator was a member of the victim's family.
  - In over 1 case in 8 the perpetrator was a boy-friend or girl-friend of the victim.
  - In less than 2% of the cases was the perpetrator a caregiver for the victim.
- Regarding the uses of stolen identities:
  - The most popular use of a victim's stolen identity was to acquire a credit card, or some other credit card fraud, with over a quarter of the incidents citing this use.
  - The second most popular use of a victim's stolen identity was to acquire mobile telephone equipment and/or service.
- There is a fairly strong positive correlation between the rate of index crimes and the rate of identity theft. As such, one would expect to find relatively higher rates of identity theft in areas where the general crime rate is high.
- There is a slight negative correlation between median household income and the rate of identity theft. As such, one would expect to find slightly higher rates of identity theft in poorer areas, and slightly lower rates of identity theft in wealthier areas.

## Reported Incidents of Identity Theft

Although the data appears to indicate that identity theft incidents peaked in 2004 with a downward trend since then, this is not exactly correct. Prior to 2004, consumer credit reporting agencies generally required identity theft victims to file a police report before they would place a fraud alert on the victim's credit file. Thus, victims filed these reports so they would have a record of the crime and have the fraud alert in place. Beginning in 2004, these police reports were not required by the credit reporting agencies in order to obtain a fraud alert. So, even though data shows a downward trend in identity theft incidents, it is probably due to the change in policy by the credit reporting agencies rather than an actual decrease in the number of identity thefts.

The median age of identity theft victims in this study is 36 years of age. Young adults were the age group most likely to be victimized. A recommendation of the study was the need for education and awareness focused at young adults to help prevent their becoming victims.

## Victims' Discovery of Identity Theft

The victims in this study generally discovered the identity thefts as a result of these circumstances:

- Received a bill for goods and services not purchased
- Received a collection notice for goods or services not purchased
- Reviewed their consumer credit report
- Were denied credit
- Received notice from a credit card company
- Served with legal process or other legal papers
- Learned about the identity theft through some other manner

Strikingly, fewer than 10% of the victims learned of their victimization through review of their credit reports. Although this detection technique is repeatedly told to consumers as an early warning system, it may not be resonating. The good news is that credit card companies are doing a good job of monitoring their card members and finding unusual patterns of activity that may be indicative of fraud.

## Use of Stolen Identities

The perpetrators in this study used the stolen identities for these fraudulent purposes:

- Acquire a credit card or other credit card fraud
- Acquire a mobile phone or cellular service
- Conduct bank or financial institution account fraud
- Acquire utilities service other than cellular service
- Place magazine subscriptions
- Perpetrate loan fraud
- Acquire government documents in the identity of the victim
- Perpetrate employment fraud
- Other unknown purposes

The most popular use of a victim's stolen identity was for credit card fraud. This is no different from what we first saw in the 1970s, when identity theft was in its infancy. The second most popular use was to acquire mobile telephone equipment and service. According to the study identity thieves focus on obtaining cell phones for two reasons:

1. By going through the application process for a new mobile phone, the thief can quickly learn if the victim is creditworthy.
2. By obtaining a cellular number, the thief gains some degree of perceived legitimacy and can use the number for additional, and potentially large, identity frauds.

### Perpetrators of Identity Theft

The study determined the means by which the identity theft was perpetrated within the universe of the case reports. The six categories include identity theft:

1. By a friend or relative
2. As a result of a purse snatching or wallet theft
3. As a result of mail theft
4. As a result of a burglary or robbery (other than a purse snatching or wallet theft)
5. By computer use or through the Internet
6. By some other means or method

The most common perpetrator was either a friend or relative. That makes sense because of the availability and access to the victim. The thief has the benefit of knowing the background of the victims and whether they are a good target for this crime. They may also have easy access to credit card information, personal data, and other information that can be stolen. Victims may not suspect a friend or relative, at least not at first.[4]

## THE PRESIDENT'S IDENTITY THEFT TASK FORCE

On May 10, 2006, President George W. Bush established by Executive Order the President's Task Force on Identity Theft. Recognizing that the problem of identity theft was already extracting a serious toll on individuals and businesses alike, the Task Force was charged with crafting "a strategic plan aiming to make the federal government's efforts more effective and efficient in the areas of identity theft awareness, prevention, detection, and prosecution."[5]

The Task Force brought together the major government departments including the Department of Justice, Federal Trade Commission, Department of the Treasury, Department of Homeland Security, Postal Service, Securities and Exchange Commission, Social Security Administration, and others to develop this vital plan. The Task Force examined the tools that law enforcement was using to combat the problem, surveyed education efforts by both government agencies and the private sector, and demonstrated how government can better safeguard personal data. The Task Force's report entitled *Combating Identity Theft: A Strategic Plan* was released on April 11, 2007 and key portions of the Executive Summary are reprinted here.

The Task Force recommends

a plan that marshals government resources to crack down on criminals who traffic in stolen identities, strengthens efforts to protect personal information of our nation's citizens, helps law enforcement officials investigate and prosecute identity thieves, helps educate consumers and businesses about protecting themselves, and increases the safeguards on personal data entrusted to federal agencies and private entities."[6]

The Plan focuses on four key areas to reduce the incidence of identity theft as follows:

- keeping sensitive consumer data out of the hands of identity thieves through better data security and more accessible education;
- making it more difficult for identity thieves who obtain consumer data to use it to steal identities;
- assisting the victims of identity theft in recovering from the crime; and
- deterring identity theft by more aggressive prosecution and punishment of those who commit the crime.[7]

The Task Force makes a number of recommendations. Among those recommendations are the following broad policy changes:

- that federal agencies should reduce the unnecessary use of Social Security numbers (SSNs), the most valuable commodity for an identity thief;
- that national standards should be established to require private sector entities to safeguard the personal data they compile and maintain and to provide notice to consumers when a breach occurs that poses a significant risk of identity theft;
- that federal agencies should implement a broad, sustained awareness campaign to educate consumers, the private sector, and the public sector on deterring, detecting, and defending against identity theft; and
- that a National Identity Theft Law Enforcement Center should be created to allow law enforcement agencies to coordinate their efforts and information more efficiently, and investigate and prosecute identity thieves more effectively.[8]

Following are the recommendations [to reduce the occurrence of identity theft] from the President's Task Force on Identity Theft.[9]

## Prevention: Keeping Consumer Data Out of the Hands of Criminals

Identity theft depends on access to consumer data. Reducing the opportunities for thieves to get the data is critical to fighting the crime. Government, the business community, and consumers have roles to play in protecting data.

Data compromises can expose consumers to the threat of identity theft or related fraud, damage the reputation of the entity that experienced the breach, and carry financial costs for everyone involved. While "perfect security" does not exist, all entities that collect and maintain sensitive consumer information must take reasonable and appropriate steps to protect it.

## Data Security in Public Sector

- Decrease the Unnecessary Use of Social Security Numbers in the Public Sector by Developing Alternative Strategies for Identity Management
  - Survey current use of SSNs by federal government
  - Issue guidance on appropriate use of SSNs
  - Establish a clearinghouse for "best" agency practices that minimize use of SSNs
  - Work with state and local governments to review use of SSNs
- Educate Federal Agencies on How to Protect Data; Monitor Their Compliance with Existing Guidance
  - Develop concrete guidance and best practices
  - Monitor agency compliance with data security guidance
  - Protect portable storage and communications devices
- Ensure Effective, Risk-Based Responses to Data Breaches Suffered by Federal Agencies
  - Issue data breach guidance to agencies
  - Publish a "routine use" allowing disclosure of information after a breach to those entities that can assist in responding to the breach

## Data Security in Private Sector

- Establish National Standards for Private Sector Data Protection Requirements and Breach Notice Requirements
- Develop Comprehensive Records on Private Sector Use of Social Security Numbers
- Better Educate the Private Sector on Safeguarding Data
  - Hold regional seminars for businesses on safeguarding information
  - Distribute improved guidance for private industry
- Initiate Investigations of Data Security Violations
- Initiate a Multi-Year Public Awareness Campaign
  - Develop national awareness campaign
  - Enlist outreach partners
  - Increase outreach to traditionally underserved communities
  - Establish "Protect Your Identity" Days
- Develop Online Clearinghouse for Current Educational Resources

## Prevention: Making It Harder to Misuse Consumer Data

Because security systems are imperfect and thieves are resourceful, it is essential to reduce the opportunities for criminals to misuse the data they steal. An identity thief who wants to open new accounts in a victim's name must be able to (1) provide identifying information to allow the creditor or other grantor of benefits to access information on which to base a decision about eligibility; and (2) convince the creditor that he is the person he purports to be.

Authentication includes determining a person's identity at the beginning of a relationship (sometimes called verification), and later ensuring that he is the same person who was originally authenticated. But the process can fail: Identity documents can be falsified; the accuracy of the initial information and the accuracy or quality of the verifying sources can be questionable; employee training can be insufficient; and people can fail to follow procedures.

Efforts to facilitate the development of better ways to authenticate consumers without burdening consumers or businesses—for example, multi-factor authentication or layered security—would go a long way toward preventing criminals from profiting from identity theft.

- Hold Workshops on Authentication
  - Engage academics, industry, entrepreneurs, and government experts on developing and promoting better ways to authenticate identity
  - Issue report on workshop findings
- Develop a Comprehensive Record on Private Sector Use of SSNs

## Victim Recovery: Helping Consumers Repair Their Lives

Identity theft can be committed despite a consumer's best efforts at securing information. Consumers have a number of rights and resources available, but some surveys indicate that they are not as well-informed as they could be. Government agencies must work together to ensure that victims have the knowledge, tools, and assistance necessary to minimize the damage and begin the recovery process.

- Provide Specialized Training About Victim Recovery to First Responders and Others Offering Direct Assistance to Identity Theft Victims
  - Train law enforcement officers
  - Provide educational materials for first responders that can be used as a reference guide for identity theft victims
  - Create and distribute an ID Theft Victim Statement of Rights
  - Design nationwide training for victim assistance counselors
- Develop Avenues for Individualized Assistance to Identity Theft Victims

- Amend Criminal Restitution Statutes to Ensure That Victims Recover the Value of Time Spent in Trying to Remediate the Harms Suffered
- Assess Whether to Implement a National System That Allows Victims to Obtain an Identification Document for Authentication Purposes
- Assess Efficacy of Tools Available to Victims
  - Conduct assessment of FACT Act remedies under FCRA
  - Conduct assessment of state credit freeze laws

## Law Enforcement: Prosecuting and Punishing Identity Thieves

Strong criminal law enforcement is necessary to punish and deter identity thieves. The increasing sophistication of identity thieves in recent years has meant that law enforcement agencies at all levels of government have had to increase the resources they devote to investigating related crimes. The investigations are labor-intensive and generally require a staff of detectives, agents, and analysts with multiple skill sets. When a suspected theft involves a large number of potential victims, investigative agencies often need additional personnel to handle victim-witness coordination.

### Coordination and Information/Intelligence Sharing

- Establish a National Identity Theft Law Enforcement Center
- Develop and Promote the Use of a Universal Identity Theft Report Form
- Enhance Information Sharing Between Law Enforcement and the Private Sector
  - Enhance ability of law enforcement to receive information from financial institutions
  - Initiate discussions with financial services industry on countermeasures to identity theft
  - Initiate discussions with credit reporting agencies on preventing identity theft

### Coordination with Foreign Law Enforcement

- Encourage Other Countries to Enact Suitable Domestic Legislation Criminalizing Identity Theft
- Facilitate Investigation and Prosecution of International Identity Theft by Encouraging Other Nations to Accede to the Convention on Cybercrime
- Identify the Nations that Provide Safe Havens for Identity Thieves and Use All Measures Available to Encourage Those Countries to Change Their Policies

- Enhance the United States Government's Ability to Respond to Appropriate Foreign Requests for Evidence in Criminal Cases Involving Identity Theft
- Assist, Train, and Support Foreign Law Enforcement

## Prosecution Approaches and Initiatives

- Increase Prosecutions of Identity Theft
  - Designate an identity theft coordinator for each United States Attorney's Office to design a specific identity theft program for each district
  - Evaluate monetary thresholds for prosecution
  - Encourage state prosecution of identity theft
  - Create working groups and task forces
- Conduct Targeted Enforcement Initiatives
  - Conduct enforcement initiatives focused on using unfair or deceptive means to make SSNs available for sale
  - Conduct enforcement initiatives focused on identity theft related to the health care system
  - Conduct enforcement initiatives focused on identity theft by illegal aliens
- Review Civil Monetary Penalty Programs

## Gaps in Statutes Criminalizing Identity Theft

- Close the Gaps in Federal Criminal Statutes Used to Prosecute Identity Theft-Related Offenses to Ensure Increased Federal Prosecution of These Crimes
  - Amend the identity theft and aggravated identity theft statutes to ensure that identity thieves who misappropriate information belonging to corporations and organizations can be prosecuted
  - Add new crimes to the list of predicate offenses for aggravated identity theft offenses
  - Amend the statute that criminalizes the theft of electronic data by eliminating the current requirement that the information must have been stolen through interstate communications
  - Penalize creators and distributors of malicious spyware and keyloggers
  - Amend the cyber-extortion statute to cover additional, alternate types of cyber-extortion
- Ensure That an Identity Thief's Sentence Can Be Enhanced When the Criminal Conduct Affects More Than One Victim

### Law Enforcement Training
- Enhance Training for Law Enforcement Officers and Prosecutors
  - Develop course at National Advocacy Center focused on investigation and prosecution of identity theft
  - Increase number of regional identity theft seminars
  - Increase resources for law enforcement on the Internet
  - Review curricula to enhance basic and advanced training on identity theft

### Measuring the Success of Law Enforcement
- Enhance the Gathering of Statistical Data Impacting the Criminal Justice System's Response to Identity Theft
  - Gather and analyze statistically reliable data from identity theft victims
  - Expand scope of national crime victimization survey
  - Review U.S. Sentencing Commission data
  - Track prosecutions of identity theft and resources spent
  - Conduct targeted surveys

---

## FEDERAL TRADE COMMISSION'S 2006 SURVEY REPORT

The Federal Trade Commission (FTC) is at the forefront in protecting consumers and businesses from identity theft. The FTC "operates the Identity Theft Data Clearinghouse, which houses the federal government's centralized repository for consumer identity theft complaints" and "analyzes identity theft trends, promotes the development and efficacy of identity fraud prevention strategies in the financial services industry, and identifies targets for referral to criminal law enforcement." The FTC also "operates a call center for ID theft victims where counselors tell consumers how to protect themselves from identity theft and what to do if their identity has been stolen [1-877-IDTHEFT (1-877-438-4338); TDD: 1-866-653-4261; or www.ftc.gov/idtheft]."[10]

As part of its work in analyzing identity theft trends and developments, the FTC conducts detailed studies on the prevalence of victimization, impact on victims, actions taken by victims, and prevention measures to reduce the incidence of identity theft. The 2006 Identity Theft Survey Report, released in November 2007, was the second such study of its kind conducted by the FTC. The study was conducted through telephone calls using a random sampling methodology between March 27 and June 11, 2006, and covered the period of 2005.

### Prevalence

The study determined that 8.3 million Americans, or 3.7% of the population, were victims of identity theft in 2005. The associated frauds were broken into three categories: new accounts and other fraud (1.8 million Americans or 0.8% of the population); misuse of existing non-credit card account or account number (3.3 million American or 1.5% of the population); and misuse of existing credit or credit card number 3.2 million Americans or 1.4% of the population).

The results only slightly contrast with the 2003 FTC study, which found that 4.6% of the survey population were victims of identity theft. The report concluded that the difference between the 2003 and 2005 study rates was not statistically significant "given the sample sizes and variances within the samples."[11]

## Financial Gain for the Identity Thief

The 2006 survey found that the estimated total loss from identity theft was $15.6 billion. Although this amount is significantly lower than the $47.6 billion estimate in the 2003 survey, there is a good explanation. Due to differences in survey methodology between the two surveys, the FTC was unable to "determine whether total losses have actually dropped significantly between 2003 and 2006."[12]

Interestingly enough, the median value of the financial gain for the culprits across all categories of identity theft was only $500. In 10% of cases, the financial gain for the culprit was $6,000 or more, and in 5% of cases, the gain was $13,000 or more. The financial gain in each of the three individual categories was somewhat similar, except in new accounts and other frauds. In this category, the culprit received at least $30,000 in the top 5% of cases.

There is a difference in the average financial gains received by identity thieves between the two studies. "Both the 2003 and 2006 surveys asked victims for their best recollection of the amount of money obtained by the thief. In the 2006 survey, the average amount obtained by the thief was $1,882, whereas the average was $4,789 in the 2003 survey."[13] The study provided an explanation for the dramatic differences between the two studies related to survey methodology:

> *Although we believe that these methodological changes improve the reliability of the estimated values, they tend to cause lower estimates as compared to the 2003 survey. Thus, the differences in the estimates between 2003 and 2006 may, at least in part, be due to the changes in methodology as opposed to changes in consumers' actual experiences. We cannot, therefore, be confident that the difference between the 2003 and 2006 estimates represents an actual drop in the average amount obtained by identity thieves.*[14]

## Cost to Victims

As much as is made about the billions of dollars in losses from identity theft, the FTC study found that in more than 50% of incidents, victims did not incur any out-of-pocket expenses. The FTC defined these potential expenses as lost wages, legal fees, payments of fraudulent debts, and other miscellaneous expenses. For those who did incur expenses, the out-of-pocket expenses ranged from a low of $1,000 to more than $5,000. Victims spent a median value of four hours of their personal time resolving the many problems stemming from identity theft. Approximately 25% of victims were able to resolve issues stemming from identity theft within one day of discovering their victimization.

Victims faced tangential issues they needed to resolve. Thirty-seven percent experienced problems including denial of credit, inability to use existing credit cards, harassment by collection agencies, utilities that were turned off, criminal or civil investigations, and, worst of all, arrest for the crimes committed by the identity thief. These potentially long-term impact issues are far more serious than the financial losses.[15]

## NOTES

1. Research and survey findings included in this section found at the Privacy Rights Clearinghouse, www.privacyrights.org/ar/idtheftsurveys.htm.
2. Saint Xavier University, Press Release, "Study Finds No. 1 Source of Identity Theft Is Relative or Friend," May 22, 2007, www.sxu.edu/relations/news_story.asp?iNewsID=608&strBack=%2Frelations%2Fpress%5Freleases%5F2007%2Easp.
3. From the Saint Xavier University Study of Identity Theft Incidents Reported to the Chicago Police Department, 2000–2006.
4. William Kresse, Kathleen Hanold Watland, and John Lucki, *Identity Theft, Findings and Public Policy Recommendations From the Saint Xavier University Study of Identity Theft Incidents Reported to the Chicago Police Department, 2000–2006*, Saint Xavier University, Graham School of Management, Chicago, IL and the Institute for Fraud Prevention, 2006, www.theifp.org/research grants/ID Theft in Chgo - Final Report_press.pdf. Selected sections reprinted with permission from Saint Xavier University, Graham School of Management.
5. The President's Identity Theft Task Force, *Combating Identity Theft: A Strategic Plan*, April 2007, viii, www.idtheft.gov/reports/StrategicPlan.pdf.
6. Ibid., 3.
7. Ibid., 4.
8. Ibid., 4.
9. Ibid., 4–9.
10. Federal Trade Commission, www.ftc.gov/bcp/bcppip.shtm.
11. 2006 Identity Theft Survey Report, Federal Trade Commission, November 2007, 8.
12. Ibid., 9.
13. Ibid., 8.
14. Ibid., 9.
15. Ibid., 6–7.

# CHAPTER 19

# The Center for Identity Management and Information Protection

The text of this chapter includes material reproduced from the Utica College/CIMIP study *Identity Fraud Trends and Patterns: Building a Data-Based Foundation for Proactive Enforcement.*[1]

## ABOUT CIMIP

The Center for Identity Management and Information Protection (CIMIP), housed at Utica College in New York, is a research collaborative of major academic and government partners dedicated to furthering a national research agenda on identity management, information sharing, and data protection. Founded in June 2006, its ultimate goal is to impact policy, regulation, and legislation, working toward a more secure homeland.

CIMIP's stakeholders are committed to working together to provide resources, gather subject matter experts, provide access to sensitive data, and produce results that will be acted upon. Completing research and publishing papers based on the results is not enough. The results must be put into action in the form of best practices, new policies, regulations, and legislation, training opportunities, and proactive initiatives for solving the growing problems of identity fraud and theft, secure sharing of information, and information protection. To learn more about CIMIP, visit www.cimip.org.

## CIMIP AND UTICA COLLEGE

CIMIP is a logical outgrowth of Utica College's academic programs and its Economic Crime Institute (ECI). Utica College is the forerunner in providing academic programs in economic crime investigation and economic crime management on the undergraduate and graduate levels. Its undergraduate degrees in criminal justice and cyber security complete the suite of programs that endeavor to provide government and private industry with a well-educated, cutting edge workforce. Graduates of these programs are currently employed at all levels in both the private and public sectors, including the United States Secret Service, United States Immigration and Customs Enforcement, the United States Mint, LexisNexis, Bank of America, JPMorgan Chase, AIG, and several local law enforcement agencies.

The Economic Crime Institute of Utica College (ECI) drives leading-edge thinking on economic crime issues faced by business and government through educational programs, policy guidance, research, and solutions. The Institute fosters a rich learning environment that positions graduates to assume key roles in the fields of economic crime, fraud, and risk management. Founded in 1988, the Institute is a forum for the exchange of ideas, solutions, and technology for managing the risk of economic crime and fraud. The ECI Board of Advisors consists of individuals at the top of their fields from national and international corporations and government agencies. They come together twice a year to provide expertise and share ideas about Utica College's academic programs and initiatives. As such, they are uniquely positioned to provide guidance for CIMIP, as well.

### Mission

The Center for Identity Management and Information Protection will facilitate a national research agenda on identity fraud and theft, information sharing policy, and data protection. The Center is committed to providing thought leadership by conducting studies and conferences that will promote new prevention strategies, improved information sharing, innovative information use, enhanced technological solutions, and drive policy, regulatory, and legislative decisions.

### Goals

- Study the trends, causes, early detection, and prevention of identity fraud and theft.
- Understand the evolving threat from cybercriminals, insiders, and organized crime groups.
- Assess the impact of policy decisions, legislation, and regulatory actions.

- Improve identity authentication systems to reduce fraud and improper payments, and protect national security.
- Study the use of information, its protection, and the role of enabling technologies to facilitate privacy and information sharing.

## IDENTITY FRAUD TRENDS AND PATTERNS: BUILDING A DATA-BASED FOUNDATION FOR PROACTIVE ENFORCEMENT

On October 22, 2007, CIMIP released the results of a landmark study of closed U.S. Secret Service cases involving identify theft. The study entitled *Identity Fraud Trends and Patterns: Building a Data-based Foundation for Proactive Enforcement* is truly unique in both scope and results. The authors of the study were Gary R. Gordon, Ed.D., Donald J. Rebovich, Ph.D., Kyung-Seok Choo, Ph.D., and Judith B. Gordon, MLS. The study aimed to provide a better understanding of the threat that identity fraud and theft pose to personal and national security. The study revealed new findings about identity theft perpetrators, victims, and methods, and marked the first time the United States Secret Service allowed a review of its closed case files on identity theft and fraud.

CIMIP reviewed 517 closed cases investigated by the Secret Service between 2000 and 2006. In the vast majority of the cases, federal jurisdiction was established by 18 United States Code 1028 (Identity Fraud), and 18 United States Code 1029 (Access Device Fraud). "The information revolution has intensified focus on our personal and financial information as a valuable commodity. Whether information is being collected and brokered by a legitimate company or stolen by an identity thief, it has value," said Secret Service Assistant Director of Investigations Michael Stenger. "By working closely with CIMIP, we are able to gain insight on patterns and trends we can share with other federal, state, and local law enforcement representatives, as well as international police agencies. This partnership approach creates a comprehensive network of intelligence sharing, resource sharing and technical expertise that bridges jurisdictional boundaries."

Funding for the study was provided by the Office of Justice Programs, Bureau of Justice Assistance, with a $173,948 grant to Utica College's Center for Identity Management and Information Protection. Businesses, law enforcement, and individuals can benefit from the study's findings relative to identity theft methods, victims, perpetrators and prevention recommendations. Utica College and CIMIP graciously gave me permission to reprint and reference this important study and related commentary. Selected sections are included in this chapter. For the full study, please visit www.utica.edu/academic/institutes/cimip/research.cfm.

## EXECUTIVE SUMMARY

The purpose of this study was to provide empirical evidence on which law enforcement can base enhanced proactive identity theft control and prevention efforts. It focuses on identity theft offenders, which sets it apart from previous surveys and other research which have centered on identity theft victims. As a result of the study of closed United States Secret Service cases with an identity theft component (2000–2006), empirical data concerning the key factors relevant to the criminal behavior of identity thieves and the conditions under which that behavior occurs are available to law enforcement agencies, corporate security, and fraud investigators for the first time.

The results fill a gap identified in the President's Identity Theft Task Force report issued in April 2007. The report states, "Unlike some groups of criminals, identity thieves cannot be readily classified. No surveys provide comprehensive data on their primary personal or demographic characteristics."[2] This study gathered and analyzed comprehensive data on identity theft offenders in order to provide both the public and private sectors with information they need to combat these crimes.

For the purposes of this study, the definition of identity theft is aligned with that presented in the President's Identity Theft Task Force report, *Combating Identity Theft: A Strategic Plan*. "Although identity theft is defined in many different ways, it is, fundamentally, the misuse of another individual's personal information to commit fraud."[3] Personal information includes name, address, Social Security number, and date of birth, but excludes credit cards, debit cards, and other bank cards. The data for the study was collected at the Secret Service headquarters by the four authors of this report. Data was collected from 517 cases with an identity theft component, which were opened and closed between 2000 and 2006.

## Findings

After the data collection and analysis were completed, the findings were separated into four categories: the case, the offenders, the commission of the crime, and victimization. Highlights of these areas follow.

## The Cases

Case characteristics include Secret Service classification, Secret Service region, referral to Secret Service, jurisdiction, statutes violated, disposition, actual dollar loss, timing and duration, and geographical scope.

- Many of the cases were classified as "Fraudulent Use of Account Number" and "Identity Theft."
- The highest percentage of cases was from the Northeastern United States.
- The cases were referred to the Secret Service from various sources.
  - Approximately 47% were referred by local and state law enforcement agencies.
  - Corporate security and/or fraud investigators referred about 20% of the cases.
- Most cases fell under federal jurisdiction, with criminal statutes Title 18, United States Code, Section 1028, Identity Fraud, and Title 18, United States Code, Section 1029, Access Device Fraud, most frequently violated.
- Approximately half of the defendants in the cases were sentenced to incarceration, often in combination with probation and restitution.
- The median actual dollar loss was $31,356.

## The Offenders

The data analysis showed more diversity among the age, race, gender, and criminal backgrounds of offenders than the picture held by conventional wisdom.

- 42.5% of offenders were between 25 and 34 years of age at the time that the case was opened.
  - The 35–49 age group made up 33% of the offenders.
  - 18.5% were between 18 and 24 years old.
  - The remaining 6% were 50 years old and older.
- 53.8% of the offenders were black; 38.3% were white.
  - One third of the offenders were female.
- 24.1% of the offenders were born outside of the United States.
- 71% of the offenders had no arrest history.
  - Of those who did, a third of the arrests were for fraud, forgery, or identity theft.
- The most prevalent motive of the offenders was personal gain. It took several forms including using fraudulently obtained personal identifying information to:
  - Obtain and use credit
  - Procure cash
  - Conceal actual identity
  - Apply for loans to purchase motor vehicles

## The Commission of the Crime

The data was examined to determine the modus operandi of the offenders, the organized nature of the crimes and offenders, and identity theft through employment.

- In most of the cases, the identity theft facilitated other offenses.
  - The most frequent offense that was facilitated by identity theft was fraud.
  - The next most frequent was larceny.
- Organized group activity was found in 42.4% of the cases, involving from 2–45 offenders.
  - The roles that the defendants took varied, but most frequently involved stealing or obtaining personal identifying information and using it for personal gain.
  - In cases with three or more offenders, there is definite coordination and organization, allowing the group to take advantage of criminal opportunities, to create opportunities for crime, and to avoid detection.
- In approximately half of the cases, the Internet and/or other technological devices were used in the commission of the crime.
  - Within the half with no use of the Internet or technology, non-technological methods, such as change of address requests and Dumpster diving were used in 20% of the cases.

- The limited number of cases opened in 2005 and 2006 prevented any trending analysis of Internet and technological use.
- The point of compromise for stealing personal identifying information or documents was determined in 274 of the cases.
  - In 50% of those cases a business (service, retail, financial industry, or corporation) provided the point of compromise or vulnerability.
  - A family member or friend was the point of compromise in approximately 16% of the 274 cases.
- Approximately a third of the cases involved identity theft through employment.
  - The most frequent type of employment from which personal identifying information or documents were stolen was retail and service (stores, car dealerships, gas stations, casinos, restaurants, hotels, hospitals, doctors offices)— 43.8%.
  - Private corporations were vulnerable to insider identity theft in about 20% of those cases.

## Victimization

Although most of the media attention surrounding identity theft and fraud has focused on individuals, they did not make up the largest percentage of victims in this study.

- Over a third (37.1%) of the victims were financial industry organizations: banks, credit unions, and credit card companies.
- Individuals accounted for 34.3% of the victims.
- 21.3% of the victims were retail businesses (stores, car dealerships, gas stations, casinos, restaurants, hotels, hospitals, doctors' offices).
- Victimization of organizations took several forms:
  - The financial services industry was most frequently victimized by offenders using fraudulently obtained personal identifying information to obtain new credit card accounts, to apply for and obtain fraudulent loans, to pass checks, and to transfer funds.
  - The retail industry was victimized by the use of stolen identity information to open store accounts and by purchasing merchandise with fraudulent credit cards.
- The data show that most individuals were victimized by individuals they did not know.
  - 59% of the victims did not know the offenders.
  - 10.5% of the victims were customers or clients of the offender.
  - 5% of the victims were related to the offender.
- 20.3% of the 939 offenders in the cases committed identity theft at their place of employment.
  - Of those offenders, 59.7% were employed by a retail business.
  - 22.2% were employed by a financial services industry organization.

While the Internet, with its chat rooms, electronic banking and payments, phishing and pharming, malware, and spyware, has certainly added a dimension to the crime, the basics are also still employed by identity thieves: common theft, mail theft and change of address, Dumpster diving, database and network hacking, and insider theft. The purposes for which identity thieves can use the stolen personal identifier information has been exacerbated by the Internet, as online credit applications, purchases, bank transfers, and the like eliminate the need for face-to-face contact.

The findings presented here must be used to improve and increase proactive measures that law enforcement and fraud investigators use to combat identity theft, including investigation, prevention, detection, and prosecution. The information concerning offender characteristics and modus operandi should be used in law enforcement training. The picture that this study paints of identity theft offenses and offenders should be used in prioritizing and managing cases and resources. Law enforcement executives will be able to use this information to develop policy, allocate resources, and advocate training.

## Secret Service Case Classification

Exhibit 19.1 displays the most frequent primary case types represented by the 517 cases. Fifty percent of the cases were classified as Fraudulent Use of Account Numbers, Fraudulent Access Device Applications, Stolen Bank Issued Cards, Financial Institution Fraud (FIF) Involving Check Fraud, Counterfeit Bank Issued Credit Cards, Counterfeit Commercial Checks, and Counterfeit State Driver's licenses. A quarter

**Exhibit 19.1  Most Frequent Primary Case Type**

| Primary Case Type Description | Frequency | Percent |
|---|---|---|
| Fraudulent use of account number | 78 | 15.1 |
| Fraudulent access device | 58 | 11.2 |
| Stolen bank-issued cards | 36 | 7.0 |
| All other cases involving financial institution fraud investigation | 35 | 6.8 |
| Financial institution fraud involving check fraud | 34 | 6.6 |
| Counterfeit bank-issued card | 27 | 5.2 |
| Counterfeit commercial checks | 23 | 4.4 |
| Counterfeit state driver's license | 22 | 4.3 |
| Fraudulently obtained genuine ID/Social Security card | 19 | 3.7 |
| Manufacturing commercial/counterfeit check | 15 | 2.9 |
| Account takeover access/bank card | 14 | 2.7 |
| Stolen/forged commercial/personal check | 12 | 2.3 |
| Fraudulent retail business card application | 11 | 2.1 |
| All others | 133 | 25.7 |
| **Total** | **517** | **100** |

of the cases (listed as other) were of primary code types ranging from altered documents to other counterfeit documents to various types of financial institution fraud.

## Motivating Factors

The data collection included a paragraph summary or synopsis of the case, based on the description of the investigation in the files, for 503 of the cases. These summaries provided information about the factors which motivated the offenders to commit the offense that provided them with fraudulently obtained or fictitious personally identifying information. In most of the cases there was more than one motive. Exhibit 19.2 shows the frequency and percentage of the eight most prevalent motives for committing identity theft or fraud.

### Exhibit 19.2  Motivating Factors

| Use Stolen ID to: | Number | Percent |
|---|---|---|
| Obtain and use credit | 228 | 45.3 |
| Procure cash | 166 | 33 |
| Conceal actual identity | 114 | 22.7 |
| Apply for loans to buy vehicles | 105 | 20.9 |
| Manufacture and sell fraudulent IDs | 39 | 7.7 |
| Obtain cell phones and services | 23 | 4.6 |
| Gain government benefits | 19 | 3.8 |
| Procure drugs | 11 | 2.2 |

It is clear that the primary motive of the offenders in these cases was financial gain. With the possible exceptions of using the fraudulent information to conceal actual identity and to obtain cell phones and services, all of these motives point to a need or desire for money. Some of the offenders were involved in perpetuating the offenses as a profitable business. Others simply wanted the ability to purchase a car or other merchandise or pay their bills. In some cases, drug addicts used identity theft offenses as a means of supporting their habits.

## Insider Identity Theft

By and large, these offenses were not perpetrated by insiders (e.g., employees of entities housing the identity information/documents stolen). In 65.9% (341) of the cases, the offenses were not committed through the employment of the offenders, while the point of vulnerability was the offenders' place of employment in 34.1% (176). Identity theft through employment occurred most often among offenders employed in the retail industry—stores, gas stations, car dealerships, casinos, restaurants, hospitals, doctors' offices, hotels, and the like. Offenders stole personal identifier information from these places of employment in 77 cases—43.8% of the cases involving identity theft through employment. It occurred 36 times in private companies (20.5%).

## Individual Activity versus Organized Group Activity

The data collected from the Secret Service cases included the number of defendants and the roles which they played in the commission of the crime. The actions the defendants took were:

- Steal or obtain personal identifying information (e.g., personal identifying information that could be captured from credit card databases, client and employee records, credit card receipts, bank statements, stolen mail, checks)
- Steal or obtain personal identifier documents (e.g., driver's licenses, birth certificates, Social Security cards, employee badges)
- Steal or obtain bank cards (credit, debit, ATM)
- Alter identification documents (e.g., driver's licenses, Social Security cards, birth certificates, employee badges)
- Produce counterfeit identification documents (e.g., driver's licenses, Social Security cards, birth certificates, employee identification cards)
- Distribute personal identifier information to others (so that they could use it for personal gain)
- Sell identification documents (genuine and counterfeit)
- Use identification documents for own use (The offender used genuine or counterfeit documents for his or her own personal gain.)
- Use identification documents to obtain more identification documents (e.g., using a utility bill and birth certificate to procure a driver's license)
- Direct others' activities (within an organized crime group, giving instructions or orders to the others in the group)
- Other (includes credit card skimming, encoding or re-encoding bank cards)

It is clear that the majority of the 517 cases involved a single offender as 57.6% (298) of the cases were ones in which there was only one defendant. In close to a quarter of the cases (22.8%, 118), however, two offenders worked together to commit the identity theft offenses. There is a significant drop in the frequency of cases with more than two offenders. There were three in 7.9% (41) cases, and four in 3.5% (18). From there the number of cases with multiple offenders continues to decrease. Seven cases had 10 or more offenders, with the largest number being 45.

As the results show, the most common types of identity theft cases in the sample are those in which one individual operated alone or worked with one other person to initiate and complete an offense(s) of identity theft. These cases generally entailed obtaining or stealing personal identifying information and using it for their own use. Based on more detailed qualitative information provided in case investigation notes, those cases in which only one offender was involved were often driven by criminal opportunities that were assessed as desirable by the offender, with no recruitment of or consultation with criminal others. These offenders started with identity theft to lead to other criminal activity, and took on several roles.

## Utilization of Methods by Offenders

- **Internet.** There were 102 cases that included the use of the Internet. Unspecified Internet use occurred most frequently—in 51 cases. It was used to search databases in 27 cases, for email in 16 cases, and for online identification document purchase and/or sale in 19 cases. In some cases more than one method of Internet use was used and therefore, recorded during data collection. For that reason, the number of uses totals more than 102.

- **Technological devices,** including computers and the other items listed above, whether used alone or in conjunction with the Internet and/or non-technological means, were used in 192 cases. Computers were most frequently used for producing documents—in 106 cases. They were used for scanning documents in 62 cases and for unspecified purposes in 93. Computer printers were used in 68 cases for producing documents, checks, and currency. Other frequently used technological devices were photocopiers (31 cases), telephone (31), and other, including access device readers (28). Again, there were combinations of computer uses and of computers and other technological devices in some of the cases, so the numbers total more than 192.

- **Using Computers to Produce Documents.** Here is an example where the defendant used a computer to create phony identification documents. The defendant procured personal identifying information by placing ads in newspapers stating that he was hiring and would accept applications at a local hotel. He would interview the individuals and collect their applications which included Social Security numbers, dates of birth, and bank account information for direct deposit of a payroll check. He would then create birth certificates and employment cards on a computer and use them to get driver's licenses with his photograph and others' names. He used the driver's licenses to open bank accounts. He then manufactured counterfeit checks with the victims' names on the computer.

- **Non-technological means**, including mail theft, mail rerouting, and Dumpster diving were used in 106 cases. The most frequent of these was the rerouting of mail through change of address cards and change of address for credit cards and bank accounts. It occurred in 62 cases. Mail theft was an element of 46 cases and Dumpster diving was employed in 12 cases. Again, these means were used in combination in some cases, so the numbers total more than 106.

## Patterns of Offender Methods

The data was examined to track variations in the use of the Internet, technological devices, and non-technological means according to the year in which the case was opened. The Secret Service opens cases once they have been referred to them and accepted. The year the case is opened is generally the year in which the crime was detected. Unfortunately, any trending analysis is premature, as there are very few 2005 and 2006 cases which are now closed. A continuation study is planned that will collect the necessary data to provide for this level of analysis. The following preliminary findings were observed.

- There is very little variation in the use of the Internet to commit identity theft from 2001 through 2004. The data indicate that in approximately 20% of the 2001–2004 cases the Internet was used.

- An interesting pattern in the use of technological devices was observed during a similar time period. There is a steady decline in the use of technology other than the Internet in the cases opened between 2001 and 2004. In 2001, 42.2% (27) of the cases involved the use of a technological device. That number dropped to 30% (17) in 2004. The decrease was steady in the intervening years: 38.5% (60) in 2002 and 34.8% (46) in 2003.

- The use of non-technological means remained fairly steady across the 4 years (2001–2004). The percentages were in the low twenties for this period. Offenders continued to use low-tech means such as mail theft, mail rerouting, and dumpster diving, but only in a small percentage of the cases. It should be noted that in some cases, the non-technological means were used in combination with the Internet and/or other technological devices.

- The limited data provided by closed 2005 and 2006 cases indicate the potential for shifts in the patterns above. However, the numbers are too small to draw any conclusions at this time.

## Offender Relationship to Individual Victims

It is stated in the President's Identity Theft Task Force report that "identity thieves have been known to prey on people they know, including coworkers, senior citizens for whom they are serving as caretakers, and even family members."[4] In collecting data for this research project, special attention was paid to the relationship between the offender and victim. The categories into which the relationships were classified include:

- Stranger (The victim had never met the offender.)
- Customer/Client (includes retail customers, client lists, and the like)
- Family (immediate and extended—spouses, parents, siblings, grandparents, aunts, uncles, nieces, nephews, cousins)
- Friend/acquaintance
- Coworker/employer
- Unavailable (There was no indication of the victim-offender relationship in the file.)

Exhibit 19.3 shows Offender and Victim Relationships. The majority of offender/victim relationships involved an individual or individuals whom the offender did not know.

As the President's Identity Theft Task Force reported, identity thieves often prey on people they know, but in most of the Secret Service cases they did not. However, there were cases of offenders taking advantage of the people for whom they were caring—both disabled and elderly, as well as cases in which spouses, parents, children, and extended family members were victimized.

**Exhibit 19.3    Offender and Victim Relationships**

| Category | Number | Percent |
| --- | --- | --- |
| Stranger | 540 | 59.4 |
| Customer/Client | 95 | 10.5 |
| Family | 46 | 5.0 |
| Friend/Acquaintance | 28 | 3.1 |
| Coworker/Employer | 28 | 3.1 |
| Unavailable | 172 | 18.9 |
| **Total** | **909** | **100%** |

## THOUGHT LEADER IN IDENTITY THEFT RESEARCH

### Donald Rebovich

Donald J. Rebovich, Ph.D., is executive director of Utica College's Center for Identity Management and Information Protection (CIMIP). He is also an associate professor and director of Economic Crime Undergraduate Programs at Utica College. Before joining Utica College, Dr. Rebovich served as research director for the National White Collar Crime Center (NW3C) and research director for the American Prosecutors Research Institute.

Dr. Rebovich is the coeditor of the book *The New Technology of Crime, Law and Social Control* and the author of the book *Dangerous Ground: The World of Hazardous Waste Crime,* which presented the results of the first empirical study of environmental crime and its control in the United States. He is the assistant editor of the *Journal of Economic Crime Management.* His background includes research in identity theft, economic crime victimization, white-collar crime prosecution, and multijurisdictional task force development.

Dr. Rebovich has served as advisor to the U.S. Department of Justice on tribal technology and information sharing and on environmental crime control. He obtained his B.S. degree in psychology from the College of New Jersey and received his M.A. and Ph.D. degrees in criminal justice from Rutgers University. Here Dr. Rebovich provides his thoughts and commentary on the CIMIP study.

IMPRESSIONS ON THE CIMIP/SECRET SERVICE STUDY

In 2007, CIMIP undertook its most challenging research endeavor: the empirical analysis of over 500 U. S. Secret Service identity theft cases. The goal was to collect investigative case file data from completed identity theft cases spanning from the years 2000 through 2006 and, from this data, document key characteristics of the offense, the offender and the victim. Up until 2007, most of the research findings on identity theft were confined to information submitted by victims through surveys or other forms of victim information submission. While valuable, conclusions drawn from findings were often limited by factors such as variable interpretations of identity theft definitions and low response rates. Further, this information did not include incidents unknown to victims nor did it include incidents of crimes against organizations or agencies (e.g., businesses, government). Finally, the view was strictly from the perspective of the victim, only addressing peripheral characteristics of the offender and the offender's modus operandi. Many questions remain around who the typical offender is and how he/she commits the crimes of identity theft and identity fraud.

The results of the study were released on October 22, 2007 and were met with an interesting mix of curiosity and surprise. Contrary to some of the preceding victim surveys, the CIMIP study found that most victims did not know their offenders. The median loss for a case was found to be over $30,000, much more than average estimates drawn from victim surveys. (Both findings can be partly attributed to the inclusion of private businesses and public organizations in the study sample.) A full one-third of offenders were found to have committed their crimes at their place of employment, spotlighting the special problems of unscrupulous "insiders" who would use personal information for criminal purposes. Close to half of the crimes depended on offenders working in concert. And the criminality itself was not confined by racial or gender boundaries; over half of the offenders were found to be black and a third were female.

The results shattered some preconceptions many held about identity theft and identity fraud. The fundamental insight furnished by the study results was that the theft of information used to commit identity fraud was predatory and pervasive, perpetrated by many different types of people from all walks of life. Furthermore, the criminals proved to be patient observers of opportunities that would allow them entree to source information upon which they could build criminal careers. These identity thieves would settle into a convenient routine of shuttling between the cultivation of data and the conversion of the data into counterfeit documents and identification cards in order to reach the ultimate goal of the fraudulent use of that data.

The study findings impressed upon me the stark realities of identity theft in our modern society. Many of the crimes were carried out by individuals using simple forms of scams, trickery, misrepresentation (e.g., phishing), and basic theft (e.g., Dumpster diving, mailbox rifling) to procure seed information for their later acts of fraud. These were crimes of individual victim manipulation. However, the crimes resulting in the most monetary loss to individuals and businesses alike proved to be more acts of *system* manipulation committed by loosely constructed criminal groups exhibiting, in many instances, remarkable skills at exploiting system vulnerabilities. A common characteristic of these cases was the specialization of criminal skills (e.g., paper document experts, laminating experts, check forgers) and the portability of those services depending on the criminal group's needs. Too often, the individual in control of the "criminal spigot" was the insider, the gatekeeper to personal information of clients and customers.

*(Continued)*

289

A variety of sources (public service announcements, commercial advertising) periodically remind U.S. citizens about the threats of identity theft and the personal actions that can be taken to help insulate oneself from identity theft victimization. One disquieting story that emerges from the CIMIP study results is that no matter how vigilant we are in following a formula for protecting ourselves from falling victim to identity theft, there is only so much the average citizen can control. Our personal information is legitimately collected and housed, daily, by numerous private and public sector entities. The successful protection of that information is contingent on the exercising of robust policies for the safekeeping of it by the information guardians themselves. Absent such policies (strong employee screening strategies, comprehensive employee monitoring programs), organizations "invite" attempts at information theft by those entrusted to protect it. Some of the findings of the CIMIP study point to a key threat to identity security as coming from "within;" the insider ready to exploit perceived system vulnerabilities. As expressed by one arrested insider in case interview notes, "It was so easy." It is hoped that studies like this one will impress Americans with the urgency of implementing proven methods to make committing identity theft "not so easy."

## IMPLICATIONS FOR LAW ENFORCEMENT[5]

The CIMIP study's findings furnish the law enforcement community with fresh, empirically obtained knowledge for the development of enhanced proactive identity theft control and prevention. The study's recommendations, derived from the findings, are designed to ensure that the CIMIP study will serve the utility of improving proactive measures that law enforcement and fraud investigators can use to control identity theft. The recommendations center on areas such as detection enhancement, interagency collaboration, the effective use of resources, training, executive briefings, and future research.

CIMIP research study results form a critical knowledge base for proactive measures in identity theft investigations. More precisely, the information gleaned from the study can play an instrumental part in equipping law enforcement with the tools needed to effectively and efficiently detect identity theft. The results serve to enhance the ability to spot "red flags" of identity theft, particularly for local law enforcers. Police face a multitude of responsibilities and may not always be focused on identity theft.

### Recommendation

Local and state law enforcement leaders should encourage more cooperation with federal law enforcement where it has begun and foster it where it is not occurring.

The manner in which the criminal justice system addresses the cases in their nascent stages underscores the integral role of local law enforcement in the referral of cases to the Secret Service. Identity theft investigations, as evidenced in the study sample, could begin with an ordinary vehicular stop for exceeding the speed limit on a rural county highway or could, just as easily, begin as an investigation of what, on the surface, appears to be the work of a small-time burglar. Recognizing the signs of identity theft at this earliest stage, with the local law enforcement officer acting in the role of an identity theft "first responder," can spell the difference between the cracking of an identity theft ring or an important enforcement opportunity missed.

Clearly, referrals to the Secret Service may result from victim reports of identity theft to local law enforcement, but, more likely, would be the product of the alertness of local officials in recognizing telltale signs of identity theft while investigating unrelated crimes. Results of the CIMIP study can help assist local police and sheriffs' departments to act as conduits to successful federal investigations and prosecutions of these cases. This can be achieved by sensitizing local enforcement to the range of clues for recognition of the presence of identity theft and the steps required affecting successful investigation and referral. The study results also uncover a trend towards a collaborative approach to investigating identity theft cases that will likely be perpetuated in the future. Most of the study cases were prosecuted under federal jurisdiction—a further indication of the cooperative and collaborative enforcement approach.

In terms of empirically-grounded characteristics of the identity theft offender, there is much that law enforcement can learn. The findings reveal that identity theft offenders are characteristically diverse in terms of their age, race, and gender. The results confirm that there is no perfect criminal "stereotype" that fits the moniker of identity thief. The results certainly do not reflect the image sometimes portrayed by the media of a devious white, young male staring at a computer screen. The frequency of women participating in these crimes is markedly unlike the level of female activity in other types of crimes; it is strikingly more pronounced.

Most of the offenders did show evidence of having prior arrest records, but of those who did, most of the past crimes were for related offenses such as fraud or theft of property. Some of these offenders freely admitted that they had shifted over from other crime areas because of their belief of the ease of the commission of identity theft and the chances of increasing their illegal profits in shorter periods of time. These prior criminal activities included drug trafficking and robbery. Once again, the results remind law enforcers that they, as crime control agents, cannot overlook the possibilities that suspects are engaged in deeper and more lucrative criminal enterprises than what would appear on the surface.

The study results also point to the practical nature of new legal tools at the disposal of identity theft law enforcers. While most of the cases were prosecuted federally, the reliance on newly enacted identity theft statutes figured prominently in the charging of offenders both on the federal and state jurisdictional levels. At the state level, identity theft statutes were the most frequently used in charging practices. At the federal level, violations of access device fraud and identity fraud statutes were charged the most. Wire fraud and mail fraud were at one time seen as the most logical and convenient paths towards prosecuting identity theft offenders; however, they were found to be used less frequently in the CIMIP study. The study also underscored the special resources needed to investigate identity theft cases, as these cases can easily go on for two years. The results of this study allow law enforcement to see a spectrum of identity theft cases, rather than dealing with one at a time. Law enforcement managers can use this information to effectively assign resources and prioritize cases.

The findings of the CIMIP study should help law enforcement executives more accurately assess where and how to allocate their identity theft control dollars. Previous enforcement strategies used loss amount thresholds as the litmus test to determine which cases would and would not be investigated or prosecuted. Research findings here demonstrate that there is clear value in pursuing identity theft cases even if the dollar loss is minimal or non-existent. CIMIP study findings on the geographical distribution and scope of identity theft also demonstrate that these crimes occur fairly evenly across the United States. It should, therefore, deserve equal enforcement prioritization throughout the land. Further, the scope of the offenses was found to be just as likely to be local as state or interstate. This information, along with information about referral patterns from local and state law enforcement, can be invaluable as law enforcement managers attempt to effectively allocate personnel and funds.

Research findings of the CIMIP study also pave the way for the establishment of standardized case classifications for identity theft and identity fraud. Doing so would help facilitate interagency sharing of case information, collaboration on investigations, and improved prioritization and management of cases. Consideration should also be given to the inclusion of identity theft as a primary classification code.

The information gained from the CIMIP study results should, ultimately, be channeled into up-to-date law enforcement training programs that capitalize upon what is recommended by the report and for which materials can be provided. The hope is that relevant findings would be disseminated to law enforcement executives so that they can develop policy, allocate resources, and advocate training based on empirical research.

Organized briefings on the research findings should be made available geared to aid law enforcement executives in developing and implementing policies and procedures for optimized investigation and prosecution of identity theft crimes. These briefings should accentuate conclusions drawn from the findings in the areas of offender methods, points of compromise, organized crime activity, insider criminal activity, and the victims. Such briefings could also highlight the points of compromise and vulnerabilities which provide opportunities for employees to steal personal identifying information, as well as the methods employed to perpetrate the thefts. This information can be turned to for the development of policies and procedures created to prevent, detect, and mitigate identity theft and fraud.

Logically, the pioneering research represented by the CIMIP study should represent a launching pad for a series of like-minded research endeavors. The analysis of closed Secret Service cases culminated in the construction of a rich data set which will be used to aid law enforcement agencies and corporations in their war against identity theft and fraud. The reality is, however, that wily criminals are constantly adapting to law enforcement investigative techniques and strategies by experimenting with new methods for committing such crimes while avoiding detection. Unfortunately, some have successfully reached their goals of undermining enforcement efforts. It is, therefore, incumbent upon today's law enforcement community to draw upon timely empirical information on trends, patterns, and groups, both current and emerging, to evolve from a reactive control posture to a proactive one. This iterative model for identity theft research should not be confined to U.S. Secret Service cases, but should also be applied, widely, to cases investigated by local, state, and other federal law enforcement agencies. Incrementally building on the baseline created through the CIMIP research, future longitudinal studies of identity theft, on all government levels, should be undertaken to ascertain trends and patterns of this crime area in the near past and to accurately anticipate future trends and areas of vulnerability to improve the system's chances of containing identity theft and identity fraud.

## NOTES

1. Utica College/CIMIP study *Identity Fraud Trends and Patterns: Building a Data-Based Foundation for Proactive Enforcement.* © Center for Identity Management and Information Protection. It is reproduced here with the permission of the Center for Identity Management and Information Protection of Utica College.
2. The President's Identity Theft Task Force, *Combating Identity Theft: A Strategic Plan* (April 2007), 12, www.idtheft.gov/reports/StrategicPlan.pdf.
3. Ibid., 2.
4. Ibid., 12.
5. The content for this section was provided by Donald J. Rebovich, Ph.D.

# CHAPTER 20

---

# Preventing Identity Theft: 21 Rules You Must Use

I learned early in my law enforcement career the value of prevention. As a young federal agent, I wanted to arrest every criminal I could find to stop fraud. Although the goal was noble, it did not work. No matter how many we arrested, new fraudsters just took their places and the crimes continued. Prosecutions put crooks behind bars but were ineffective in reimbursing consumers and businesses for their financial losses. I came to embrace the importance of prevention in limiting victimization from fraud, especially in the case of identity theft.

Nothing will guarantee that you will never become an identity theft victim. With the widespread availability of personal information and the increasing exposure from data breaches, the risk is ever-present. But there is much you can do to protect yourself, your family, and your business. Robust prevention activities can limit your chances of becoming a victim of identity theft. I say "limit" because there is no perfect guarantee against victimization. Nevertheless, using the many recommended prevention rules will definitely make you less of a target.

First, do not panic. Just because you lost your wallet or purse, do not assume you will automatically become an identity theft victim. The same goes with data breaches. Investigators discovered only 800 cases of fraud among the more than 163,000 identities exposed in the ChoicePoint data breach in 2004. Statistics are on your side. Prevention techniques can provide you safety and peace of mind.

I offer a robust set of proactive and reactive rules to fraud-proof and protect your good name. The "21 Rules You Must Use" are the most important things you need to do now and on an ongoing basis to prevent identity theft. There are also rules to follow if you become a victim. Consider these rules as further hardening of your defenses. Learn these rules and use them religiously. Tell your family, friends, and work associates. If you employ all these rules, you will significantly lessen your identity theft risk and be prepared to act if you are victimized.

## 1. Safeguard Your Social Security Number

Your Social Security number (SSN) is the key to your personal and financial vault. It provides access to your bank and brokerage accounts, credit reports, medical records, and so much more. The SSN is often the entry point for identity theft. Do not carry your Social Security card in your wallet or purse. Do not write your SSN on a piece of paper in your wallet or purse either. Guard it always and do not give it out unless absolutely necessary. Do not be afraid to strongly question why anyone needs to know your SSN. Also protect your other personal information, such as your passport, birth certificate, voter registration card, alien registration card, and other forms of identification.

## 2. Protect Your Other Personal Information

Locking down your SSN is the first step in protecting your personal information. The same safeguards are needed for your credit card numbers, bank and brokerage accounts, retirement accounts, and others. Do not give your credit card number or other personal information to people who call you, no matter how legitimate or enticing the offer may sound. Always limit to whom you give your date of birth, mother's maiden name, or other confidential personal information. Again, do not be afraid to question why someone needs this information.

Minimize the amount of information you carry with you. Do not carry more than two credit cards at any one time. Do not write your personal identification number (PIN) on your automated teller machine (ATM) card. Go through your wallet or purse and remove old deposit slips, blank checks, and other information that you may not need to carry. Do not keep account information or passwords in your cell phone or personal digital assistant. Cancel credit cards that you do not need.

Check your credit card after each use. Always check that you have received your own credit card back after making a purchase, although this is not a frequent problem. In some instances, corrupt clerks have switched credit cards. The clerk knows that the particular credit card is good since it was approved for the purchase; criminally minded clerks can use the card or sell it to others.

Always guard your other passwords and PINs. Do not provide your address or telephone number on credit card transaction slips. Some states actually prohibit retailers from asking you for this information. When purchasing from online retailers, do not allow them to maintain your credit card number or other personal information for future transactions. The less information that you allow them to store, the less information can be adversely impacted if a data breach occurs.

Keep unnecessary information off your checks. I have seen people print their SSNs and home telephone numbers on their checks. There is no need to do this; it only exposes more personal information. Limit the information to your name and address. Rather than having new or additional checks for your checking account mailed to your home address, consider having them delivered to your bank for pickup. This is especially recommended if you do not have a locking mailbox.

Some credit card issuers allow card holders to place their photograph on their cards. This can be a good if the card is lost and then used by a thief. Of course, we have to assume that whoever receives the card for purchases will actually look at the face of the card and compare the signature on the back of the card with the signature provided at time of use. In some cases, people have signed "Mickey Mouse" on their credit card receipts without the cashiers ever noticing.

Protect personal information that you leave in your car. Do not leave any items with personal information, such as insurance cards, vehicle registration, wallets, purses, or laptops in your vehicle, especially in plain view. Thieves will break into vehicles to obtain this information. In addition, remove or hide from view your garage door opener. The garage door opener and vehicle registration with your home address provides thieves with the tools they needed to locate and easily enter your house while you are away. Properly secure financial instruments and important documents in your residence or business, or bank safety deposit box. Better yet, install a home alarm system for further protection. Residential and commercial burglaries have been carried out to obtain SSNs, birth certificates, and account information.

## 3. Review Your Credit Reports

If you follow only one recommendation from this book, this should be the one. Carefully reviewing your consumer credit report on an ongoing basis is the best way to learn if you are a victim of identity theft. Consistent scrutiny of your credit reports can detect identity theft early and minimize potential damage. Often reviews find errors that have nothing to do with fraud but need to be corrected nonetheless.

In 2003, Congress amended the Fair Credit Reporting Act to allow consumers access to their credit scores and a free copy of their credit reports each year. You can access your credit reports from the three major credit bureaus with one call or email request. Annualcreditreport.com is the central online site available to consumers to request these credit reports. It can be accessed at: www.annualcreditreport.com/cra/index.jsp. Note: It is the only official site for the free annual credit report. Another Web site offers a "free" credit report, but it is run by one of the credit bureaus. Users must purchase a credit monitoring service in order to receive the "free" credit reports.

Review your credit report each year from the three major credit reporting bureaus, Equifax (www.equifax.com), Experian (www.experian.com), and TransUnion (www.transunion.com). Rather than reviewing all three reports at the same time each year, spread them out. Order one report in January, a second in May, and the third one in September. This way you continuously self-monitor your credit from the major credit agencies.

Look for credit inquiries and issuance of credit that you did not authorize. If any are found, make immediate inquiries and notifications. If you do not know how to read a credit report, helpful resources are available online. Review the credit reports for your children just in case their personal information has been compromised by identity thieves. Once they leave home, encourage them to check their credit reports regularly.

### Exhibit 20.1 Avoid Becoming a Victim of Identity Theft

The United States Department of Justice recommends that consumers think of the word "SCAM" to minimize their risk of becoming victims of identity theft.

S - Be Stingy about giving out personal information.

C - Check your financial information regularly.

A - Ask periodically for a copy of your credit report.

M - Maintain careful records of financial accounts.

Source: United States Department of Justice, www.usdoj.gov/criminal/fraud/websites/idtheft.html

### 4. Buy a Good Shredder and Use It

One of the easiest prevention techniques to thwart Dumpster diving is to buy and use a shredder. They are relatively inexpensive and the best protection from someone acquiring personal information that is discarded in the trash. People discard all sorts of sensitive information without thinking of the consequences: preapproved credit card offers, convenience checks, bank statements, canceled checks, deposit slips, and correspondence containing SSNs and other information. Do not forget to shred receipts for prescriptions too. Thieves who are addicts may break into your home if they find evidence that you have certain prescription narcotic drugs they can use to get high.

Get a shredder that provides a confetti cut. Confetti is virtually impossible to reassemble. Cheaper shredders cut paper into strips that industrious fraudsters can piece together. Put a shredder in your kitchen, office, garage, or other convenient spot. Ultra-small models are available. When the mail arrives, shred unwanted credit card offers and other documents immediately. Do this every day.

Businesses also need to shred sensitive documents. Businesses produce confidential documents that could put them at risk if they were lost or stolen. Everything from medical records to internal business memos can put a company at risk. Privacy concerns, legal compliance requirements, and the threat of corporate espionage can be better addressed if everything that needs to be discarded is properly shredded. Document destruction companies have specially equipped document-shredding trucks that visit the workplace, collect documents for destruction, and shred the material on-site. Collection boxes are placed throughout the office for employees to place documents that need shredding.

### 5. Reduce Your Exposure to Mail Theft

Mail theft has been a problem ever since the origin of the Postal Service in the 1700s. For much of the last 30 years, mail theft has been a contributor to identity theft. The good news is that in a Federal Trade Commission (FTC) survey released in November 2007, only 2% of victims reported that the theft of their identity was connected to the U.S. mails. This shows that t the Postal Service's prevention initiatives are working. But that does not guarantee that you will never be a victim of mail theft.

Always use a locking mailbox. Mail theft, although it is occurring less often, is still a significant threat to your identity. Take precautions to protect your mail from theft. Mail is something we all receive six days a week, each and every week. The daily delivery and volume make mail an inviting target for fraudsters. Thus, it is important to have the most secure mailbox as possible. If you cannot obtain a locking mailbox, consider using a Post Office box or a box at a private mail receiving agency, such as The UPS Store.

The U.S. Postal Inspection Service is the federal law enforcement agency responsible for protecting the public and the Postal Service from mail theft. It has long been working to reduce the number of break-ins of individual house mailboxes and neighborhood mailbox units in affected areas. The public's assistance is also needed in helping to reduce the losses from these thefts. Take these measures to help protect yourself from becoming a victim of mail theft:

- Retrieve your mail as soon as possible after delivery to the mail receptacle. Do not leave mail in your mailbox overnight or on weekends.
- Use collection boxes or letter slots at the Post Office to mail letters instead of leaving them in your residential box for carrier pickup. This is especially true for outgoing mail containing payment checks. Payment checks are prime targets for mail thieves who can alter the checks and negotiate them. Thieves steal outgoing and incoming mail to obtain bank account numbers, bank routing numbers, names, addresses, SSNs, and other information.
- Always remember that the red flag up on rural boxes can alert would-be crooks that there is mail in the box. I often say that the red flag in the up position screams "steal me" to mail thieves.
- If your employer allows it, take your outgoing mail to work and place with the company's outgoing mail.
- If your mail receptacle has a locking device, make sure it works. If it does not, install either a new lock or a new secure mailbox with a sturdy lock.
- Notify your post office to issue a hold on your mail during vacation or business trips so that mail does not accumulate in your box. You can now do this online at https://holdmail.usps.com/duns/HoldMail.jsp.
- Report any suspicious activity around your mail receptacle, your letter carrier, his or her vehicle, other residential mailboxes, and collection boxes, to your local police department and the Postal Inspection Service. Postal Inspectors actively investigate mail theft complaints.
- Report nonreceipt of valuable mail as soon as possible by calling the bank or financial institution, credit card issuers, and the Postal Inspection Service.

The U.S. Postal Inspection Service offers a reward up to $10,000 for information and services leading to the arrest and conviction of any person for mail theft. Mail theft is a federal felony and upon conviction may be punishable by a fine of up to $250,000 and imprisonment up to five years, or both. If you suspect anyone of mail theft, please contact the Postal Inspection Service.

## 6. Practice Computer and Internet Safety

Ensure that your computer has adequate firewall protection and current operating system software. Organized identity theft groups are remotely loading spyware, malware, and Trojan horses on victim computers. These programs transmit your keystrokes and other stored computer files to suspects. The newest trend in identity theft is botnets. People who do not maintain current versions of their operating software and firewall software are susceptible to being a part of a botnet.

Be on the lookout for phishing and related scams. Always be suspicious of unsolicited emails asking for personal or financial information. Do not respond to phishing emails from financial institutions requiring an update of personal and banking information. Legitimate requests for personal information are generally not conducted by email. Suspect emails requesting this information will contain an internet hyperlink that directs the victim to a suspect Web site containing fields for victim personal information. Do not use public computers in libraries, hotels, coffee shops, or other public venues for online financial transactions. Public computers may be infected with spyware and viruses that may subject you and your personal information to fraud and misuse.

Never open unknown attachments or download questionable software. Never open attachments or download any software from sites that you are not 100% certain of. The same goes for pop-ups. Criminals may offer you free music, antivirus protection, or other applications. If you fall for it and download this, spyware may be installed on your computer. Once installed, identity thieves can use this spyware to record your keystrokes and obtain passwords, bank account information, and other sensitive information. Keep your computer safe by installing updated antivirus and antispyware software, and adequate firewalls.

Enable password protection on your personal computer. Use a password to log on to your computer and a password to get back on after your screen saver goes on if you leave your computer on. Encrypt your home wireless computer network. Fraudsters will drive around residential neighborhoods and businesses to locate unsecured wireless networks. They use these unsecured networks to facilitate fraud and other unauthorized activity. Microsoft (www.microsoft.com/security) offers excellent tips, guidance, and software for individuals and businesses on improving security of their computers and networks.

Always use strong passwords to protect against unauthorized access. Do not use words, names, or phrases that can be easily connected to an individual. The longer the password, the better. It should be at least eight characters in length; 14 characters or more is best. Random letters, numbers, punctuation, and symbols that are not repeated are the strongest. Microsoft offers an excellent password checker to gauge the level of security for any given password. Simply go to www.microsoft.com/protect/yourself/password/checker.mspx and enter your password. The strength of the password will be displayed as either weak, medium, strong, or best. Also be sure to change passwords on a regular basis.

**Exhibit 20.2   NCL's Six Tips for Shopping Safely Online**

The National Consumers League (NCL) has been advocating for consumers for more than a century. The NCL provides government, businesses, and other organizations with the consumer's perspective on a wide variety of social issues including fraud prevention and privacy concerns. Here are the NCL's Six Tips for Shopping Safely Online:

1. **Get the scoop on the seller.** Check complaint records at your state or local consumer protection agency and Better Business Bureau. Get the physical address and phone number to contact the seller offline. Look for sellers belonging to programs that encourage good business practices and help resolve complaints.

2. **Use a credit card.** It's the safest way to pay because you have the legal right to dispute charges for goods or services that were never ordered, never received, or misrepresented.

3. **Ask your credit card issuer about "substitute" or "single-use" credit card numbers.** This new technology allows you to use your credit card without putting your real account number online, protecting it from abuse and hackers or dishonest employees of the seller.

4. **Look for clues about safety.** When you provide payment information, the "http" at the beginning of the address bar should change to "https" or "shttp" (the "s" stands for secure). Your browser may show whether the information is being encrypted, or scrambled, as it is being sent. See what Web sites say about how they safeguard your information in transmission and storage. Don't provide sensitive information by email.

5. **Know the "real deal".** Get all the details before you buy: a complete description of the item, the total price (including shipping), the delivery time, warranty information, the return policy, and what to do and who to call if you have any problem.

6. **Keep proof handy.** Always print and file the information in case you need proof of this purchase later.

Source: National Consumers' League Six Tips for Shopping Safely Online, www.nclnet.org/shoppingonline/ shoppingtips.htm

Be extra careful when online. The Internet is your entrance to the marketplace for the world from the comfort of your home or office. While it is the way we do business and communicate today, there are also safety concerns when it comes to identity theft and fraud. Never use your credit or debit card at any Web site unless it offers a secure transaction. Secure or encrypted transactions have an icon of a miniature lock that appears in the Web browser. Yet just seeing the miniature lock may not be enough. Highly skilled scammers can replicate the miniature lock on sites, giving the false impression of a secure site. If in doubt, click off any suspicious Web sites. In addition, the URL address for the Web page changes from "http" to "https" indicating a secure site for you to input your personal information.

Deal only with reputable online merchants, and always use your credit card in case of fraud. By using your credit card rather than a debit card or check, you are covered for fraud losses, should they occur. Federal law limits consumer losses to a maximum of $50, but credit card companies rarely enforce this.

## 7. Be Cautious at ATMs

Identity thieves have been known to place skimming devices over ATM slots to steal card account information. Look for suspicious devices on the front of the ATM. Check for exposed wires, tape, or loose connections. Look for hidden cameras on the sides of the ATM that criminals use to record ATM passwords. If the ATM card slot, keypad, or any part of the ATM does not look right or if you can move or remove them, do not use the machine and alert the bank representatives. Be aware of those people who may have too much of an interest in your ATM transaction—the ones who are trying to look over your shoulder to see what you are doing. They may be shoulder surfers attempting to see your account balance or PIN. A recommended practice is to use one hand as a shield to cover your other hand as you enter your PIN.

Be extra careful when using ATMs with an unfamiliar brand name and suspicious-looking card readers. Always be aware of the threat of skimming devices at other places, such as restaurants, convenience stores, hotels, gasoline stations, and public places outside banks. If in doubt about using a particular ATM, go to another one. The same applies to purchasing at restaurants and other locations. You can always consider paying in cash to limit possible data loss.

Be on the lookout for shoulder surfers at locations other than ATMs. At the store checkout line when you are writing out your check for the cashier, make sure that someone is not looking over your shoulder to obtain your checking account number or other information from your driver's license.

Do not leave your receipts at the ATM. Although they usually do not contain your complete information, they often have the last four digits of your account and list your balance. Why leave any amount of information for others to see? The same goes for receipts at stores or gasoline stations. Take them with you and shred them when no longer needed.

## 8. Opt Out of Sharing Your Information

Consumers generally have the choice regarding how much information they want to share with marketing firms, companies, and certain government agencies. In this information age, information about you is frequently shared with multiple business partners for product offerings, services, and promotions. You can "opt out" of having your personal information disclosed to others. For example, by removing your name from the major commercial marketing databases, unsolicited mailings, including catalogs, will be reduced.

The FTC has created a one-page information site that provides detailed information and links to allow consumers to opt out of information sharing related to credit bureaus, various state departments of motor vehicles, and direct marketers. This excellent resource site can be found at www.ftc.gov/privacy/protect.shtm. A sample opt-out form letter is also available at the FTC site. The information that is found at the FTC site is summarized in the following paragraphs.The Direct Marketing Association (DMA) is the leading global trade association of business and nonprofit organizations involved in direct marketing. As it states on its Web site, the DMA advocates industry standards for responsible marketing and their "Mail Preference Service (MPS), which was created in 1971, is designed to help consumers decrease the amount of nationally generated commercial or nonprofit mail they receive at home."[1] In simple terms, this is the ability to opt out of direct mail marketing, telemarketing, and other direct email marketing from many national companies. The DMA offers various ways to opt out, including via the U.S. mail, telephone, or email.

You can opt out of direct mail marketing by sending a letter to:

Direct Marketing Association
Mail Preference Service
PO Box 9008
Farmingdale, NY 11735-9008

Further information about opting out of direct mail marketing can be found at www.dmachoice.org/MPS/mps_consumer_description.php.

You can opt-out of telemarketing calls by sending a letter to:

Direct Marketing Association
Telephone Preference Service
PO Box 9014
Farmingdale, NY 11735-9014

Further information about opting out of telephone marketing can be found at www.dmachoice.org/TPS/.

You can opt-out of direct email marketing at www.dmachoice.org/emps.php.

The three major credit bureaus offer you the opportunity to opt out of receiving preapproved credit offers. This can be done by calling one telephone number: 1-888-5-OPTOUT (1-888-567-8688). This one call will cover all three credit bureaus. As an alternative, you can mail a letter to each credit bureau requesting that it not share personal information with others for promotional reasons. A sample opt-out letter can be found at www.ftc.gov/privacy/cred-ltr.htm. The mailing addresses for the three credit bureaus to request an opt-out are:

Equifax, Inc.
PO Box 740123
Atlanta, GA 30374-0123

Experian
Consumer Opt-Out
701 Experian Parkway
Allen, TX 75013

Trans Union
Name Removal Option
PO Box 97328
Jackson, MS 39288-7328

## 9. Keep a Credit Inventory

Prepare an inventory of everything you carry in your wallet or purse. Write down or photocopy the account numbers of credit cards, expiration dates, credit card verification numbers, the names of the issuers, and the 800 contact telephone numbers to call to cancel your existing accounts in case of loss or theft. The credit card verification number on an American Express card is the four-digit number imprinted on the upper right side of the front of the card. For MasterCard, Visa, and Diners Club, it is the last three numbers on the signature panel on the back of the card.

Do not keep this inventory list in your wallet or purse. Keep it in a secure place in your residence that you can access easily if necessary. Photocopy the fronts and backs of your credit cards as well as all other identification documents. In addition, keep a detailed list of all your bank and brokerage account numbers and numbers to call if you suspect they have been used fraudulently. Back up your personal digital assistants (PDA); better yet, do not keep any personal or financial information on them. If you do, be sure to have them password protected.

## 10. Review Your Financial Statements Each Month

Make sure you thoroughly review and reconcile all the charges on each of your credit card accounts and other financial statements each month. Even if you do not find unauthorized charges that may be indicative of identity theft, you may find double charges or other mistakes that need to be corrected. Cancel credit card accounts that you do not use or need. Be aware that doing this can affect your credit score, especially if the card is one that you have had for many years.

Guard your checkbook. Report any lost or stolen checks to your bank or financial institution immediately. Properly store or dispose of canceled checks. Take a few minutes to review your canceled checks when they are returned with your monthly statement. Look to see if the payee name or amount paid was changed. Provide your checking account information only to reputable businesses or individuals. Do not provide this information to someone you do not know, even if he or she claims to be from your bank.

If you have had your checking or bank accounts compromised, contact the check guarantee company TeleCheck at the toll-free telephone number (800-366-2425) or online at www.firstdata.com/support/telecheck_consumer_services/telecheck_forgery_ idtheft.htm. Your account will be flagged so that counterfeit checks will be refused.

Know the billing cycles for your credit cards. Identity thieves have been known to submit change-of-address orders to the Postal Service in order to obtain the mail of potential victims. The diverted mail is received at a location controlled by the scammer, either a mail drop or a temporary residence used for this purpose. The indication will be that you are not receiving mail. More often, industrious fraudsters "cherrypick" your mailbox after the mail carrier delivers your mail but before you pick it up. This is more common with rural mailboxes or house letter boxes that do not have locking mechanisms. Be on the lookout for credit card, bank, and brokerage statements that do not arrive or arrive late. Identity thief Jeffrey Webster Lawson, profiled in Chapter 3, specialized in recycling stolen mail.

## 11. Destroy Your Old PC's Hard Drive Before Discarding

When you buy that brand-new desktop or laptop, what will you do with your old one? Many people and businesses discard them with the hard drive intact. That is a recipe for disaster. Studies have found that fewer than 25% of disposed computers have their data erased. That means that your most sensitive personal and financial information is available to whoever obtains the computer. In 2000, former Beatle Paul McCartney's banking information was discovered on a computer discarded by a financial services firm in the United Kingdom. The company had done nothing to delete the sensitive information from the computer.

A few years ago, a privacy expert purchased 158 hard drives on eBay to see how much data was left on them by their former owners. To his amazement, he found more than 5,000 credit card numbers, financial accounts, medical records, email, and other personal information. Even more surprising, on the 51 hard drives that supposedly had been wiped clean, 19 had data he was able to recover.[2] Computer owners need to know that deleting a file does not completely erase it. Although the file is not visible in the directory, the data is still on the drive. "The data is still available, and the drive writes over it, but not completely," says a representative of hard drive manufacturer Maxtor. "Only recording over this data many times with a random series of ones and zeroes will remove the original."[3] Even doing that is no guarantee that erased data cannot eventually be recovered.

Software is available to wipe hard drives clean, but computer forensic experts have been known to recover information even on wiped drives. There continue to be instances of people who sold their old PCs on Internet auction sites or donated them to charity with supposedly completely wiped drives but the deleted information was easily recovered by forensic specialists. Identity thieves are doing the same so you must protect yourself. Always remove the hard drive (or drives if your computer has more than one) and physically destroy it. Drill holes through it or smash it with a hammer into little pieces. The same goes for your PDA, cell phones, flash drives, and other portable digital devices that you are discarding.

## 12. Be Careful with Product Warranty Cards

When you buy an appliance or other type of home electronics, you normally receive a product warranty card to complete and mail in to the manufacturer. The stated purpose is to register the product that consumers purchase. In most cases, the information on the warranty cards is used for marketing databases. These cards can yield significant personal information that can be sold for marketing purposes. The amount of personal information requested, such as questions on annual income and other sensitive financial information, can be excessive and are not needed except for marketing purposes. There is a good chance that any information you provide will find its way into the hands of a marketing firm.

Although they are usually called product warranty cards, you generally do not have to submit them for the product warranty to be in effect. Most manufacturers provide limited warranties on their products. Under federal law, a company can require a purchaser to register their products in order to receive the limited warranty, but in reality this is not very common. Some states, such as California, prohibit manufacturers from making the warranty contingent on registration with the company.

Often the warranty cards are postcards that, if returned, could potentially expose your information to anyone processing the card. My suggestion is not to return any warranty cards unless absolutely necessary. If you must complete one, be sure it is sealed in an envelope before mailing. That will keep prying eyes away but will still expose your information to marketing databases and future contact.

## 13. Review Your Social Security Earnings and Benefits Statements

Carefully review your Social Security Earnings and Benefits Statements when received each year. Review them for accuracy as well as indications that someone else may be using your SSN. These U.S. government forms are usually mailed out approximately three months prior to one's birthday. If you suspect fraud involving this statement or your SSN, contact the Social Security Administration's Fraud Hotline at 800-269-0271.

In addition, the Social Security Administration advises that you will not automatically receive a Social Security Statement if:

- you are under age 25, or
- you are already receiving Social Security benefits, or
- a current mailing address is not on file, or
- you are age 62 or older and receiving Social Security benefits on someone else's record, or
- you are a Medicare beneficiary, or
- you requested a statement within the past 11 months.

## 14. Use Privacy Screens

Buy and use a privacy screen on your laptop when traveling, at coffee shops, and at other public spots. These screens ensure the privacy of your on-screen data by making it visible only to someone directly in front of the screen. Such screens can keep prying eyes off your personal documents especially when you are traveling in cramped spaces, such as on airplanes. Although privacy screens are very effective in limiting what others can see, it is always good to be vigilant. You may not want to work on an extremely sensitive document on an airplane or in a public place even if you have a privacy screen.

## 15. If It Sounds Too Good to Be True, It Is

Scam artists often use the mails and the telephone, as well as the Internet, for misrepresentations and deception. They will offer "free" five-day, four-night cruises to the Bahamas, expensive consumer electronics, and other prizes to obtain personal and financial information for identity theft. They may pose as government officials, bank officers, or representatives of legitimate companies and use high-pressure sales tactics. These fraudsters are trying to sell you the "sizzle but not the steak" and are intent on defrauding you. Do not fall for their trickery.

Do not respond to emails soliciting advance-fee business arrangements. These solicitations ask recipients to provide bank account information in order to transfer a large sum of money. Recipients supposedly will be paid a percentage of the money as an administrative fee. Do not respond to emails soliciting overseas reshipment arrangements. These solicitations also ask recipients to act as an import/export business and reship product (usually electronics) overseas. The products victims ship are usually fraudulently purchased and may involve credit card fraud and identity theft. Victims pay the shipping costs and are promised reimbursement at a later time. Do not respond to email solicitations where you will receive financial instruments, such as checks and money orders, that you have to deposit in your bank account. In such cases, you are asked to send a portion back to the solicitor but are allowed to keep a percentage of the total funds as an administrative fee. The financial instruments are counterfeit.

These "dialing for dollars" criminals use their silver tongues to get unsuspecting victims to part with their money, financial information, and identities. Always be careful to whom you give your credit card number or other information, whether over the telephone or via the Internet. If in doubt, do not give your number. No matter how fraudsters reach out to you, it is always wise to remember that if something sounds too good to be true, it usually is.

## 16. Watch Out for Skimming

Although this is not the easiest thing to do, attempt to minimize the use of credit and debit cards in restaurants and retail establishments where employees take possession of your card and walk across the room to complete the transaction. Criminals involved in identity theft will retrieve the data stored on your credit card by swiping your card on a credit card skimming device. These devices are small enough that they can be secreted in a subject's pocket. The data is then downloaded to a computer and used for identity theft.

If you can, try to keep a restaurant server in sight or pay at the register. If in doubt, pay cash and avoid the use of cards. Wireless technology that will allow diners to swipe their cards in a handheld device at their table is slowly making its way to restaurants. This innovation will limit the opportunity for skimming.

## 17. Prevent Data Breaches

Data breaches and the resulting damage can be reduced if businesses and government agencies take these safeguards:

- Limit the amount of sensitive data stored on employee laptops. Far too much personally identifiable information (PII) than is necessary is kept on laptops.
- Implement company polices around data storage, data breaches, laptop security, and use of encryption.
- Install and require the use of encryption software on laptops that contain sensitive data.
- Educate employees about the benefit of encryption and hold them accountable if they fail to use it.
- If existing computers cannot enable encryption due to age or other limitations, replace them with newer ones that can.
- Require employees to certify that they have encryption installed, are trained in its use, are using it, and understand the consequences for noncompliance.
- Consider disabling USB ports and the use of portable digital devices as appropriate.
- Use secure Internet locations at all times when traveling.
- Do not use computers or digital copiers in hotel office centers.
- Consider using biometric authentication, such as fingerprint scans, in order to log on.
- Turn off computers when leaving the office at the end of the day.
- Although the use of cable locks to secure laptops is better than using nothing, it is better to lock the computer in a desk or cabinet.
- Secure peripherals such as backup drives, flash drives, and other storage sites used for data.
- Do not leave laptops in a hotel room when traveling. Lock them in the room safe or the hotel safe if possible. At last resort, place them in locked luggage. The vulnerability of laptops to theft is but one more reason for encryption.

## 18. Place Fraud Alerts

Fraud alerts are notifications placed on credit reports to alert creditors that a person's personal and financial information may have been compromised. This allows creditors to personally contact the registrant and verify all credit applications prior to approval. Fraud alerts are advisory in nature and good only if the credit bureau sees them and follows up with the victim. While they often work, in some instances lenders either did not see the notices or chose not to act on them. Credit bureaus have made it easier to place fraud alerts on a consumer's credit file but have no way to enforce action on a fraud alert request.

There are two types of fraud alerts, initial and extended. The initial fraud alert is in effect for at least 90 days and is generally used when there is a suspicion of account compromise and identity theft, such as responding to a phishing scheme. Consumers are entitled to one free credit report from each of the three major credit reporting agencies after requesting an initial fraud alert. The extended alert stays in effect for seven years. This form of alert is used after confirmation of identity theft victimization. To be eligible for extended alerts, consumers must provide credit reporting agencies with a copy of an identity theft report filed with a local, state, or federal law enforcement agency. With extended alerts, consumers also receive free credit reports.

You can also subscribe to a credit monitoring service, which notifies you via email, text message, or telephone of any change to your credit report. Any changes, such as credit inquiries and new credit accounts, are reported to the subscriber for appropriate action. A number of credit monitoring services offering protection from identity theft have sprung up in recent years. For a fee, they monitor your credit reports for red flags of fraud and then take action on your behalf. Much of what they do is readily available to all consumers through free services. One widely advertised credit monitoring service has become the focus of media scrutiny and civil lawsuits for its identity theft protection claims. More details on this story can be found in the next chapter. If you decide to use a credit monitoring service, make sure you do research and decide if it is in your best interest.

## 19. Use Credit Freezes

Credit freezes are a relatively new way to block your credit from potential misuse and identity theft. Credit freezes block a prospective credit card issuer or lender from issuing new credit in a person's name without obtaining specific approval from that person. A credit freeze prevents credit bureaus from issuing your credit score. Without that information, few if any lenders will issue credit. It effectively blocks the issuance of instant credit, as is often seen when stores offer big discounts on purchases if a new credit card is opened at the same time.

Credit freezes are expected to become significant weapons to lessen the spread of identity theft. "The credit freeze, out of anything else that's been conceived, has the potential to be the most effective tool for preventing crooks from fraudulently using your Social Security number," said a cofounder of an identity protection firm.[4] Only time will tell if this is true; for now, credit freezes are another prevention strategy to consider.

## 20. Stay Informed

The best way to prevent identity theft is to stay informed about the problem. Government agencies are doing a very good job at telling the public about how to prevent identity theft. In February 2008, the United States Postal Service embarked on a national education campaign, sending a mailing providing identity theft awareness materials to every home in the United States. The letter advised that a recent FTC survey found only 2% of all victims reported the theft of their identity connected to the mail. Still, the Postal Service wanted to do even more to reduce that number. The letter discussed the role of the Postal Inspection Service in investigating identity theft, and protecting the mail and postal customers. Inserted in the envelope was the FTC's excellent brochure entitled *Detect·Detect·Defend: Avoid ID Theft*. The brochure contained helpful tips, telephone numbers, Web sites, and steps to take to prevent identity theft. That information can also be found at www.ftc.gov/idtheft.

**Exhibit 20.3   FTC's Tips for Organizing Your Case**

The Federal Trade Commission offers these excellent tips on organizing your case if you become a victim of identity theft.

Accurate and complete records will help you to resolve your identity theft case more quickly.

- Have a plan when you contact a company. Don't assume that the person you talk to will give you all the information or help you need. Prepare a list of questions to ask the representative, as well as information about your identity theft. Don't end the call until you're sure you understand everything you've been told. If you need more help, ask to speak to a supervisor.

- Write down the name of everyone you talk to, what he or she tells you, and the date the conversation occurred.

- Follow-up in writing with all contacts you've made on the phone or in person. Use certified mail, return receipt requested, so you can document what the company or organization received and when.

- Keep copies of all correspondence or forms you send.

- Keep the originals of supporting documentation, like police reports and letters to and from creditors; send copies only.

- Set up a filing system for easy access to your paperwork.

- Keep old files even if you believe your case is closed. Once resolved, most cases stay resolved, but problems can crop up.

Source: *Take Charge: Fighting Back Against Identity Theft*, Federal Trade Commission, February 2005, www.ftc.gov/bcp/edu/pubs/consumer/idtheft/idt04.shtm

## 21. If You Become a Victim

If you learn that you are a victim of identity theft, immediately contact the fraud departments of the three major credit bureaus as well as the related credit card companies and financial institutions. Request that the credit bureaus place a fraud alert in your file as well as a credit freeze.

Order copies of your credit report from the three major credit bureaus to determine the extent of your victimization. Thoroughly review your reports for fraudulent activity. Besides fraudulent accounts opened, look for listed "inquiries" that are indicative of either opened or about-to-be-opened accounts. Contact those affected accounts for reporting and closing. By closing the affected accounts, you will be protected from any fraud that may occur. Order new cards and account numbers as appropriate. It is a good idea to request credit reports again several months later to confirm that the credit bureaus made the necessary corrections by removing the fraudulent accounts.

Always report the crime to the local police and obtain a copy of the report. If the police agency does not want to take a report or provide a copy, be persistent. Police reports are important in establishing the criminal activity and the facts. Also make a report to the federal law enforcement agencies focused on identity theft crimes such as the Postal

Inspection Service and the Secret Service. Both agencies have national jurisdictions and can easily investigate cases involving activity in multiple states. Both agencies are also actively conducting investigations outside of the United States as identity theft becomes international in scope.

File an identity theft complaint with the Federal Trade Commission. The FTC is mandated by legislation as the federal clearinghouse for identity theft complaints. It does not conduct criminal investigations based on the complaints but provides detailed information and assistance to victims to resolve financial and other problems resulting from victimization. The FTC does provide complaint information to other government agencies and private organizations for possible follow-up action. The FTC complaint form and related information can be found at www.ftc.gov/bcp/edu/microsites/idtheft/consumers/filing-a-report.html.

If your identity theft was the result of a data breach, there are additional things you can do. Check your data breach notification rights. These rights vary by state, but a number of states have notification requirements. These requirements include the details of the breach, what data was stolen, and steps to protect yourself. California was the first state to enact a data breach notification law, and it has served as a model for other states. There are two excellent online sites for information on the varying state laws on breach notification. They are: www.consumersunion.org/campaigns/Breach_laws_May05.pdf and www.ncsl.org/programs/lis/cip/priv/breach.htm.

Take identity theft seriously. Simply reporting the fraud by telephone is not enough. People have short memories, and representatives of financial institutions can move from job to job. Document the events in writing and create a paper trail that you can refer to if necessary. Do not assume that your work is over once you report the occurrence to law enforcement, your banks and credit card companies, and the major credit bureaus. Continuous follow-up is required, possibly for years, to ensure that your identity is not still being fraudulently used. It is your responsibility to monitor your accounts and history.

## NOTES

1. Direct Marketing Association, Consumer Information and Preference Services, www.dmachoice.org/consumerassistance.php.
2. Jefferson Graham, "Erased Hard Drives Can Bite You," *USA Today*, February 5, 2003, www.usatoday.com/tech/news/2003-02-05-drive_x.htm.
3. Ibid.
4. Byron Acohido and Jon Swartz, "Credit Bureaus Fight on State, Federal Levels against Freezes," *USA Today,* June 26, 2007, 1B.

# CHAPTER 21

# Future of Identity Theft

Identity theft is the world's fastest-growing crime. It was the crime of the 1990s and now it is the crime of the new millennium. Nothing has been able to stop its spread. Its impact is felt by individuals, businesses, and governments everywhere. Almost everyone knows someone who is a victim of this crime or else has been a victim him- or herself. Not a week goes by when there is not some mention in the media of an identity theft case, an unauthorized disclosure of personal information, or a congressional outcry about this unrelenting crime. The sad fact is that identity theft has grown and evolved into a worldwide problem.

Consumers and businesses are continually warned about the need to be vigilant against this threat. Protecting your personal information, checking your credit, and improving your computer security are vital requirements for identity theft avoidance. "Identity theft is most often a crime of convenience. If you can make it difficult to steal your information, a thief may look elsewhere for an easier target."[1] Robust prevention is the best answer we now have, and Chapter 20 presented a multitude of prevention approaches. Although these approaches can be very effective in protecting pathways to vulnerability, there are no guarantees that one will never fall victim to identity theft because so much of identity theft is beyond the control of potential victims. You can follow all the prescribed prevention practices detailed in this book, but one corrupt employee in a credit reporting service can supersede your best deterrence efforts.

Technology may one day advance to such a degree that identity theft is no longer an issue, but that day is not in the foreseeable future. Technology definitely plays an important role in protecting us—maintaining a strong firewall, installing antivirus software, and updating computer software—but there is still another element at play: the human factor. "The most insidious Internet security problems today rely on human gullibility, not tricky software."[2] The term often used is "social engineering," which is a fancy phrase for conning victims into providing information they normally would not supply. Fraudsters are masters of deceit. Reformed fraudster Barry Minkow is fond of saying that fraud "is the skin of the truth stuffed with a lie," and that sums it up pretty well. Why else would a smart person willingly provide personal information to someone who calls on the telephone or sends a phishing email? Human greed, naiveté, and frailty ensure that fraud and identity theft will be around for quite a while. We as a society need to get much better at education and awareness to reduce human gullibility.

Biometrics has long been looked to as a cure-all, but it has not gained universal acceptance. The term "biometrics" is defined as the biological identification of a person using that person's specific body characteristics, such as fingerprints, iris and retinal patterns, voice, facial shape, and hand measurements for authentication purposes. Laptops are available with fingerprint sensors, but they are not common. The same applies to cell phones. Biometric locks have a very limited availability in the United States. Other countries have a different perspective. In Japan, for example, "cell phones are increasingly used as a mobile 'wallet' to pay for goods and services—they can be swiped over payment processors for everything from subway rides to Big Macs— fingerprint sensors are used to unlock the phones' data and payment capabilities."[3] Americans must join their consumer cousins in Japan and adapt this new biometric technology to protect against fraud.

## PREDICTING THE FUTURE

Much to my chagrin, in articles I authored and speeches given in years past, I predicted many of the issues we see today. Identity theft would become a problem in other countries as criminals used stolen identities globally. High-net-worth individuals would continue to be targeted due to their high profiles, financial status, and availability of their personal information. The widespread use of the Internet and easy access to personal information would contribute to cyberstalking and online bullying. Violence will play a role in some identity theft cases—albeit and luckily a very small number. In the most serious instances, victims may be forced to obtain a new Social Security number (SSN) and credit profile.

There have been other trends. Culprits have committed serious crimes and used stolen identities for identification when apprehended by the police. For 17 years, a man in Salt Lake City lived a nightmarish existence when a career criminal took over his identity and committed a string of crimes including burglary, assault, making a bomb threat, vandalism, and driving under the influence. Each time the fraudster was arrested, he used the stolen identity. In another case, a Pennsylvania man learned that a violent felon who had murdered a police officer was booked under his stolen name when appre-hended. The defendant was charged and convicted of murder in his name. Imagine having to live with the stigma of your good name associated with a cop killer.

Scammers are filing bankruptcy claims using stolen identities to avoid paying debts, and stop evictions, and foreclosures. Some identity thieves are using this approach after they have run up large debts using the name and credit of others. Once a bankruptcy case is filed, an automatic stay goes into effect. This effectively stops all debt collection proceedings against the person filing bankruptcy (the identity thief). Ultimately, this fraudulent bankruptcy claim comes back to haunt the victim of the identity theft. The unknowing victim now faces all the implications of identity theft as well as bankruptcy proceedings. One serious consequence is the court record of filing a bankruptcy action will appear on the victim's credit report, thus impacting credit.

The evolution of identity theft is producing new types of the crime. *Synthetic identity fraud* combines true and phony identifying information to establish new identities for fraudulent purposes. For example, a legitimate SSN may be paired with a different name and different date of birth to open bank and credit accounts. There is a dispute about how common this new fraud is. ID Analytics, a San Diego–based analytic software and risk management services company, reported in 2005 that synthetic identity fraud was responsible for 88% of all identity theft occurrences, including opening fraudulent financial accounts and change-of-address orders. Yet a February 2008 Identity Fraud Survey Report from Javelin Strategy & Research called synthetic identity fraud a very rare form of crime. Either way, we can expect to see this and other variations of identity theft in the future.

There is also the question as to whether the occurrence of identity theft is growing or declining. Credit card fraud, a crime closely tied to identity theft, has steadily increased from $1.46 billion in 1997 to $5.49 billion in 2007.[4] If we are to believe the Javelin Strategy & Research February 2008 study, identity theft is on the decline: "Although both the total number of victims and overall monetary losses have steadily decreased over the past four years, consumers and their financial institutions must continue to take protective measures against this serious crime."[5] The study interviewed 442 victims by telephone and came to this remarkable conclusion. A related Javelin Strategy & Research study from May 2008 states: "Once noted as the nation's fastest growing crime, identity fraud will experience a steady decrease in number of victims and total one-year fraud amounts from 2008 to 2013."[6] It should be noted that these studies examined identity theft in the United States; they did not address the march of identity theft elsewhere in the world. If these studies were truly global in nature, I have no doubt that the findings would be far different.

The end result of the evolution and variations of identity theft are many, and all are bad. Ruined credit, denial of employment or a place to live, getting arrested for crimes you did not commit, garnishment of wages, loss of a driver's license, along with financial loss, emotional toll, and reputational harm are but some of the results. When people supposedly in the know tell you not to worry because identity theft is on the decline or the average dollar loss is small, be skeptical. Clearly, they have never faced firsthand the nightmares of so many victims.

## MAKING MONEY FROM IDENTITY THEFT

Identity theft is a very lucrative crime. It is extremely profitable for fraudsters, but it is also big business for opportunistic entrepreneurs who offer a slew of protection services. Over the last few years, numerous identity theft protection service companies have sprung up, intent on protecting consumers and businesses from identity theft, all for a fee. These companies offer credit monitoring, fraud alerts, credit freezes, and database mining of public records to determine if personal information is inappropriately available. These firms advertise their services widely through various media venues. Many consumers have signed up for ongoing monitoring of their credit reports and other services.

But many questions beg to be answered regarding these services. Are they as effective as advertised? Are people already at risk by identity thieves now being taken advantage of by a new group of opportunistic individuals? Just who are the operators of these businesses and what are their backgrounds? Are consumers really getting a beneficial service for which they have to pay that they could easily get for free?

The new companies, including Debix, LifeLock, TrustedID, among many others, plus new services from the three major credit bureaus have attracted many new customers. Start-up companies have raised tens of millions of dollars in venture capital funds to start and expand their businesses.

The most prominent of these companies is LifeLock, which advertises heavily on the Internet, radio, television, and in print. In these commercials, the company's chief executive, Todd Davis, openly publicizes his SSN as a sign of faith in his company's ability to protect his identity. He has even gone so far as to shout it out via megaphone while walking down crowded city streets. These attention-getting devices have brought the company a tremendous amount of notice as well as notoriety.

LifeLock works by setting up fraud alerts for the customer. "When fraud alerts are established with the major credit bureaus, creditors are required to verify [one's] identity before opening any new lines of credit, issuing new cards or increasing [one's] credit limit."[7] LifeLock, like other credit-monitoring companies, monitors customers' credit to detect signs of identity theft. The company also automatically renews fraud alerts, which expire after 90 days. In addition, LifeLock offers services that "scour known criminal websites for the illegal selling or trading of your personal information," and alert customers to unauthorized address changes.[8] If identity theft does occur, LifeLock offers a $1 million guarantee to remedy any incidents. According to the LifeLock Web site:

> *If your Identity is stolen while you are a member of LifeLock, we're going to do whatever it takes to recover your good name. . . . If you lose money as a result of the theft, we're going to give it back to you. We will do whatever it takes to help you recover your good name and we will spend up to $1,000,000 to do it.*[9]

Looking beyond the hype, how much do consumers really know about LifeLock? Todd Davis and Arizona businessman Robert J. Maynard founded the company in 2005. Davis, LifeLock's present pitchman, is well known for hawking his SSN, but what about Maynard? The allegations surrounding the company, and in particular cofounder and former marketing executive Maynard, should be enough to give any potential customer pause.

Maynard "claimed he got the idea for LifeLock after spending a week in jail in 2003,"[10] after, as he put it, he was falsely arrested for failing to pay back a $16,000 loan to a Las Vegas casino. Allegedly, "[o]ne of the guys who stole Maynard's identity and the casino's money is doing time for murder. Maynard was released after seven days, but he spent more than $20,000 and countless hours on the telephone trying to clear his name."[11] Maynard and Davis presented this story far and wide as the ultimate nightmare in identity theft;[12] however, unlike the many similar stories described here, this was no case of mistaken identity. An investigation by the Phoenix, Arizona, *New Times*, confirmed by the District Attorney's Office in Clark County, Nevada, revealed that the person who took out the casino marker was . . . Robert Maynard. Maynard used his own driver's license to obtain the marker, which under Nevada law acts just like a check.[13]

The rest of Maynard's story is true, just not the way he presents it to be. He was arrested and ultimately did have to spend more than $20,000 to clear up the case. Nevada law allows violators to avoid criminal charges if they pay back the loan plus fees, which is why Maynard was not convicted. Furthermore, according to Bernie Zadrowski, Chief Deputy District Attorney in Clark County, Maynard never filed a police report for identify theft nor did anyone involved in the case every suggest it was a case of mistaken identity. In fact, due to the high prevalence of identity theft in Nevada, "forgery packets" are given to anyone claiming to be a victim of identity theft.[14] As Zadrowski put it, "We could show beyond a shadow of a doubt that [Maynard] was the one who committed the crime."[15]

Maynard has filed for bankruptcy several times, including once for his company Internet America, an early Internet service provider.[16] Maynard was also banned by the Federal Trade Commission (FTC) in 1997 from engaging in the credit repair business after the FTC and the State of Arizona sued Maynard's company National Credit Foundation for fraud and misrepresentation.[17] In one of the case's more shocking allegations, especially considering the amount of personal information customers must entrust to LifeLock, the FTC charged that Maynard and the other defendants withdrew money from consumers' accounts without authorization.[18]

In 1999, someone ordered an American Express card in Maynard's father's name and had the bills sent to an address that matched that of Maynard's company at the time. His father, while unable to offer significant details regarding the case due to ongoing litigation, "says the 'premise' that his son fraudulently ordered the card is accurate."[19] LifeLock publicly stated that there was no merit to the claims made against Maynard, but he resigned in June 2007. Nevertheless, Maynard retained his 10% stake in the company and continued to provide marketing services as an outside consultant.[20]

The failed businesses, the bankruptcies, the arrest for an unpaid debt, the action taken by the FTC to forcibly remove him from the credit repair business, and the allegation of identity theft should make customers question whether LifeLock, Maynard's creation, should be the one to protect them from scammers.

As evidence of the comprehensive security of his company, Davis has consistently stated that his identity had never been stolen or compromised. However, after numerous media outlets reported on the frequent identity theft attempts against him, including a successful case in Texas, Davis publicly acknowledged the attempts. In this case, a Texas man used Davis's SSN to obtain a $500 loan; the payday loan company acknowledged that it did not run the proper checks on the SSN. Davis stated that the "'incident proves that LifeLock works, because I was never out a dime of my own money or a minute of my own time.'"[21] Davis's statements regarding this incident seem to indicate that it was inconsequential and had no bearing on the company's effectiveness or credibility. But LifeLock's actions severely undermine its own assertions.

According to Fort Worth, Texas, police, Davis and his associates interfered with the police investigation, to the point that their actions forced local prosecutors to drop the case. A private investigator hired by LifeLock ran a parallel investigation into the case. While the police awaited subpoenaed records to solidify the case, Davis and others, despite police warnings, personally confronted the suspect and videotaped his confession.[22] According to Fort Worth Sergeant J. D. Moore, they "yelled" and "browbeat" the suspect, a mentally disabled man, until they coerced a confession from him. Police and the Tarrant County District Attorney's Office determined that the confession would be inadmissible in court due to the coercion and dropped the charges.[23]

This question has also been raised by numerous lawsuits filed against LifeLock. Class action lawsuits have been filed in several states, including New Jersey, Maryland, West Virginia, Florida, and California. As stated in court filings:

> *The proposed class action lawsuits address the deceptive business practices and fraudulent advertising campaign employed by LifeLock. . . . In actuality, the services and one million dollar service guarantee offered by LifeLock are not what they seem and do not provide the level of protection that is advertised in its deceptive marketing campaign.[24]*

The suits allege that the company dramatically overstates the effectiveness of its identity theft monitoring service and that fraud alerts cannot provide the comprehensive protection claimed. LifeLock's use of fraud alerts only protects against credit-based identity theft, not any other type. Fraud alerts are not an infallible method of protecting against identity theft, since "creditors are not legally required to contact [customers], even if they have fraud alerts in place."[25]

The $1 million guarantee against identity theft loss is also not what it appears to be, according to David Paris, the attorney for the class actions. "'In actuality, once you get beyond the limitations and disclaimers, you find that the guarantee is limited to fixing failures in LifeLock's services and paying third parties to attempt to restore subscriber losses,'" says Paris.[26] According to the complaint, LifeLock's $1 million guarantee covers only those losses resulting from LifeLock's failure to properly place a fraud alert, not from any other type of loss.[27]

The suits make other allegations, including that over 20 driver's licenses have been fraudulently obtained through the misappropriation of Davis's personal information. Additionally, a background check on Davis revealed that his personal profile has been compromised and now contains incorrect data.[28]

LifeLock has also been sued by the credit bureau Experian. "According to Experian's complaint, 'LifeLock's scheme costs Experian millions of dollars every year in processing large numbers of improper initial fraud alerts, mailing mandatory notices to consumers, and providing free credit reports to consumers who are not eligible for such reports.'"[29] Of course, Experian is a LifeLock competitor, as it offers its own, competing monitoring service, so its allegations should be taken with a grain of salt. Experian has also

*been under fire from the FTC over its FreeCreditReport.com site, which provides a free credit report if you sign up for Experian's (not free) service. The FTC says the site is uncomfortably close to AnnualCreditReport.com, which actually does provide free credit reports.[30]*

In response to these suits,

*Davis cites LifeLock's industry leader status as the reasons for several lawsuits recently filed against the company. "Obviously, I can't comment on ongoing legal matters, but this is what happens when you're the leader in your field. . . . We were ready and believe the suits will be proved to be without merit."[31]*

Referring to the New Jersey lawsuit plaintiffs, Davis said, "From what I know, they've never had an issue with LifeLock. They've never attempted to make a claim [for identity theft] and they don't say that in the suit."[32]

Despite the negative publicity, LifeLock has signed up approximately 1 million customers and has continued to raise significant amounts of venture capital funds even as competitors try to encroach on its success. This author sent a letter to LifeLock CEO Davis in October 2007, prior to learning of the lawsuits and any of the issues discussed here. In the letter, I stated I was writing a book on identity theft and that I had seen their many advertisements and wanted to profile what they were doing to protect consumers from identity theft. LifeLock did not respond.

In the end, consumers should always follow the maxim *caveat emptor*, "let the buyer beware." Consumers should understand what their needs are and what their risk level is, do their due diligence, and research their options before deciding for themselves whether LifeLock or any other company is right for them. Potential customers should also know that many of the services offered are available for no charge. Yet they may appreciate the convenience factor of having someone else take care of the monitoring and be available to answer questions. Being an educated consumer is always a best practice.

If you do sign up for LifeLock's service, do not emulate Davis and publish your SSN to show faith in the company product. Doing so would violate the terms and conditions of your contract and will result in termination of your service.[33]

## PROACTIVE APPROACH AND EDUCATION OUTREACH

The best approach to fighting identity theft is a public and private sector partnership that combines coordination of government agencies and the business community, public outreach and ongoing communication of prevention techniques, effective law enforcement, protecting victims, and needed legislation. The Washington State Attorney General's Office is a leader in addressing identity theft head-on and has used this approach for several years. The Attorney General has made the war on identity theft a main priority of his administration with a continuous and high-visibility outreach program. The program is a great example for other state and local jurisdictions to follow.

The Attorney General's proactive approach included holding a statewide summit bringing together hundreds of experts on identity theft from the public and private sectors. This summit discussed in detail the many issues involved in identity theft and came up with numerous proposals to fight the problem. Among the many proposals were these:

- Coordinate a public education campaign that includes a tool kit for consumers and businesses, mass communication and training.
- Determine and promote a one-stop location of resources and assistance for identity theft victims.
- Enhance existing methods of coordination and develop new methods of coordination to investigate and prosecute identity theft cases.
- Establish a safe harbor provision for law enforcement and business to share information about identity theft suspects and victims without being subject to liability if they have cooperated in good faith.
- Develop regulations to help ensure that private sector entities, particularly those with headquarters outside Washington, provide information relevant to local criminal and civil investigations.
- Better define identity theft and increase penalties for those convicted of identity theft crimes.
- State government workers who handle personal information, including driver's license data and Social Security numbers, should be subject to background checks as a condition of employment.
- Incorporate biometric data into driver's licenses and state identification cards.
- Establish a means for business and private sector groups to voluntarily help fund criminal justice positions and programs for the prevention, investigation, and prosecution of identity theft crimes.[34]

Another aspect of the outreach program is "Guard It! Washington," a multiagency campaign sponsored by the Washington State Attorney General's Office to educate residents and businesses about ways to reduce identity theft. The campaign travels around the state throughout the year. Presenters include the Attorney General and experts from the FTC, AARP (the American Association of Retired Persons), and the Attorney General's Consumer Protection Division. A "Shredathon Event" is often held in conjunction with the education campaign dates. Consumers can bring their sensitive documents containing personal information for shredding done by commercial shredding services on site.

There is no doubt that identity theft has the attention of elected officials and law enforcement. It is great to see that they are partnering with other government agencies, service organizations, the business sector, and the public to fight identity theft. This partnership must be an ongoing priority that is permanently embedded in daily business operations. On the federal level, the Postal Inspection Service is taking both a proactive and a reactive approach to the identity theft epidemic. A senior executive and experienced law enforcement professional from the Postal Inspection Service provides additional strategies and prevention practices in the next thought leader profile.

## THOUGHT LEADER IN FINANCIAL CRIMES PREVENTION

### Kenneth R. Jones

As the Deputy Chief Postal Inspector, Kenneth R. Jones is responsible for all headquarters operations, including all investigative programs for the U.S. Postal Inspection Service, one of the oldest federal law enforcement agencies in the United States. Over the last 25 years, Inspector Jones has led the efforts in some of the most far-reaching corporate fraud investigations, including market timing and late trading collusion. He has investigated identity theft; revenue fraud against the U.S. Postal Service; insurance fraud and other types of fraud; armed robberies; burglaries; child sexual exploitation; narcotics use/distribution; workplace violence mitigation; embezzlements; a wide variety of misconduct investigations; workers' compensation fraud; and money laundering.

His enterprise risk management and security responsibilities include: revenue protection, facility design, personnel security, access control systems, employee screening reviews, mail room security, management of armed Postal Police Force and unarmed contract security personnel, facility risk-rating and facility security reviews, armed robbery and burglary countermeasures and prevention, airport security reviews, biohazardous detection systems, emergency and disaster management, integrated emergency management plans, incident command structure, workplace violence/threat assessment teams and security consultation for the various industries doing business with the Postal Service.

Inspector Jones holds a B.A. in criminology from Mansfield University (PA) and a M.A. in criminology from Indiana University of Pennsylvania and the Certified Protection Professional credential through the American Society for Industrial Security.

Inspector Jones is a respected law enforcement professional and recognized thought leader in fraud prevention. Here he opines on the "fraud gap" and future expectations for financial crimes, including the serious impact of identity theft.

WHAT IS THE FRAUD GAP?
There has always been a gap between law enforcement and criminals, in that criminals are continually finding new schemes and variations on old schemes to defraud individuals, corporations, and governments. I refer to this gap as the fraud gap. The gap refers to law enforcement lagging behind on trying to identify and dismantle the schemes and the criminal organizations that commit these crimes.

*(Continued)*

Corporate security has emerged as an important and highly professional entity over the past years and has joined this fight to close the gap. Over the years, this gap has widened and narrowed as schemes evolve or as law enforcement has given aggressive attention to a particular type of fraud or has come up with ways to prevent certain crimes.

The fraud gap is wider now than it has ever been. Two factors, globalization and the use of the Internet and computer technology, indicate that the gap will continue to widen at an alarming rate if governments, industry, law enforcement, and consumer advocates don't react in a coordinated worldwide fashion. The identity theft epidemic has been a contributing factor to this problem.

A new class of organized criminals has globalized to commit international fraud. In fact, they have distinct advantages over any multinational corporation. They don't pay taxes to any government, and they obviously do not concern themselves with labor laws, privacy laws, civil litigation, or the public good. The use of the word "family" and some of their criminal activities are clear indications that these groups have modeled themselves after the organized crime groups that have come before them, such as the Mafia. I refer to these new groups as international financial organized crime.

The other major reason the fraud gap is widening is the efficient and effective use of the Internet and computer technology by this new group of organized criminals. Some of the best examples are the "carder" sites on the Internet that offer stolen personal information to those willing to pay. Certain cells of the criminal organizations provide hacking services, personal identifying information, full-track credit card data, software, spamming services, and more. Others in the criminal network do their own type of security background checks on those allowed to use the site, or their customers. They do the due diligence to ensure the "family" (using their own words . . . does this sound like organized crime to you?) site is protected from undercover law enforcement efforts. Also, the "family" clears those providing the services before they are allowed to sell their illegal services.

Law enforcement, particularly in the United States, is more like a dysfunctional family. Agencies don't openly share with each other, worry about protecting their own "turf," and when they do share, it is not in a coordinated or automated fashion. International law enforcement lacks the appropriate legal venues to share intelligence and to coordinate investigative efforts in an efficient and timely manner.

Two of the most common ways for a person's identity to be stolen are computer intrusion and what I refer to as "infiltration." Computer intrusion is obvious, and there have been far too many examples of large corporations, universities, and governments around the world that have lost personal identifying information to computer intrusions. "Infiltration" is the act of either getting someone hired in a corporation/government where enormous amounts of personal identifiable data are kept or bribing an existing employee to provide that data.

How Do We Narrow the Gap?

How do we narrow the fraud gap? First, to be very honest, I am concerned that politics, egos, and the territorial nature of law enforcement, corporations, and governments will impede our success, if not doom us to failure. The fraud gap is widening at a tremendous pace, and I do not yet see the sense of urgency and the coordinated effort necessary to address the problem. However, there is reason to believe we can dramatically narrow the fraud gap. Here are some opportunities to do so.

1. **Comprehensive global strategies.** A recent Postal Inspection Service Global Counterfeit Financial Instrument initiative seized over $2.5 billion in counterfeit checks that would have been used to defraud financial institutions and consumers. The Re-Shipping Initiative dismantled organized groups using your identity and credit to buy high-end computer merchandise and sell those items on the black market.

2. **Consumer awareness.** We must take an aggressive stance to educate consumers and corporations. It is no longer only the greedy and the unassuming who become victims. These are clever criminals and many savvy people and corporations have become victims. Postal Inspectors followed the Counterfeit Financial Instrument Initiative with an extensive consumer awareness campaign known as www.fakechecks.org. This was a massive public service effort that included television, newspaper, and online segments to publicize the problem of counterfeit checks. There is no legitimate reason why anyone would give you a check or money order and ask you to wire money anywhere in return. Once again, we did this in partnership with the financial services industry. By the way, we used money seized from criminals to fund the consumer awareness campaign. Our first objective is to always give money back to the victims. When we cannot identify victims, the courts have allowed us to use some funds for consumer awareness. It is our intention to have a similar consumer awareness campaign following the Re-Shipping Initiative.

3. **Enterprise risk management (ERM) and comprehensive security plans.** Fraud, in one form or another, often makes the top of the list when a company conducts a risk assessment. If not fraud in the purest sense, then cyber security usually makes it to the top of the risk list. Keep in mind one of the common ways for your identity to be stolen is computer intrusion. As mentioned earlier, one of the other ways is infiltration into a company, and this is where "personnel security" and "physical security" come into play. The three elements of corporate security—cyber, physical, and personnel— are all interrelated. As we know from all too many cyber breaches, personnel practices (such as background checks and sensitive clearances) and physical security policies (such as access control) have a relationship to cyber security.

*(Continued)*

4. **Self-audit of personal identifying information in a corporation.** Two tools have been developed to assist corporations in protecting their brand, their revenue, and their customers from identity breaches. These tools were developed with significant participation from the FTC, numerous financial institutions, and the Postal Inspection Service. The first is a self-audit for corporations, and it is scalable to the size of the corporation. Essentially, it examines how personal identifying information (PII) comes into a company, is stored, shared, distributed, destroyed, and so on. This is a low-cost tool to conduct an assessment of your risk in this area. The link to the U.S. Postal Inspection Service Business Checklist for Securing Personal Information can be found at http://postalinspectors.uspis.gov/radDocs/BusChecklist.html.

5. **Information Compromise Response Plan.** The second tool, the Information Compromise Response Plan, is necessary because any corporation, university, or government agency can be compromised. Let me repeat, anyone can be compromised. It's what is done after the compromise that will protect your brand, help you retain customer loyalty, and avoid larger costs and litigation expenses. This is no different than many disaster management plans and integrated emergency management plans that are now in place in most corporations. Inquiries from media, government agencies, customers, and employees can largely be anticipated and incorporated as part of a prepared Information Compromise Response Plan.

6. **Intelligence, cyber security, and cyber investigations.** These areas must be approached in a partnership among industry, law enforcement, and academia. The National Cyber Forensic and Training Alliance (NCFTA) is one of the best examples where corporations gain valuable intelligence to protect their infrastructures (and your identity) and where law enforcement gains valuable data to go after the criminals. We need more NCFTAs, both domestically and internationally. Academia has seen both the need and, from its perspective, the opportunity to partner with industry and law enforcement to create undergraduate and graduate-level degree programs in the area of cyber security.

7. **Homeland Security and the postal/shipping sector.** The U.S. Postal Service, FedEx, UPS, and others make up this shipping sector and are considered part of the critical infrastructure of the United States. Great strides have been made to protect the country from terrorist attacks in this sector. As a result, a significant positive relationship has been established in the area of fraud prevention in an effort to protect our employees and our customers.

8. **Department of Justice's International Organized Crime Initiative.** In the spring of 2008, U.S. Attorney General Michael B. Mukasey announced the intention of the Department of Justice to renew an effort to focus on "International Organized Crime." The Department of Justice taking the lead on this initiative is absolutely critical to closing the fraud gap, and I

commend Attorney General Mukasey for doing so. However, it is imperative that this initiative transcend the tenure of any one attorney general. It must be a sustained initiative, crossing several administrations, and we must all be ready for a long war.

9. **Major corporate ownership.** The major corporations of the world must also take a primary role in this war against the new international financial organized crime families. Many are stepping up to the plate. Microsoft, eBay, Google, and others are greatly supporting law enforcement, creating systems to combat online and Internet fraud, and exchanging intelligence with both law enforcement and industry partners. The key here will be to maximize these efforts in a coordinated way. Clearly one way would be to involve these and many more corporations in the NCFTA model and to create international versions of the NCFTA.

Narrowing the fraud gap is more than a daunting task. Success will take both diplomacy and international resolve. A tremendous amount is at stake, including the safety of our citizens, the integrity of the financial services industry, and the impact to commerce. As discussed, there is reason for hope, but the next administration in the White House, particularly the Department of State and the Department of Justice, will have to make fraud and identity theft prevention one of their top priorities for us to win this war.

## NO COUNTRY FOR IDENTITY THIEVES

In the 2007 crime thriller *No Country for Old Men*, the Anton Chigurh character portrayed by actor Javier Bardem is an unrepentant, psychopathic killing machine. Even worse, he is methodical as well as maniacal. He is a plague on the land, destroying everything in his path to locate the $2 million in cash he seeks. This to me is the evil that is identity theft: an unrelenting, unstoppable force committed to stealing and destroying our good names for financial gain.

What is even worse than the criminal nature and actions of identity theft is the aftermath: the loss of one's reputation, the feeling of violation and helplessness that someone is running around the country and the world with your name and identity, the knowledge that your name is no longer your own. Iago's passage from *Othello* as recounted in Chapter 3 is the perfect statement of that helplessness:

*But he that filches from me my good name,*

*Robs me of that which not enriches him,*

*And makes me poor indeed.*[35]

Knowing what identity theft is and what it does is not enough. Everyone has a vested interest in defeating this monster. We cannot bury our heads in the sand by believing that identity theft cannot happen to us. It can and does. We must take every precaution and teach all of our family members, friends, and associates to do the same to limit their risk of being victimized.

In this volume, I have endeavored to provide the history, growth, and transformation of this extraordinary crime. Investigating and preventing identity theft has been a part of my life for most of my career. I have a vested interest in seeing it defeated. I hope that everyone will consider and put into effect the findings of the many case studies, strategies, and prevention recommendations I discuss. I truly hope that together we can make this a "No Country, or World, for Identity Thieves." I believe we can.

## NOTES

1. *Help Protect Yourself against Identity Theft*, www.microsoft.com/downloads/details .aspx?FamilyID=bc58a88c-2fa3-4923-b9ff-762b1ec2c952&DisplayLang=en.
2. Walter S. Mossberg, "How to Avoid Cons That Can Lead to Identity Theft," *Wall Street Journal*, May 1, 2008, D1.
3. Lynn Cowan, "ID Firms Aren't a Sure Bet," *Wall Street Journal*, April 28, 2008, C3.
4. Joseph Pereira, "Credit Card Security Falters," *Wall Street Journal*, April 29, 2008, A9.
5. Rachel Kim, *2008 Identity Fraud Survey Report: How Consumers Can Protect Themselves*, Javelin Strategy & Research (February 2008), 1, www.idsafety.net/ 803.R_2008%20Identity%20Fraud%20Survey%20Report_Consumer%20Version. pdf.
6. Rachel Kim, *2008 Identity Fraud Forecast: Fraud Techniques Will Evolve in Tandem with Industry Defenses*, Javelin Strategy & Research (May 2008), www .javelinstrategy.com/uploads/808.R_2008IdentityFraudForecast_Brochure.pdf.
7. "How Does LifeLock Protect My Identity," LifeLock.com, www.lifelock.com/ lifelock-for-people/what-we-do/how-does-lifelock-protect-my-identity.
8. "How LifeLock Works," LifeLock.com, www.lifelock.com/lifelock-for-people.
9. Ibid.
10. Ray Stern, "What Happened in Vegas . . . ," *Phoenix New Times*, May 31, 2007, www.phoenixnewtimes.com/2007-05-31/news/what-happened-in-vegas/full.
11. Ibid.
12. See, e.g., "Interview with Todd Davis, CEO of LifeLock," Techrockies, February 13, 2007, www.techrockies.com/story/0007560.html.
13. Stern, "What Happened in Vegas."
14. Ibid.
15. Joseph Menn, "An Awkward Ad by Fred Thompson," *Los Angeles Times*, June 9, 2007, C1, http://articles.latimes.com/2007/jun/09/business/fi-lifelock9.
16. Ibid.; Stern, "What Happened in Vegas."
17. *FTC v. Maynard, et al.,* Final Judgment and Order for Permanent Injunction with Respect to Defendant Robert J. Maynard, Jr., United States District Court for the District of Arizona, CIV-96-2374-PHX-ROS, www.ftc.gov/os/1997/04/maynard .htm.

18. FTC Press Release, "National Credit Foundation Settles FTC Charges over Credit Repair Fraud," April 10, 1997, www.ftc.gov/opa/1997/04/ncf-4.shtm.

19. Stern, "What Happened in Vegas."

20. Kim Zetter, "LifeLock Founder Resigns amid Controversy," *Wired,* June 11, 2007, http://blog.wired.com/27bstroke6/2007/06/lifelock_founde_1.html. It should be noted that in a May 2008 interview, Davis stated that a year after his departure, Maynard "has no bearing, no involvement, zero, in the company." See Thomas Claburn, "ID Security Firm LifeLock Sued for Misleading Marketing," *InformationWeek*, May 2, 2008, www.informationweek.com/news/security/client/show Article.jhtml?articleID=207500392.

21. "Does LifeLock Really Work?" LifeLock.com, www.lifelock.com/todd-davis.

22. Deanna Boyd, "Officials Say They Can't Prosecute Phony-Loan Case," *Fort Worth Star Telegram*, July 25, 2007. *See also* Kim Zetter, Police Say LifeLock Coerced Unusable Confession from Identity Theft Suspect," Wired, July 25, 2007, http://blog.wired.com/27bstroke6/2007/07/police-say-life.html.

23. Deanna Boyd, "Officials say they can't prosecute phony-loan case," *Fort Worth Star Telegram*, July 25, 2007.

24. LifeLock Class Action, www.lifelockclassaction.com/.

25. *Pasternack v. LifeLock,* Class Action Complaint and Jury Demand, State of New Jersey Superior Court Law Division, Middlesex County, March 28, 2003, 9.

26. Press Release from Marks & Klein, LLP, "NJ Class Action Lawsuit Filed Against LifeLock Alleging Deceptive Marketing Regarding Limited Level of Protection Against Identity Theft," March 31, 2008, www.lifelockclassaction.com/lifelock release.pdf.

27. *Pasternack v. LifeLock,* 14.

28. *Falke v. LifeLock,* Class Action Complaint, Washington County (MD) Circuit Court, April 17, 2008, 2–3.

29. Matthew Schwartz, "ID Theft Monitoring Services: What You Need to Know" *InformationWeek,* May 9, 2008, www.informationweek.com/news/security/privacy/showArticle.jhtml?articleID=207501091&cid=RSSfeed_IWK_Security.

30. Ibid.

31. "Does LifeLock Really Work?" LifeLock.com, www.lifelock.com/todd-davis.

32. Thomas Claburn, "ID Security Firm LifeLock Sued for Misleading Marketing," *InformationWeek*, May 2, 2008, www.informationweek.com/news/security/client/showArticle.jhtml?articleID=207500392.

33. "LifeLock Terms and Conditions," LifeLock.com, www.lifelock.com/about-us/about-lifelock/terms-and-conditions. See also Ray Stern, "Money for Nothing," *Phoenix New Times*, July 19, 2007, www.phoenixnewtimes.com/2007-07-19/news/money-for-nothing/full.

34. Washington State Attorney General's Office Identity Theft Advisory Panel, *2005 Identity Theft Summit Summary and Recommendations*, Office of Attorney General Rob McKenna, January 26, 2006, www.atg.wa.gov/uploadedFiles/Home/Safeguarding_Consumers/Consumer_Issues_A-Z/Identity_Theft_(Privacy)/IdentityTheft Report.pdf.

35. William Shakespeare, *Othello*, Act 3, Scene 3, 155–161.

# APPENDIX

# Designing an Effective Identity Theft Red Flags Rule Compliance Program

The Fair and Accurate Credit Transactions Act (FACTA) of 2003 requires financial institutions and creditors to design and implement an effective Red Flags Rule Compliance Program to detect, prevent, and mitigate identity theft pertaining to covered accounts. This is both a compliance requirement for FACTA, as well as for protecting the interests of businesses and customers alike. The deadline for compliance was November 1, 2008.

This Appendix is prepared from the FACTA Red Flags Rule Program and is intended to provide a broad overview for related program requirements and compliance. For full details and all aspects of compliance requirements, please refer to the Identity Theft Red Flags and Address Discrepancies of FACTA. Implementation of such a program should be done under the auspices of an entity's general counsel, outside counsel, or compliance department.

## DEFINITIONS

### Financial Institution

A financial institution is defined as a state or national bank, savings and loan association, mutual savings bank, state or federal credit union, or any similar financial entity.

### Creditor

A creditor is a lender such as a bank, finance company, automobile dealer, mortgage broker, utility company, or telecommunication company that participates in credit decisions, regularly extends credit, or arranges for the extension of credit.

### Customer

A customer is any person that has a covered account with a financial institution or creditor.

### Covered Accounts

A covered account is an account offered by a financial institution or creditor (1) primarily for personal, family, or household purposes, that involves or is designed to permit multiple payments or transactions, or (2) any account for which there is a reasonably foreseeable risk to customers or the safety and soundness of the financial institution or creditor from identity theft, including financial, operational, compliance, reputation, or litigation risks. Each financial institution and creditor must periodically determine whether it offers or maintains a "covered account."[1] Covered accounts include checking, savings, and credit card accounts; installment loans; mortgage loans; margin accounts; utility bills; and cellular service accounts.

### Identity Theft

Under the final rules, identity theft as it pertains to FACTA is defined as "a fraud committed or attempted using the identifying information of another person without authority."[2]

### Red Flags

A red flag is "a pattern, practice, or specific activity that indicates the possible existence of identity theft."[3]

### Service Provider

A service provider is a person or entity that provides a service directly to a financial institution or creditor

## ESTABLISHMENT OF AN IDENTITY THEFT PREVENTION PROGRAM

Every financial institution or creditor that offers or maintains even one covered account must develop and implement a written Identity Theft Prevention Program "designed to detect, prevent, and mitigate identity theft in connection with the opening of a covered account or any existing covered account."[4] The program must be tailored to the entity's size, complexity, and the nature of its operations. There are four basic elements that must be part of any effective compliance Red Flags Rule Program. They are:

- Identify relevant red flags for the covered accounts that the financial institution or creditor offers or maintains, and incorporate those red flags into its program;
- Detect red flags that have been incorporated into the program of the financial institution or creditor;
- Respond appropriately to any red flags that are detected to prevent and mitigate identity theft; and
- Ensure the program is updated periodically, to reflect changes in risks to customers, or to the safety and soundness of the financial institutions or creditor from identity theft.[5]

### Administration of the Program

An important aspect of the program is an ongoing administration requirement to ensure successful implementation. The board of directors must assign specific responsibility for the compliance program. Oversight includes approving the compliance program and ensuring continuous oversight of the "development, implementation, and administration of the Program."[6] Further oversight includes review and approval of related reports and material changes in the program. The following actions are necessary for continued administration:

- Obtain approval of the initial written program from either its board of directors or an appropriate committee of the board of directors;
- Involve the board of directors, an appropriate committee thereof, or a designated employee at the level of senior management in the oversight, development, implementation and administration of the program;
- Train staff, as necessary, to effectively implement the program; and
- Exercise appropriate and effective oversight of service provider arrangements.[7]

The program must be flexible to address changes in identity theft risks as they arise. On an annual basis, the board or designee needs to report on various issues including the existence and effectiveness of policies, service provider arrangements such as the existence of written contracts, significant identity theft incidents, and recommendations to improve detection, prevention, and mitigation of identity theft.

The training plan should include both new and existing employees. New employee orientation is an excellent opportunity to train new hires in the program. Modifications and updates to the program must also be communicated via appropriate training sessions. Employee completion of training should be documented and the training program and content should also be periodically assessed for relevance. Consideration should be given to providing or encouraging training for service providers.

## Risk Assessment

There is a program requirement that each financial institution or creditor conduct a risk assessment to identify relevant red flags. The risk assessment must periodically determine whether it offers covered accounts including:

- Types of covered accounts it offers or maintains
- Methods it provides to open accounts
- Methods it provides to access its accounts
- Its previous experiences with identity theft.[8]

Additional aspects of the risk assessment must include:

- Incidents of identity theft that the financial institution or creditor has experienced
- Methods of identity theft that the financial institution or creditor has identified that reflect changes in identity theft risks
- Applicable supervisory guidance.[9]

## Detecting Red Flags

An effective program must involve the detection of red flags with the opening of covered accounts and existing accounts. This includes:

- Obtaining identifying information about, and verifying the identity of, a person opening a covered account, for example, using the policies and procedures regarding identification and verification set forth in the Customer Identification Program rules of the USA PATRIOT Act
- Authenticating customers, monitoring transactions, and verifying the validity of change of address requests, in the case of existing covered accounts.[10]

The following are 26 examples of Identity Theft Red Flags and Address Discrepancies as documented in FACTA that financial institutions or creditors may consider incorporating into their identity theft prevention compliance programs in connection with covered accounts.

## Alerts, Notifications, or Warnings from a Consumer Reporting Agency

1. A fraud or active duty alert is included with a consumer report.
2. A consumer reporting agency provides a notice of credit freeze in response to a request for a consumer report.
3. A consumer reporting agency provides a notice of address discrepancy.
4. A consumer report indicates a pattern of activity that is inconsistent with the history and usual pattern of activity of an applicant or customer, such as:
   a. A recent and significant increase in the volume of inquiries
   b. An unusual number of recently established credit relationships
   c. A material change in the use of credit, especially with respect to recently established credit relationships
   d. An account that was closed for cause or identified for abuse of account privileges by a financial institution or creditor.

## Suspicious Documents

5. Documents provided for identification appear to have been altered or forged.
6. The photograph or physical description on the identification is not consistent with the appearance of the applicant or customer presenting the identification.
7. Other information on the identification is not consistent with information provided by the person opening a new covered account or customer presenting the identification.
8. Other information on the identification is not consistent with readily accessible information that is on file with the financial institution or creditor, such as a signature card or a recent check.
9. An application appears to have been altered or forged, or gives the appearance of having been destroyed and reassembled.

## Suspicious Personal Identifying Information

10. Personal identifying information provided is inconsistent when compared against external information sources used by the financial institution or creditor.
    a. The address does not match any address in the consumer report.
    b. The Social Security Number (SSN) has not been issued, or is listed on the Social Security Administration's Death Master File.

11. Personal identifying information provided by the customer is not consistent with other personal identifying information provided by the customer. For example, there is a lack of correlation between the SSN range and date of birth.

12. Personal identifying information provided is associated with known fraudulent activity as indicated by internal or third-party sources used by the financial institution or creditor.

    a. The address on an application is the same as the address provided on a fraudulent application.

    b. The phone number on an application is the same as the number provided on a fraudulent application.

13. Personal identifying information provided is of a type commonly associated with fraudulent activity as indicated by internal or third-party sources used by the financial institution or creditor.

    a. The address on an application is fictitious, a mail drop, or a prison.

    b. The phone number is invalid, or is associated with a pager or answering service.

14. The SSN provided is the same as that submitted by other persons opening an account or other customers.

15. The address or telephone number provided is the same as or similar to the account number or telephone number submitted by an unusually large number of other persons opening accounts or other customers.

16. The person opening the covered account or the customer fails to provide all required personal identifying information on an application or in response to notification that the application is incomplete.

17. Personal identifying information provided is not consistent with personal identifying information that is on file with the financial institution or creditor.

18. For financial institutions and creditors that use challenge questions, the person opening the covered account or the customer cannot provide authenticating information beyond that which generally would be available from a wallet or consumer report.

**Unusual Use of, or Suspicious Activity Related to, the Covered Account**

19. Shortly following the notice of a change of address for a covered account, the institution or creditor receives a request for a new, additional, or replacement card or a cell phone, or for the addition of authorized users on the account.

20. A new revolving credit account is used in a manner commonly associated with known patterns of fraud.

  a. The majority of available credit is used for cash advances or merchandise that is easily convertible to cash (e.g., electronics equipment or jewelry).

  b. The customer fails to make the first payment or makes an initial payment but no subsequent payments.

21. A covered account is used in a manner that is not consistent with established patterns of activity on the account. There is, for example:

  a. Nonpayment when there is no history of late or missed payments;

  b. A material increase in the use of available credit;

  c. A material change in purchasing or spending patterns;

  d. A material change in electronic fund transfer patterns in connection with a deposit account; or

  e. A material change in telephone call patterns in connection with a cellular phone account.

22. A covered account that has been inactive for a reasonably lengthy period of time is used (taking into consideration the type of account, the expected pattern of usage and other relevant factors).

23. Mail sent to the customer is returned repeatedly as undeliverable although transactions continue to be conducted in connection with the customer's covered account.

24. The financial institution or creditor is notified that the customer is not receiving paper account statements.

25. The financial institution or creditor is notified of unauthorized charges or transactions in connection with a customer's covered account.

### Notice from Customers, Victims of Identity Theft, Law Enforcement Authorities, or Other Persons Regarding Possible Identity Theft in Connection with Covered Accounts Held by the Financial Institution or Creditor

26. The financial institution or creditor is notified by a customer, a victim of identity theft, a law enforcement authority, or any other person that it has opened a fraudulent account for a person engaged in identity theft.[11]

### Preventing and Mitigating Red Flags

The program's policies and procedures should provide for appropriate responses to the red flags the financial institution or creditor has detected that are commensurate with the degree of risk posed. In determining an appropriate response, a financial institution or creditor should consider aggravating factors that may heighten the risk of identity theft, such as a data security incident that results in unauthorized access to a customer's account records held by the financial institution, creditor, or third party, or notice that a customer has provided information related to a covered account held by the financial institution or creditor to someone fraudulently claiming to represent the financial institution or creditor or to a fraudulent Web site. Appropriate responses may include:

- *Monitoring a covered account for evidence of identity theft*
- *Contacting the customer*
- *Changing any passwords, security codes, or other security devices that permit access to a covered account*
- *Reopening a covered account with a new account number*
- *Not opening a new covered account*
- *Closing an existing covered account*
- *Not attempting to collect on a covered account or not selling a covered account to a debt collector*
- *Notifying law enforcement*
- *Determining that no response is warranted under the particular circumstances[12]*

## Updating the Program

Financial institutions and creditors should update the program (including the red flags determined to be relevant) periodically, to reflect changes in risks to customers or to the safety and soundness of the financial institution or creditor from identity theft, based on such factors as:

- *The experiences of the financial institution or creditor with identity theft;*
- *Changes in methods of identity theft*
- *Changes in methods to detect, prevent, and mitigate identity theft*
- *Changes in the types of accounts that the financial institution or creditor offers or maintains*
- *Changes in the business arrangements of the financial institution or creditor, including mergers, acquisitions, alliances, joint ventures, and service provider arrangements[13]*

Compliance with the FACTA Red Flags Rule is mandatory. Since the deadline for compliance was November 1, 2008, any financial institution or creditor not in compliance risks adverse governmental actions. In addition, the failure to design and implement a robust compliance program may result in financial and reputational harm.

## NOTES

1. Identity Theft Red Flags and Address Discrepancies Under the Fair and Accurate Credit Transactions Act of 2003; Final Rule, Federal Register, Part IV, November 9, 2007, www.federalreserve.gov/reportforms/formsreview/RegV_20071109_ffr.pdf.
2. Ibid.
3. Ibid.

4. Ibid.
5. Ibid
6. Ibid.
7. Ibid.
8. Ibid.
9. Ibid.
10. Ibid.
11. Ibid.
12. Identity Theft Red Flags and Address Discrepancies, Fair and Accurate Credit Transactions Act of 2003, 159-162, www.ftc.gov/os/2007/10/r611019redflags frn.pdf.
13. Ibid.

# INDEX